MARINE TANK BATTLES
IN THE PACIFIC

MARINE
TANK BATTLES
IN THE PACIFIC

Oscar E. Gilbert

DA CAPO PRESS

Originally published by Combined Publishing in 2001.

Copyright © 2001 Oscar E. Gilbert

Cataloging-in-Publication Data is available from the Library of Congress.

ISBN 1-58097-050-8

Printed in the United States of America.

First Da Capo Edition 2001.

EBA   01 02 03   10 9 8 7 6 5 4 3 2

CONTENTS

ACKNOWLEDGEMENTS

It is a pleasure to be able to thank the many people who furthered the considerable work involved in preserving this bit of history, particularly the men whose stories make up the core of this book. Their names are listed separately in the section "Back In The World." Don Gagnon, editor of the *Marine Corps Tankers' Association Newsletter*, was instrumental in the effort, suggesting many key people for interviews and inviting me to the annual reunions of the association as his guest. My early conversations with William "Mac" McMillian (CWO USMC, ret.) and Ed Bale (Colonel, USMC, ret.) confirmed my suspicions that much of what had been written about Marine Corps tank operations in World War II contained serious factual errors. Their early cooperation encouraged me to continue in the work, and they both provided me with copies of contemporary records and introduced me to other knowledgeable veterans.

Steve Zaloga supported me in many projects over the years, and inspired me to begin this one—although neither of us knew it at the time. Research librarian Debbie Gumienny and the staff of the Maude Marks Branch of the Harris County, Texas, Public Library tracked down and obtained many hard to obtain references. The late Curtis Everett of Houston loaned me important references that helped jumpstart the project, and Lena Kaljot of the Marine Corps Historical Center and the staff of the National Archives were most helpful in tracking down historic photographs. Charles Bell provided a photocopy of his company First Sergeant's field notebook, which he fortunately saved from the trash following the battle of Iwo Jima. Akira Takizawa translated some material from Japanese and shared the results of his research into Japanese archives.

Dr. Jim Pickens reviewed the manuscript at an early stage, and both he and Steve Smith of Sarpedon Publishers, now an imprint of Combined Publishing, were instrumental in encouraging me to reduce the original ponderous manuscript to a managable scale. Alvin Hubert reviewed the final manuscript and offered valuable suggestions, and has been a friend and sounding board over the years. Several anonymous reviewers provided

6

valuable criticisms that led to restructuring of and additions to the manuscript. I would particularly like to thank Ken Estes (Lieutenant Colonel, USMC, ret.) who shared the results of his research on the history of armored fighting vehicles in Marine Corps service and corrected significant errors in the final draft. Jim Curtin converted the completed manuscript from one computer format to another, a formidable task.

It is customary to thank the family, but in this case it is perhaps more appropriate than is usually the case. My children—Jordan, Bill, and Jillian—have, over the years, served as size references in photographs, drivers, runners of errands, providers of technical services, and performed many other tasks that needed to be done. Last but not least, of course, is my wife Cathy. Through 30 years of married life she has been dragged through military bases and museums, toured old battlefields in all weather, been stranded in strange places, and tolerated my sometimes lengthy absences on professional business with good grace.

PREFACE

THE RESEARCH that resulted in this book began when I read a then recently published account of the first battle involving Marine Corps tanks on the tiny island of Tanambogo in the southern Solomons. The story was distinctly different from previous accounts of the battle, and I was aware that there were similar discrepancies in the published accounts of the very influential actions of the tanks in the short and extremely violent battle on Tarawa in the Gilbert Islands.

When I compared the various accounts, I discovered that there were as many as five mutually contradictory versions of the stories of both battles. Additional reading revealed another bothersome trend. Although tanks were a fundamental part of the Marine Corps combined arms team in World War II, they have slowly disappeared from the history books. In most recently published histories of the Pacific War tanks are seldom mentioned, if at all. The exception to this trend is the work of Steve Zaloga, who has carried this torch virtually alone for years.

Like other crusaders before me, I set out to write "The Definitive Book of Everything You Ever Wanted To Know about Marine Corps Tanks in World War II; operational history, technology, Japanese countermeasures, and the human experience of tank warfare." I began by interviewing World War II tank veterans, and researching the secondary sources. The result was a manuscript that reached monstrous proportions, even before I began to really research primary sources.

Fortunately Jim Pickens and Steve Smith, among others, helped me to find the real center of interest, the human experience of the men who fought in the tanks. The final result is a broad overview of the operational history of Marine Corps tanks in the southwestern and central Pacific fighting, but one which incorporates the experiences of the fighting men, as told in their own words.

Historical researchers may legitimately question the accuracy of memories of events that took place nearly 60 years ago. However, I feel that I have been more lucky than clever in avoiding that trap. The men I interviewed have been amazingly forthright in sorting out the details of what is accurately remembered, what is forgotten because it seemed unimportant, and what is too painful to recall. Some have contacted me following their interviews to correct recollections that they, upon further reflection, considered incorrect. Others were encouraged to conduct their own research into past events that were of interest to them personally.

Then there is the issue of conscious or unconscious embellishment, the retelling of a story until it becomes "fact." Marines call these apocryphal tales sea stories. (The definition of a sea story is that a fairytale begins "Once upon a time..." while a sea story begins "This ain't no shit, buddy...")

Here too, I was fortunate. Most, but not all, of the interviewees are members of the Marine Corps Tanker's Association, and cheerfully provided cross checks on each other's stories. In fact, my main problem with most of these men was to get them to talk at all, because for the most part they are unexpectedly modest and reluctant to talk to writers. I quickly determined that it was writers, and not these men, who were more likely to embellish a story to make it more "dramatic."

Whenever possible I have also attempted to corroborate stories with separate accounts (seldom really possible), to determine whether a story is plausible, and I have interviewed some men a second time to clarify points and eliminate inconsistencies. It is in most cases impossible to reliably place a specific event on the precise day or in the exact location on the battlefield, so I hope the interviewees and the reader will forgive me if I err in that regard.

In the final analysis, I felt that the story of these men was worth telling. I am confident that there are errors in my telling of it. But the only foolproof way to avoid error is to do nothing, and that would be the greater error.

Ed Gilbert
Katy, Texas
June 2000

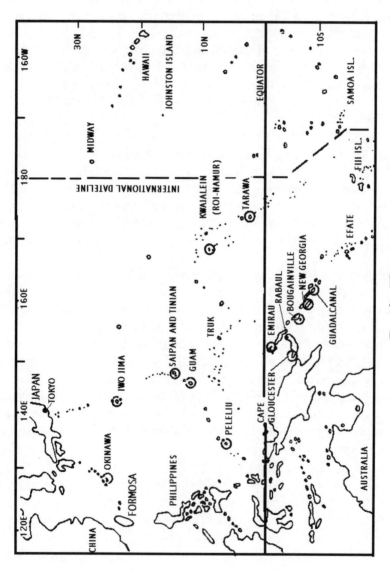

Pacific Theater

PROLOGUE

"Next to his rifle, the infantryman cherished the tank, which like a lumbering elephant, could either strike terror into a foe or be a gentle servant to a friend. On the open field, hospital corpsmen, moving behind a tank, could get to the wounded and safely bring them off. In attack, the Marine tank-infantry team felt itself unbeatable, and the Saipan experience added confidence. The medium tank would precede the riflemen, who, in return, protected the tank from Japanese antitank grenades. Each half of the team needed the other."

> Henry I. Shaw Jr., Bernard C. Nalty,
> and Edwin T. Turnbladh, in *Central Pacific Drive*,
> Volume III of the official history of
> Marine Corps Operations in World War II

ON THE SWELTERING AFTERNOON of 9 July 1944, a Sherman tank named *Bonita* nosed through the thorny underbrush of Saipan. The tank commander rode with his head exposed, risking death from a sniper or machine gun to guide his otherwise blind tank as a ragged line of riflemen, survivors of a decimated rifle company, picked through the tangle on either side. The dense vegetation hid a deadly warren of enemy trenches and pillboxes, and cunning waist-high tunnels cut through the bushes. A rifleman knew he had stumbled into one of these fire tunnels only when bullets cut his legs from beneath him.

Machine-gun fire spattered against the steel hull of the tank, and the sergeant reflexively told his gunner to traverse right, toward the blinking muzzle flashes. He raked the underbrush with his own roof-mounted machine gun as the turret slowly turned, then leaned out over the side to wave the riflemen away. The muzzle blast of the big cannon could kill or injure at close quarters. Distracted, he never saw the grenade that arced up from the ground to his front, and clanged onto the roof of the turret.

The missile bounced off the top of the turret, and dropped into the narrow gap between the sergeant's face and the rim of the hatch. From the instant the baseball-sized grenade cleared the rim of his hatch, Sergeant Grant Frederick Timmerman was a dead man. The question was how many others would die with him. The explosion of the loose grenade amid nearly a ton of fuel and ammunition inside the tank would turn it into a fiery tomb for the five-man crew.

Timmerman grasped the grenade and hugged it to his chest. In the instant remaining to him, Timmerman turned his face to the steel wall of the turret. His chest torn out by the blast, Sergeant Timmerman of the 2nd Marine Tank Battalion became the second tank commander to win a posthumous Medal of Honor on this terrible island.

Within the year the deadly proficient Marine Corps tank-infantry teams would capture two of the most staunchly defended pieces of military real estate in the world, Iwo Jima and Okinawa, and stand poised for the invasion of Japan. Yet less than two years earlier, when this same tank battalion had helped spearhead the first American offensive against the Axis powers, the tank battalions had been the orphans of the Marine Corps. Inadequately trained, using obsolete equipment, and unable to communicate with the infantry, they had not been in any true sense members of the division combat team. They had come far indeed.

The first Marine Corps tank units had gone poorly trained and inexperienced into combat in the southern Solomons, and paid a bloody toll. Unskilled in working with infantry, the tanks often charged ahead and were trapped. Only once did their impetuosity pay off in decisive victory; on other occasions the tanks suffered prohibitive losses at the hands of the seemingly fearless Japanese.

On Guadalcanal, New Georgia, Bougainville, and Cape Gloucester the Marines defied all logic and learned to operate their unwieldy steel monsters in the most terrible jungles and swamps in the world. In the end the problem was not so much the usefulness of tanks in the jungle as that there were never enough of them.

November 1943 was a pivotal point in the history of the tank units. At Tarawa Atoll tanks were first used as intended, in support of a direct frontal assault from the sea. The tanks had no real experience in working with infantry, and most tank commanders had never even met the leaders of the infantry units. Worse, they were assigned no specific tactical mission.

In the first 24 hours of this holocaust the rifle battalions were ravaged, and the tank companies suffered 87 percent losses. The surviving Marines justified their legendary reputation, reorganizing their shattered units, and quickly learned how to use tanks in desperate close-quarter combat. In three days of the most concentrated savagery in the history of the world, the Marines suffered, persevered, prevailed. And learned.

From Tarawa the Marines moved always forward through a series of struggles, some epic, some nearly forgotten—Kwajalein, Saipan, Tinian, Guam, Peleliu, Iwo Jima, Okinawa. In each the riflemen always had the protection of their armored angels. The great fleets of aircraft carriers and strategic bombers may have "won" the war, but only after the sacrifices of the riflemen and tankers carried them within reach of the enemy.

Marine tanks and their crews saved countless American lives as they blundered forward to blast and sear defensive works manned by some of the world's most tenacious fighting men, and fought off the enemy's armored counterattacks. But that was only what was expected of them. They also hauled ammunition and medical supplies to units trapped by enemy fire, and dragged the wounded to safety in their armored bellies. They launched assault bridges under fire, and bulldozed paths through minefields. They fought naval battles with Japanese armored barges. They welded steel pontoons to their sides to swim ashore, and one rammed a destroyer. They piled up ramps of dirt to raise their snouts and fired as makeshift artillery.

The tankers suffered alongside the infantrymen they protected. They were sprayed with red-hot fragments when antitank rounds went in one armored flank and out the other. They were torn and burned when the enemy struck with explosive charges and grenades. They died without leaving a body for burial when huge mines lifted their 35-ton tanks high into the air, gutted them, and tossed them aside like empty cans. They shivered with malaria and baked inside sealed tanks in the 110 degree heat, drowned in flooded tanks and were crushed when tanks broke loose and slid about in the holds of storm-tossed ships. But in the end, they triumphed. They were United States Marines.

CHAPTER 1

NOVICES AT WAR:
BIRTH OF THE TANK CORPS AND THE
COMING OF WAR

The enemy's power lies in its tanks.

> *Lt. General Mitsuru Ushijima*
> *Commander, Japanese 32nd Army*
> *Okinawa, 1945*

OFFICIAL HISTORIES written in the immediate aftermath of World War II considered tanks a fundamental part of the combined arms team, and captured Japanese documents provided ample proof that the enemy considered them a primary threat. Today the role of tanks in the Pacific war is all but forgotten. Popular histories now mention tanks only in passing if at all, but in actuality tanks played a fundamental role in the war against Japan. They made the cost of winning the war morally and politically acceptable to the American people.

A key aspect of the Japanese war strategy was to take advantage of what they perceived as superior martial spirit and willingness to sacrifice lives in the pursuit of military and political ends. Their plan was to seize a vast area rich in natural resources, then establish a defensive perimeter through the Central Pacific, and around the East Indies, Burma, and much of China. They believed that faced with the immense human cost of breaching this strategic barrier, the Americans would lose the will to bring the war to its final conclusion.

The bloodbath at Tarawa in November 1943 was the first portent of the price America would have to pay to defeat the Japanese Empire. In 76 hours the 2nd Marine Division suffered more casualties than total losses in the six-month campaign for Guadalcanal. But Tarawa also demonstrated that tanks could play a fundamental role in reducing casualties. The tank units endured stunning casualties, but proved to be the key to successful assaults on the Japanese defenses. In the battles that followed the Marine Corps tank-infantry team grew increasingly deadly, and the tanks played an increasingly important role in division combat teams.

By early 1945 United States military forces had achieved a clear ascendancy, and from the Japanese perspective the most painfully visible manifestation of American material superiority was the medium tank. Colonel Hiromichi Yahara was the most senior Japanese Army officer captured in World War II, and was briefed by General Atomiya, vice-chief of staff for *Imperial Army Headquarters* before his assignment to Okinawa. Atomiya stated that "… the greatest threat above ground is enemy tanks."[1] The 1945 Interrogation Report on Colonel Yahara states that the absence of massive American tank attacks on Okinawa "… came as a great relief to the Japanese. Col. YAHARA is, however, of the opinion that Blue (American) superiority in tanks was the single factor most important in deciding the battle of OKINAWA."[2]

The history of Marine Corps tanks also illustrates the often-unorthodox ways in which the Marine Corps adapts to the challenges that confront it. In 1940 and 1941 the armies of the world stood in awe of the Nazi *blitzkrieg*, the slashing tank attacks that had brought down Poland and France. The Western allies organized armored forces after the German pattern, but the problems that the Marine Corps faced were far different.

The concept of the *blitzkrieg* was to find the open flank, bypass opposition, and cause the collapse of the enemy by isolating his positions and raising havoc in his rear areas. On the small islands of the Central Pacific there were no open flanks. Every attack would be a frontal assault. Bypassed Japanese soldiers would never surrender, every Japanese position would have to be eliminated.

The United States Marine Corps solved this problem by defying orthodoxy. They developed an entirely new doctrine of frontal assault from the sea, a concept that flew in the face of every current military principle, but one which proved fundamental in the destruction not only of Imperial Japan, but of Nazi Germany as well. The Marines also moved forward by looking backward, refining the doctrine of the slow-moving infantry tank.

This was accomplished despite enormous problems. The first Marine Corps tank crews were trained by one-on-one tutelage as individuals within units. The enormous expansion of the Marine Corps in 1941–1942 swamped this system, and until formal schools were established the tank units were especially typical of Allan Millett's assessment that "... specialists learned their skills in the field, often under fire."[3]

But before the Marine Corps faced the Japanese Empire, it first had to face a more dangerous foe—the United States government.

The publicity garnered by the Marine Brigade in World War I aroused deep resentment among influential Army officers, who felt that the achievements of the Army had been unfairly overshadowed. In the aftermath of the war, military experts declared the United States Marine Corps both obsolete and redundant. While the Army and Navy struggled to modernize and maintain readiness in a time of declining budgets, the Marine Corps struggled to survive.

The United States had in fact ended the Great War in a degraded global strategic position. Before 1914 the islands of the Central Pacific, in the hands of a weak naval power like Germany, had posed no threat to American interests. In 1914 Japan eagerly took control of Germany's small Pacific empire, and gained permanent trusteeship over most of Germany's far eastern possessions following the 1919 Treaty of Versailles. As early as 1920 the U. S. Navy concluded that their next war might likely be against Japan.

The U. S. Army refused to deal with the problems posed by a potential Pacific war. In any area of potential conflict, like Europe or China, the assumption was that the Army could either land through existing ports or land at some undefended spot, then march overland to a decisive battle. The logistical implications of supporting a field army over open beaches were clearly not considered. With their strategic eyes fixed upon the great land masses of Europe and Asia, the Army had neither plan nor intent to provide support for a naval campaign by seizing advanced island bases.

Concerned by this doctrinal disjunction, in 1920 the Chief of Naval Operations advised Marine Commandant George Barnett that the Navy's new War Plan Orange called for the creation of a Marine expeditionary force to support offensive operations across the Pacific, with a smaller force to support Atlantic/Caribbean operations. For the Navy, the Marine Corps was the natural choice. They had traditionally provided shipboard security and small landing parties, and since the Spanish-American War had functioned as the Navy's advanced base force, charged with the capture and defense of naval facilities.

Politics and bureaucratic infighting resulted in Barnett's resignation in 1920, and the secretary of the navy selected John Lejeune as his successor, probably the single most fortunate personnel choice in the history of the Corps. Lejeune brought the Marine Corps into the modern age, and persuaded a miserly Congress to fund an increase in troop strength.

Lejeune embraced the concept of the Marine Corps as the Navy's advanced base force, and assigned a young Alabama lawyer, Major Holland M. Smith, to the Navy War Plans Division.

Influential among Lejeune's cadre of visionaries was Major Earl H. "Pete" Ellis. Ellis had been obsessed by Japanese expansionism prior to the Great War, and after observing Japan's absorption of the former German Pacific colonies, was near maniacal on the subject. By May 1921 he and others produced *Advanced Base Operations in Micronesia* (Operations Plan 712), a blueprint for the seizure of the Marshall, Caroline, and Palau island chains as steppingstones to Japan. A corollary to War Plan Orange, this document provided a detailed outline of the specialized equipment, organization, and tactics necessary for a successful amphibious campaign.

A key item in Ellis's plan was adequate gunfire support. The single most fundamental lesson of every armed conflict from the the American Civil War to the Great War of 1914–1918 was that accurate gunfire support capable of destroying specific enemy defensive positions was vital. For amphibious assaults the need was particularly critical, since opportunities for maneuver or withdrawal were non-existent.

The story of Marine tanks is also the story of the failure of big guns in the waning days of the battleship navy. The enormous guns of the battleship were the obvious weapons of choice to substitute for artillery in support of amphibious assaults. Yet technical problems in gunnery and the reluctance of admirals to risk the big ships prevented the battleship from fulfilling this obvious and crucial function.

The solution to the fire support problem was the tank, which, if it could be successfully put ashore, could engage enemy positions with direct fire. The tank had been invented to solve an identical problem, the failure of conventional artillery to destroy specific enemy strongpoints on the Western Front. Marine Corps officers serving in the

Army's 2nd Division had almost certainly observed operations of the Tank Corps, and were familiar with the potential of the tank.

Procuring suitable tanks was but a small part of a much bigger problem. Also fundamental to the Corps' plans were the landing boats required to put an "all-arms" force onto a defended beach. In 1921 plans to land heavy equipment over open beaches still lay in the realm of science fiction.

Ellis himself never lived to see the fruits of his vision. In May 1923 he died, apparently of alcohol toxicity, while on a covert intelligence mission to the Japanese-controlled Palau Islands.

A major fleet landing exercise in 1924 provided the first test of the Ellis doctrines, and also tested the first American amphibian tank, designed by J. Walter Christie. The vehicle was not really a tank, but a self-propelled gun mount, and either a 75mm M1897 gun or a 37mm M1916 Infantry Gun could be fitted to fire through the prow-shaped front plate. Although the vehicle was successfully unloaded from a battleship and swam ashore, observers considered it to be unseaworthy and inadequately armored. Christie redesigned and rebuilt the vehicle but could never overcome the resistance of the Navy Department.

More obscure but vastly more important was the Experimental Tank Platoon that helped defend the base at Culebra, Puerto Rico. This unit was raised at Quantico on 5 December 1923 under Captain Leslie G. Wayt, and included Second Lieutenant Charles Finch, 22 enlisted personnel, and three M1917 light tanks armed with 37mm cannon; Finch commanded the unit at Culebra.[4]

The Six Ton Tank Model 1917 was an extensively reengineered version of the versatile and popular French Renault FT-17, manufactured by the Van Dorn Iron Works of Cleveland, Ohio. It could be armed with either a Browning machine gun or a 37mm M1916 Infantry Gun.

The tactical experience gained from the use of these tanks on Culebra was negligible because the terrain limited operations, but it did demonstrate the potential value of the tanks. The unit was issued additional tanks armed with machine guns, and eventually reached a strength of nine vehicles.[5]

In 1927 the Nationalist Chinese forces moved north against the warlords who controlled much of northern China. Nationalist troops pillaged property and killed foreigners in Nanking, so two regiments of Marines were dispatched to help defend American interests. Caught among Chinese Nationalists, Communists, warlords, and common bandits, the Marines were also plagued by their increasingly belligerent Japanese "allies." Based in the river port of Tientsin, the U. S. Army's 3rd Brigade and the 15th Infantry were tasked with the rescue of the American community in Peking should a crisis arise. This meant projecting a truck-or rail-mounted force across 100 miles of open country. The brigade wanted armored cars, but the Corps had no suitable vehicles.[6]

On 27 May a part of the Corps' small tank force, now under Captain Nathan Landon, arrived.* Brigadier General Smedley Butler organized a relief force that could move on Peking at short notice aboard a fleet of trucks escorted by the tanks, but refused to undertake regular patrols of the roads or railway line. This was just as well because the old tanks were nearing the end of their service life. In September 1928 the Tank Platoon sailed for San Diego, where it was disbanded. The expedition had provided experience in shipping and operating tanks in the field, but no tactical experience.

The onset of the Great Depression hamstrung the further development of the Marine Corps. President Hoover, an isolationist and fiscal conservative, advocated "disarmament by example" and ordered crippling cuts in defense spending, pitting the Army and Navy against each other for funds with the Marine Corps caught in the middle. Even a major increase in the Japanese depredations in China failed to sway his isolationist resolve.

The situation improved under the Roosevelt administration, and fleet exercises resumed in 1934. A particularly intractable problem was poor naval gunfire support. Battleships were still the queens of the fleet, and to risk their loss in support of secondary goals—even the seizure of bases for them—was anathema to the Navy.

Gunfire support for the Marines was sparingly and grudgingly delivered, and contemporary naval gunnery doctrine precluded delivery of precise fire on specific defensive works. Navy ships could not deliver the pinpoint accuracy necessary to destroy specific defensive positions and beach obstacles.

The obvious solution was the tank, and so a major part of the effort to build the Marines into a balanced fighting force was the development of an armored component. The independent development of a

---

* The unit was now designated Light Tank Platoon, Marine Corps Expeditionary Force, MCB Quantico. As far as can be determined five tanks, three with machine guns and two with cannon, were dispatched to China. (Ken Estes, personal communication)

Marine Corps armored force was nonetheless hampered by Navy requirements. The Navy specified that all landing boats and the equipment carried therein would be limited to what could be accommodated by the dimensions and lifting-capacity of existing boat davits and cranes.

The predictable result was Boat Rig A, a prefabricated timber ramp assembled on the beach by shore parties. The top of the ramp mated to the bow end of a wooden platform built atop a standard 50-foot motor launch. The problems are obvious in retrospect. A heavy vehicle or gun perched high atop a narrow-hulled, round-bottomed boat made for a topheavy craft. The boat's narrow, keeled hull made it unstable when grounded on a hard beach, so mating with the ramp and maneuvering the load off the boat were harrowing experiences.

Boat Rig A was directly responsible for one of the Marine Corps' major misdirections, the Marmon-Herrington CTL turretless light tank series. The 10,155-pound gasoline-powered CTL-3 had a two-man crew, and was designed specifically to fit within the Navy-prescribed weight and dimension limits.

Rowland Hall, then a second lieutenant in the Marine Corps Reserve, volunteered to transfer to the new tank unit. He said that the CTLs were "a real compromise. They had three bow machine guns, a .30 caliber in front of the driver, a .30 caliber in front of the gunner, and in the middle a .50 caliber. Very difficult [to operate]. No rotating turret: they just stuck out in the front. They were a makeshift thing, but they were the best the Marine Corps had at the time."

John M. Scarborough enlisted from Dublin, Georgia, and his route to the fledgling tank units was fairly typical: "I was in the infantry to start with, and I went out for boxing. The lieutenant in charge of boxing was in charge of the tanks. They only had five tanks in the Marine Corps at the time." His succinct assessment of the CTL-3 is that "they weren't anything to go to war with, that's for sure."

The Marines procured five of these tiny vehicles and nicknamed each after one of the famous Dionne quintuplets.[7] The CTL-3s were organized as 1st Tank Company, 1st Marine Brigade, activated on 1 March 1937. The Marines persisted with the development of this vehicle through 1941, and acquired both new and rebuilt designs, culminating in the three-man CTLS-4TAC, with two .50-caliber machine guns in a rotating turret and a reliable diesel engine. No matter how much the vehicle was upgraded, everyone knew that as a tank it was a farce.

The 1937 west coast FLEX-3, with the 1st Marine Brigade and the Army's 30th Infantry Regiment, involved only infantry and proved a near disaster as boats foundered and radios malfunctioned. Brigadier General James C. Meade, the commander of the 1st Marine Brigade, personally investigated the effects of naval gunfire and found that the heaviest naval bombardment left wire obstacles and simulated gun positions virtually unscathed.

Fortunately for the Marines more suitable means of getting heavy equipment ashore was being developed. Andrew Jackson Higgins of New Orleans had developed the Eureka boat, a shallow-draft wooden craft, to support construction and oil exploration activities in the swamps and shallow waters. The Navy was emphatically uninterested in this craft because it would not fit existing boat davits, but Navy and Marine Corps representatives continued to work with Higgins, and showed him intelligence photos of a Japanese landing barge with a bow ramp. Higgins used his own funds to build the prototype of the LCVP (Landing Craft, Vehicle, Personnel lightweight wooden landing boats), the most versatile and widely used landing boat of World War II.

By 1939 the Marines were experimenting with the Army's M2 light tank, and finally convinced the Navy that a self-propelled lighter capable of carrying a tank was a necessity. The Navy Bureau of Ships decided upon a 45-foot lighter of its own design, capable of carrying the 15-ton M2 light tank. A contract was let for 96 of these craft, even though the prototype capsized during testing.[8]

On 1 August 1940 the 1st Tank Company, 1st Marine Brigade at Marine Corps Base Quantico took delivery of 18 new M2A4 light tanks, each armed with a 37mm cannon and four .30-caliber machine guns, and powered by a radial aircraft engine.*

The M2A4 was a formidable vehicle in comparison to the old CTLs, but was already obsolete by the standards of European tank design. Crew comfort was a joke. "They were pretty darned sparse machines," said Rowland Hall. "They were crowded inside. They had four people in them, and they tried to put as much as they could [inside] ... The only ventilation that you really got, you had oil cooler heat exchangers built into the bulkhead between the fighting com-

---

* Some sources suggest that some had radial diesel engines but Ken Estes has concluded that the M2A4s were likely all gasoline models. Sources and documentation are frustratingly vague and incomplete.

partment and the engine compartment. The [heat exchanger] cooling fan pulled some air through the fighting compartment, which I guess just sort of leaked in through various places. There were no inlet vents. They were hot. We had no periscopes, just slits with a sliding piece of armor that you were supposed to look out of. They were pretty simple. Pretty crude."

As a platoon leader Hall experienced the problems that faced the new tank units firsthand: "From the first time we got the M2A4s, both east coast and west coast, we were expanding like everything. The training that was going on, first of all, was to teach the people how to drive the doggone things, and how to fire the weapons in them."

Shortly thereafter the company was shipped to Guantanamo Bay, Cuba, which offered better training facilities.[9] "We spent one afternoon out on a sort of a flat area near Guantanamo Bay, and for the first time fired the machine guns. I guess we fired five rounds out of the 37. It may seem strange, but we never fired either the machine guns or the 37 [again] until January of 1942. We never fired them, because practically all of that time we were taking huge influxes of recruits and trying to teach them their positions, their jobs, in the tanks. The training … was mostly small unit stuff. It was not until we got to Australia, after Guadalcanal, that we started really having any realistic tank-infantry coordination. All that time, we were training in the most basic things."

Before Hall's unit could absorb its new vehicles and personnel, it was off for its first potential mission, a rumored invasion of the main Vichy French possession in the West Indies. Hall:

In November we mounted an expedition that as far as we could determine was to be an invasion of the island of Martinique. Off we went, with ammunition and a great task force of aircraft carriers. The night before we were scheduled to land, we turned around and headed back west again and did some landing exercises at Culebra. The big problem was that we had four or five, maybe six, of these Navy Bureau of Ships landing craft which were sort of clunkers. They had twelve-cylinder Lincoln Zephyr automobile engines. The big problem was that the engines were always breaking down. They weren't very fast, and you didn't have enough of them. If you got two tanks ashore, that was a real big deal.

My tanks were aboard one ship, and I was on another one. We never saw our tanks until we got back to Guantanamo shortly before

Christmas. The training and development was hampered by the lack of these landing craft, but I'm sure a lot was learned from it.

In the three different times that I took my group over to Culebra, only on one occasion did we get to land my tanks, and then only two of them. The terrain on Culebra didn't lend itself to any sort of tank-infantry cooperation. What you were really learning was the timing, and how the heck to get the tanks ashore along with the leading waves of infantry, which was the doctrine then. In many cases you had to tow the darned tank lighters with other landing craft.

[The shortcomings of the Navy tank lighters led to desperate improvisations.] I remember one case ... when they took a 500 ton lighter, a big flat steel scow, cut a ramp in one end of it that would lower down, and towed it with a big Navy tug. The idea was that we were going to pile all the tanks aboard that thing and then haul it to shore. We would go off that, because we had nothing else. It was an unpowered vessel, and it was towed from Guantanamo by this great big salvage tug, the Seminole. It was makeshift, because we didn't have anything else.

Nobody really knew very much about how we were going to do this thing. The Landing Force Manual was talking about using the ship's boats and things like that. The changes were occurring so fast that you sort of made up things as you went.

Hall's wanderings had been part of FLEX-7, division-scale exercises involving the new 1st Marine Division. The underpowered Navy tank lighter had been an abject failure, taking more than three hours to carry an M2A4 light tank ashore and return to its mother ship—when it worked at all.

On New Year's Day 1941, Hall's unit was redesignated Company A, 1st Tank Battalion, part of the new 1st Marine Division, FMF. The 1st Division was shipped back from Cuba in April 1941.

Staff planners at Quantico were busily developing an organizational structure for the FMF tank battalions. Although the Marine divisions would function as light infantry, the organization of the tank battalions was influenced by the organization of mechanized units in European armies, and by the Army's experimental Armored Division. The Division Scout Company was included as D Company of the tank battalion, and equipped with motorcycles, scout cars, and light tracked vehicles for mechanized reconnaissance.

The four-wheeled, open-topped White Scout Cars were organized into three-vehicle sections attached directly to each of the tank companies.[9] The obsolete Marmon-Herringtons were assigned to the Scout Company.*

Bob Neiman joined the Marines as a member of the first Marine Corps Officer Candidate Class in May 1941, and upon graduation was assigned to the motorcycle platoon of the Scout Company. The company commander decreed that all officers would know how to operate all vehicles, so a Lieutenant Mattson was to give driving lessons for the CTL-3.

"I was having a ball," recalled Neiman. "We pulled up to the top of a rather steep hill, and he asked me if I was ready to take over control, and I said 'Sure.' Very confident. He had second thoughts, apparently, and said 'Maybe I'd better get down to level ground, and then you can take over.' With that, he pulled the right lever all the way back, and we made this complete about face."

A board of inquiry later determined that when Mattson executed the in-place turn, the track snagged on a stump hidden in the tall grass, pushing the small tank sideways.[10] Neiman:

> The next thing I knew we were rolling down this steep hill, over and over, sideways. The last thing I recall before I lost consciousness was that my crash helmet fell off, and I grabbed my head to try to protect it. The next thing I remember the tank has come to a halt. I don't know how many revolutions it made, probably four or five.
>
> I came to, and the reason I came to was that my feet are up in the air, my head is down, and Mattson is looking right down at me. Blood is pouring out of someplace in his head onto my face, and that's what brought me to. I hit him as hard as I could with my open palm … I didn't know whether he was alive and unconscious, or dead. It was also obvious to me that the tank was on fire. There was only one way in or out. That was on the top, and I didn't know whether we were upside down or not. If we were, our goose was cooked, so to speak.

---

* Actual tank battalion organization often did not conform to any official pattern. In actuality D Company appears to have been organized to absorb additional Marmon-Herringtons. In the 2nd Division the reconnaissance formation continued to be called 2nd Scout Company, and an E Company was authorized to replace A Company, at that time on detached duty with 1st Marine Brigade (Provisional). (Ken Estes, personal communication)

Fortunately the tank was lying on its side, and Mattson managed to open a hatch. Neiman: "I could see the grass around us was burning pretty well, and he said 'Move it!' I don't think my feet touched the ground 'til I reached the extremity of the ring of fire. I turned around to see him stepping out of the tank. Flames were coming up higher than his knees, but he was very unconcerned. He reached back in, and I heard a hissing noise. I thought 'My God, it's blowing up.' I hit the deck. He trotted over to me, and said 'What the hell are you doing on the ground?'"

The noise Neiman heard was the manual fire extinguisher system. No one had foreseen the need for an extinguisher system that worked while the tank was lying on its side. The efforts of a fire truck were ineffective, "… and that was *Marie's* last ride."

The Navy at last recommended that Andrew Higgins be invited to produce a prototype tank lighter by equipping a 45-foot Eureka with a bow ramp. Higgins produced a prototype within the week, but the Navy ordered 131 copies of a new 47-foot Navy model that had never been built as a prototype.

The August 1941 exercises at New River, North Carolina, involved the new Amphibious Force Atlantic Fleet, built around the 1st Marine Division and the 1st Infantry Division. The ambitious experiment proved to be beyond the capabilities of the joint Army-Navy-Marine Corps force. One of the few bright spots was the experimental Higgins tank lighter, and Rowland Hall recalled these exercises in a more favorable light: "We got a little bit better in the summer of '41, when we did the landings off North Carolina, off what is now Camp Lejeune. We had a bunch of tank landing craft made by Higgins, and they were far superior to the Bureau of Ships landing craft. We had a fair number of those, and we were able to get the entire complement of the company ashore, and maneuver there."

There still could be no meaningful tank-infantry exercises because the tanks were too busy working out the basic task of getting ashore. Hall and another officer acquired indirect experience in tank warfare when they were assigned as observers to follow the July and August 1941 maneuvers of the Army's new Armored Division in Louisiana and East Texas.[11]

On 1 September 1941, Rowland Hall was assigned to raise B Company, 1st Tank Battalion, to be activated in November. This company was equipped with M3 light tanks, a refined version of the M2A4. It retained the awkward internal layout in which the drive shaft from the radial engine ran down and forward through the crew compartment to the transmission mounted beside the driver.*

This layout meant that the two-man turret crew had to aim and fire the guns, and avoid tripping over the drive shaft as the turret traversed relative to the hull. Bill Finley later trained in these tanks: "It was bad. When you turned the turret you had to crank it manually, then find a place to step going around."

Another feature that few liked about the early light tanks was the poor communications. The radios were difficult for the crews to maintain, so that the tanks often communicated with signal flags, and there was no useful internal intercom. Bill Finley: "You didn't have any communications. The tank commander would be over on the [left] side where he could reach the driver. If he wanted the driver to go forward, he would just kick him in the back of the head. Of course you would have a helmet. If he wanted to stop, he would mash his foot down on his head. If he wanted to turn right, you mash on the right shoulder, left, mash on his left one ... That's kind of primitive communications." The gymnastic feats required to signal the driver while traversing the turret defy imagination.

Jim Carter, also a light tank driver: "Let some silly bastard up there get excited and then you really had trouble figuring out what he was doing ... When they wanted you to stop, they'd push your head right down between your knees, and you couldn't pull the levers back to stop. You wanted to kill 'em...."

The gasoline-fueled vehicles had self-starters, but cranking the diesel engine was a lengthy and awkward process. Finley said that to start the engine "... you had to ratchet them over with the drive shaft that came through right between the driver and assistant driver. You had a deal [like a wrench] that fit over that, and you had to turn it over ten, fifteen times sometimes." When the engine was stopped for several hours, oil pooled in the lower cylinders. If the oil was not manually redistributed, the high-pressure cranking process might bend the valve shafts or even blow off a cylinder head.

Finley: "Then you had a cartridge about six inches long, bigger than a shotgun shell. You put it in a breech behind you and locked it,

---

* The British Army nicknamed the M3 and later the M5 light tanks the "General Stuart" after the Confederate cavalry general of the American Civil War. The term "General Sherman" was later applied to the M4 series medium tanks. American troops seldom used these terms, and most veterans still do not use them. However, the terms are used here because of their familiarity to modern readers.

then mashed two toggle switches. It fired real loud, and the engine would go to turning over. Sometimes it would start, and sometimes you'd have to do it all over again."

Being kicked in the head or cranking the engine with a hand wrench was far from the worst indignity that the light tanks had to offer. Unexpected problems with the cramped little tanks revealed themselves only in actual combat. "Like going to the bathroom," said Carter. "It's amazing how people never think about that. If you got out you got killed, and if you stayed in there you shit your pants. You had a problem. Of course, no more than we were eating, it wasn't near as big a problem as it would have been. Unless you had diarrhea.

"It was kind of a personal choice. You either dirtied your pants, or got out and took a chance on somebody shooting you. It wasn't a place to be if something bothered you a whole lot."

On 1 January 1942, Rowland Hall was given the task of forming C Company at New River. This company was equipped with yet another model of light tank, the M3A1. The greatest improvement from the crew's point of view was the integral turret basket, with seats for the commander and gunner, which rotated with the turret. No more stepping over the drive shaft. Harold Harrison's unit later used the M3A1 on Bougainville, an extremely harsh environment for tanks: "The M3A1s ran quite well. If they were in good condition, unless there was some kind of abuse or some kind of hit, the maintenance was no problem. They were a very dependable tank."

The real problem with all the light tanks was the little 37mm main gun. The armor-piercing round was completely inadequate, and the high explosive round too small to be effective against pillboxes and bunkers. William McMillian, another prewar tank crewman, said that the joke was that "... it wouldn't knock the bark off a tree." The canister round was another matter, though. The deadly shotgun-like blast of steel pellets was devastating against infantry.

The new tank lighters could carry any of the light tanks in service by late 1941, but advances in tank design were making further 40-foot class boat design effort pointless, as none of the boats could carry the new 30-ton medium tanks. In December 1941 the tank lighter requirement was changed, and both Higgins and the Bureau submitted designs for a 50-foot medium-tank lighter. Before any prototypes were built, America was at war. In early April 1942 President Roosevelt ordered the procurement of sufficient tank lighters for

Operation Torch, the invasion of North Africa, set for September 1942. The Bureau of Ships ordered 1,100 copies of its own design.

Since Operation Torch was to be an Army operation, they were keenly interested in comparative tests of the prototype lighters held on 25 May 1942, near Norfolk, Virginia. Each boat would carry a medium tank. The tank in the Navy boat was carefully lashed down, the one in the Higgins boat merely chock-blocked.

Both boats completed the prescribed speed trial over a measured calm-water course without incident. When the two boats headed out into the more exposed bay en route to the test-landing beach, nature stepped in to override the Navy's decision-makers. In a gusting wind that raised choppy two-foot waves, the Navy boat began to wallow. As reported by the Army observer, the Navy boat began to porpoise into the low waves and take water over the sides, forcing the crew to man the pumps. When the Navy boat attempted to return to safety by making a wide turn that took it broadside to the wind, the boat heeled over on its beam. The crew rushed to the weather side, the better to jump overboard in anticipation of capsizing. The helmsman stepped outside the wheelhouse, desperately trying to steer from a position near the rail. The Higgins lighter was adding insult to injury by circling about the stricken Navy boat and making preparations to rescue its crew.

After the Navy boat regained control and turned back toward safety, the Higgins prototype chugged merrily to the test site and landed its tank. The coxswain allowed the boat to broach in the surf, but regained control and the Higgins craft backed off the beach under its own power. The Navy quietly suspended production of the Bureau model, and the Higgins design was standardized as the Landing Craft, Mechanized (LCM).

In late 1941 the biggest problems that still faced the tank battalions were organization and integration into the combined arms team. The individual tank companies were brigaded with rifle regiments, and functioned semi-independently. Despite all the planning and effort the Marines had yet to field a fully integrated tank battalion.

By 7 December 1941, the U. S. Marine Corps had already established in theory how it would crush the Japanese Empire. Specialized equipment had been developed, and was trickling through the procurement system. Among the most serious shortcomings were the absence of a suitable tank force, and an adequate means of getting it ashore. Worse, Marine tanks and infantry had never actually worked together in any but an abstract sense, and so despite heroic efforts, the Marines did not yet actually know how to use tanks to support the rifleman fighting his way up the deadly beach.

* * *

Elements of the Marine Corps had been sent in harm's way long before Pearl Harbor. To forestall a German attack on neutral Iceland, the British had garrisoned that critical mid-Atlantic position. In July 1941 the 1st Marine Brigade (Provisional) assumed the British 79th Division's responsibilities. Brigaded with the 6th Marine Regiment were a dozen light tanks, the 1st and 2nd Platoons of A Company, 2nd Marine Tank Battalion.[12]

Robert Swackhammer, a maintenance officer with the tanks in Iceland: "Down below our camp—Camp Whitehorse—at a little village called Aldufoss was a woolen mill fed by one of these hot water streams. During the noon hour the girls who worked in the woolen mill would come out there to go skinny-dipping. They paid no more attention to us than if we weren't even there. That was their attitude in general. They were neutral right from the word go, and they wanted to maintain their neutrality. Don't blame them for that. In order to do it, they didn't communicate very well with anybody as a general rule."

The tanks did very little combat-related training. "We were pretty well tied down acting as stevedores and that sort of thing," said Swackhammer. The aurora borealis impeded radio communication with the outside world, so "it took us a while to learn that the Japanese had bombed Pearl Harbor."

After an uneventful occupation, army units relieved the brigade. The tanks were shipped to southern California, where the Corps had established a training center on a former vegetable truck farm. Max English, a former machine gunner and a veteran of four years in the Army's horse cavalry, had also been with the tanks in Iceland. He was made a staff NCO in charge of driving instruction. "We came back to Jacques Farm, near San Diego. Anyone who was ever in tanks knows Jacques Farm. We went through every tank that the army or anyone else was building. They would bring one of them out there and we used them in our training."

At Jacques Farm the Marines took the first tentative steps toward development of a new doctrine for the infantry tank, and to systematize the training of tank crews. English: "We didn't run out 800 miles trying to fight something. We worked with the infantry. We went in slow. We went in first gear."

The Marine Corps had also started to systematically select potential tank crewmen. On 7 December 1941, G. G. Sweet was a sergeant in the Marine Corps, and a gun captain on the battleship *Nevada* at Pearl Harbor:

> The reason why I went to sea was that you could get fast promotions. In the infantry you couldn't get anything in those days. When the war came along, I was on a 5/25 [a five-inch caliber gun with a 125 inch-long tube] antiaircraft gun. I won't tell you I knocked any airplanes down, but we were doing the best we could. They were knocking us. We weren't doing too much damage to them.
>
> I got wounded three different times that day ... I got shipped to the Bremerton [Washington] Naval Hospital. That's when they decided they were going to survey me [declare him unfit for service] and send me out selling War Bonds. I was just too much of a gung-ho Marine, and I told them I could make it, and I didn't want to be surveyed. I wanted to see how many friggin' Japs I could kill. That's just the way I felt. I had trained all these years for just this one thing, you know.
>
> Anyway, about that time they started to check records on the old Marines, and they were starting to give us tests. They called it a GCT test. I was real high mechanically. Then they decided they thought I could go into artillery or something. Somebody mentioned tanks, and I said "That sounds good to me." They let me stay in the service—I was a platoon sergeant by this time—and sent me to tank school ... I was sent to A Company, I Corps Medium Tank Battalion at Camp Pendleton, California.

Unfortunately the tankers already headed for the Pacific would have to learn their trade through bloody on-the-job training.

In early 1942 the great worry of Allied leaders was that the seemingly invincible Japanese would invade Polynesia and cut the shipping routes to Australia. If Australia and New Zealand or the big islands of southern Polynesia were lost, a meaningful offensive against the Japanese would be impossible.

Rowland Hall's C Company, 1st Tank was given orders to join the 7th Marines: "Back in March of 1942 the 3rd Marine Brigade was formed, and its mission was to go out to British Samoa and help defend the communications line to Australia. My company was designated to become part of that operation. I was the junior company commander in the battalion. I was still only a second lieutenant, but they chose my company, I guess because it was the best-prepared." Hall's company was also the best-equipped, with new M3A1 light tanks, the best the Marines had.

The Japanese presented the Americans with an opportunity that changed the course of the war when they decided to invade tiny Midway. The Japanese allocated an overwhelming force of four fleet carriers to destroy the American fleet's remaining carriers. Forewarned by intercepted Japanese messages, the Americans had no intention of yielding Midway and girded for a decisive battle.

Midway was defended by about as many combat troops as could be crammed onto Sand and Eastern Islands. The fate of the 1st Defense Battalion on Wake had clearly demonstrated the folly of deploying these units without a maneuver element, so the battalion on Midway was reinforced with infantry and tanks. Thomas Cheshier was shipped to Hawaii Territory as part of the 2nd Separate Tank Company, with three platoons of M2A4s: "They split us up. One platoon went to the 6th Defense Battalion on Midway. One platoon went to the 1st Defense Battalion on Palmyra, and one platoon went to the 16th on Johnston Island, which I was a member of."*

The Japanese suffered a stunning defeat at Midway. As a parting gesture a Japanese submarine fired eight rounds from its deck gun at Midway, and similar gestures were made at other objectives, including Johnston Island. "A submarine came up out there one morning and fired three rounds at us," said Cheshier. "No damage, except that one of them went right through the mess hall. It was all over so fast."

After the brief excitement Johnston was "… pretty quiet. It was lonely duty. We used to do tank tactics with the infantry, running up and down the runway."

It was imperative to go on the offensive before the Japanese could recover from the Midway blow. The most critical place to blunt the Japanese advance seemed to be at their point of furthest advance in

---

* The history of the 2nd Separate Tank Company is one of the more confusing items in the history of Marine Corps armor. Ken Estes suggests that the Defense Battalion tank platoons were not a part per se of the company, but were administratively associated with the 2nd Separate Tank Company before being deployed as separate platoons. The 2nd Separate Tank Company went to Samoa, fought in the Marshalls campaign, and eventually was absorbed as B Company, 6th Tank Battalion. (Ken Estes, personal communication)

the southern Solomon Islands, where they were building bases to threaten the America–Australia lifeline.

First and foremost among Allied concerns, however, was not an offensive, but the defense of the communications route.[13] The victory at Midway might have opened a window of opportunity, but it was an opportunity the Allies were not mentally prepared to exploit to the fullest. Still wary of enemy capabilities, Chief of Naval Operations Admiral Ernest J. King instructed the area commander, Vice Admiral Robert L. Ghormley, that he must at all costs hold on to the big logistical bases on New Caledonia, Samoa, and Efate in the New Hebrides. Ghormley felt hobbled by this restriction, and would allocate only limited resources to the offensive.

As a result, the first American attack on the advanced Japanese positions in the southern Solomons would be a cobbled-up compromise. MacArthur would provide some air and naval support, but all ground troops would be drawn from Nimitz's command. This provision had serious repercussions for the Marine Corps. Both Nimitz and MacArthur had fully intended to use the Marines as amphibious shock troops, with the Army taking over for lengthy land campaigns. There were, however, only two Army divisions in Nimitz's Pacific Ocean Area, and neither was trained for amphibious operations.

Ghormley was reluctant to risk the Army divisions in the Solomons, and held back not only the Army divisions, but also the 3rd Marine Brigade. The brigade included C Company, 1st Tank Battalion which, not by coincidence, was equipped with the newest M3A1 tanks.

Ed Hutchinson volunteered for a transfer from infantry to tanks on Samoa. He was unusually well qualified by the standards of the time, with a background as a truck driver and mechanic. "I was just put in a tank and told to try and shift it and so forth." Such was the sum total of formal tank crew training for the men of the Fleet Marine Force who would now carry the war to Japan.

CHAPTER 2

BLOOD ON THE TRACKS: GUADALCANAL AND THE SOUTHERN SOLOMONS

T HE STAFF OF THE 1ST MARINE DIVISION clearly perceived the tanks as an important component of the division in the campaign to come. The shortages of shipping required that much heavy equipment, including the division's 155mm howitzers, the counterbattery detection and ranging gear, and all the 2½ ton trucks be left behind, yet the tanks went along. They were in theory a part of the combined arms team, though they had never actually exercised with the rifle units, and the practical details of tank warfare were still a mystery to both the tankers and the infantry.

A bigger problem was that American military men were still laboring under the *blitzkrieg* model for the employment of tanks, and had yet to learn that vastly different tactics would be required to deal with the peculiar courage and dedication of the Japanese soldier. The Japanese soldier's offensive tactics would prove inflexible and often fatally predictable, but in the defense he neither panicked nor became discouraged when surrounded, and could never be forced into surrender when his flanks collapsed. Instead, he simply hunkered down to die in place and make his enemy pay dearly for the mistake of leaving him alive.

The biggest problems of the southern Solomons operation as a whole were the timidity of the naval commanders and a confused command structure. Because Ghormley husbanded troops for the defense of his base areas, the 1st Division could take only two of its own rifle regiments, plus the 2nd Marines of the 2nd Division. A handful of relatively modern M3A1 light tanks would support the 2nd Marines, but only the old M2A4s and M3s would be placed at

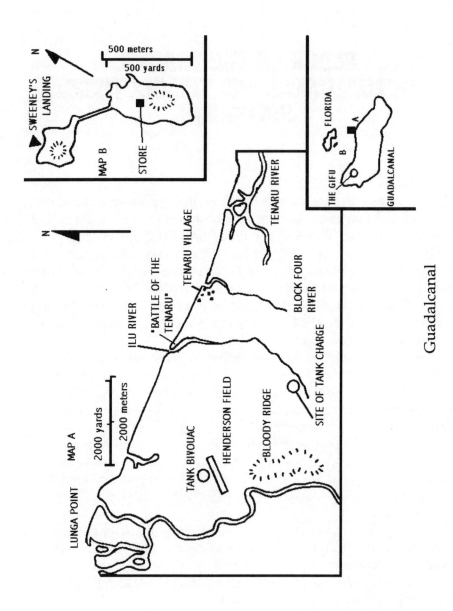

Guadalcanal

risk. The participants derided the offensive as "Operation Shoestring."

Vice Admiral Frank Fletcher, nominally Ghormley's subordinate, refused to commit his three aircraft carriers to the area for longer than two days, and apparently perceived the entire operation as just another carrier raid.[1] Ghormley and Rear Admiral Richmond Kelly Turner (commander of the Southwest Pacific amphibious force) made the operation needlessly complex by their insistence that the landing force also capture the smaller islands of Tulagi, Gavutu–Tanambogo, and Florida, which had anchorages and sites for floatplane bases that the Navy coveted. The Marines argued that a quick seizure of the main objective and completion of the airfield would allow them to dominate the smaller islands and take them at their leisure, but the admirals were adamant. The 2nd Marines, designated as the reserve for the operation, were diverted to the capture of secondary objectives.

These sideshow assaults on the small islands across the channel from Guadalcanal would be the first American landings against prepared defenses of World War II, the first amphibious tank assault by U.S. forces, and the first ever action involving Marine tanks. In the best military tradition, the tanks had to wait. Because of the shipping shortage the light tanks of C Company, 2nd Tank Battalion were administratively loaded, underneath lighter-weight cargo.

GAVUTU–TANAMBOGO

At 0740 on 7 August 1942, Company B, 1st Battalion, 2nd Marines, 2nd Marine Division* splashed ashore on Florida Island, and became the first American unit to land on enemy-held soil in World War II. The Japanese fled into the jungle-covered interior.

The small twin islands of Gavutu and Tanambogo, just to the north, were joined by a narrow 300-yard-long causeway and occupied by a handful of Japanese. Gavutu is only about 300 by 500 yards, Tanambogo slightly smaller. With no option to flee, the defenders of these small islands fought savagely and tenaciously.

---

* Marines refer to themselves by their regiment. For example, the 5th Marines refers to the 5th Marine Regiment of the 1st Marine Division. Regiments may be attached to other divisions, but are not permanently reassigned. The abbreviation system refers to units by company/battalion/regiment, for example above is B/1/2.

The plan was to land on Gavutu, subdue the defenders, then attack across the causeway. At 0613 on 7 August 1942, the light cruiser *San Juan* opened fire against the Japanese seaplane base. At 0800 hours Gavutu was attacked by the 1st Marine Parachute Battalion, which went ashore in three waves of landing boats.

As the first wave hit the beach the defenders poured a withering fire into the faces of the men in the boats and the parachutists were pinned on the beach with heavy casualties. With no way out but to advance and destroy the enemy, the parachutists clawed their way inland. By 1430 hours they had secured the small hill that dominates the little island, but with 10 percent casualties and many officers down, the 1st Parachute Battalion was hardly in a position to assault Tanambogo. All attempts to approach the causeway were driven back by machine-gun fire.

A hastily organized amphibious assault on Tanambogo by B/1/2 was bloodily repulsed, leaving 13 men pinned on the beach, unable to make it back to the boats. In the predawn darkness of 8 August this small group crept out through the shallow water beside the causeway.

The infantry commander ashore called for reinforcement and tank support, and the men of 3rd Platoon, C Company, 2nd Tank Battalion began to burrow into the holds for their tanks. The process of digging the tanks out from under a mass of other cargo and lifting them over the side with the ship's cranes lasted well into the day.

On the afternoon of 8 August the Marines organized a two-pronged attack on Tanambogo. K/3/2 landed on Gavutu and would attack across the fire-swept causeway. Only two tank lighters were available, so Item Company, reinforced by two M3A1 tanks under Lieutenant E. J. Sweeney, would land on the opposite shore.

At that time a tank platoon was organized with a four-man head-quarters section, five tanks with four-man crews, and a six-man maintenance section.[2] Sweeney decided to lead the small expedition himself. He left Platoon Sergeant William F. McMillian in charge aboard the transport ship and took over Sergeant Marsh's tank, number 11. He would be accompanied by tank number 14 under Sergeant Leon C. Richardt. Richardt was an experienced Marine who had served in China in the 1930s, then reenlisted after Pearl Harbor. The plan was for the lighters to return and shuttle more tanks ashore.[3]

McMillian was another old-timer who had enlisted in 1933. "I had just returned from China when we formed C Company. I applied for it. I didn't know anything about tanks. I was always infantry, but I was intrigued by the German *blitzkrieg* and all that. We had been getting news and magazine articles on that for several years, since '38 ... A Lieutenant Colonel Fellows, he knew me, and when I went in to volunteer to go to tanks, he says 'Tanks? Tanks? What do you know about tanks, Mac?' I said, 'I don't know anything, but I can learn.' He said, 'You know what's going to happen to you? During this war, you're going to be sitting back in a tank park somewhere, and we're gonna be out there winning the war!'"

The destroyer *Buchanan* shelled the defenders with its five-inch guns. At 1620 the riflemen waded ashore and moved inland through the trees. The ground was littered with fallen trees, stumps, and the wreckage of buildings, all smoldering from fires started by the *Buchanan*'s shells.

The bulk of the Japanese combat troops were busy defending the end of the causeway, but the defenders facing Item Company counterattacked in one of the first of the screaming *banzai* charges that would become all too familiar.

The niceties of tank-infantry coordination were poorly understood, and the surprising vulnerability of tanks to close infantry assault was known to Americans only in theory. The tragedy that ensued is understandable in light of the Marines' inexperience. Several versions of what happened next have been published, and some sources have stated that the two tanks had deliberately separated. McMillian doesn't accept this. Coordination between tanks was difficult because of the unreliable radios, and there was little room for maneuver among the trees, but both Sweeney and Richardt were experienced and level headed.[4]

The two tanks were advancing in front of the riflemen, covered by their fire according to doctrine. With no means of communicating with the infantry, the tanks pulled too far ahead, and when heavy fire drove the infantry to ground for a few critical minutes the tanks were unprotected. In later battles the tankers would learn to survive these traps by "scratching each others backs" with light machine-gun fire, or going back-to-back like fighters in a barroom brawl to protect each other's blind sides.

McMillian reconstructed the story from talks with the survivors: "He [Sweeney] was trying to operate his two tanks as a section ... I do know that from the rubbish and the smoke and haze, visibility was very bad. In fact visibility was very bad in the M3A1 light tanks anyway. The periscopes had not been perfected, and about the best sight the lieutenant could get would be a one-eyed squint through the gun sight. A man has a tendency when he gets into a position like that to fight for sight like a smothering man would for air."

Lieutenant Sweeney opened his hatch to orient himself and to coordinate with Richardt's tank. McMillian: "He stuck his head up once too often, and it was a very clean wound in his forehead. He probably died instantly. The radioman-loader that was in the turret with him was [Corporal] Fellows. I don't know whether the driver knew whether he was dead or just dying, just wounded, but the driver took him back down to the beach, behind the lines of the [infantry] company."

The number 11 tank was now out of the action because the commander aimed and fired the main weapons, the 37mm cannon and the coaxial machine gun. "The other tank, he backed up. Danley was the driver and Richardt the tank commander. Just as fate would have it, there was a coconut stump just the right height behind. As those light tanks backed up, the rear end reared up. He backed into this stump, and then when he started to go ahead again, it [the back of the tank] came back down. It just caught a flange, about four inches high, on the bustle of the tank back near the exhaust. He couldn't move forward or backward. He was trapped."

The infantry reported that the Japanese who set upon the stranded tank had jammed the tracks and tried to set fire to the tank with burning rags. "It is true that the Japanese were mostly working party people, not real troops. In there they had a bunch of laborers, and they did throw some crowbars into his track, which wouldn't have stopped him had he had mobility. At what point Richardt opened his hatch, I don't know. He apparently fired his Thompson submachine gun quite a bit. At some point they threw some kind of projectile, I don't know what kind of grenade it was, inside. Those M3A1s used 100-octane aviation gasoline, and there was of course ammunition inside and what have you.

"Richardt was cremated inside, and so was Danley.* The radioman, Moore, and the assistant driver [Pugsley] got out through the escape hatch. As far as I know, neither were wounded with gunshots. They were beaten, and later evacuated." Nearby infantry reported that the Japanese had beaten the two tankers, and even picked one up and

---

* MacMillian later pointed out that Danley may have actually been killed outside the tank, although most accounts state that he died inside.

smashed him repeatedly against the side of the tank. "They lay there and played dead."

It rained heavily during the night, and at some point, the two battered survivors from Richardt's crew managed to crawl back into friendly lines.[5]

McMillian waited until 1600 hours, but the tank lighters never came back for more tanks so he hitched a ride ashore, where he learned about the fate of his two tanks. The night was pitch black with heavy clouds and rain:

> I got the word that night, and I went over to battalion headquarters. It was still pretty hot around there, lots of shooting. The battalion commander told me I couldn't get over there to Tanambogo that night. I believed him, and I bunked down there at the battalion CP on Gavutu, there very near to where the old British store was.
>
> The next morning it got to be quite a battle. I didn't say goodbye to anybody. I made my way down to the causeway. The tide was low, so I got down beside the causeway, on the seaward side, and made my way, waded over to Tanambogo, to Company K.
>
> I saw the men of the crew that Sweeney was in, and talked to those people. I saw the lieutenant laying among the killed in action. The two boys from Richardt's tank that had been beaten and left for dead out there came to some time during the night, and how they crawled into our lines I'll never know. They were already evacuated.
>
> Later in the day I made my way out to the tank. It was still smoldering a little bit, warm to the touch. It had burned to a hulk. I counted right around it 41 bodies. I don't know how many of them the tank crew took care of. Knowing Richardt, I would believe that with a Thompson submachine gun, he took care of quite a few of them. But I wouldn't know how many, and of course I wouldn't know how many the infantry who were within sight distance of them took care of.
>
> I left there and went back down to the Company [K]. They had sent one tank lighter out to pick up the one operable tank that we still had, the one Sweeney was in. I took my crew, and we went aboard that lighter back out to the USS *President Adams*. They started loading it in the hold where my other tanks were. We hadn't more than got it slung aboard when we up-anchored. You know the story of how on that third morning the Navy ships left and took much of the heavy gear with them. There was, from Japanese air strikes, one of our ships burning. We got out of there, and went down to Espiritu Santo.

The Marine tankers had learned that the Japanese had little fear of tanks, and that their own tank-infantry coordination left a great deal to be desired.

GUADALCANAL

On the main island the Japanese fled into the interior, abandoning the airstrip which the 1st Division quickly renamed Henderson Field. The tanks of A and B Companies, 1st Tank Battalion were at first held as a division reserve, to be committed only upon direct orders of General Vandegrift. The tanks were released for operations, and A Company supported 1/5 in its advance along the coast, crossing what they thought was the Ilu River. These large patrols stumbled onto some enemy resistance, but the Japanese tended to melt away.

The Allied naval command had seriously underestimated the speed and ferocity of the Japanese reaction. Vice Admiral Gunichi Mikawa immediately set sail from Kavieng, New Ireland, with elements of the *8th Fleet*. Admiral Frank Fletcher feared for the safety of his aircraft carriers (three of the Navy's four surviving carriers in the Pacific), and retreated. When Fletcher informed the amphibious group commander, Rear Admiral Richmond Turner, of his departure Turner felt he had no choice but that the amphibious force also retire, even though fully half the Marines' supplies and heavy gear were still afloat.

In the early morning hours of 9 August a Japanese naval force slipped undetected through the Allied destroyer screen and inflicted the most one-sided defeat ever suffered by the U. S. Navy in wartime. Incredibly, Mikawa failed to follow up on his victory and fall upon the defenseless transports. Destruction of the troops, equipment, and supplies still afloat, but most of all the transports themselves, would have been a deadly blow to the Allies. On the afternoon of 9 August, as Mikawa steamed triumphantly away, Turner completed the victory for him as the last Allied naval vessel slipped over the horizon.

With the ships went not only the 2nd Tank Battalion vehicles, but ammunition and food, troops, barbed wire, coast-defense guns, radar units, and the heavy equipment needed to complete the airstrip. The troops ashore were left with rations for 17 days, and ammunition sufficient for four days of fighting.

The Marines had landed their SPMs (World War I vintage 75mm guns mounted on halftracks) of the 1st Special Weapons Battalion, and the elderly light tanks of A and B Companies, 1st Marine Tank Battalion. To defend the vital airstrip General Vandegrift established a 20-mile perimeter, far too long to be held by his limited force but necessary to establish lines along easily defensible terrain. The senior tank officer ashore was Captain Harvey Walseth, the commanding officer of A Company.[6] The tanks were held near the airstrip, where their mobility would at least give Vandegrift a limited ability to reinforce threatened points along the lengthy perimeter.

The Japanese underestimated the size of the American force on Guadalcanal, but realized that the Americans had to be thrown off the island. Their worst mistake was in attempting to do it with forces thrown piecemeal against the Marines. Another was to dispatch one of the foremost sufferers of the "victory disease"—overconfidence—to lead the counteroffensive.

Colonel Kiyono Ichiki commanded the *Ichiki Butai* (Ichiki Detachment), an elite combat team built around the *28th Infantry Regiment*, with attachments of engineers and artillery. Colonel Ichiki and 900 men landed about 40 kilometers east of Henderson Field, with orders to scout the American positions and await the balance of the *Ichiki Butai*, scheduled to come as soon as transport could be arranged.

Colonel Ichiki was so confident in the superiority of his men over the Marines that he decided to disobey his orders and exterminate the Marines before the balance of his troops arrived. He hatched a strikingly simple battle plan: march down the beach and through the heart of the Marine defenses. He even wrote out the appropriate diary entries in advance: "18 August, landing; 20 August, march by night and battle; 21 August, enjoyment of the fruits of victory."[7]

The defense in Ichiki's path rested on the western bank of the Ilu River. Because of the confusing maps the Marines thought it was the Tenaru, which actually lay about 3,600 meters to the east beyond the small Block Four River. To add to the confusion, the village of Tenaru sat on the western bank of the Block Four River, between it and the Ilu.

The Ilu, like most of the sluggish rivers on the island, has a mouth bar—really a part of the beach about 40 yards wide—across the river mouth. Behind the bar the Ilu was a stagnant, crocodile-infested stream about 30 yards across. Upstream a small wooden bridge spanned the stream, bearing the foot track connecting the villages of Lunga, Tenaru, and Block Four. Deep irrigation ditches traversed most of the area.

41

Reacting to information from his patrols, Vandegrift shifted the full strength of 2/1 to the sector of the perimeter along the river, with 1/1 in reserve. Artillery was registered on the coconut groves east of the river, and B Company's tanks moved forward. Rusty barbed wire, laboriously stripped from fences, was restrung to block the near end of the stream mouth bar. Two 37mm antitank guns were positioned to fire onto the bar, and two SPMs from the Special Weapons Battalion were brought up.

At 0310, 200 of Ichiki's men suddenly charged across the sandbar, right into massed machine-gun and rifle fire and devastating blasts of canister from the 37mm guns. A handful made it into the Marine positions where they were killed in hand-to-hand combat. Other Japanese tried repeatedly to cross the river itself. Japanese mortar and machine-gun fire silenced Marine machine-gun positions by firing at the muzzle flashes of the American guns. Snipers picked off the crews of the 37mm guns. Mortars dueled across the river, joined by two Japanese 70mm howitzers.

At daybreak the bar was covered with enemy bodies, some half-buried by the rise of the tide.

At 0800 Vandegrift released the reserve 1st Battalion to the 1st Marines' regimental commander, Colonel Clifton Cates, for a counterattack. The battalion and two platoons of B Company tanks were to cross upstream and envelop the remnants of the *Ichiki Butai* while artillery bombarded the open groves. The tanks became mired in the swamps and maze of irrigation ditches and came under intense fire.

John Scarborough was now a platoon sergeant and an acting lieutenant in one of the tank platoons that tried to get across upstream: "A tank slipped over in an irrigation ditch ... and couldn't get out. Sergeant Mallory had his tank pull up there. He jumped out, grabbed his cable, hooked it onto the other one, and pulled the thing right out. He was awarded the Navy Cross for that action." The encircling attack proved impractical for the tanks, but the infantry closed off any chance for the Japanese to escape.

The *Ichiki Butai* defended the grove as stubbornly as it had attacked the river line, and soon the riflemen of the 1st Battalion were locked in a deadly struggle. Colonel Cates ordered the remaining platoon of five tanks under 1st Lieutenant Leo Case to cross the sandbar and attack the enemy in the grove.[8] This was risky, but Ichiki's survivors were dispirited and vulnerable, the open grove allowed more room for maneuver, and five tanks allowed better mutual protection.

The tanks clattered across the bar, blasting the Japanese with machine guns and canister. Cates later said that he had intended that the tanks move onto the beach to close off the Japanese escape route.[9] Case instead took his tanks into the grove. If tanks are truly the heirs of the cavalry, then this day they were doing one of the jobs that the cavalry did best—slaughtering the remnants of broken infantry formations. The tanks pursued enemy infantry around the trees, playing the part of demons in a vision of hell. Observers noted that the rear plates of the tanks "… looked like meat grinders"[10] covered not just with the usual mud and sand, but with blood and gobbets of flesh and bone thrown up by the churning tracks.

The panicked survivors of the *Ichiki Butai* tried to flee into the jungle, but were driven back by the 1st Battalion. They fled into the surf, only to be driven back by the weapons of the 2nd Battalion firing along the beach. In the melee the Japanese disabled a tank, and there was no question of the crew making a run for safety.

Bob Neiman of D Company later joined the battalion on Guadalcanal and discussed this action with Case: "One of the Japanese stuck a rifle barrel into the suspension of one of Leo Case's five tanks, and stopped it. Leo had three tanks circling around that one tank. One tank moved directly behind it. The tanks had escape hatches in the bottom. There were four men in the tank. They would evacuate one man through the escape hatch and into the other tank that was right up against it. Then that tank would pull out and start circling, and another tank would move in. They evacuated all four men from the tank with no casualties."

Colonel Cates radioed the tank detachment to withdraw only to be told, rather tersely, to "Leave us alone. We're too busy killing Japs." Finally the tanks withdrew, and the riflemen of the 1st Battalion moved in.[11]

The surviving Japanese refused to surrender, and were hunted down one by one. Only a handful managed to escape. Colonel Ichiki burned the regimental colors, then shot himself. Fifteen survivors of the *Ichiki Butai*, all badly wounded, were captured.

Over 850 Japanese lay dead on the small battlefield, and the fight was the high-water mark of Marine tank operations on the island. The next day John Scarborough's 1st Platoon of B Company tanks assisted the infantry in a sweep down the beach to the point where Ichiki's men had landed. "There was a shot or two fired, but I think that any Japanese left just ran."

Both sides continued to reinforce the island, and the belated Japanese awareness of the threat resulted in dispatch of larger units. The bulk of General Kawaguchi's *35th Brigade*, including strong anti-tank detachments, landed near Taivu Point in early September.

The tanks continued to function as the division reserve, stationed near the airfield, which made them inadvertent targets for Japanese aerial and naval bombardments. Eugene Viveiros was another pre-war Marine who had transferred from the infantry to become one of the first tankers. He had been around bulldozers during a hitch in the Civilian Conservation Corps before joining the Marines in 1938, and thought that "… it beat walking, anyway."

Viveiros, a sergeant in Headquarters Platoon of A Company: "We were subjected to quite a bit of naval shelling by the Japanese. They would cruise through The Slot there, and during the daytime you could just about set your watch around noontime when the bombers would come over … Washing Machine Charlie, he'd float around all evening. He'd drop a bomb. It was more or less a harassing kind of deal to keep you all worked up and not getting too much sleep."

The small Military Police detachment, organized as infantry, assisted in patrolling the beach, so the tankers assumed some of their normal duties. Scarborough said that during this period "there wasn't much for us to do, so we looked after the maintenance of our tanks, and took over the guard for the Division headquarters. Every night we would go up there in the dark and set up positions."

The designers of the old light tanks had never considered the problems inherent in trying to maintain their product in a steaming jungle, ankle-deep in brackish water. Scarborough: "One problem, you got in the salt-water or salt atmosphere, the suspension would freeze. We had to remember to get out and drive over logs to keep it exercised, because we knew what would happen once they froze."

The fuel for the tanks had gone away with the Navy ships, but the Japanese had abandoned stocks of gasoline that varied from 60 to 90 octane. Eugene Viveiros said that in the absence of the proper aviation-grade gasoline the tankers "… started mixing in what gasoline we recovered that the Japanese had [left] there. The tank was fine, but you could tell the difference as far as the engine and its power."

For the first 20 days or so the Marines were on very short rations. Viveiros:

We captured quite a bit of supplies in what they called Kukun Village. These were distributed, and consisted of canned fish, rice, stuff of this nature. I know that for a period there until we got our own ships back in to bring supplies we were down to what they classified as about a quarter ration.

We would get kind of a gruel, a mush made out of rice and so forth, in the morning, with a couple of hardtack crackers that the Japanese had. They had some jams, and you'd get a third of a canteen cup of coffee. That would be your morning meal.

Then in early afternoon you'd go by and there'd be an evening meal quite similar to what you had for breakfast. The rest of the time you filled up on coconuts.

On 8 September the 1st Parachute Battalion and 1st Raider Battalion were dispatched to raid a Japanese base area. Kawaguchi had already marched into the jungle for an attack against the inland flank of the American perimeter, but among the booty captured were several antitank guns.*

Kawaguchi had drafted an elaborate plan for attacking the perimeter simultaneously at three separate points. The main attack would be delivered against what the Marines would later call Bloody Ridge, where the perimeter lay closest to the airfield. The usual poor Japanese communications, delays in moving through the jungle, and incessant prodding from higher commands to attack as soon as possible caused Kawaguchi's attacks to be delivered on three different nights. On 13 September Kawaguchi's main attack was defeated by American infantry and artillery fire; the tanks could not get up onto the ridge because of the dense jungle and deep ravines.

On 13 September two companies of the Japanese *2nd Battalion, 4th Infantry* attacked 3/1 near the headwaters of the Ilu River, 2,500 yards to the east of Bloody Ridge. Here the American positions fronted on a grassy river flood plain cut by deep ravines, and the Marines had burned off the dry grass to give clear fields of fire.

Here too the repeated Japanese attacks were broken up by machine-gun and howitzer fire. By morning the survivors were keep-

---

* Some sources list four 47mm guns and one 37mm antitank gun captured; other sources state that no 47mm guns were captured here.[12] No records document the presence of 47mm guns on Guadalcanal.

ing up a sporadic fire from trees and underbrush that rimmed the steep riverbanks and ravines on the far side of the field. The Marine rifle companies had not scouted this ground, and were unaware of the ravines.

The five tanks of Lieutenant Finan's 2nd Platoon, B Company, and another from the company's Headquarters Platoon, were sent to reinforce the position during the night. Neither the tank officers nor the infantry battalion commander realized their mistake when they formulated a plan to have the tanks attack the Japanese. The tanks clattered onto the open ground, unprotected by infantry. The Japanese opened fire when the tanks were about halfway across.

John Scarborough summarized the action as it related to him: "That was bad. They started drawing fire from the other side there, and the lieutenant was hit in the chest. It was an armor-piercing shot that pierced the armor and hit him. It killed him, of course."

"They shot a hole right through the turret," said Rowland Hall, "and killed him and a guy named Paul Lind, who had been one of my radio operators." The attack had located the remaining Japanese antitank guns.

One Japanese soldier in the bushes near a ravine set his own tank trap. Scarborough said that "the Japanese, if he saw an opportunity to sacrifice his life to get you, he didn't hesitate one bit. Nobody knows exactly what happened, because all the witnesses are dead now. He [the Japanese] jumped up and started waving and shouting at a tank. In my opinion, the driver, he just said 'We'll get you if we don't get anybody else' and he just barreled into the wooded area. Of course the Japanese didn't mind getting killed. The tank ran over the bank of the river, and there was about a 20 foot drop down there. The tank plunged down there and landed tracks-up. No way the men could get out of there. It was the platoon sergeant's tank that flipped over into the river."

Another tank was disabled, and only two tanks were able to head back toward the shelter of the infantry line. One threw a track about 50 yards from safety, and the crew hastily abandoned the tank and scrambled into the infantry positions. "Several [tanks] were disabled," said Scarborough. "We had a Captain there, Cooper (Francis Cooper was the B Company commander). He got a tank and ran out there and rescued as many men as he could. Some of them were bayoneted by the Japanese. He did a really heroic thing in getting all the men out that he could. There was a command sergeant, we called him

'Matty' Matthews, he crawled all the way back to our lines. The skin was rubbed off his forearms."

Once again an unsupported tank attack had proven a tragic fiasco. Obviously there was more to the effective use of tanks than charging into the teeth of the enemy, but later events would demonstrate that neither the Marines nor the Japanese were through making this mistake. Another lesson learned from this action was that the prominent white markings on the tanks were a serious tactical liability, as they made excellent aiming points. "They had big white stars painted on the turret ...," said Rowland Hall. "They had hit that thing right through there. I saw the tank after we all went back to Australia."

Repairs were simple. Hall: "They put a big plug in the hole. You just had a hole about an inch and a half in diameter. They just milled out a steel plug, and stuck it in the hole. Just like a cork."

The tank that had crashed into the river belonged to Sergeant Bronson, a friend of Eugene Viveiros:

[Two days later] I had orders to set up, on foot, a defensive perimeter while these maintenance people from B Company went in to try to retrieve that tank. Of course the bodies [of the men] that had all got killed were still in that vehicle. . .

There was a strange occurrence. We had an open area to cross before we got to the heavy foliage part where the tank had busted through and went into the river. Just before we got to that point I recall that there was an odd sound. Something I wasn't familiar with.

We got across this open space and then set up a defensive perimeter while the maintenance crews that were behind us from B Company were going to extract that tank. The sound that I was hearing was just a multitude of flies, blowflies trying to get into the tank that was bellied up, with the turret down into the water ... The buzzing of thousands, millions maybe, of flies, trying to get through the hull, to get at the bodies.

Both sides continued to pour fresh forces into the campaign, but the issue ashore would ultimately be decided by a series of savage naval engagements. The battle of the Eastern Solomons (23–25 August) cost the Japanese the carrier *Ryujo*, and forced the transport group it was escorting to turn back. The night action called the battle of Cape Esperance (11–12 October) failed to interrupt Japanese resupply efforts, but gave notice that the balance of power was shifting.

The next night a large Japanese force shelled Marine positions for 80 minutes on the infamous "Dugout Sunday." The tanks were in the prime target zone. Viveiros:

> It was the largest working-over we encountered. Within our own tank CP area we had quite a bit of the twelve-and fourteen-inch naval shells that landed.
>
> One ... evidently was armor-piercing. Its trajectory went through the machine shop that was part of our organizational equipment at that time. I remember that the machinist was almost in tears ... The shell trajected right down through the overhead of the machine shop, cut through where he had his lathe and all his instruments and tools and so forth on his workbench.
>
> Under several of the tanks within the dispersement, a few of the shells had penetrated. You could see where they went in under these tanks, but never did explode. We called the demolition team and they came up and checked it. We didn't know whether we should move these tanks, whether the vibration of starting up the tanks would cause an "activity" ... They said nah, they're okay, so we were able to move our tanks to different positions.

The massive bombardment covered the landing of nearly a full Japanese division west of the Matanikau River. By mid-October the battered, disease-ridden Marines had also been resupplied, and reinforced by the 164th Regimental Combat Team.

For their final counteroffensive the Japanese brought in 20,000 men of the *2nd (Sendai) Division*, two battalions from the *38th Division*, heavy artillery, heavy mortars, and the *1st Independent Tank Company*, attached to the *Sendai* to make it a "heavy" division. Like most Japanese tank units it was under strength, and landed on Guadalcanal with only 12 vehicles, two *Ha-Go* and 10 of the heavier Type 97 *Chi-Ha* medium tanks with low-velocity 57mm main guns. Two vehicles were damaged or disabled during the confused night landings.*

During October the reinforced Marines began to take the offensive, extending the perimeter to the west around the base of Mount

---

* There is a discrepancy between Japanese and American accounts of this unit. Japanese sources state that only 10 vehicles were successfully landed, while American reported a total of 13 destroyed.[13]

Austen, and encountered forces commanded by General Tadashi Sumiyoshi, including the tank company.

In another overly complex plan, Sumiyoshi was to fix the attention of the Americans on the Matanikau River crossings while General Maruyama hacked his way through the jungle to attack Henderson Field from the south.

Japanese tanks were first encountered in the fighting at the mouth of the Matanikau on 20 October, when an enemy patrol supported by two tanks hit the 3/1 defenses on the east bank. An American anti-tank gun destroyed one tank. Near sunset on 21 October nine tanks attacked across the sandbar at the mouth of the river. An American antitank gun destroyed one, and the others uncharacteristically retreated.

Maruyama had underestimated the difficulties of moving through the jungle and had overestimated the abilities of his troops, most of whom were seriously debilitated by disease and hunger. Maruyama delayed his attack from 22 October to the 23rd, and then to the 24th.

Sumiyoshi kept probing the Marine positions near the mouth of the Matanikau. At 1800 hours on 23 October the Japanese shelling increased sharply, and nine Japanese tanks led Sumiyoshi's main attack.

The deep river channeled the attack across the mouth bar, and the Marines had positioned several 37mm antitank guns to fire into the flank of any such crossing. Armor-piercing shot clanged through the thin side armor of several tanks. Within minutes, eight tanks sat burning in the wet sand.

The lone survivor rolled into the Marine positions, and a rifleman reached out and tipped a grenade into the left track. The explosion damaged the flimsy suspension, and the tank veered out into the shallow surf and stalled. An SPM fired a 75mm round into the rear of the stalled tank. The round tore through the engine compartment and exploded in the crew space, igniting the tank's own ammunition. The explosion hurled the small turret farther down the beach, opened the hull like a metal flower, and ended the Japanese tank threat on Guadalcanal.

Another attempt to cross the river inland was also beaten off, but in a sense Sumiyoshi did succeed. The Marines reinforced the river positions, because neither long-range patrols nor air reconnaissance had detected Maruyama's main force struggling through the terrible jungle.

Just after midnight on 25 October Maruyama's main attack surged out of the jungle south of Henderson Field. The night battle finally tipped in favor of the defenders when the Army's 3/164 Infantry was fed in to reinforce the thin Marine line. By morning, over a thousand of Maruyama's troops lay dead.

With the destruction of the *Sendai Division*, Japanese power on Guadalcanal was broken. Despite the best efforts of the *Imperial Navy*, the Japanese garrison of the island was dying of neglect. Guadalcanal was now a campaign in which American troops had to root a stubborn but immobile foe out of carefully constructed bunkers set into the jungle slopes.

North of the Matanikau the rough, hilly spine of the island extends nearly to the coast, and numerous streams cross the narrow coastal lowland. The worn-out light tanks were unable to maneuver over the steep slopes covered with slimy mud and dense jungle, and the puny 37mm cannons were not powerful enough to deal with the log and earth bunkers. After mid-January the light tanks were no longer worth the effort of pushing them through the jungle.

The exception was the effort to subdue a defensive complex on the western slopes of Mount Austen that both the Japanese and U. S. Army called the *Gifu*. This was the strongest defensive position ever encountered on Guadalcanal, a 500-meter oval with 45 interlocking and mutually protecting pillboxes. The complex resisted repeated attacks for a month, and the attack on the *Gifu* eventually consumed five battalions of Army infantry.

On 25 January the Army obtained several surplus Marine light tanks, crewed by men of the 25th Division Reconnaissance Troop. Three tanks started up a steep, tortuous trail toward the crest of the mountain, 455 meters above sea level. Rejects when the Marines got them, and worn out by five months of constant operations in the jungles and swamps, two broke down.

On the morning of 22 January the lone tank, supported by a squad of infantry, advanced along a ridge from the northeast and punched through the defenses of the *Gifu*. It destroyed three pillboxes. Turning around and breaking out, the tank-infantry team looped around to the side, and in midafternoon punched another hole in the *Gifu*. The *Gifu* was doomed.

Unknown to the Americans, and to the defenders of the *Gifu*, on 14 January General Hyakutake had received orders that Guadalcanal was to be abandoned. Thirteen thousand Japanese slipped away in a spectacularly effective evacuation on the nights of 1–2, 4–5, and 7–8 February 1943.

The tanks had not played a pivotal role in this first offensive, but Guadalcanal had not been the type of operation for which the Marine divisions had been trained.

For the tankers, lessons had been cruel. William McMillian: "There hadn't been enough tank-infantry training, as a tank-infantry team. Then of course, the tank-infantry team's no good if you don't have communications. We learned a lot of lessons." John Scarborough: "It [tank-infantry coordination] was something we had to work out as we went along."

The first American amphibian tank designed by J. Walter Christie being unloaded from a battleship onto a submarine during the Fleet Landing Exercise of 1924. The submarine would submerge, allowing the tank to float off the deck frame. (*Marine Corps Historical Center*)

An M3A1 of Rowland Hall's C Company, 1st Tank Battalion, comes ashore from a Higgins Tank Lighter (LCM-1) at New River, North Carolina, 1941. The tank still carries an Army serial number (USA W-308903) in light blue. (*National Archives*)

An assortment of vehicles at Tutuila, Samoa. The two tanks on the left are M3s. The vehicles on the right are Marmon-Herrington light tanks of the Division Scout Company. The first in line is a CTL-6, the two behind are CTM-3TBDs with boxy turrets mounting a single light machine gun. (*Marine Corps Historical Center*)

An M3 light tank of B Company, 1st Tank Battalion, entrenched and camouflaged near Henderson Field, Guadalcanal. At this time the airfield was under regular air attack. The turret has a white band, with an interrupted circle surrounding the number 2, also in white. (*National Archives*)

A mixed column of light tanks on Guadalcanal. The first vehicle is an M2A4 of A Company, 1st Tank Battalion, followed by two M3s of B Company. (*National Archives*)

Crewmen pose beside their M3A1 light tank. C Company, 1st Tank Battalion, was not initially deployed to Guadalcanal. The square and number 2 are in red. (*National Archives*)

Two M3A1 light tanks of the 1st Tank Battalion at an improvised re-fueling station on Samoa, March 1943. (*National Archives*)

A light tank of the 9th Defense Battalion Tank Platoon and Army infantry advance through typical New Georgia terrain. (*Marine Corps Historical Center, Army Signal Corps*)

Lt. Robert Blake (kneeling) and his crew examine damage caused by a Japanese Type 99 magnetic mine on New Georgia. (*Marine Corps Historical Center*)

Light tanks patrol the outskirts of the airfield at Munda. The crewmen in the lead tank are wearing two different types of the old-fashioned tanker's helmet. The second tank in the column carries the inscription "Peggy" on the side of the turret. (*National Archives*)

Japanese 37mm Type 94 antitank gun captured on New Georgia. This example is missing the gun shield, but shows the awkward driven spades that prevented rapid traverse, and the old-fashioned design. The ammunition case holds an armor-piercing (left) and a high-explosive round. (*National Archives*)

A 47mm Type 01 antitank gun captured on New Georgia. This was the most modern gun in the Japanese inventory, although it retained the driven spades. It could penetrate the armor of American medium tanks, but the small bursting charge inside the round often failed to explode. (*National Archives*)

M3A1 light tanks of the 3rd Tank Battalion replenish fuel and ammunition on the beach at Bougainville, 15 November 1943. The men are removing 37mm rounds from their waterproof storage tubes. (*National Archives*)

Near the junction of the Numa Numa and Piva Trails, Bougainville, November 1943. 1st Lt. Leon Stanley's tank snagged the vine dangling across the center of the photo, which detonated a mine that ripped off the track. When the officer dismounted he was shot, and lies dead under the back of the tank. (*National Archives*)

An M3A1 of B Company, 3rd Tank Battalion, waits on the Numa-Numa Trail on Bougainville. When both Lt. Stanley's tank and the accompanying tank were knocked out of action, this vehicle and two others were sent to the rear with a load of wounded. (*National Archives*)

"The light tanks were all knee-deep in mud."— G. G. Sweet. (*National Archives*)

CHAPTER 3

A JOB FOR THE ARMY: THE NEW GEORGIA CAMPAIGN

T HE NEW GEORGIA CAMPAIGN, fought largely by the Army's light infantry divisions and Marine Corps Raider Battalions, is one of the "forgotten battles" of World War II. Sharing in the obscurity of this grim struggle was another band of forgotten warriors, the Marine Defense Battalions, who provided heavy artillery and tank support.

The Japanese began construction of an airfield at Munda Point on the western tip of New Georgia on 21 November 1942. The airfield was seldom used by the Japanese, as United States Marine and Army Air Corps squadrons on Guadalcanal pounded it on a regular basis.

The Munda Point facility had strong natural defenses. The broad Roviana Lagoon extends out to low-lying islands, so that any attack from the sea would have to struggle through an uncharted maze of small channels. To the east and west is nearly impenetrable jungle, assuring a long slog for any force attacking overland. A narrow trail extended north to Bairoko on the north coast, assuring that personnel and some supplies could always reach the position from big depots on Kolombangara.

The garrison, elements of Major General Noboru Sasaki's *17th Army*, included about 3,000 men of the *229th Regiment*, the *10th Independent Mountain Artillery Regiment, 15th Air Defense Unit*, two antiaircraft machine-gun companies, two regiments of pioneers, and coastal guns. At Bairoko on the north coast was the *6th Kure Special Naval Landing Force*.

The American military in World War II favored simple strategic and tactical plans: concentrate on the minimum number of critical objectives, and strike with overwhelming power. At New Georgia limited resources, the absence of any formations fully trained in

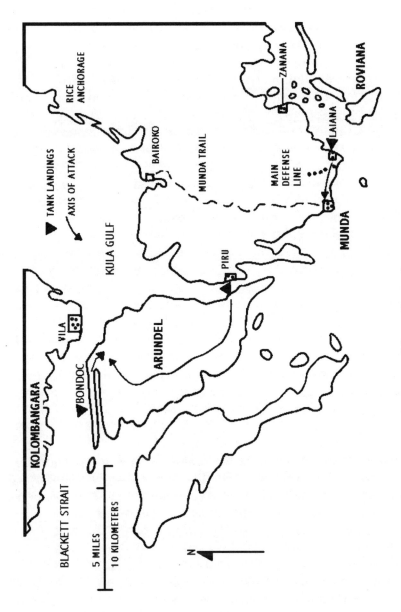

New Georgia

amphibious operations, and geography limited the ability to strike directly at a single key objective.

The overarching issue, however, was doctrine. To Army leaders raised up in the bloodbaths of the Western Front, a Marine Corps-style frontal assault was anathema. The "school solution" was to land at some distance and march overland to the attack. For this reason the New Georgia campaign evolved into one of the most bewilderingly complex operations of World War II and a prolonged and horrific struggle in the jungle.

The original plan was based on ignorance of actual conditions on New Georgia, and envisaged establishment of a logistical center at Segi on the southernmost tip of New Georgia, followed by an overland advance on Munda on the northwestern tip. Every experience on Guadalcanal and New Guinea argued that long approach marches involved a protracted struggle with the jungle, a far more implacable enemy than the Japanese.

Admiral William Halsey's staff formulated a more realistic plan, but one that still involved a lengthy overland approach. An Eastern Force would seize Segi, and several other small anchorages as bases and logistical centers. The main Western Force would land on Rendova Island, from which Munda could be bombarded by long-range guns. Rendova Harbor would provide an advanced base from which to interdict enemy reinforcement from the big bases on Kolombangara. This force would include the 43rd Infantry Division, 136th Field Artillery Regiment, detached from the 37th Infantry Division, the 24th Naval Construction Battalion, the 9th Marine Defense Battalion, O Company of the 4th Marine Raider Battalion, and the 1st Commando of the Fiji Guerrillas.

Three Marine defense battalions would play a disproportionately important role in the campaign. Hastily converted to what amounted to heavy weapons brigades, they would augment the Army divisions, which possessed inadequate artillery and no heavy vehicles.

The 9th Defense Battalion was formed at Parris Island and served on Guadalcanal from November 1942. Prior to the New Georgia campaign it was in part reorganized as a heavy field artillery unit with two four-gun batteries of long-range 155mm M1A1 "Long Tom" guns. The antiaircraft batteries received new 90mm, 40mm, 20mm, and .50-caliber guns. It already had a reinforced platoon of eight M3A1 light tanks. The 10th Defense Battalion would eventually contribute its tank platoon, as would the 11th Defense Battalion.

Defense battalions were raised on a catch-as-catch-can basis. Sixteen-year-old Ed Sahatjian quit school to join the Marines, and was assigned to the 9th Defense Battalion as an antiaircraft machine gunner: "The drill instructor was telling me 'Lead the target, lead it, lead it.' Well, I led it too far and put a hole in the fuselage of the airplane that was carrying the target, so I was shanghaied to motor transportation. In other words, they didn't want me to shoot the .50 caliber. We got our tanks on Guadalcanal, because we could operate those engines, [which were] like tractors and bulldozers."

Sergeant Bob Botts was shipped from California to what is now Camp Lejeune, North Carolina as part of the cadre for a new rifle regiment: "[Some of the men were] ... in the tent there one night. I come tearing out of the tent and [hit] this first lieutenant and knocked him right flat on his back out there in the sand." Botts helped the officer up and apologized. After a brief conversation Lieutenant Irving P. Carlson produced a letter from the commanding general authorizing him to take suitable personnel for a new tank platoon in the 11th Defense Battalion.[1] Botts soon found himself in a tank.

Japanese action forced the premature opening of the offensive when they sent a reinforced company against Segi Plantation on the southeastern tip of New Georgia to flush out a particularly aggressive Coastwatcher. New Zealander Donald Kennedy called for help on 18 June, and an odd assortment of troops was dispatched to protect him. The rescue force landed on 21–22 June, and the infantry moved far inland without encountering a significant enemy force.

Sasaki, convinced that the Americans would launch an amphibious attack directly across the Roviana Lagoon, pulled his scattered units back into the main Munda perimeter.

On 30 June the main Allied attacks fell. Two companies of the 169th Infantry secured the small islands at the eastern end of Roviana Lagoon. Two more companies of the 169th Infantry, with Tonganese and Fijian Scouts, landed unopposed near Zanana Village, only 9,000 yards east of the main Japanese airfield, establishing a beachhead near Munda ahead of the original schedule.

In the dissipation of effort that characterized this campaign, a Marine Raider regiment and army troops that were to serve as the operational reserves were committed to what became known as the Dragon's Peninsula campaign, intended to sever the overland route between Munda and Kolombangara. The plan was to make an unopposed landing, then march overland to capture the small barge bases at

Enogai and Bairoko on the northwestern coast. On 4 July the 1st and 4th Battalions of the Raiders landed at Rice Anchorage, north of Munda on the opposite coast of the island, and on 7 July the 1st Battalion and the Army's 3/145th Infantry moved south to attack Enogai.

This force did not succeed in cutting the Munda Trail until 2 August, in part because of faulty intelligence; there was a branch of the trail unknown to Allied intelligence, and this was the main route used by the enemy. Bairoko was eventually captured three weeks after the fall of Munda.

By 4 July, 1/172 had crossed from Rendova to Zanana, and the Long Tom guns were shelling Munda. On 6 July the 172nd launched its cautious attack westward toward Munda, with the 169th on the inland flank, followed by engineers who built a single-lane corduroy road through the swamps.

On 8 July the tanks of the 9th Defense Battalion were brought into Zanana by barge. The arrival of the tanks coincided with a raid by 16 Mitsubishi bombers and their fighter escort. Shells from the 9th Defense Battalion's 90mm antiaircraft guns detonated the bomb load of one of the bombers, starting a chain reaction of explosions. The wreckage of 13 bombers and a fighter rained down on the beachhead.

Much precious time was lost because of the slow and methodical advance, and in a postwar interview General Sasaki marveled that "... the speed of the infantry advance was extremely slow. They waited the results of several days of bombardment before a squad advanced."[2] There was a price to be paid for this caution. Ten days later the soldiers were within 2,500 yards of the main airfield, but faced Sasaki's main defensive line embedded in a range of low hills. Japanese construction troops had built lines of interlocking bunkers into the rough ground. Not surprisingly the 169th stalled, badly depleted from the constant ambushes and exhausting struggle with the jungle in the advance from Zanana.

The debilitated troops captured Laiana on 13 July, and on 14 July the M3A1 light tanks of the 9th Defense Battalion, held at Zanana to preserve the log road, were transported by boat to Laiana. From the first day life had certain grimly routine elements. Ed Sahatjian: "We got bombed every day, every single day, for 120 days. I was more or less diving under my tank, and then I realized they were aiming for the tanks. I dove into a hole nearby, and landed on a dead Jap. Cripes, it smelled like a bad tooth. I couldn't get that odor out of my clothing, and had to jump in the ocean."

On 15 July a three-tank section under Lieutenant Robert W. Blake, the commander of the Tank Platoon whom Sahatjian described as "a real tough hombre," supported 2/172 along the coast. Three other tanks under Gunnery Sergeant Charles Spurlock worked with 3/172 on the inland flank. Each tank had infantry assigned to guard it against close attack and Solomon Islanders as foot guides to spot targets in the dense jungle. About 100 yards forward of the starting line the tanks encountered the first defenses.

The infantry and foot guides marked enemy emplacements with tracer, but heavy undergrowth hid targets from the tank gunners. Enormous stumps and fallen trees formed a maze through which the tanks had to maneuver. Tangles of smaller logs were traps for the tanks, and the ground was so rugged that the tanks could not elevate or depress their guns sufficiently to fire on targets dug into the slopes.

All day the tanks engaged in a deadly game of hide and seek, stumbling forward as the infantry was repeatedly driven to ground. The tanks would inch forward only to be struck by a hail of machine-gun fire, often from several sides at once. Looking out an open hatch to spot the source of fire, or to pick a path through the tangled ground, was not an option.

In the cramped turret Ed Sahatjian and his fellow crewmen had to "... load, unload, throw the shells out of the base [of the turret]. All the smoke was inside the turret" since the small tanks did not have ventilators. Each time the cannon breech was opened the backdraft sucked acrid powder smoke into the turret. Despite the danger from stray rounds, the crews sometimes had to open a hatch in order to breathe.

Sahatjian: "We worked with leather helmets and glasses. It was hot, everything was hot. But you know when you're a young man you can take it. We wore something like ski glasses, with a rubber base that fit under your eyes. Every time we came out of a small battle, we were black from our nose down."

Not only was there the threat of random rounds entering the vision ports or hatch, but there was the constant threat from suicidal attackers armed with flamethrowers and Type 99 *Hakobakurai*.

The *Hakobakurai* magnetic grenade-mine was a canvas pouch containing a 12cm disc of molded TNT, with four small magnets sewn into the cover and a time-delay fuse screwed into the side. The user snapped the protruding fuse head initiating a four-second delay. In theory the user could throw the device against the side of the tank, and the magnets would hold it in place until it exploded. It usually bounced off, and it was common for Japanese attackers to hold these devices in place until they exploded.

The Type 99 would theoretically blow a hole through 12mm of armor, and so could barely penetrate the deck armor of the light tanks. In fact, it would punch a six- or seven-inch diameter hole in the deck or rear armor. When placed on the engine access doors under the overhanging rear deck, the explosion would damage the cooling fans, causing the engine to overheat.[3]

The enormous consumption of 37mm ammunition became a problem, as canister rounds were used to shred the thick underbrush, but slowly the bunkers were revealed and blasted out at point-blank range. The tanks closed to within 10 yards, where the gunsights for the 37mm cannon were useless.[4] By nightfall Blake's tanks had broken the seaward flank of the defenses. Spurlock's tanks and riflemen discovered an extremely strong position, with multiple bunkers linked to the rear slope of the hill by trenches. By dark, Spurlock's tanks had fought their way to the base of the first hill, and blown out five bunkers on its forward slope.

In the tangled jungle the enemy was not the only problem. Thick undergrowth hid gullies and huge bomb craters. Ed Sahatjian's tank "… hit a 500 pound bomb crater, and rolled over. We only had a slot to look through, plus I had a periscope. I never used it; I used the slot. The driver had a slot. You could hear the bullets hitting the turret."

The platoon leader, Lieutenant Robert Blake, tried to describe the relentless brutality of one day's fighting.* In a five-minute duel with a heavy machine gun, Blake had already slaughtered several enemy gunners in succession, when yet another tried to reach the abandoned gun: "I align the sight pipper on the Jap's shoulder and press the electric contact. When the smoke drifts off, the pile of Japs has blossomed out. An arm is lying on the trail. Even as I search the littered remains for further signs of life, a helmet bobs along behind the embankment. I level my sights on the enemy gun and wait. Without hesitating to look at the tank, the Jap crawls quickly over the bodies of his comrades and takes his place behind the gun. I cannot believe it. His

---

* Blake's "Death On The Munda Trail" and "Battle Without A Name," originally published during World War II, are some of the few contemporary accounts of tank combat written by a tank crewman. Written at a time when euphemisms were the norm, they are surprisingly modern in their graphic descriptions of the stress and savagery of close combat.

hands and knees must be sopping with their blood. He must be sitting in it!"

The enemy soldier struggled to reload the damaged gun, then opened fire on Blake's tank. As the rounds drummed on the armor, Blake's crew urged him to continue the slaughter. Looking his enemy in the face was an unusual experience for a tank crewman.

> A live Jap, so close I could almost touch him. He is wearing a quilted cover over his helmet, for camouflage. I can see the sparse growth of moustache across his upper lip. What can he be thinking? It is frightening enough behind this armor. Think of the livid terror in that man's heart, knowing and waiting for the shell to come spinning into his face, to smash through his eyes and splash his brain like a gray paste on the leaves. What magnificent courage! But wasted. They probably think they can bait us in with that gun, and then jump us with mines.
>
> The Jap lowers his eyes to check the lay of his gun, then straightens up to fire again.
>
> I let him get his first shots away, then knuckle down on the trigger. When the smoke thins, he is sprawled on his back against the bodies of the other gunners, his heels pounding the ground and his arms clutching convulsively at the air.[5]

Blake marveled at the courage of the enemy, but when he dismounted he found himself standing among the swollen and blackened bodies of dead Americans, including a party of stretcher-bearers and wounded, gunned down by the same Japanese machine guns several days before. Aghast that his tanks had crushed some of the bodies in the confusion of the attack, Blake's sympathy for the enemy quickly evaporated.[6]

On 16 July the Americans changed tactics. On the inland flank three tanks and a squad of infantry punched a narrow hole in the defenses. Spurlock's tanks moved around the hill and into a saddle behind. As the tanks retired, one tumbled into a hidden hole and a log drove through the belly escape hatch, breaking Spurlock's leg.

On the left the tanks supporting 2/172 outflanked the enemy positions by moving along the firm beach, advancing 200 yards only to discover that the infantry had been driven down near the start line. The tanks returned to collect their charges and went back into the underbrush only to be left unprotected when the riflemen were again driven down. The tank crews thought the men they saw in the underbrush were friendly infantry, but they were not. Japanese infantry swarmed over the unprotected tanks.

The tanks defended themselves by circling, spraying the thick underbrush and each other with machine-gun fire. Type 99 mines damaged all three tanks. The tanks, still machine gunning the underbrush at random, broke free and fought their way back to friendly lines, though one broke a track and had to be recovered after dark.

That night the fresh 3/103 relieved the battered and diseased 2/172. The exhausted tank crews worked all night to replenish ammunition and do what repairs were possible, but one tank had to be sacrificed for parts and unwounded crewmen.

On 17 July Blake's section again went forward against the troublesome thicket near the beach. Thirty riflemen were assigned to protect each tank as they advanced in a column. The infantry eventually were stripped off by close-range ambushes, and bullets striking the tanks sounded like "... hail on a roof."[7] A Japanese sprayed Blake's tank with flamethrower fuel, but was gunned down as he struggled with the awkward cartridge igniter.[8] Others rushed out of the jungle with *Hakobakurai*. The following tanks managed to rake the enemy off the two lead tanks, but the trail tank had no such defender, and an enemy soldier placed a mine on the roof next to the turret ring. The blast caved in the armor, jamming the turret and critically wounding two crewmen.

Although the underbrush was swarming with enemy infantry one man dismounted and hooked a tow cable to the crippled tank. The tanks managed a slow fighting withdrawal and reached safety by 1400 hours. Further attacks were called off for the day, and the tanks sent to the rear to recover.

During the vicious struggle in the hills Sasaki was organizing a counterattack. He sent the *Tomonari Force* on a three-day march through terrible jungle to fall upon the American rear as part of a complex, coordinated attack. The *6th SNLF* would launch an amphibious assault behind the American lines. The defenders of the hill line would attack to roll up the Americans when the *Tomonari Force* and the *SNLF* severed their support services. Again the old Japanese bugaboo of complex plans with poor communications asserted itself. The troops in the hills were too disorganized and battered to play out their part, and American shelling disrupted the amphibious landing. Only Tomonari launched his attack on schedule.

Tomonari found himself among the vulnerable support units strung along the beach, and the main medical collecting station, engineer camps, the 172nd Regiment Anti-Tank Company, and the 9th Marine Defense Battalion's antiaircraft positions were hard-hit. By dawn the Japanese had been driven off, though for weeks the survivors launched scattered raids. The Japanese were on the ropes, but the American infantry was also close to collapse. Unit strength was below 50 percent from casualties and disease, and the 43rd Division was afflicted by the highest incidence of "combat fatigue" in the Pacific Theater.[9]

In late July the tanks and infantry faced the last high ground before the airfield, a terrain feature called Bartley Ridge. The fight was nightmarish, and Sahatjian, like so many others "… did things I don't want to remember." When the tanks broke into enemy positions "I'd kill everybody in the area, machine gun them with .30 caliber. My radioman did that. All of a sudden I ran into a payroll place, there was payroll money all over the place. I took it all, millions of dollars. Then I found out it was all occupation money. No good, you know."

When the tanks literally overran the enemy in these horrid little encounters, "You can hear them popping. Heads cracking, screaming, everything else…. You're laughing from ear to ear while you're doing it. I don't know what got into us at that point. Maybe it was just a cop out, a way out of the picture."

The American drive was delayed until 24 July while fresh troops were brought in, including the Tank Platoon of the 10th Defense Battalion. One clear lesson from the fighting thus far was that although better tank-infantry coordination was needed, the tanks were the weapon most able to deal with the sturdy enemy bunkers.

There was no respite for the tankers, and the five surviving light tanks of the 9th Defense Battalion were back in action on 24 July in support of the 172nd Infantry. The enemy unexpectedly abandoned two Type 01 47mm antitank guns and fled. The right flank of the American line had pushed about 500 yards ahead of the left or seaward flank, and the first goal was to straighten the line. The tanks struggled up a bunker-covered hill against heavy enemy fire, where repeated hits by a particularly proficient sniper crippled one tank by wrecking the gunsight periscope. Others were troubled by low quality fuel, and over-revving the engines to compensate for the lowered power output caused the radial engines to overheat.

In this attack Ed Sahatjian was injured when his tank was hit and overturned into yet another bomb crater: "When I tipped over the tank, I crawled out. A hatch or something hit my leg. It broke my kneecap. I crawled into the woods with my tank driver. His arm was off, so he was hurt pretty bad. He died." Only two tanks remained in action, but the hill was secured. The Japanese fell back 500 yards to repeat the bloody performance.

On 26 July the 9th's tanks were again in action, destroying 74 pillboxes as the 103rd Infantry moved against the collapsing enemy. The heaviest fighting was inland, where the 10th Defense Battalion's tanks under Lieutenant Bailey were supporting the 161st Infantry in their attack on Bartley Ridge. Six tanks went into the attack, deployed in a line of three backed by a second line of three, with infantry in direct support. They drove straight into a Japanese trap. Flanking fire immediately drove the infantry down, and a Japanese placed a magnetic mine on the deck of one of the leading tanks, crippling it and wounding two of the crew.

The survivors kept fighting their way slowly forward for another five hours until another tank bogged down, and had to be abandoned when fuel and ammunition ran low. As they retreated, two of the surviving tanks became disoriented and veered off into the jungle, where one fell victim to an enemy tank-killer team.

Bailey led his three surviving tanks back and attempted to extricate his lost vehicles, but was forced to pull back ahead of the coming night. The next morning Bailey found one tank damaged beyond repair and set it afire, towing the other to safety.

On 27 July the scene of action shifted back to the left flank. A morning attack in support of 103rd Infantry stumbled into an antitank ambush in thick jungle. A round fired by a 47mm antitank gun struck the lead tank in the column and the wounded driver stalled the engine. He restarted the engine, but in the confusion abruptly backed up and rammed the second tank, just as another tank was struck and crippled by the antitank gun. Two following vehicles moved up to provide protection, and were rushed by suicide troops. One tank absorbed seven magnetic mines, and the other was damaged by a shaped-charge grenade.

The Japanese Type 3 (1943) Conical Hand-Thrown Mine was a simple shaped-charge grenade with a tail of hemp fiber, or sometimes just a tuft of local grass, intended to make the grenade fly head-first at the target. The Type 3 was not very satisfactory in the best of circumstances, since it was hard to get close enough to a tank to use it effectively.[10]

In addition to killed and wounded, this action resulted in five disabled tanks, of which three would run but were no longer fit for combat. The Japanese abandoned another 47mm gun, but the combined tank platoons had lost eight tanks, four permanently. The following day the 9th had only three bedraggled tanks back in action supporting 3/103's attack along the coast.

The 43rd Division commander sent a personal emissary forward to convey specific instructions for the next attack. The handful of surviving tanks would be provided with an entire company of infantry to protect them, and a squad with automatic rifles and a flamethrower would accompany each tank. The tanks were to be followed by a heavy weapons company assigned to hold the ground taken. It is a credit to the exhausted and disease-ridden infantry that on this day they and the tanks rapidly advanced some 500 yards in the face of heavy resistance, destroying 40 enemy positions. Bailey's tank was hit three times by a 37mm antitank gun, but survived to ram the gun and destroy it. The tanks ranged ahead another 400 yards, where another was damaged by an antitank gun and two crewmen killed. The tanks were forced to pull back because there was insufficient infantry to hold the ground.

Farther inland, the Army infantry continued to hold positions in front of a dominating feature they called Horseshoe Hill, in part because they were required to send troops to the rear to hunt down troublesome survivors of the *Tomonari Force*.

The final collapse of the Munda position was anticlimactic. By 1 August the 43rd Division had driven to the edge of the airfield complex, outflanking Horseshoe Ridge. Sasaki was ordered to withdraw overland to the north coast. While most of his men fled, some held out at Munda.

With the tank platoon of the 9th Defense Battalion all but extinct, the tanks of the 11th Defense Battalion were brought forward on 3 August. "We went up on an LST," said Bob Botts. "We were kidding the skipper up there, said 'Look, dadgummit, don't park out there in the middle of the damn ocean. Get us up there. We don't wanna get our feet wet.' So he opened the bow doors, and dropped that anchor. He put that sucker up on the beach, and tried to let the ramp down. It went into the trees. He said 'Okay boys, you won't get your feet wet, but you'll have to slide down on a rope. Cut them trees, and you can get your equipment out.'"

Hal Rogers commented: "When we got up there we found that our platoon leader was senior. First Lieutenant Irving P. Carlson at that time. He was senior to both Lt. Blake of the 9th Defense Tank Platoon, and Lt. Bailey of the 10th Defense Tank Platoon. He took over and we operated as a Provisional Tank Company. We weren't as large as a regular company, but we were pretty close to it. The 9th had one tank knocked out. She took a round through the side of the turret, through the port side … Other than that they had taken hits on some of their other tanks. They only had about three tanks on duty."

Bob Botts recalled that on 4 August, "the day that we pulled into the airfield, the lower end of it, we hadn't secured it yet, there were three Jap dive bombers came right over. They were low enough that they tipped their wings and looked at us. I mean they were nowhere, just a couple of hundred feet [up]. You could see the expressions on their face and everything. Well, we knew they would be back bright and early next morning. We set up what machine guns we had, a couple of 50s and a whole bunch of 30s."

Hal Rogers said that the antiaircraft machine-gun mounts on the light tanks were of little use: "It was on the rear of the gun turret, and you practically had to get out of the turret to use it. We took the crowbar, each tank had one, and jammed it into the ground next to a coconut stump. We had leather straps that we usually used to fasten stuff onto the outside of the tank. You could put two or three of those together, and go around the coconut stump and the bar. We strapped it on there, and then took the antiaircraft gun mount and set it down on the crowbar. It would rotate on there, and it was up in the air a little ways. It was not an ideal mount, but it worked."

When the enemy aircraft returned, Botts said, "Instead of shooting at airplanes, we just put up a blanket of fire, and we got one of them when he came back. The other two … just peeled up and dumped their bombs. They came down in a big arc, but they lit short of us about a hundred yards."

The enemy stragglers were scattered about the airfield and on Kokengola Hill, a large rocky feature in the center of the triangular runway complex. For two days the tanks of the 10th and 11th Defense Battalions, and the lone surviving tank from the 9th, roamed the airfield ahead of the infantry. In the words of Hal Rogers, they were "… shooting at anything that moved, or looked like it might move. In that area we were out there where the Japanese couldn't crawl up on us."

Botts's tank was patrolling the airfield when they drew fire: "We couldn't pick up where it was coming from." They circled back to where friendly infantry was sheltering. "We came back and said we were getting some pretty good fire out on the other side, and could they see where it was coming from? They said 'Yeah, them [Japanese] have got a little field gun in there, in that airplane.'" The Japanese had placed a small howitzer inside the waist gun position of an abandoned bomber; they would slide the door open, fire, and then quickly close the door to avoid detection.[11]

The little gun could not damage the tanks except with a lucky hit, but was dangerous to the infantry. Botts:

> We went around and just blew up every [Mitsubishi Type 1] Betty bomber in there, and then we caught hell from the navy. Those were the first intact Betty bombers they had come across.
>
> Just as we were coming back around and coming back to where the infantry was … there were three Marine Corps Corsairs landed. One of them jumped out and he said, "What airstrip is this?"
>
> I said, "This is Munda, why?"
>
> "Well, we were just flying over and saw it."
>
> I said "Well buddy, you better get your ass out of here, 'cause we don't know really who owns this thing yet. By the way, who won the pool?" All them guys … had pools going on who could land on these captured airfields first. He just grinned and jumped back in his airplane and took off.

The last positions to fall were those on Kokengola Hill. On 5 August the last caves were dynamited shut, and at 1410 hours the airfield was declared secure.

Botts and his gunner checked out the abandoned control tower, where they found "… very large binoculars—with six-inch lenses and the tripod to hold it. These binoculars were used by Marines when they moved the 155mm Long Toms to Piru Plantation . . ."

Sasaki's men still held the hills overlooking the airfield, and Hal Rogers remembered that "they retreated up a general trail that went from the airstrip, that taxiway, up to the northwest … Our tank got stuck, and I got out on one flank, and one of the other fellows got out on the other flank, and we provided cover while they yanked that thing out of there."

Over the next few weeks the infantry repeatedly called for help from the tanks. Bob Botts:

> They called us out half a dozen times I suppose to help an infantry group break up a strongpoint. We did a lot of that in that jungle ... it was up in the ridges and the mountains. We followed trails. When there wasn't any trail, we would just start through the jungle. When we got balled up so much we couldn't go anywhere, we'd back off and with the canister ammunition shoot a hole big enough to drive the tank through.
> We got up in the hills, and it was dense jungle. It was raining in there almost all the time, and those guys were soaking wet most all the time. They sent us up there and I got hold of this company commander, and it was kind of a break. They were getting ready to move up and relieve another bunch. We were settin' there eatin' lunch, and stuff [was] dropping out of the trees. We got to looking, and there was a dead Jap in there. It was maggots dropping out of the trees. It don't even spoil your lunch at that point. We had a lot of that to put up with. We were chasing that bunch across the island, but we never did catch up with 'em.

On 9 August the 27th Infantry linked up with the Marine Raiders advancing from the north coast, isolating the last of Sasaki's stragglers. The combined tank platoons of the 9th, 10th, and 11th Defense Battalions could now muster only 13 functional tanks. Hal Rogers and the others "... withdrew our tanks down to the airfield and dug them in right across Munda Point in case of an attempted invasion [counter]landing. We would sit there and watch the SBDs [dive-bombers] come in with the arms of the gunners hanging over edges of the rear cockpit. They lost a lot of those boys."

On the evening of 23 August the last of 19 barge loads of Japanese slipped out of Bairoko Harbor to safety on Kolombangara. On 27 August, the 172nd Infantry landed unopposed on the southern end of Arundel Island.

Arundel was militarily worthless, covered by boggy jungle and rimmed by tangled mangrove thickets, but Sasaki had plans for another costly delaying action. In a protracted struggle against mines, booby traps, and incessant counterattacks the Army rifle battalions slowly drove the Japanese into the northeastern corner of Arundel. In a last-ditch effort to hold a corner of Arundel, Sasaki landed two additional battalions on the night of 14-15 September, and immediately threw them into an unsuccessful early morning counterattack. The survivors went to ground in a ring of tough defensive positions along the north coast.

To drive this final enemy presence into the sea, on 16 September a battalion of the 27th Infantry and all surviving tanks were dispatched to the Bomboc Peninsula, on the northern coast of Arundel. Landing in a heavy rain that masked their noise, five tanks of the 11th Defense Battalion followed their commander's jeep.

Hal Rogers found, like tankers before and since, that his own communications troops could be as dangerous as the enemy: "We came to a road junction. I was up in the gun turret, and I came damn close to getting decapitated. That road junction had a network of phone lines coming from all three roads and crossing over each other in a general rat's nest at that road junction. I didn't pay attention. Someone hollered 'Duck,' and I ducked. The wires grabbed the antiaircraft gun and spun that around, and oh boy did we hear some choice words from the Army Signal Corps people."

On the morning of 17 September the five tanks and C/1/27 took the Japanese by surprise, and a strongpoint that had held up the Army riflemen for several days was quickly eliminated. A counterattack disintegrated in the face of the tanks. That afternoon the mixed force pushed another 500 yards into the Japanese defenses, for the loss of one tank to mechanical problems.

The next morning the Japanese were waiting for the tanks. Bob Botts: "We lost two tanks in there. They had moved a 37mm gun in there, and my tank got hit first and set on fire.* The first one [round] came through right between the driver's feet, hit the axle that goes across underneath his seat, then came back through the turret and punctured one of our fuel tanks. I put it out the first time."

The front of the tank was raked by enemy fire, blocking the escape of the driver and radioman. Carlson reported that Botts had to manually traverse the turret to one side to let the radio man escape through the turret hatch, then to the other side to allow the driver out while the tank filled with gasoline vapors.[13]

Bob Botts: "Everybody was out but my gunner and myself, and my gunner was about to leave. I was trying to keep some fire going, to

---

* Irving Carlson later wrote that the gun was a 47mm, although official accounts say it was a 37mm.[12] Both were deadly to the light tanks at short range.

keep some heads down, so those guys could get back safe. Then that thing caught on fire again, so we just bailed out and took off."

Botts got out just before the ammunition ignited, and received first degree burns.

Hal Rogers said his tank

... got hit right in the final drive ... I didn't even know we had been hit. All of a sudden the driver, who was right next to me, said he couldn't shift. I think he ended by saying 'I think we've been hit.'

I should have known it. I felt some pretty sharp stuff in my left ankle, and it was burned as well as having some steel in there. It went through the outer layer of armor, but didn't go through the inside of that final drive. I think there was some spalling on the inside, and I got a couple of fragments in the ankle.

Point blank. The gun was right outside the tank, we found out afterwards. They let us get right up on top of them. I probably got two or three of them with the bow gun without really realizing it.

The gun holed the tank four times, but miraculously did not seriously wound any of the crew.

The third tank, commanded by Lieutenant Carlson, became disoriented in the confusion and headed off into the enemy-infested jungle. Botts attracted his attention and led the surviving tank out, pursued by fire from the gun.[14]

Hal Rogers and his crewmates got safely away from their tank, but he said, "after we abandoned it, one of the turret hatches was [left] open. The skipper thought it would be a good idea if we destroyed it." The crew ventured back into the underbrush and set their tank afire.

On the morning of 19 September two tanks from the 9th and four from the 10th Defense Battalion joined the two survivors in another attack. Falling back on a proven tactic the tanks attacked on a narrow front, moving in two waves of four tanks followed closely by infantry. The lead tanks shredded the underbrush with canister to flush out defenders, while the tanks of the second wave protected the lead tanks.

Bob Botts was back that day: "Another tank commander ... he couldn't go, so I took his tank and went back in there and got that gun the next morning. They were set up in a big banyan tree grove. I mean they had set up housekeeping, and there was a regular camp. We went in with canister ammunition, and you could have played soft-ball in that place in just about 30 minutes. We cleaned that out in just about two hours." In the process Botts's replacement tank was also hit and immobilized.[15]

This attack pierced a deep hole in the Japanese defenses, allowing infantry to flood through and roll up enemy positions from the rear. This was the last straw for Sasaki, who ordered the evacuation of Arundel.

The Japanese expected the next blow to fall upon Vila, their big base on the southern tip of Kolombangara, but Admiral Halsey intervened to put a stop to the slow bloodbath. On 15 August elements of the 35th Infantry and 4th Defense Battalion landed on lightly defended Vella Lavella, the most northwesterly large island, bypassing Kolombangara.

New Zealand infantry pressed the Japanese into the northwest corner of Vella Lavella, closing in on the last big pocket of resistance on 5 October. Stubborn Japanese resistance covered the withdrawal of major units, and the New Zealanders' final assault closed upon an empty pocket.

Despite their obvious value, the light tanks with their little 37mm cannons had proven less than desirable in terms of firepower. When the fighting ended, the tankers were working with Navy Seabees to remove the wrecked turret from a 9th Defense Battalion M3A1 and replace it with a 75mm pack howitzer protected by a shield made of mild steel.[16] Hal Rogers: "You would have had almost no traverse, only elevation ... Anything would have helped that would have thrown something bigger than a 37mm."

The overall failures on New Georgia were of leadership at high levels, and not in the courage or leadership at the front end. The men in the lines had again proven that they could endure incredible hardships, and finally outlast the Japanese soldiers whose bravery and offensive vigor availed them little against equally courageous American tank-infantry teams.

The New Georgia operation had provided the first true insight into the value of the tanks. Army sources stated that the tanks were "... instrumental in saving the lives of many infantrymen," and General Sasaki "... complained that the Marine tanks often actively stopped or neutralized his fires."[17]

CHAPTER 4

THE DEFENSIVE OFFENSIVE: BOUGAINVILLE

THE CAPTURE OF BOUGAINVILLE was the campaign in which the Marine tanks played the least significant role. The tanks had proven their utility in jungle warfare, but there are limits to anything.

Bougainville was selected as the next Allied objective because it was not the logical choice. The obvious targets, air bases on Choiseul, would be bypassed. Bougainville would be the last step before the assault on the huge fortress of Rabaul on New Britain.

The Japanese had built airfields on the northern and southern tips of the huge island, and although the attrition of their own air power made these bases useless to them, the Japanese were painfully aware of their potential value to the Allies. Lieutenant General Haruyoshi Hyakutake knew he could never hope to defend all potential landing sites on the huge island, and concentrated his troops around the airfield complexes. The only Japanese presence on the south coast was a contingent of civilian rice farmers protected by 300 soldiers.

His opponent Halsey had his own resource problems. A direct attack on the airfields would be a play against Japanese strength. An assault on the lightly held north coast would require sealift capacity he did not possess, and expose his ships to air attack from Rabaul.

Halsey was determined not to repeat the mistakes of the New Georgia campaign, and ordered detailed reconnaissance of potential airfield sites along the south coast. He finally settled on the Cape Torokina area, near the center of the south coast. The site was isolated from the major Japanese bases by tens of miles of implacable jungle, and the attacking Japanese would be forced to wear themselves out in a cross-country struggle with nature.

I Marine Amphibious Corps could make available only the new 3rd Marine Division. The division had been formed in the United

Bougainville

States, and the 3rd Tank Battalion formally raised on 16 September 1942. The medium tank companies of I Marine Amphibious Corps Tank Battalion had been assigned to each of the three Marine divisions currently in the Pacific area, and B Company was assigned to the 3rd Tank Battalion. Only 12 assault transports were available, and the ships could transport only light tanks. The medium tanks would have to be left behind.[1]

At 0712 hours on 1 November the 3rd Marine Division landed at Cape Torokina on an enormous 8,000-yard frontage, with one ship assigned to each of 12 beaches. Only six hours were allotted to unload all personnel and supplies.

On the exposed left beaches rough surf wrecked 64 LCVPs and 22 of the precious LCMs. On the right Puruata Island sheltered a small Japanese garrison, who fired into the rear of the assault boats with their machine guns, and the infantry landings were scrambled.

Cape Torokina on the extreme right held 15 bunkers arrayed in depth and manned by 270 Japanese. A 75mm mountain gun destroyed six landing boats, but Marines with flamethrowers and SPMs wrecked the bunkers and silenced the guns. The men of the tank companies were busy unloading supplies. The defenders had achieved about all that could be hoped for, throwing the landings into disarray and spreading the alarm.

The terrain was the more powerful enemy, and opportunities to utilize the tanks proved limited. Harold Harrison, a light tank crewman in the 1st Platoon, A Company: "We couldn't go back through the swamp. We just turned around and faced for what they called 'Condition Black,' facing to the ocean in case of invasion."

The first serious attempt to defeat the Marines with a land attack was typical of Japanese doctrine. A two-pronged attack by battalion-scale forces would be directed against the two ends of the American perimeter. The first attack, a counterlanding in the west, would draw off Marine reserves, followed by the main attack from the east. The forces were small, but fighting spirit was expected to help them massacre an American division.

On 7 November a Japanese infantry force landed from barges 150 yards west of the Marine perimeter. The Japanese thought they were several miles from the Marine positions, but the Americans held fire all through the noisy landing operation because in the darkness the barges looked like American craft.

At 0820 a hastily organized attack by two platoons of K Company and a platoon from the regimental Weapons Company stalled in the face of enemy fire. Repeated attempts to turn the Japanese flank bogged down in thick jungle.

At 1315 two companies of 1/3 attacked, supported by light tanks that fired canister rounds to shred the thick foliage. The infantry moved in the lee of the tanks, hurling grenades to point out targets, and six machine-gun positions were destroyed.[2] Still the enemy held on, so on the morning of 8 November five batteries of artillery shelled the jungle positions, followed by an attack by a fresh rifle battalion and tanks. The Marines pushed forward about 150 yards, and on 9 November air strikes pounded the enemy survivors.

On the eastern end of the perimeter the 2nd Raider Battalion established a trail block on the Piva Trail, a footpath that led inland to hook up with the main Numa Numa Trail. On the afternoon of 8 November a battalion-scale Japanese attack struck the exposed Raiders. All day long on 9 November the two forces hammered at each other in a series of futile attacks and counterattacks. Efforts to move tanks and SPMs up the narrow, steep track failed in the gluey mud and they withdrew, carrying cargoes of wounded Raiders. On 10 November 2/9 drove the enemy back in a full day of bloody hand-to-hand combat, capturing Piva Village, a questionable prize.

The M3A1 light tanks were again proving less than ideal vehicles, and a decision had to be made whether to commit the medium tanks. G. G. Sweet, who had come from IMAC Tank Battalion with the medium tanks, was in the advance party: "I made a reconnaissance to Bougainville, from New Caledonia, with the colonel, a warrant officer, and myself. We went to Bougainville, and decided that medium tanks couldn't be run there, because the light tanks were all bogged down. They were all knee-deep in mud."

The enemy continued to launch aerial counterattacks, and night raiders accomplished more damage than daylight attacks. The planes dropped their bombs indiscriminately. Harold Harrison: "We were hit by some bombs. There was a 90mm [antiaircraft battery] right there on the beach with us. They didn't follow safety procedures. One [bomb] hit where they had stored ammunition too close, and started a chain reaction. Blew everything all to hell. Of course we were down in our foxholes, but it killed about eleven men around there."

Army and Marine ground forces concentrated their efforts on expanding the perimeter. On the morning of 13 November E/2/21 inadvertently triggered what became known as the Coconut Grove Battles when they were ambushed and cut off while advancing up the Numa Numa Trail.

The surrounded company held out through the night, and on the morning of 14 November five light tanks of 2nd Platoon, B Company and the remainder of 2/21 tried to effect a rescue. In the confusion, rain, and dense jungle the nervous tankers began to fire at the flitting, half-seen targets to their front. An infantry officer jumped onto one of the tanks and hammered on the turret hatches. They were firing on their own infantry. In the rest of the day's fighting two of the tanks were disabled by magnetic mines, and the enemy slid farther back into the bush.

Patrols discovered yet more Japanese blocking positions astride the Numa Numa Trail, and on the 18th five tanks moved up to support an attack by 3/3. The two lead tanks advanced along the trail, and the turret of the Platoon Leader's tank snagged a dangling vine. The vine was a trigger for a mine buried in the trail, and the blast severed the tank's track. When Lt. Leon Stanley dismounted to check the damage, a machine gun concealed in the thick jungle opened fire, and the officer fell mortally wounded. Marine riflemen outflanked and destroyed the gun position, but in the confusion the other tank was disabled by a *Hakobakurai* mine. The other three tanks withdrew down the trail, burdened with wounded.

The light tanks were withdrawn after the abortive action on 18 November, although the crews continued to serve in other capacities. A protracted struggle for the hill complexes east of the beachhead was fought on dry (for Bougainville) ground, but the slopes themselves would have presented formidable obstacles for the tanks. Harold Harrison:

> After the swamp, there were hills. Part of the crew, like me and the assistant driver, would be on a working party. We would carry ammunition up the hills ... The planes would try to drop rations and it would all just go to hell. You would have hash and beans all over the place.
>
> It was either swamp or hills, and most of the infantry fought up on these hills. They were steep. You couldn't run a tank up them, or a vehicle. Some of them I don't think you could get a mule up. Bougainville was hot, but we were young, and we sweated a lot. They [the hills]

were so steep you were limited in what you could carry, but every little bit helped the guys up there. It was pretty hot, and I think that was
the most malaria-infested place in the world.

Following the battles for the hills, the Americans were content to let
the starving enemy roam the jungle, harrying them with long-range
patrols. On 10 December the first airfield was operational, followed
by two more on 9 January.

The last expansion of the perimeter was the fight for Hellzapoppin'
Ridge, a complex of high hills about 2,000 yards farther east, that
dominated the big East-West Trail. This ghastly action lasted from 10
through 24 December, when the enemy finally withdrew.

The 3rd Division received the best possible Christmas present. The
bulk of the troops were withdrawn between 25 December and 9
January, and the final elements were gone by 16 January 1944,
replaced by the 37th and Americal divisions.

The end result of the Bougainville operation was the isolation of
40,000 Japanese, and the first decisive step in the strangulation of the
great Japanese base at Rabaul.

CHAPTER 5

DROWNING ON THE REEF: TARAWA

I N LATE 1943 the Marine Corps' amphibious assault doctrine was still untested, since the landings up to this point in the war had been unopposed (Guadalcanal, New Georgia), or across lightly defended beaches (Bougainville). The test came in November 1943 on Betio, the main island of Tarawa Atoll. The bloody assault on this flyspeck island served as a preview of future assaults on the islands of the central Pacific.

The fight for Betio Island was the turning point of the war for Marine Corps tanks. The operations of the light tanks in the Solomons had been limited by the terrain and by the frailty and limited firepower of the tanks themselves. Those protracted struggles had also been orthodox campaigns, not the amphibious assaults for which the Marines had studied and trained.

The Japanese Empire took control of the Gilberts in the second week of December 1941, but delayed construction of significant facilities. On 17 August 1942, the 2nd Marine Raider Battalion landed on Butaritari at Makin Atoll, and almost annihilated the small Japanese garrison. The embarrassed Japanese fortified Betio and transformed it into the administrative center for the Gilberts. In September 1943 Admiral Keiji Shibasaki assumed command of the Betio garrison, which included combat veterans of the *7th Sasebo Special Naval Landing Force*, *3rd Special Base Force*, *111th Pioneers* and the *4th Construction Unit*.

Trenches, fighting holes, antitank ditches, and wire entanglements protected 500 bunkers and pillboxes built of concrete or resilient coconut logs. These positions held 20 heavy cannon, 25 field guns, 31 heavy machine guns, and hundreds of light machine guns, automatic rifles, and antitank rifles. Beach defenses were sited so that attack-

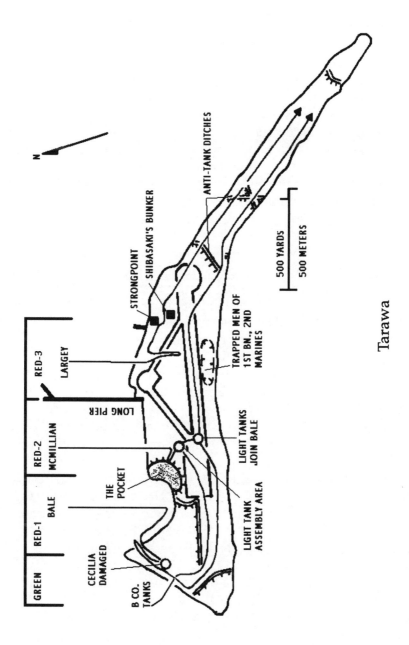

Tarawa

ers would be exposed to machine-gun fire from front and flanks. Wire fences in the waist-deep water would slow attacking infantry, holding them in the crossfire.

Around the rim of the island was a coconut log seawall high enough to stop tracked vehicles, or expose their vulnerable bellies as they reared up to surmount it. More machine guns were sited to sweep the top of the wall. A counterattack force included seven Type 95 *Ha-Go* light tanks.

The goal of the defense was to delay the enemy and buy time to launch a naval *yogaki* or "waylaying attack." Admiral Nimitz instructed Raymond Spruance, commander of the task force, to get in and out fast. This haste to have the naval units quit the scene would have considerable impact on operational planning.

The Navy-Marine planning team outlined a series of special problems that they knew would bedevil the Betio landings. Heavier defenses and high waves on the seaward side of the island meant that the landings were best launched from the lagoon side. The planners suggested capturing one of the nearby islands so that Betio could be subjected to several days of land-based artillery bombardment. The loss of surprise would be more than outweighed by the advantages of systematic artillery support. Admiral Spruance quickly vetoed this plan because of the threat of the *yogaki*.

The least tangible problem was the dodging tide. Major Frank L. G. Holland, a New Zealander and former resident of the atoll, repeatedly warned of unusually low tides that occur in late November. At a dodging tide, landing boats would ground on the far edge of the reef, leaving the troops to struggle across the broad reef under intense fire.

Senior naval officers argued that the landings were unlikely to encounter the lowered tides, a position Holland disputed to the point of tears.[1] Lieutenant Colonel David Shoup suggested that tracked amphibian cargo carriers, or LVTs, could be used to carry assault troops; if the tides were low, the LVTs could drive up onto the reef and carry the men to the seawall. Naval officers resisted until Holland Smith gave his ultimatum. No tractors, no Marines.

The 1st Amphibious Tractor Battalion could field 75 functional, if decrepit, LVT-1s. The Navy provided 50 new LVT-2s, enough to carry the first three assault waves.

The landing force would for the first time have the support of medium tanks. The deployment of the bigger tanks was limited both by the Army's demand for tanks, and by problems of how to transport and land such heavy vehicles. In late 1943 the Marines could procure only diesel-powered M4A2s, a model the Army would not accept for overseas service.[2]

The Army had cited reliability and high maintenance burdens as objections to the diesel engine, but the Marines did not find either to be a problem. In addition, the commonality of fuel between landing boat engines and the tanks simplified beachhead logistics.[3]

The new tanks were equipped with powerful 75mm cannons that could fire high explosive, armor-piercing, or the far less popular canister rounds. According to Bill Finley, a sergeant and tank commander who used the Shermans at Peleliu and Okinawa, the canister round was six or eight inches long, and filled with "... pellets about the size of an English pea. You could just nearly mow the grass with one of them."

The 75mm canister projectile casing was easily damaged. "They were pretty bad about coming loose in your 75. When you threw it in there [the chamber], sometimes it would come loose. I was a little bit leery of that."

The 75mm round was light enough to maintain a prodigious rate of fire, and the guns and rounds were very reliable. "We had very little trouble. They only recoiled about ten to twelve inches. The loader sat over there [on the left side of the turret]. He just sat the nose of one [round] up in there. The breech opened on the side; it didn't open up and down. The loader just sat that end in the barrel, then took his fist and slammed it in there and closed it, and we were ready to go."

The gun was equipped with a gyrostabilizer that allowed the tank to fire its cannon on the move. Crews were instructed to destroy the device if the tank had to be abandoned.[4]

The medium tanks equipped I Marine Amphibious Corps (IMAC) Tank Battalion. First Lieutenant Ed Bale was the commanding officer of C Company. Originally the leader of the light tank platoon of the 51st Composite Defense Battalion (a segregated formation, with black enlisted men and white officers), he had been sent to a tank maintenance course at Fort Knox, Kentucky:

> It was there that I met other Marine students, including then-Major A. J. "Jeb" Stuart, who was the executive officer of this First Corps Medium [Battalion]. When I got back to Lejeune after the course was over, had been back there maybe a month, they disestablished this

tank platoon, disestablished the infantry company, and just called the thing the 51st Defense Battalion. It was at this point in time that I asked for transfer to the west coast, to the medium tank battalion, of which the Marine Corps only had one. The transfer went through, so that's how I ended up in the First Corps Medium Tank Battalion.

I reported in out there in early May of '43 to Camp Elliot [California], which was Area Command. I was taken to see the Area Command Chief of Staff, then-Colonel Erskine. I was a really young, green, and ignorant lieutenant. He said to me, "Now we can send you up to Pendleton to this tank battalion, but you'll probably be leaving the States in 60 days." I said, "Send me," and I went up there. I was the senior first lieutenant in the battalion, so I took over C Company.

Bale liked the diesel-powered M4A2 Sherman medium tank:

I do know that one of the Marine Corps considerations was ... the availability of diesel fuel when working with the Navy. We never had a problem with that engine.

The decision [to use the M4A2] had been made, to the best of my knowledge, back in December '42, maybe January '43. The battalion commander, a Lieutenant Colonel Ben Powers, and the battalion maintenance officer, who was a Captain Charlie Dunmore ... went back to the Detroit area. They had almost an open checkbook, because they bought tank recovery vehicles,* the first the Marine Corps had. They even shipped the turrets that came off the hulls [of tanks converted to recovery vehicles], and the guns that had come out of the turrets. When I left the States, I had all that stuff—an extra turret, and an extra gun. They bought machine shops. Even in a tank company in this battalion we had a full machine shop. All kinds of stuff.

I didn't know any better then, but now I figure that nobody in the Marine Corps knew what to buy and what not to buy ... We took spare track, and all kinds of stuff in the company, and we did all the maintenance in the company.

We trained—I used to have it right down to the day—something just short of 60 days, and we sailed out of San Diego.

---

* Tank recovery vehicles were modified tanks fitted with cranes and winches to recover damaged vehicles. They were also called retrievers, or more commonly VTRs (Vehicle, Tank Recovery) by the Marines.

Melvin Swango, a member of Bale's Reconnaissance Platoon: "When I was leaving boot camp I received a questionnaire from the Marine Corps and they asked what would be your first choice of service, and your second choice. I never thought it would amount to anything, but I said I might like to be a radio operator or a member of a tank crew." Much to his surprise, Swango became a radio operator in a tank. "While we were in training in California we formed this new Reconnaissance Platoon. I liked that because we had halftracks and jeeps, so I was a radio man with reconnaissance."

Doug Crotts was assigned to the fire department at Camp Pendleton, and had been harassing his captain for a transfer to the Fleet Marine Force. He won a five-dollar bet on the Rose Bowl, and accepted a transfer to the tanks in lieu of cash.[5]

Ed Bale: "C and D Companies left San Diego first. We got all new tanks before we left San Diego. The tanks that the battalion had used in training were left at Pendleton ... We went on a Liberty ship—it seemed like it took forever—down to Noumea, on New Caledonia. The rest of the battalion followed on two ships in about three weeks time."

The biggest problem for the medium tanks was the inadequate training imposed by the operational schedule, and the absence of suitable training areas. Bale:

> We got down there and we had to park the tanks at one location, and the troops and all were billeted in a First Corps transit center. After the rest of the troops came in, we moved out to an area where there was a camp that the Raider Battalion had been in. It was about 15 miles to where the tanks were. It was a miserable situation, and there was no place where you could train with the tanks. We spent most of our time trucking back and forth to the tank park to do maintenance, and when we weren't doing maintenance it was hikes and this kind of thing. On one occasion the battalion communications officer and I took a jeep and went way up the island looking for areas where maybe some arrangement could be made with the French so that we could train. [The main guns of the tanks had not been fired in four months.][6]

> We found some [locations], but then in the middle of the negotiations, I got orders to take this Company and go to New Zealand to join the 2nd Division ... That's all that the plan called for. They wanted one company of medium tanks.

I was on a hike with my company when the battalion commander came back from First Corps Headquarters and called a meeting, and I wasn't there. He announced that one company was going to leave and was going somewhere to join a Marine division. Where they were going, and what Marine division, were classified. They were going to draw straws … The battalion exec [Stuart] drew for me, and I don't know to this day whether I got the long or the short straw.

We loaded out on a freighter that had been converted to carry heavy equipment as well as troops, and we never unloaded … The reason we never unloaded was that the *Ashland*, which was the first LSD that the U. S. had, was coming down from Hawaii. There was not time enough for it to come to New Zealand and load us out and get back north in time for the operation. So we stayed there about a week, and then we went back and unloaded back in Noumea, New Caledonia, and three or four days later the *Ashland* came in and picked us up.

The medium tanks were too heavy for any ship's crane, so the Navy had designed the Landing Ship, Dock or LSD. The U.S.S. *Ashland* was the first ship of this class.

Ed Bale: "While in New Zealand I was taken up to the Division Headquarters in a hotel, I believe the name was the Windsor Hotel … and met some of the Division people. I was taken by the [2nd] Tank Battalion commander, Al Swenceski, out to where the tank battalion was … We had to be back by dark, so we had lunch and talked. We unloaded two [medium] tanks, which went with an infantry battalion on a short exercise up to a place called Hawke's Bay. We sent those tanks up there because I was quizzed extensively as to how much water that thing [the M4A2] could ford, and I didn't know. All I could do was refer them back to the manual. These two tanks were sent up to Hawke's Bay to see how much water they could ford. It turned out they could ford 40 inches, like the manual said."

Bale was grilled in detail because Major Holland had also warned that the reef was "dished," and water would be slightly deeper between the edge of the reef and the beach.[7] Bale:

"There was no waterproofing in the Pacific at that point in time. None. The two tanks were put on an APA [troop transport] after this Hawke's Bay exercise, and rejoined us at Efate for the rehearsal, which in the case of the tank company consisted of coming out of the well of the LSD and unloading on the beach. You couldn't leave the beach, because of various restrictions imposed on heavy vehicle traffic. The rehearsal really didn't do much for us, except give us a chance to move the vehicles out of the landing craft.

[The hastily organized task force suffered from the problems inherent in attaching one unit to another at the last moment.] When we joined the the Division at Efate in the Hebrides, Swenceski and his executive officer, a Major Worth McCoy ... and the battalion staff joined us on the *Ashland*.

What was the command relationship? To be very candid about it, I didn't know, and I don't know to this day. It was a strange thing. We were attached to the 2nd Marines, but the only contact I ever had with the 2nd Marines was at a briefing in a conference aboard one of the APAs at Efate, during the rehearsal period. Of course they were in turmoil because that's where the regimental commander got relieved, and Dave Shoup took over the regiment. I met the three battalion commanders, and the leaders of the tank platoons met them. We arranged to have a liaison NCO land with them.

There was no training with the infantry. None at all. Looking back on it, it was a strange, strange thing. I was getting most of my instructions from a Major ... Tommy Tompkins, who was the assistant G-3 of the Division ... Our orders were simply to land on the three beaches behind the three battalions. [The combat role of the big tanks was in fact never clarified.]

We landed with radios that were incompatible with the infantry radios [below the battalion level]. Most tanks were equipped with a radio used by naval aviation. I don't know what they stood for, but they were RU-GF, we called them "Ruji-Fuji." They had all these coils, and the coil covered a certain spectrum. We had a box of coils, but we didn't have a damned thing that would work with the infantry.

The light tanks had been part of the division for months, yet coordination was little better. Jim Carter was 16 years old when he enlisted, and was a driver of a light tank in B Company of the 2nd Tank. "We were still operating pretty much with the Army manual, as cavalry, where you dashed here and dashed there."

In a map view Betio looks like a dead parrot lying on its back, with its head to the west and a long tail extending to the east. The three landing beaches were, from west to east, Red-1 in the small embayment between the bird's beak and the neck, Red-2 on the bird's breast west of the pier, and Red-3 east of the pier.

On D-day, 20 November, things began to go amiss almost immediately. In the darkness and confusion landing boats and waddling amphibious tractors became separated from their mother transports, air attacks were poorly coordinated, and the command ship *Maryland*'s main guns had knocked out its own radio communications.

The first inkling that things had gone catastrophically wrong was when a single LCVP carrying an advance party that was to eliminate any Japanese on a long pier that extended to the edge of the reef found that it could not maneuver alongside the pier. The aerial observer for the *Maryland* banked in to examine the landing areas and reported the tide was so low that some parts of the reef were emergent.

The Japanese defenders took the LVTs under fire 3,000 yards offshore. When the first wave of LVTs clambered up onto the reef machine-gun and cannon rounds began to tear through the thin sides, shredding drivers, gunners, and passengers. Major Drewes, the commander of the LVT battalion, took over a machine gun when the gunner was hit, and seconds later was shot through the head.[8] When the first LVT-1 ashore tried to mount the seawall the thin front and belly plates were ripped out by point-blank machine-gun fire, killing and wounding most of the passengers.

More tractors were hit on the reef, spilling dead and wounded into the water. At 0922 the main body of LVTs hit the seawall, and the Marines climbed over the high sides and straight into massed machine-gun fire. Some rifle companies suffered 50 percent casualties just getting to the seawall. The worst carnage was on Red-1, where the tractors were caught in a deadly three-way crossfire as they churned into the embayment. Along most of the beaches the Marines were stalled at the seawall, but by now the LCVPs of the fourth wave were grinding to a stop against the coral.

At the edge of the reef the boats dumped their passengers into the firestorm. Surviving LVTs carried wounded out and loaded them onto the LCVPs, exchanging them for loads of infantry for a second passage across the deadly reef. As the number of tractors dwindled, most of the infantry were forced to wade in across the fire-swept reef, leaning forward into the sheets of fire like men in a rainstorm.

The deadliest enemy fire was coming from a cluster of Japanese positions at the juncture of Red-1 and Red-2, beating on the left flank of the Marines trying to make shore on Red-1. Major John Schoettel decided that his remaining men could not get ashore through the deadly crossfire, and held the follow-on troops of the fourth and fifth waves aboard the boats. Most of the radios, immersed in water during the trip across the reef, had failed. The men on Red-1 were completely cut off.

SPMs of the Special Weapons Battalion landed with the first waves on Red-2. One LCM took a direct hit from a coastal gun and sank with its SPM in deep water. One SPM drowned in a pothole on the reef, another bogged down in soft sand near the beach. Other boats carrying SPMs were waved off.[9] At close range the thin armor could be penetrated by machine-gun fire, so attempts to use the SPMs as assault guns proved nearly suicidal.

The medium tanks of Ed Bale's company were scheduled to land ahead of the fourth assault wave. The reinforced 1st Platoon would land on Red-1 with six tanks (including Bale's two headquarters tanks); the 2nd and 3rd Platoons with four tanks each would land on Red-2 and Red-3 respectively.

The light tanks of "Gunner Mac" McMillian's* 2nd Platoon, C Company, 2nd Marine Tank Battalion, reinforced by a single tank from the company headquarters platoon, were to land on Red-1, expected to be the toughest of the beaches. The allocation of light tanks was governed by availability of space on the transport ships, and each light tank company was split among several ships.[10] McMillian: "My platoon was loaded on the *Thuban* (AKA19). They had room for six light tanks, so they put another on. The logistics had more to do with that than anything tactical."

McMillian's efforts to get his platoon ashore proved an ordeal of frustration: "About first light we were loaded into tank lighters ... There were regular boat coxswains, [and] one commissioned officer who had the little wave the tanks were in. I was on another boat. We moved in like everybody else, and then circled around and ran into all that opposition. We had all figured that it was pulverized, that we would just walk in on that island. As it turned out, it wasn't. We had also hoped to ride over the reef ... We probably could have gone in, except we had that offshore fire."

---

* Marine Gunner was a rank that reflected the role of ship's Marine detachments in the "dreadnought Navy" when the Marines manned the ship's secondary batteries. The grade was later renamed Warrant Officer to parallel Army rank structure, but the "old breed" Marines who held the rank were proud of the tradition embodied in the title.

The lighters carrying McMillian's tanks searched in vain for a suitable landing site on Red-1, then moved farther down toward Red-3, where they were singled out by the Japanese guns for special attention: "We approached that reef the better part of a mile offshore. The first thing off, it happened to be the boat I was in, got hit right down around the waterline, and the ramp just fell. That little ol' boat with that light tank in it sank mighty fast. Me and the boys, and the sailors too—two of them, the coxswain and the boat hook man—we swam around. Very quickly they pulled us out of the water onto this other one [an LCM].]."

As bad as things were for the tanks, they were worse on the reef. Colonel Shoup, commander of the assault rifle regiment, was still aboard an LCVP. McMillian: "About an hour [later] with my tanks, we started back toward that reef. It was at that time that Colonel Shoup, he knew me by name, he hollered across to me that they would wait and try to get in over by the side of the pier. Actually that's where they went in . . ."

Shoup commandeered an LVT, and his small command group worked their way ashore as the tank lighters continued to circle in the lagoon. "Then we had another one hit, and we picked them up. [There was] nobody killed of ours. Finally, there was some more fire, and this time I got sunk again. This time they were a long time getting to us. All of us were pretty good swimmers, I guess, [but] I had to let loose of all my gear, and then I took off my shoes."

This time the boat wave commander's vessel picked up McMillian: "The lieutenant j.g. had an airburst over his boat that had killed the boathook man. He said 'Let's get out of here, let's get out of here', but the second class [petty officer]—I wish I could remember his name— an older man who was the coxswain, said 'We've got to pick up these people.' He came over ... and I crawled aboard there with him. He picked everybody up." Now three of the vessels carrying light tanks had been lost, a fourth was damaged and grounded on a reef in the lagoon.[11]

The boats carrying the medium tanks arrived without loss, but also had trouble locating suitable landing points at the irregular edge of the reef.[12] The controversial commander of 3/2, Major Schoettel, was offshore when Ed Bale tried to land his tanks on Red-1 at about 1000 hours. Most accounts state that Schoettel intercepted the medium tank lighters as they were returning to the transports. Ed Bale:

At no time did Major Schoettel find any tanks headed back to the USS *Ashland*. I was embarked with one tank in an LCM-3 commanded by the Boat Officer, USS *Ashland*, who served as Wave Guide. Because of the cautions expressed by Major Frank Holland, and upon the advice of the Executive Officer, 2nd Tank Battalion, Major C. Worth McCoy, I had a boathook marked in six-inch increments up to 48 inches. We were about 15 minutes behind the third wave headed for Red Beach One when the LCM grounded on the reef. I was no more than 200 yards off the old Japanese ship, which strangely did not fire on us.* According to plan, the Boat Officer and I measured the depth of the water from the bow of the LCM. The depth of water at that point was 30 inches....

The Boat Officer and I were in the process of getting the Recon Guides in the water and ordering the other LCMs to drop their ramps and unload the tanks when Major Schoettel's boat came alongside. The Major said we should land as quickly as possible. I responded we were doing just that.

Major Schoettel may indeed have thought that the tanks were lagging, but given that the lighters were distributed along the three beaches and not in direct communication, it seems unlikely that they had all decided to draw away simultaneously. In view of the growing carnage, the reactions of both men are understandable.

Schoettel has been criticized, both during and after the war, for not landing with his troops and for holding his fourth and fifth waves offshore. Fifty years later it is seductively easy to second-guess his actions. Ed Bale more charitably said, "He made a decision, which was to stay afloat and try to keep shoving troops in there. As it turns out, it was probably a bad decision ... It's one of those things. He was particularly interested in getting the tanks ashore, because at one time he was exec of the tank battalion."

Despite the delay, Bale's tanks splashed into the water only 16 minutes after the lead assault wave arrived on the beach.[13]

Bale's Recon Platoon was in one of the first boats to hit the edge of the reef. Melvin Swango:

---

* The *Niminoa* was actually an Australian commercial vessel deliberately driven aground to avoid capture in 1941. It sheltered at least one enemy machine gun and several snipers, who took a heavy toll on the struggling infantry.

Our mission was to guide the tanks around the bomb craters on the 800 yards of reef. They outfitted us with some floats about the size of a soccer ball. We each had three floats with about a six-foot cord and an anchor. There were about 20 of us, all in one Higgins boat.

By the time we hit the edge of the reef the machine-gun fire was so intense it was tearing through the bulkheads of the Higgins boat. I would guess that maybe five or six of the men fell to the deck there, either killed or wounded. We just left them on the boat and they took them back to the ship. If the Higgins boat ever made it back to the ship. I never did know.

Sergeant Zirkle, who was in charge of our group, was hit by gunfire in the Higgins boat. He never left the boat. It didn't matter, because we knew what we had to do anyhow.

We divided up those floats, but we soon found that they were all tangled in the salt water, and we couldn't do anything with them.

They landed us right at the edge of the reef, and we started wading in. Wherever we found a bomb crater, one man would stand there to wave the tanks around it, because if a tank got into that bomb crater the men couldn't get out. It would sink like a rock.

Machine-gun fire was so intense it was like raindrops in the water all around us. Each time I looked around, there would be fewer of us. A man would simply sink beneath the water, and that would be the end of him. Most of the tanks got in ... Then it was up to us to follow the tanks in, if there were any of us left, and replace the tank crew members wherever necessary.

I only know of three of us that survived. There was myself, Charlie Kaiser, and a[nother] man ... Charlie Kaiser had his kidneys ruptured by underwater concussion while we were on the reef.

I always thought of it as a suicide mission. I don't see how any of us could have survived.

Ed Bale: "The trip to Red Beach One was a madhouse. The floats placed by the Recon Guides were floating away. The fire from the beach, mostly automatic weapons fire, was intense. The water deepened, threatening the electrical junction boxes secured to the decks of the tanks. Of the six tanks, three arrived on Red Beach One in operable condition. The other three either ran into bomb craters or the electrical systems went out as the result of salt water entering the vehicles."

Without electrical power the crews could no longer operate the main guns, and in most cases the tanks quickly flooded. Some crewmen stood atop their stalled tanks amid machine-gun and light cannon fire, and hosed the enemy with their own machine guns.[14]

Unlike Bale, Lieutenant Colonel Swenceski did not have a command tank, and unaware of the disaster that had befallen MacMillian's platoon, he proceeded to land with his command group in an LVT. Swenceski also ordered many of the support and maintenance personnel from his own battalion and Bale's medium tank company ashore, although they had no conceivable role at this stage of the battle.[15]

Halfway across the reef Swenceski's LVT was blown onto its side and everyone except Swenceski killed. Swenceski, stunned and bleeding heavily, dragged himself onto a pile of dead Marines. On this grisly little island of bodies that were already beginning to decompose in the intense heat he survived the night to be rescued 36 hours later, barely alive. Swenceski was reported to Shoup as dead.[16]

Major McCoy made it ashore with three surviving enlisted men from the battalion command group and reported to Shoup, but without radios had no way to coordinate the activities of the tanks. Each small group of tanks would fight its own isolated battle.

Ed Bale struggled to land on Red-1:

> We started inland, toward the beach, and the water got deeper ... I was in *Cecilia*, which was named after the newly-born daughter of the driver of the tank, a kid named Chavez who was later killed on Saipan ... We took a round in the left sponson, up fairly high in the sponson. Nobody was hurt or anything, but the water got deeper. I was scared, not as much that the engine would drown out as of the electrical system going out, because all the voltage regulators and everything were down near the bottom of the hull.
>
> Two tanks landed near the boundary of Red Beaches One and Two, *Chicago* and *China Gal*. My command tank, *Cecilia*, ... arrived just to the left of the center of Red Beach One. The beach was filled with bodies, wounded, individual equipment, and wrecked LVTs. We got ashore, and I got out, to try and find a way through that seawall. The plan had been that there would be an engineer team to meet us and try and blow a way through there. You know, hindsight's always better ... Of course, I never found the engineers.

The platoon leader landed west of me. His name was [William I.] Sheedy, and he landed up in the little cove." [Bale worked his way west along the beach, searching for engineers to breach the wall.]

One of the recon men who had laid the buoys in the water approached from the direction of Green Beach Two. I ordered him to work his way back ... to locate the 1st Platoon Leader [Sheedy] and have him bring tanks to my location. One tank, *Cecilia*, arrived but the crew did not know where the lieutenant was located. We later found the lieutenant and the recon man dead, side by side.

Bale's bland account neglects to mention that the narrow space below the seawall was carpeted with dead and wounded Marines, and swept by a deadly crossfire. Just moving around was courting death, and the tanks were drawing the heaviest fire.

Ed Bale: "With *Cecilia* and *China Gal* I reentered the water to avoid running over dead and wounded Marines and to get around damaged LVTs that were up against the seawall. There were almost no living Marines except badly wounded laying on that beach. So we went back in the water and ran parallel to the beach to try and find a place [to get through]."

As the tanks worked their way to the west, *Chicago* was lost when it shipped water that shorted out the electrical system.[17] Ed Bale:

About 50 yards from the intersection of Red Beach One and Green Beach we found a low spot in the seawall and were able to move through. With *China Gal* to the left of *Cecilia*, we moved inland to locate Marines. We didn't see any Marines. We saw a lot of Japanese running, and we started shooting at them with the machine guns. Then this Japanese tank popped up from behind a revetment.

The *Cecilia* gunner was excited and fired, missing the Japanese tank. Before the loader could reload, the Japanese tank fired. His 37mm round hit the end of *Cecilia*'s gun tube, broke into fragments, and came down the 75mm gun tube. The breech was open, and the fragments bounced around the inside of the turret. That thing lit up like a Christmas tree. Seven or eight different colors. Nobody got hit, but that driver like to stomped me to death trying to get out of there. I had to put my foot in his chest.

The enemy tank was quickly torn apart by the heavier gun of *China Gal*. Bale: "A look down the tube by the loader revealed the inside of the tube was damaged. So then I said 'We're going back to the beach.' Leaving *China Gal* to continue support of the badly-exposed troops, I returned to the beach with *Cecilia* to assess the damage."

One of Schoettel's subordinates, Major Mike Ryan, assumed command on Red-1. The riflemen of 3/2 recoiled from the enemy strongpoint between the Red-1 and Red-2 beaches, and were struggling inland to take control of the area behind the bird's beak. It was these men that the *China Gal* linked up with. Bale: "We went back to the beach, and got out and looked to see if we could use that gun. A big hunk [had been] taken out of the muzzle. You looked down in there the lands and grooves were gouged. I was afraid to try to fire something through there, afraid it would go off and wreck the turret. We went back and used the machine guns until we ran into *China Gal*, then I got in it and took it over."

It was probably about 1400 hours when both tanks joined with the infantry of 3/2 in trying to extend the position south along the west shore of the island. The rest of the day the two tanks worked steadily at reducing pillboxes.

On Red-3 the Recon Guides arrived almost simultaneously with the boats carrying the tanks. "Nothing went according to schedule for the next six to eight hours," said Doug Crotts. "I took about three of my close friends, and we went over to the end of the pier. We went down the pier, and got in. It must have taken us four hours. I know that by the time I got in my rifle was rusty, with the salt water and all … I remember throwing it away and picking up another from a dead Marine. The water was just about up to our chins. I suppose we would have drowned, with the equipment we had, if it had been just two or three inches deeper. We were getting shot at almost constantly. I remember one of my buddies saying 'Looky here!' He had a spent shell in his hand. He had just caught it as it came into the water."

The 3rd Platoon tanks worked their way ashore near the center of Red-3, between the long pier and the shorter Burns-Philp Company pier. Colonel Shoup hoped the tanks would help his desperate infantry to establish a defensible beachhead.

The 2nd Platoon of Bale's company tried to land on Red-2, but the first tank off the LCM plunged into water up to its turret. Two LCMs tried to make their way alongside the pier, but about 100 yards offshore the lead boat was hit, and blocked the channel. As the following boat backed away, it was hit repeatedly. It ground to a stop with its bottom on the coral, and the embarked tank somehow churned out and up onto the reef, but stumbled into a pothole hidden under the milky water. The survivors of the 2nd Platoon finally landed on Red-3, and cut across the beach into the Red-2 zone to join up with Colonel Shoup's infantry.

At about 1200 hours Shoup ordered the two 2nd Platoon tanks to attack westward, supporting an infantry assault across the airfield's west taxi strip. Operating in front of the infantry, one of the Shermans was hit by a hail of gunfire. As it maneuvered to escape, it tumbled into a crater and had to be abandoned. A few minutes later the other was damaged when a Japanese sailor ran out and slapped a magnetic mine against the sponson.* This tank was then holed several times by another gun. Colonel Shoup enjoyed the services of the tanks for less than 20 minutes before both were incapacitated.

The four tanks of 3rd Platoon fared little better. Lt. Louis Largey's command tank, *Cannonball*, took a heavy caliber hit on the slope plate that sheared away the sponson antenna and wrecked the command net radio.** Major Crowe, the commander on Red-3 was inexperienced at operating with the heavier tanks, and waved them through with instructions to "… knock out all enemy positions encountered."[19]

Sending tanks to operate unprotected was a recipe for disaster. Within the first hour *Condor* was reportedly hit and destroyed by a Navy dive-bomber.*** Wounded, *Cannonball* tried to take cover from the fire of an antitank gun by veering into a wide pit, which proved to be a Japanese fuel dump filled with barrels. The weight of the tank ruptured the barrels, and as luck would have it tracers from a strafing Navy fighter plane ignited the fuel. The crews of the tanks were trapped for a time in enemy-held ground.

Charlie fell victim to another Japanese antitank gun, which pumped several rounds through the side from near point-blank range. *Commando* took Crowe's orders literally and ranged far ahead of the protecting infantry. It defeated two antitank guns, knocked out five pillboxes, and ranged nearly to the south shore before a shell disabled it.

---

* Japanese sources state that no Type 99 *Hakobakurai* mines were available on Tarawa,[18] but numerous Marines mention these or similar devices.

** Existing photographs show the slope-plate antenna mount to be intact.

***Ed Bale disputes this assessment, pointing out to the author that photographs do not show damage to either the tank or nearby objects consistent with detonation of a large bomb.

Colorado was set afire by a hand-thrown gasoline bomb, but the quick-thinking driver raced back to the beach and out into the lagoon, drowning the flaming fuel in seawater. By 1800 hours only *Colorado* survived on Red-3.

Supplies were being funneled ashore along the relatively less exposed eastern side of the long pier. Ships' officers were dumping their holds into the landing boats, and much of what men were dying to bring ashore was useless. General Leo Hermle, the assistant division commander, took charge of organizing the effort at the end of the pier, sorting out loads of the critical materials for the surviving LVTs and human pack horses. One of the critical items lost in the shuffle was 75mm ammunition for the tanks.

At 1800 hours the Marines began to dig in for a night defense. The two surviving tanks under Ed Bale's control tied in with the infantry and prepared for the night.

Ed Bale: "Mike Ryan pulled what Marines he could find back to the beach. The Japanese were as badly disorganized as we were, because if they could have formed a counterattack and came over that seawall, they would have wiped us out that night. It was a scary night because they kept throwing mortars.* Mike Ryan and I got down for a while alongside an amtrac that had six or eight dead Marines in it. The Japanese kept throwing mortar shells at it, and we finally got up and moved. I don't know where Mike went ... I went down 60 or 70 yards down toward Green Beach."

None of the few Japanese survivors knew why Shibasaki never ordered the attack that the Marines feared. Perhaps it was the usual breakdown in communications that plagued Japanese formations throughout the war. Marine Corps historian Joseph Alexander speculated that Shibasaki was killed early in the battle, and the Japanese command structure was in disarray.[21]

The respite gave the Marines time to bring in crucial reinforcements, including four 75mm pack howitzers. On Red-3 Lou Largey took over the lone surviving medium tank, *Colorado*.

In the early morning the Japanese laid down heavy fire on the beachhead near the base of the pier. Shoup dispatched *Colorado* to bolster the line, and the tank quickly shelled several Japanese machine guns into silence.

---

* Most accounts state that mortars were little used by the Japanese in this battle.[20]

93

After waiting all night in the lagoon, the LCMs carrying McMillian's light tanks attracted still more fire: "Then there was [more] damage, and the decision was to go back out to the *Thuban* and take [off] all the excess people and to take the lieutenant and turn him over to somebody else, too ... We went back out." McMillian took the dead sailor's shoes—which didn't fit—and bumped one of his tank commanders to get a vehicle.

At 0615 the first of five waves of LCVPs carrying the men of 1/8 grounded on the reef off Red-1. The Japanese fire from the strong-point again shredded the advancing Marines. To Ryan's men huddled on the beach, the carnage seemed as bad or worse than that on D-day. Shortly after 0700 hours Major Lawrence Hays reported to Shoup. Many of his men, pinned by the intense fire, would not be ashore until 1430 hours. Shoup ordered Hays to use his relatively fresh men to try and establish contact with any survivors on Red-1.

At noon Hays's men launched their attack, only to be driven to ground by sheets of machine-gun fire from the knot of interlocked positions in back of the Red-1/Red-2 boundary. For six hours the Marines launched attack after attack under the broiling sun.

Attacking from the direction of Red-1, the damaged *Cecilia* used its .30-caliber machine guns to fire into the enemy positions raking the cove.[22] Maneuvering parallel to the beach, the bad-luck tank skidded sideways into a crater and shorted out the electrical system. With the tank canted sideways, the crew could not even manually traverse the turret to bring its guns to bear, and it was abandoned.

The critical need was for a secure route by which reinforcements could be landed without fighting their way ashore. To secure a beach not covered by enemy fire, Mike Ryan planned to attack south from Red-1 to clear the Green beaches. At 1120 hours the Marine infantry and *China Gal* moved south on a 100-yard-wide front. The Japanese defense was poorly organized, and these Marines were quickly learning how to work with Bale's tank.

Ed Bale: "Along about daylight, I took *China Gal* and we started across parallel to Green Beach. We never went out on Green Beach. People write about the fight along Green Beach, but I don't know anybody who ever went out and moved along Green Beach. They moved parallel to it, because what emplacements were there were facing the beach. You were going in behind these emplacements ...."

Within two hours they had secured the entire western shore of the island. Ryan's scratch force and Bale's lone tank had forged the single biggest contribution of the day, and perhaps of the entire battle.[23]

Ed Bale: "We went across with the infantry, and then there was a halt called. Of course it was slow going because everybody checked every hole, every emplacement. We fired a lot of ammunition. The big bunkers were not only concrete, but they were covered with deep sand. We finally realized that if you could find the opening, and fire into the opening [we could destroy them], and that's what we did. Before dark that night, we pulled back almost all the way back to Red Beach, and holed up for the night. We had a few infantrymen nearby, and we slept under that tank."

The next task for Ryan and Bale was to rescue a large contingent of trapped infantry. On D-day remnants of two companies of 1/2 crossed the wide, flat west taxi strip and occupied the central triangle of the airfield. The Japanese had discovered their mistake, and positioned heavy machine guns to seal off this route with deadly grazing fire. When Shoup ordered an attack to the south on 21 November, the 200 or so men in the central triangle crossed the wide main runway and into a tangle of dense underbrush along the south shore. Cut off by the failure of the follow-on attack across the taxiway, the small American force held a 200-by 50-yard area and was completely surrounded. A strong counterattack from the east forced the isolated Marines to expend much of their ammunition.

Behind Red-3 Major Crowe spent the day trying to reduce Japanese positions around the foot of the Burns-Philp Pier. *Colorado* eliminated a series of enemy positions that had come back to life inside the beachhead, working with a bulldozer to blast the positions at point-blank range, then cover them over with sand.

The new task of the Recon Guides was to scout targets for the tanks,[24] and Doug Crotts was working with Lou Largey. Crotts:

> At one stage he said, "Doug, you've got to get in the tank and go with me. I've got to show you what we're looking at here, so when you give me signals you'll know what I can see and what I can't see, and what happenstance will enable me to see."
>
> I got in ... I said, "Lou"—I was turned around, not being familiar with the inside of a tank—"is this our lines straight ahead?"
>
> He said, "Oh, no. Japanese."

I said, "Well there's Japanese soldiers going over a little mound, one after another."

He threw the turret over in that direction. The Japanese were just like marching, only on their stomachs. Lou just took a machine gun, and he could almost just close his eyes after the timing started. It was almost like a dance. As they would climb over he'd just roll them over. After they quit coming he just threw a 75 into the group.

He said, "I just want you to see." I thought boy, I'd rather be outside than in this thing … I think I had claustrophobia, to tell the truth. I never did relax inside. I felt better outside.

[The guides moved ahead of the tank, dragging dead and wounded Marines out of its path.] We'd move them, and they would protect me while I was out there with my two friends, clearing the way for them.

Anything that we thought they ought to see, I would lay my rifle down as if I were sighting … He could look at my rifle, and then I would hold up fingers for how many yards out there it was.

One problem was attracting the attention of the tank crew when he found a target. The brass casings from expended cannon rounds, shoved out the pistol port on the side of the turret, made excellent bells. Crotts: "I took a 75mm shell and beat on the tank until they acknowledged that they saw us. That was very risky. Those Japs saw you out there and they knew damn well what you were telling them."

By late morning it was obvious that Ryan on Green Beach was making the most headway, and General Julian Smith decided to reinforce success. The infantry of 1/6 and the light tanks of Captain Frank Stewart's B Company, 2nd Tank Battalion were ordered to land on Green Beach.

The first wave found the southern stretch of the reef heavily mined, and one of the accompanying LVTs carrying heavy communications equipment was blown up. The rest of the battalion was diverted north, adding to the delay and confusion. Finally, at about 1900 hours 1/6 was ashore as an intact fighting force, the first such on the island.

The confusion was worse for the tankers because their light tanks were deep in the holds of three different transports. In the mad scramble of the previous day the tanks had been further buried under random piles of other cargo.

When the LCMs reached the seaward edge of the reef off Green Beach, scouts found that the reef shelved off on the landward side into deeper water, and there were numerous potholes. A shifting current and heavy surf made it almost impossible to hold the LCMs against the edge of the reef long enough to unload the tanks. Lieutenant Bill Barry's reinforced platoon did not get onto the reef until 1830 hours, and the other two platoons were diverted to the Red beaches.

Charles Frederick, a crewman in one of Barry's tanks: "Somebody screwed up and they let us out with our tanks too damned soon. We were supposed to go there at high tide so we could get right up to that seawall. We came in on low tide, and they dropped us off 700 yards from where they were supposed to."

Robert Thompson, a driver in the same platoon:

> We had five tanks. Two of us got ashore out of the five. My Platoon Sergeant [Walter Fiegeth] was a guinea pig. He got out and waded ahead of his tank. I was two tanks behind him ... Fiegeth's tank and my tank were the only tanks that were rolling. A couple of them got right to the beach before the water got to them. They were missing and sputtering. We had the old aviation engines in them. Any time water hit that fan, it hit the whole engine.
>
> [Frederick's tank] ... happened to hit a hole there and the tank drowned out, 'cause we didn't have them sealed or anything. We started stripping the guns and ammunition, and throwing it out into the sea. [We] swam in to the beach, and there was coral reef and we got cut up. There was some barbed wire, too. When we hit the seawall we stayed there for a night before we could get over the seawall.

The remnant of C Company's light tanks landed on Red-2 at 1700 hours, losing one of the remaining tanks in a shell hole near the pier. The two remaining tanks reported to Shoup and McCoy, and were ordered to dig in near the head of the pier. The light tank assembly area, established in an abandoned Japanese aircraft revetment, came under heavy mortar fire.

At 1700 the daily summary report included a description of the ground held: southwest from the short Burns-Philp Pier to the south coast, along the south coast for a short distance, then back up to a point near the Red-1/Red-2 boundary. The report did not mention that the small force on the south coast was cut off, but concluded with a now-legendary summary: "Casualties: many. Percentage dead: unknown. Combat efficiency: we are winning. Shoup."[25]

The remnant of Bill Barry's platoon linked up with McMillian at the revetment. Frederick: "The ones that came in there with their tanks, they just had to dig a foxhole and crawl underneath the tank. My whole crew crawled under somebody's tank, because we didn't have a tank to put over our heads. We had orders, anybody walks around is gonna get shot, because it started getting dark. At night some people were walking around, and we started shooting at them. In the morning there were several Japs laying there dead."

The B Company tanks were desperately searching for a place to land, and Platoon Sergeant Leonard Sines's section arrived off Red-2 just after 0200 hours. One tank shorted out its electrical system and refused to start, so one of the others towed it ashore, where it was quickly disabled by mortar fire.

In the early morning hours the B Company tanks continued to dribble ashore on Red-2. Another section arrived at about 0730 and made it safely ashore, but three more that arrived at 0800 all drowned on the reef.

Shoup worked through the night of 21–22 November to prepare a coordinated attack. At 0400 runners carried the plans to the battalion commanders.

Without a tank, Jim Carter and the gunner from Frederick's tank had been made company runners: "You carried messages from one place to another. Communications weren't very good in those days, so a lot of company runners were used to get messages from one command post to another ... Actually you were a kind of bodyguard for the command post, too."

The job of runner was extremely hazardous, because the runners had to move around, sometimes through enemy-held ground: "You got shot at. You had to move, you had to expose yourself, to get from one place to another."

The tenacious Japanese defenders between Red-1 and Red-2 still held out, and Shoup's first priority was to eliminate this threat. His second was to attack east down the main axis of the island.

At 0700 Major Hays's 1/8 launched another attack into the stubborn hellhole that had stalled his attacks of the previous day. McMillian's three surviving light tanks and Barry's two were assigned to support the attack. Any movement on the part of the tanks attracted torrents of mortar rounds. One mortar round struck the turret ring of a B Company tank, putting it out of action.[26]

Without telephones or radios the tanks had no way to communicate with the infantry, and the Japanese defenders would hold their fire when the tanks appeared.[27] One solution was for an infantryman to scout the ground, then climb into the tank and guide them to the target. McMillian:

> On two occasions infantry people mounted up with me and took me to show me things they thought we could take care of. There was a Lieutenant Martin Tomlinson from A Company, of the Eighth.
>
> That was dangerous, crawling in and out of tanks like that. There wasn't any place to go into defilade, and it was very dangerous. In fact, I had to mount and dismount quite a few times, and I had two occasions when they [bullets] fanned my face. I was just lucky. There were some pretty accurate snipers out and around there somewhere, and I think they were looking for people crawling in and out of the tanks.
>
> I leapt off that tank. I got away in a hurry. I came down, and I hurt my foot on a piece of coral … I didn't have the right size shoes on anyhow, and my foot got to swelling. I was limping around, [and Major McCoy said] "What's wrong with you, Mac?"

McMillian managed to talk his way past McCoy, but after the battle was evacuated with a broken foot.

The small tanks approached to within yards of their target through a hail of gunfire, putting round after round from their little 37mm cannons into the targets. Some poked the muzzles of their cannons up to the embrasures of pillboxes. The 37mm guns simply did not have the needed punch. McMillian:

> There were eight, maybe ten, rounds fired one right after the other right into this pillbox. You would think there wasn't anybody in there, but about that time the Japanese, through another exit, they showed up. One of the other tanks threw two rounds of canister in on them, and got every one of them. Thirty-seven canister was pretty effective.
>
> We had lots of tracer, .30 caliber, and we shot through old trucks, tin [roofing], and debris. I don't know how effective we were, but we created enough diversion that other people could work … enough diversion that other people could get in with their flamethrowers and such.
>
> [Ultimately Tomlinson's luck ran out.] He had been in and out before. He rode with us and we got pretty well acquainted. Nice fellow. I hated to see him go like that. He was coming in to go on another lit-

tle sashay with me. He had gotten down and reported, and they reported to him, gave him a little fire mission in other words. He wasn't talking to them on the radio. They didn't have any radios. There was a captain, I can't remember his name, came over with him. We all discussed what we were gonna do, and were all ready to go at it.

The tank crewmen would dive through the hatch, but the infantry officer paused too long. Shot through the chest, the mortally wounded officer dropped into the cramped interior of the turret, right on top of McMillian. "We didn't go on that fire mission. We canceled it."

Another of McMillian's tanks was lost when a Japanese soldier ran out and tossed a Type 99 magnetic mine onto the engine deck.* The explosion ripped open the thin deck armor and set fire to the fuel tanks.

Hays pulled the light tanks out of the fight and committed two of the regiment's SPMs. Although more powerfully armed, the open-topped SPMs could not press home attacks amid a shower of grenades and mortar rounds. Hays's troops battered at the enemy positions for the rest of the day.

Back at Green Beach, Bale and *China Gal* were back in action. "Come daylight, we started back to find Ryan and that little command group he had formed, and we ran into Bill Jones and his battalion of the 6th Marines. Then we started working with them."

At 0815 Major Jones's 1/6 launched an attack to relieve the isolated perimeter on the south beaches. Jones was the inheritor of the most powerful tank force on the island, *China Gal* and seven light tanks. Jones decreed that under no circumstances were the tanks to operate more than 50 yards in front of the infantry, and were to remain under his personal control. He improvised a way to communicate with the light tanks by holding one at his command post to act as a radio base-station.[28] The attack was delivered on a very narrow front of about 100 yards, through the underbrush south of the airfield runway.

"By that time there were some light tanks from one of the companies of the 2nd Tank Battalion ashore," said Bale, "and what we did was to team up like a mother hen with two or three chicks. We would go places, and they would protect us with their machine-gun fire. We went down that [south] side of the airstrip. In fact, we ran a lot on the airstrip, firing off the airstrip."

---

* Again, note that Japanese sources say that this weapon was not used on Tarawa.

The infantry led the tanks from one position to another, but unable to communicate with the riflemen, Bale had to improvise: "It meant that the tank commander—me—either got out of the tank to talk to the infantry, or an infantryman crawled up on the turret. We would turn the turret away from the Japanese. The tank commander's hatch was on a rotating ring in those days, and I would rotate that, and put one of those hatch covers between me and the Japanese. [It protected us] from one direction, but God knows, you could have gotten hit from anywhere."

The attack made steady headway. At 1100 hours they had advanced some 800 yards, and relieved the isolated perimeter. The fighting had the strange aspect of having two battalions attacking in opposite directions along parallel axes. Hays's 1/8 was attacking toward the west on the north side of the runway, while Jones's 1/6 was attacking toward the east on the south side. A man could be as easily killed or wounded by stray rounds from across the runway as by those fired by the enemy to his front. Bale said, "It could have gotten real hairy. It was hairy, but it could have gotten worse."

Frederick and some of his crew were set to work cleaning out enemy stragglers. Frederick:

> They had trenches dug under the ground, and we had to go through there and throw hand grenades in ... We walked right across dead bodies and everything else.
>
> We had several of our people got shot in the legs. We started throwing smoke and grenades down there, and here 12 Japs came out of there. And that was one of those dugouts that I had walked through ... They were still in there. That's when I got scared. They might have been alive when I walked across them. I don't know.
>
> My buddy, _____, had a Thompson sub. When they lined 'em up, he just mowed 'em all down.
>
> There was another bunker there that had nothing but coconut logs protecting it. People were throwing in all the fire they could get ... They bombed it, they put dynamite in there and blew it up, and everything else. Finally he came out, waving a white flag, and he was bleeding from the ears and everything else.

Adequate supplies could now be landed, but no ammunition for the 75mm guns of the Sherman tanks was being brought ashore. On Red-3 Largey, Crotts, and others scavenged from disabled tanks, but *China*

Gal was far from the remains of the other vehicles. Ed Bale: "Once they began to get supplies ashore we had adequate machine-gun ammunition. Seventy-five millimeter gun ammunition? We fired a lot of 75mm pack howitzer ammunition, which didn't seat properly, but it worked … Whatever the stuff was fused with, we used. It didn't matter, because the object was to shoot as much as you could."

Major Crowe's 2/8 launched its long-awaited attack to the east of Red-3, against the formidable positions at the foot of the Burns-Philp Pier. The positions blocking this advance, and that had tormented Crowe's men for two days and nights, included Shibasaki's huge command bunker and two sturdy pillboxes that protected it. About 0930 a mortar round penetrated the roof of the most inland of the three positions, causing a huge secondary explosion. *Colorado* rolled forward to deliver a close-range attack on the other pillbox, pumping several rounds at the now-exhumed steel box. One round finally penetrated, and the way was clear to attack the big bunker.

Charles Frederick was reassigned as an impromptu ambulance attendant: "[They] put me on with another tank, going out and picking up wounded people and bringing them back. One guy I threw on the back end of the tank to haul him up to the bivouac area to where some corpsmen were, he got shot right between the legs. I never saw so much blood on anybody in all my life."

At 1100 hours Lieutenant Colonel McLeod's 3/6 landed across Green Beach and moved into reserve behind the advancing 1/6.

At nightfall the decimated rifle battalions established a continuous north-south front across the island east of the airfield, held by the survivors of 2/8, 3/8, and 1/6. The stubborn Japanese pocket at the Red-1/Red-2 boundary still defied all attempts at reduction. Anticipating another grim day of bloody frontal attacks, the Marines stockpiled grenades, ammunition, and water. A tank was used to haul the cargo.[29]

At 0300 on 23 November several machine guns opened fire against B/1/6, and at 0400 hours nearly 400 Japanese rushed B Company. Most were killed by concentrated fire from mortars, machine guns and rifles, and by bayonets and knives in the hand-to-hand struggle that followed.

At 0700 a carrier air strike plastered the "tail" of the bird, followed by artillery and naval gunfire. McLeod's 3/6 passed through the lines of the exhausted 1/6 and moved forward for the last gasp of the conquest of Betio.

Colorado, China Gal, and the seven surviving light tanks led the attack. The fight seemed to have gone out of the defenders. Many Japanese committed suicide, others offered token resistance. McMillian: "We moved right down on them, and that was one reason the battle got over with right then. We led the infantry down through there. We went in a formation of iron. They [the medium tanks] were not out front or behind us, they were about on the same line with us."

At 1310 hours 3/6 reached the eastern tip of the island. McLeod reported that "medium tanks were excellent. My light tanks didn't fire a shot."[30] This was an obvious exaggeration, but the heavy fire-power and thicker armor protection of the medium tanks certainly made them the decisive weapon.

The pocket at the Red-1/Red-2 boundary that was responsible for most of the death inflicted on four battalions of Marines had thus far withstood the most determined attacks launched against it. On this final day 1/8 attacked west from Red-2, while the weary 3/2, with Major Schoettel once more in command, attacked from the south. No tanks could be spared from the eastern drive, so two SPMs support-ed the attack. The two battalions slowly gnawed away at the inter-locking positions, reducing them one by one.

At 1305 Shoup radioed the command ship that the island was secure. The Marine Corps had triumphed in one of the ghastliest bat-tles of World War II, but at a terrible price. Over one-third of the land-ing force were casualties.

Ed Bale's medium tank company had one more unique contribu-tion to make:

> In some of that stuff [references] they probably talk about when they raised the flag declaring the island secure. They needed a bugler, and the bugler showed up in a white Japanese [naval officer's] uniform. That was a guy named Jimmy Williams. Jimmy Williams had been a field music (bugler) on an aircraft carrier that went down during the Coral Sea. When I took over this company, we were organized along Marine Corps lines. You had a field music and all these things, and Jimmy was the field music. I put him in a tank, and he was one who was written up for standing on the back of this tank after it drowned out in the water, firing at Japanese emplacements with a machine gun.
>
> [Bale and his men] ... salvaged everything we could salvage before we left there, and hauled them back in the *Ashland*. When the *Ashland* unloaded us at Hilo, they went over to Maui or somewhere and

unloaded those tanks. A lot of them were subsequently rebuilt. Those that were usable were used by the tank company of the 22nd Marines, I think at Eniwetok.

In salvaging the tanks, we had no retriever. Our retriever was down in New Caledonia. I had a warrant officer by the name of [Roger A.] Massey ... Massey was an old Marine who had been a Motor Transport sergeant. He was a genius at keeping things running. He figured out a way of taking all the towing cables off the tanks, and rigged two or three tanks on the shore and pulled all these things out. That's *Cecilia* that's sitting out there now [in 1993]. We tried to get it out. It's the only one I know of that truly ran into a big bomb crater, and that's what it's sitting in.

After the battle I went back to it, because when I left it, I left a prayer book and a pint of Scotch in my dispatch case. I went back to get that bag.

Now hundreds of unburied bodies festered in the blistering heat. Fifty-five years later Jim Carter said of the film *Saving Private Ryan*, "They had the noise ... but they couldn't duplicate the smell. That was something else that you had to get used to. It was the dead bodies, dead seaweed, and diesel fuel."

The medium tanks had played a pivotal role in this horrid battle. However, the hasty integration of the medium tanks, lack of meaningful training, and inadequate communications had reduced their effectiveness.

Without doubt Tarawa served to highlight the worst problems in doctrine, inadequate equipment, poor communications, and poor tank-infantry coordination. The single worst problem was the poor communication between tanks and infantry, and many tank crew casualties were the result of tank commanders dismounting to talk to the riflemen.[31] Lieutenant Colonel C. Worth McCoy summarized the three major lessons of the action on Tarawa—the 37mm cannon of the light tank was completely inadequate against Japanese bunkers. The heavier medium tank had a definite place in landing operations; and the 2nd Division launched an "intense" program to improve tank-infantry coordination and communications.[32]

CHAPTER 6

SWAMP TANKS: CAPE GLOUCESTER

O PERATION BACKHANDER was the battle for control of the big island of New Britain, the ultimate prize for which the Allies had fought the protracted struggle for the Solomons. The neutralization of the great enemy base at Rabaul would deprive the enemy of their greatest logistical center and harbor in the southwest Pacific.

Most of New Britain was covered with dense jungle, broken only by a few tracts of kunai grass on better-drained terrain. The Japanese developed a small transit center near Cape Gloucester, on the extreme western tip of the island 350 miles from Rabaul, where two airfields served aircraft shuttling to and from New Guinea. The capture of these airfields would help complete a noose of air bases about Rabaul.

Major General Iwao Matsuda commanded the equivalent of three infantry regiments, an artillery regiment and parts of two others, an independent antitank company, the *39th Field Anti-Aircraft Battalion* with a dozen 75mm Type 88 guns, two machine cannon* companies, and a number of transport corps and service units. The largest local garrison was at Cape Bushing on the southern coast, which Matsuda considered to be the most likely landing site. One site that Matsuda did not bother to fortify was just east of Cape Gloucester near Borgen Bay.

Allied air reconnaissance of the Borgen Bay area indicated firm ground behind this raised strip, but the area is actually a coastal swamp. The American landings were set to take place during the monsoon, when the swamp is waist deep in fetid black water.

The reinforced 1st Marine Division was temporarily under the control of General Walter Krueger's Sixth Army. Krueger's superior,

---

* A machine cannon was a fully-automatic light cannon that fired explosive shells.

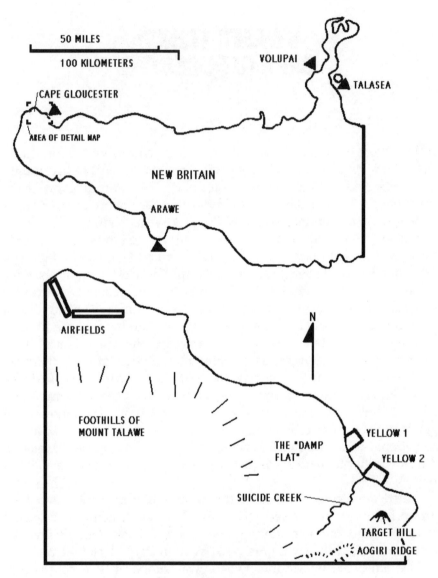

Cape Gloucester

Douglas MacArthur, frequently bypassed Krueger and communicated directly with the 1st Division commander. The 1st Marine Tank Battalion received 24 M4A1 Sherman tanks in May 1943, and these equipped A Company.* The M4A1, with a distinctive rounded cast hull, was at that time the preferred version in Army service. Able Company would be the only Marine unit ever to use this model.

The other tank companies were re-equipped with new M5A1 light tanks powered by a pair of automobile engines linked through two Hydra-Matic transmissions to a single final-stage transmission.

With the new tanks came a shipment of FM 10-channel SCR508 and SCR528 radios to replace the old aircraft radios that Ed Bale had found so frustrating. Arthur Rowe was a staff sergeant communications specialist assigned to C Company and later to Headquarters Company as a radio maintenance man.

Rowe: "The old GF-RU was originally an aircraft radio. When they got newer stuff for the Navy, we wound up with the old stuff in the tanks. It was not totally unreliable, but very difficult to keep on frequency. Most of the tankers did not like it, and as a result they did not have much faith in communications people or equipment. When the new ones came, that made a big difference. The old stuff was AM and subject to a lot of noise, whereas the FM was virtually noise-free."

Tarawa had demonstrated the value of the flamethrower, but the short range made it hard to approach the target closely enough to be effective. The obvious solution was to mount the weapon in a tank, so the first experiments involved mounting an M1A1 man-pack unit in place of the bow machine gun on the M3A1 light.

"We were up at Goodenough Island, getting ready to go into Cape Gloucester," said Rowland Hall. "They gave a demonstration with the infantry flamethrower, and that's the one where Chesty Puller made his famous remark, 'Where do you put the bayonet on the damn thing?' Seeing that thing, I said well, maybe we could put it in the tank. [We] got Ed Huckle, who was a good machinist, and the hubs of a couple of aircraft propellers and stuff like that."

The flamethrower was mounted in place of the bow machine gun, using the propeller hub as a ball mount. "It wasn't really worth a damn, because we had no napalm. All we had was the fuel that they

---

* The limited number of medium tanks in Marine Corps service were organized as the I Marine Amphibious Corps Tank Battalion. Other divisional tank battalions

used, diesel fuel and gasoline mixed together. It just created a gorgeous big ball of flame, but it was not like the napalm ... that would really shoot. We fired this stuff off, but never used it in combat."

The 1st Tank Battalion was shipped to Milne Bay, New Guinea, and then to the Oro Bay staging area. Because of the limited shipping capacity, the light tanks of B Company were left behind at Oro Bay as an operational reserve.

Following a supporting operation on the south coast, the main landings on 26 December were directed at two objectives. The Stoneface Force landed on the west coast seven miles south of the airfield complex to deny the enemy use of the coastal trail if Matsuda tried to consolidate his scattered forces.

The main landing took place at the gap in the reefs at Borgen Bay, seven miles southeast of the main airfield complex. There was no opposition because Matsuda never expected the Americans to land in an impassable swamp. There were the usual snarls inherent in any landing. The wash of waves could cause vehicles to mire up in the soft volcanic sand of the narrow beach. Arthur Rowe was bringing the Headquarters Company communications section jeep ashore:

> As I sat there waiting for the beachmaster to give me the go-ahead sign, somebody onshore hollered over to him. It distracted him for a moment ... It must have been no more than four or five seconds. When he turned back to me to give me the go ahead, that four or five seconds was just long enough for me to get caught in the back wave instead of being washed ashore in the one going.
> When I went off [the boat], the water got up to my neck ... The jeep was dead. I came out of there screaming and hollering and cussing. Oh God, it made me mad! The best I could do was get about ten or twelve Marines to help me push that thing right up.

The area behind the beach terrace, marked on the American maps as "wet flat ground" turned out to be, in the words of one anonymous Marine, "damp up to your neck."[1] The only place 2/11 could find for its howitzers was astride the trail along the top of the terrace, and other units were forced to use the narrow beach as a road.

The first organized resistance lay athwart the coastal trail west of the landing beaches, where riflemen of 3/1 stumbled upon four mutually supporting bunkers. The attack degenerated into a desperate short-range battle. Rain-sodden earth that covered the bunkers would absorb the rounds from bazookas without providing enough resistance to detonate the round, flamethrower fuel failed to ignite in the rain and fog. Delayed by the confusion on the beach, a platoon of Sherman tanks arrived too late to intervene.

On the left the 7th Marines launched themselves into the worst of the swamps. Gunners manning the 75mm howitzers of 1/11 had to deal with a nightmare as LVTs were used to knock down trees on scattered islands that protruded from an enormous stagnant lake. By 1800 hours the beachhead was secure, and the Marines settled into two separate perimeters to await the inevitable counterattack.

The landing in the swamp had thrown Matsuda off balance, and Japanese intelligence had again sorely underestimated American strength. Rather than gathering a strong force, Matsuda threw his units in piecemeal.

Takabe's battalion was not able to locate an open flank of the 7th Marines in the pitch-dark night and ground fog, and threw themselves into a night-long series of attacks against the front of the perimeter. A storm blew in from the Bismarck Sea, with driving rains and gale force winds. Brilliant flashes of lightning blinded both sides, and peals of thunder drowned the noises of gunfire and artillery. All night the Marines and Japanese infantry fought from behind trees and fallen logs, unable to dig fighting holes in the flooded ground.

Torrential rains hampered expansion of the perimeter and hamstrung the tanks. Uniforms and shoes began to rot, and the waxed wrappers from rations were as highly prized as the rations themselves: they were the only things that would burn to heat powdered coffee.[2] The constant flow of traffic broke down the coastal track into a morass, and the Shore Regiment and the Army's 592nd Engineer Boat Regiment shuttled equipment and supplies along the shore.

Bob Boardman recalled that of the three campaigns in which he participated, the Cape was the most difficult: "None of us will ever forget those living conditions, but it was not the most intense combat experiences for us." Like all new men in combat units, Boardman and the other replacements faced a cruel reception: "Many of us were new in C Company, 1st Tank Battalion, and it was our first combat experience. We were very green and scared, and didn't know what was happening. Also we were treated rather poorly by some of the veterans of C Company … We were like rookies in the NFL, so that part of it was not easy, but the discipline and so forth was good for us. We were trying to prove ourselves there on Cape Gloucester. We saw some combat but the tanks were limited because of the terrain. It was an overwhelming experience. The mud and the rain and the terrain were formidable obstacles."

Bill Henahan recalled that "… there was so much mud and stuff that the tanks were almost useless. They were so heavy that they just sank right into it."

The only men who worked in comparative luxury were Arthur Rowe's communications maintenance section. "I had charge of a standard Marine Corps trailer, about 20 feet long, four wheels, and was pulled around by anything that could pull it. In there I had a complete arrangement of maintenance equipment to repair the radios, check them out, I even had one on line all the time so I could hear what was going on. That one turned out to be a spare, so that any time one came back that spare went out as a replacement while I repaired the old one." This luxurious trailer was not a standard item for the tank battalions. "Nothing was standard in those days. What you could scrounge or what you could dig up, or how you managed to get it, was in your favor."

The 1st Marines were able to advance fairly rapidly until on 27 December they fetched up against the defenses at Hell's Point, a promontory two miles east of the airfield. A dozen solid bunkers built of logs and oil drums filled with crushed rock, and protected by aprons of barbed wire, mines, mortars, and precut fire lanes for heavy machine guns formed a line extending 300 yards inland.

The next morning's assault was delayed to allow A Company to bring up a platoon of Sherman tanks, a decision which "paid dividends."[3] At 1100 hours on 28 December the 1st Marines attacked on a two-battalion front. The 1st Battalion went into the flooded jungle to try and outflank the defenses, only to bog down in a deadly seesaw of attacks and counterattacks.

The 3rd Battalion launched a frontal attack on the bunker complex with Item Company in the lead. An echelon of three A Company Shermans led the attack.

Eugene Viveiros, Gunnery Sergeant for A Company: "We started to form tank-infantry teams there. This is where it was put together as far as my knowledge goes. We would advance with a tank plus a squad of infantrymen, busting through heavy jungle foliage."

The leading tank-infantry teams were backed by another echelon of three tanks followed by rifle squads, with two more rifle companies trailing to consolidate any gains. The tanks hammered the bunkers with cannon fire while the rifle squads protected the sides and rear of the tanks.

At 1200 hours the Japanese ambushed the lead tanks with hand-held satchel charges, sack mines, and shoulder-pack mines. Conventional Japanese satchel charges contained 10kg or more of explosive, and a favored tactic was to attack the thinner belly armor, tracks, or the undersides of the sponsons. The sponsons were used for ammunition and fuel stowage in both the Stuart and Sherman tanks.

The sack mine consisted of from 5 to 10 kg of explosive in a burlap sack. The shoulder-pack or box mine, was fitted with rope shoulder straps and held up to 10 kg of explosive. Both were equipped with a detonator and wooden pull handle; the soldier usually either tossed the device under a tank, or threw himself and the charge under a tank, then pulled the handle to initiate the detonator.[4]

Viveiros: "These guys worked in groups of three, and they would have a heavy charge all bundled up inside this straw matted stuff that they would weave. It had a neck harness. The guy who was supposed to blow the tank up, his job was to if possible get up close to the tank and affix a heavy demolition charge within the suspension, or wherever he could get it. Then he would pull his igniter, and set off the charge. In most cases this guy went to meet his ancestors along with it."

Only one tank was lost. "Hell, that one tank it must have went 15 or 20 feet straight up when that guy set that charge off. Blew the whole suspension off of one side of the tank. Tank came down and it was all burnt black on one side. We were able to rescue the crew, and other than looking kind of glassy-eyed none of them sustained any serious injuries. The tank was completely knocked out."

Attacks were less successful when directed against the side armor. Rowland Hall saw a backpack mine in use. "They had a Japanese suddenly spring out of the jungle with a big knapsack on his back, and a ripcord like you'd have on a parachute. He simply leaned up against the side of a tank and pulled that thing. There was a tremendous roar, and he got splattered all over. The concussion was pretty rough inside the tank. Scarborough was the tank commander of that one. The guys kind of shook their heads, hitched up their belts, and off they went."

The powerful 75mm tank cannons ripped apart the bunkers, and the tanks crawled up onto the log bunkers, collapsing their roofs. The enemy's little 75mm howitzers were incapable of damaging the big tanks.

Bill Finley followed the Shermans in a light tank. "The Japanese had a 77mm pack-howitzer there ... They said that this Japanese officer was just standing there with his hand on the lanyard. As soon as that Sherman tank turned where he could see it, he fired and hit that tank. It just scratched it, maybe an eighth of an inch deep, but didn't hurt it."

The tank opened fire with its machine guns, and crushed the gun under its treads.[5] "They left a pile of those dead Japanese. One of them's head, you couldn't tell it was a head. It looked like about the size of a piece sausage, about twelve, eighteen inches long. You couldn't tell the features or anything. Looked like somebody had shot about 200 rounds right through under his chin and all through his head. That was the weirdest thing I ever saw, but there were a lot of sights that weren't too pretty.

"I know sometimes we would have to go somewhere, and the only way we could go we had to drive over Japanese bodies. It didn't make it very pleasant, because when you stopped to eat it smelled pretty bad."

As the dry ground widened out, the rifle battalion commander committed K Company and another platoon of tanks, attacking on a two-company front. After destroying most of the bunkers the attack broke off when the cannons on two of the tanks malfunctioned and ammunition began to run low. The Japanese took the opportunity to abandon the few remaining positions. At about 1630 the rifle platoons and tanks dug in to await a rumored enemy armored counterattack. They waited all night. Matsuda had no tanks.

On the morning of 29 December, the 5th Marines moved into the attack but the Japanese had slipped away. By 1925 hours the rifle squads were on the big Airfield Number Two. Matsuda wisely chose to abandon the low, open ground. By stubbornly hanging on in the high ground overlooking the airfields his men could deny the Allies the use of the facilities, while minimizing the imbalance wrought by the Marine tanks and artillery.

On 30 December, the 5th Marines set about trying to clear the hills, starting with a large clearing that overlooked the airfields. Aerial reconnaissance had failed again. The clearing was in reality a steep ridge flanked by dense jungle, and a key enemy position. The exposed men came under a blistering fire from the up slope edge of the clearing, but held on to drive back a counterattack. Tanks were brought forward, and by 1130 had wrecked 30 bunkers.

At noon General Rupertus reported the capture of the airfield to General Krueger. Communications between the tanks and the infantry were still poor because the infantry's radios were neither portable nor reliable. "When the infantry boys saw a pocket that they would like the tankers to take out for them," said Arthur Rowe, "they had no way of telling them." Rowe thought that they might modify the intercom by putting another station on the rear of the tank. "All I did was extend the intercom from the inside of the tank out. When anybody on the outside pressed the button, he would break in on the intercom."

Engine maintenance personnel helped snake a rubberized intercom cable through the engine compartment, then out the ventilator on the rear corner of the hull. An extra intercom box was hung on the back of the tank. Arthur Rowe:

> What happened next was straight out of Murphy's book of laws!
> The cable contained 11 wires, including a pair of white colored ones. It was one of these that I used as a control line that operated the switch on the handset and enabled a person to "break in" to the intercom. In the tank installation, the white wires were inadvertently transposed and therefore, the mod didn't work. Before I discovered what the problem was, the person assigned to oversee the installation (a light colonel) arrived on the scene. This officer had opposed the installation from the very start for reasons I never fully understood … It would have taken only 10 minutes to correct the problem but, seeing that it didn't work, I was ordered to stop work and forget it. That is the closest I ever came to disobeying a direct order! He reported to the CO that the project didn't work and that was the end of it. I simply stopped working on that project, left the installation as it was, and went on to other things that needed my attention.[6]

In the new year the fighting shifted back east toward the shores of Borgen Bay. The Marines wanted to expand their perimeter to the east and destroy the remaining enemy, while the Japanese were still intent on driving what they thought was a small force into the sea. Unknown to each other, the combatants planned to launch their main efforts at the same spot. The Japanese *141st Infantry* would spill out of the hills directly into the face of the American offensive. The focal point of this collision would be a gory struggle for control of the banks of an unmapped and nameless creek.

On 1 January the American offensive began with what was intended to be a short hook by two battalions. On 2 January the Marines ran into heavy fire while trying to cross a small stream. Along some stretches the stream was a creek proper with high banks. Upstream it was choked with tangled vegetation and neck-deep with water from the rains. It was a fantastic defensive barrier and the enemy was determined to hold it to cover the assembly of his own attack.

Four times on 3 January the Marines clawed their way to a foothold on the east bank of the stream, only to be driven back by grenades and mortar fire. The anonymous stream acquired a name—Suicide Creek.

Engineers of C/1/17 were sweating their own river to build a corduroy road through the swamp, and at 1600 hours the engineers were able to bring up a bulldozer. Suicide Creek was already purple with the blood of dead and wounded riflemen, but now an engineer had to sit exposed atop the bulldozer to cut down the 12-foot creek bank. The driver was almost immediately shot from the seat. Two more engineers rushed out and drove the tractor by working the pedals and levers with a shovel and an axe handle. When the bank was worked down somewhat, one crawled up into the seat, was himself shot, but continued to work the dozer until nightfall.

The next morning three A Company Shermans, followed by two SPMs, nosed cautiously across and were immediately rushed by Japanese with demolition charges. The attackers were cut down by rifle fire before they could damage the tanks, which proceeded to blast the machine-gun positions raking the ford. Enemy resistance collapsed in the face of the tanks, and the Japanese withdrew leaving about 500 dead.

Captured documents indicated that the next enemy position was called Aogiri Ridge, but did not reveal which terrain feature went by that name. The Americans paused to reorganize and prepare for a systematic attack.

At 1100 hours on 6 January the advance of A/1/7 was stopped by heavy fire on the banks of another unnamed stream, and the company once more called for tank support. Again a bulldozer cut down the approaches, but this time the tanks balked, afraid of the soft ground in the stream bottom. Once across, though, the tanks quickly stifled the resistance on the far bank, but the overall advance the next day bogged in tangles and flooded gullies.

On 8 January the infantry advanced despite pouring rain and flooding that defeated all attempts to drive a corduroy road through the swamp. In a particularly dense tract of jungle the rifle squads of

3/5 started up a gently rising slope, and were smacked down by intense fire. Next morning the rifle squads of 3/5 literally clawed their way up the steep, slimy slopes, dragging themselves upward into the machine-gun fire using roots as handholds. The stubborn Japanese machine gunners were dug into natural bunkers formed by the giant prop roots of the jungle trees. Snipers covered all possible approaches.

In late afternoon the rifle squads were bloodied and exhausted, and the fight had stalled into a debilitating exchange of rifle volleys and grenades at 10 yards. An attempt to attack down the other side exposed the Marines to a series of frenzied counterattacks. The Japanese were determined to hold the ridge, which screened their big supply dumps and positions inland.

The exhausted Marines dug in for the night, and called down 75mm and 105mm artillery fire on the reverse slope. At 0115 hours the first counterattack came on in a driving rain. The Japanese came four more times in a swirling confusion of rain, explosions, lightning, and screams.

At 0800 the exhausted Marines staggered forward down the south slope, but the churned and smoking jungle held only enemy bodies. The Japanese had slipped away.

By 11 January a corduroy road had at last been driven forward, and four light tanks and two SPMs arrived to help in a four-hour battle to reduce the last big enemy position. The Japanese fought literally to the last man to defend the supply and ammunition dumps that could not be removed with their available manpower.

The Japanese fell back on Hill 660, a steep, round hill near the coastline about a mile to the south, and backed by a deep swamp. Behind the hill a narrow strip of dry ground carried the coastal trail to a river crossing south of the swamp. The Marine plan was for a frontal attack on the hill, supported by a mechanized blocking force to prevent the escape of defenders driven off the hill.

The blocking force under Captain Joe Buckley of the 7th Marines Special Weapons Company included a platoon of 37mm guns, two SPMs, two light tanks, two rifle platoons, an Army DUKW amphibious truck with a rocket launcher mounted, and a pioneer platoon and bulldozer from 2/17.

By 1030 hours on 13 January Buckley was in position at the eastern base of the hill, tied in by a telephone line through country still roamed by enemy patrols. The primary attack by Item/3/7 was already snarled in a tangle of boulder-filled ravines at the base of the northern slope. An attempt to outflank the Japanese was pinned down, and bypassed machine guns opened fire from the rear, trapping two rifle companies. About 1400 hours the engineers succeeded in getting two light tanks forward to blast out the guns and free the two rifle companies.

Bill Henahan, a crewman in one of the light tanks from 2nd Platoon, C Company:

> There was a valley that ran along one side of it [Hill 660] … They were referring to it as Death Valley. They were getting extremely high casualties when they tried to go through this valley. The Japanese had positions in there. Our light tanks went up on a ridge that ran along the opposite side of the valley from Hill 660. This wasn't a large valley, I'd say maybe 400-500 yards wide ….
>
> Our platoon of light tanks sat up on this ridge for one whole day. We shot nothing but canister ammunition down into that jungle, shredding vegetation. When we got through it looked like they had gone through and trimmed it all down. I remember there was a .50-caliber machine-gun emplacement down there, one of our .50-caliber machine guns that the Japs had set down in there.
>
> The infantry went through there after we shot that place all up with that canister. They went through there with no sweat.

On 14 January, 3/7 worked slowly up the precipitous slopes of Hill 660, but the steep slopes stymied the light tanks. Henahan: "We started up the slope, and the light tanks with this automatic transmission, they just wouldn't cut it. The one that was in the lead started up first, and the others were sitting there, seeing how he was going to progress. He never made it to the top because the transmission just petered out. We never went up there with our tanks."

At nightfall the Marines controlled the crest of the hill. Buckley's mechanized blocking force had to fight off a series of savage attacks in the dense jungle. The enemy could close within a few yards of the vehicles, but were kept at bay by the enormous short-range firepower of the SPMs with their multiple machine guns, and canister from the light tanks and 37mm guns.

The morning of 15 January dawned clear and hot, and the Marines spent the day destroying bypassed pockets of Japanese on the northern slopes of the hill. The enemy organized one last counterthrust, and at 0630 on 16 January two companies charged up the slope and into a hand-to-hand struggle with the 3rd Battalion riflemen. By late morning the *Matsuda Force* was a fleeing remnant, trying only to survive.

While the bulk of Japanese forces were being hammered to death, Major Komori's command at Cape Merkus on the south coast had concentrated on the containment of the American 112th Cavalry. The 112th Cavalry now spent 1–6 January fruitlessly attempting to break out through the strong Japanese lines, and eventually requested armored support.

General William Rupertus would not concede to the Army request for a platoon of tanks, but insisted on sending a company, the smallest self-sufficient Marine armored unit. Eighteen light tanks of B Company, 1st Tank arrived on 12 January. The tanks were to support two companies of a fresh formation, the 2/158th Infantry. The tanks and infantry spent three days working out cooperative tactics.

On 16 January two Army infantry companies, each led by five tanks, moved into the heavy jungle. The tank-infantry teams made good progress, though several tanks tumbled into craters hidden by the dense foliage, one threw a track in the rough terrain, and several tank commanders were wounded when they either dismounted or leaned out of their turret hatches to get instructions from troops on the ground. By 1600 hours the force had driven a gap through the defenses.

Major Komori was a Japanese officer who had no intent of letting his command be sacrificed in vain. He took the opportunity to slide back into the jungle. When the next cautious American attack finally came on 27 February, Komori's command had been gone for three days, taking their wounded with them. His unusual humanitarian streak, however, would not prevent Komori from fighting a series of stubborn and skillful delaying actions against the American advance.

This sideshow to the struggle for Cape Gloucester led to a major innovation for the tankers. B Company tankers solved the tank-infantry communication problem by rigging a pair of field telephones, one attached to the rear plate of the tank, the other inside .[7] The infantry could shelter behind the mass of the tank and communicate target data to the crew inside the closed vehicle.*

---

* Ken Estes has researched the use of field telephones for communication between tanks and infantry. He concluded that the idea was arrived at independently by the Defense Battalion Tank Platoons on New Georgia, the 1st Tank Battalion on New Britain, and the 4th Tank Battalion prior to the Marshalls operation.

General Matsuda started the bulk of his survivors toward the east, leaving Colonel Jiro Sato in charge of his rearguard. The remnants of the north coast forces withdrew along the coastal track, pursued by Marine patrols. On 5 March Major Komori's force linked up with Sato's survivors about 60 miles east of Cape Gloucester, and both headed toward the Willaumez Peninsula, on the north coast about halfway to Rabaul. The Americans used their tenuous control of the air and sea to leap ahead of them.

The Americans assembled an odd force for landings on the Willaumez Peninsula. The Army provided the sea transport, as the Navy was unwilling to risk shipping under the nose of the enemy at Rabaul. This operation required a heroic effort on the part of the Army's 533rd Engineer and Boat Shore Regiment.

"The boat company (sic) sailed up from Townsville, Australia," recalled Bill Henahan. "They sailed from Townsville to New Guinea, across the open sea, in these LCMs, about 600 miles. They sailed around New Guinea over to Oro Bay, and then north to New Britain, another 600 miles. They picked us up at Cape Gloucester. They picked up six light tanks, and they had LCM(s) with a platoon of Sherman tanks."

The 5th Marines were transported aboard a flotilla of LCMs, LCTs, and LCVPs. With no gunfire support ships, the Marines and boat troops chock-blocked four of 1st Platoon, A Company's M4A1 tanks into the Army LCMs to act as improvised gunboats. The tanks could fire only over the sides because of the high bow ramp. Rowland Hall said that "the turret on the M4 would swing out over the side. We were concerned about what would happen if we fired it. The tank was so doggone heavy that really nothing happened as far as moving it, but it was as if you hit the LCM with a sledge hammer. The concussion was absorbed by the short recoil of the 75, and that was transmitted down to the tracks and into the light metal of the LCM. We were going to use that, but there was no opposition."

With no naval aircraft available, and the airfields at Cape Gloucester not yet in operation, air support was limited to a single Piper L-9 observation plane.

Bill Henahan: "We didn't have any air support, except the Piper Cub that came in there … they were throwing hand grenades out as they flew over." The L-9 soon expended its full bomb load of hand grenades, and "that was our pre-invasion support."

At 0835 on 6 March the Marines landed and 2/5 moved up onto the slopes of Little Mount Worri. One Sherman bogged down in the beach sand, and the other three moved up a narrow, mud-slick jungle track along a ridge spine. A Japanese broke through the protective infantry and attacked the lead tank. The blast from his *Hakobakurai* mine killed him and a rifleman who tried to stop him.

Another Japanese apparently fired a rifle-mounted Type Two 40mm Hollow-Charge Rifle Grenade at the tank. Rowland Hall: "… they fired a grenade of some sort that hit the rear of the turret on an M4A1. It penetrated the rear of the turret, but the radios that were in there stopped it."

This unsuccessful attack led to a chain of events that would have satisfied the suicidal attackers beyond their wildest imaginings. The attack jammed the turret of the lead tank. The driver pulled the damaged tank off the trail and allowed the two survivors to pass, but when he pulled back onto the trail the tank hit a mine, breaking the track and damaging the suspension. Unable to construct a bypass on the steep slopes and soft, unstable ground, the medium tanks were trapped on the ridge, and effectively out of the fight.

The Japanese began to evacuate the small harbor at Talasea on the opposite side of the peninsula, but on their second run the boats were all sunk in a running gun battle with American torpedo boats. For several nights American landing craft fought night actions against the enemy landing barges.

To plug this escape route, a small force supported by a section of C Company's light tanks was carried around the peninsula to attack Talasea on 9 March. Rowland Hall related: "We re-embarked them [three light tanks]. As we went around the tip of the peninsula inshore we spotted some Jap landing craft. We opened up on them with the 37 and machine guns. We bagged about three of those and set them on fire. A sort of naval battle using tanks."

A Navy PT boat squadron and tender were also based at Talasea, and they were short of personnel. Bill Henahan: "They wanted anyone who had experience with .50-caliber machine guns to go out on these PT boats. Everybody in our outfit thought that was going to be great, and we were volunteering left and right to get on them. The colonel in charge of this battalion of infantry, who was in overall command, he pooh-poohed it. He said you can't send any specialists, so they only let the infantrymen go out."

The local Japanese commander, Captain Terunuma, fought skillful blocking actions at the base of the peninsula, and for four crucial days held open the door for the escape for Japanese survivors of Cape Gloucester. On 30 March a Marine spotter plane vectored a patrol to a large group of sleeping Japanese, and Colonel Sato died, sword in hand. Among the last to be hunted down was Major Komori, killed in an ambush on 9 April only 20 miles from Rabaul.

As the 1st Division pursued the Japanese on New Britain, other forces were capturing the small islands that would knit Cape Gloucester together with American forces on New Guinea. Bob Botts and other veterans of New Georgia were looking forward to a return to civilization. "We were headed for New Zealand for some much needed R&R. But when we reached ... Guadalcanal, I and two other NCOs were pulled to replace three NCOs that were killed before leaving New Zealand. So no R&R. This was B Company, 3rd Tank Battalion."

Botts's new company, commanded by Phil Morell, was redesignated Tank Company, 4th Marines, and on 20 March supported that regiment's unopposed landings on Emirau. In Morell's words, all the tanks did was "picnic. There were only 52 or 54 Japs there. We had the light tanks then, and we landed with the 4th Marines. We landed and Colonel Shapley sent my tanks to the left from the beach, all the way to the tip [of the island]. We encountered nothing, and found that these Japs had taken off in some native canoes, and a destroyer picked them up. It was a pretty neat deal, because we built an airfield there that saved us making a landing at Kavieng and Rabaul." Fortress Rabaul was now a self-managed prison.

Able Company, 1st Tank Battalion was assigned to the Army's 1st Cavalry Division on New Guinea to augment their light tanks. "We were gonna support them with the medium tanks when they went into the Admiralty Islands," said Eugene Viveiros. "But while we were there, their requested shipment of mediums arrived." The Marines were instead assigned to train the Army crews in the use of the new tanks. "The skipper that we had at the time, John Murphy, he figured that was a useless trip to be made for nothing. Whoever he talked to at the Officer's Club back at New Guinea, next thing I know we got assigned to accompany General Eichelberger's outfit. He had about three Army divisions."

On 22 April 1944, A Company landed to support Operation Reckless, 24th Infantry Division landings on the north coast of New Guinea. Both the United States and Australian Armies had successfully used light tanks to good effect in northern New Guinea,[8] but the

Allied reconnaissance failed to indicate the nature of the terrain behind the narrow beaches of Tanamerah Bay. The tanks found themselves trapped between the sea and a deep belt of swamps, and played no substantive part in the operation.

"Following that," said Rowland Hall, "we turned all that army-supplied equipment back to them."

Thanks to the superhuman efforts of the pioneers, engineers, and Seabees the tanks had been able to bring their firepower to bear some of the most terrible terrain United States forces ever faced. The greater firepower of the Sherman tank's 75mm cannon, and its near impregnability to many of the Japanese antitank weapons, justified the prodigious effort required to get it ashore and in a position to fight. Tank-infantry coordination had been far better than in previous struggles. The official assessment was that "perhaps the most significant tactical development to emerge was the adaptation of tanks, both light and medium, to jungle warfare."[9]

The light tank assembly area on Tarawa, located in an abandoned aircraft revetment, was subjected to intermittent mortar fire. Careful examination of unit markings indicates the presence of at least three different platoons of C Company, 2nd Tank Battalion. (*National Archives*)

Battered *Colorado* sits in the shallow water of the lagoon. The fates of individual medium tanks of C Company, I Marine Amphibious Corps Tank Battalion, on Tarawa were extensively documented. (*National Archives*)

An unusual photo of *China Gal* taken during a lull in the fighting. The unit marking, a white elephant with one foot upraised wearing a red blanket with the Marine Corps emblem in white and firing a cannonball out of his trunk, was one of the most distinctive of the war. (*National Archives*)

Burned-out *Charlie* shows evidence of several hits by high-explosive rounds. Note the fuel cans, and the machine-gun mount on the turret roof. Bale's company was one of the few units to actually use the roof-mounted heavy machine gun in combat. (*National Archives*)

Wrecked *Condor* shows no evidence of being hit by a large bomb dropped by a Navy plane, as pointed out by Ed Bale. (*National Archives*)

This unidentified vehicle, probably *Commando*, fell victim to a Japanese antitank gun, as indicated by at least seven and possibly thirteen penetrations of the sponson and turret front. (*National Archives*)

Lou Largey's *Cannonball* tumbled into a Japanese fuel dump and was destroyed in the ensuing fire. (*National Archives*)

A light tank of C Company halted during the initial advance near Cape Gloucester on New Britain. An earlier assault by the medium tanks killed the Japanese lying in the foreground. (*National Archives*)

A wary Marine rifle squad follows behind a medium tank during the advance to the airfield at Cape Gloucester. This was the first campaign in which rifle squads worked directly with specific vehicles. (*National Archives*)

The terrain was a major limiting factor on operations. Here a column of Able Company tanks advances toward the front. Note the crude handpainted company markings, A 3, on the rear engine doors. (*National Archives*)

First Lt. John E. Heath and his crew take a break during the fighting. Heath later became a company commander and was killed on Peleliu. (*National Archives*)

A bulldozer tries to clear a path for retrieval of an M4A1 that has slid off the trail and become mired in deep mud. (*Marine Corps Historical Center*)

An Able Company tank crosses the upper reaches of Suicide Creek on New Britain, 4 January 1944. (*National Archives*)

An M5A1 light tank moves along the beach, 16 January 1944. In the background is a wrecked Japanese landing barge. (*National Archives*)

A medium tank from A Company, 1st Tank Battalion, replenishes ammunition during the fighting on Cape Gloucester. Note the tire chains on the jeep for additional traction in the slick mud, and the pedestal-mounted machine gun. (Associated Press, *Marine Corps Historical Center*)

CHAPTER 7

THE LAST CHARGE: ROI-NAMUR AND THE MARSHALL ISLANDS

THE MARSHALL ISLANDS had to be a primary objective in any naval offensive against the Japanese Empire, as the immense lagoons offered some of the best potential naval bases east of Manila Bay. The problem was that the Japanese were expected to defend them with proportionate tenacity.

The assault plan proposed by Admiral Fletcher's staff involved a prolonged and systematic reduction of enemy defenses on several major atolls. Admiral Chester Nimitz intervened with a bold plan to go straight for the main objective at Kwajalein Atoll, and develop its air bases as quickly as possible. Land-based aircraft from Kwajalein and the Gilberts could neutralize the remaining enemy bases.

Major General Holland Smith and Admirals Spruance and Kelly Turner immediately objected. The danger, in their eyes, was that the rapid subjugation of the surrounding atolls could not be guaranteed, and Spruance's fast carriers were only scheduled to be on the scene for a few days. As a compromise, the operation was delayed until late January 1944. Spruance's continued objections also resulted in the addition of Majuro Atoll in the extreme southeast as a secondary objective, insurance in the event of an unexpectedly prolonged campaign. The almost undefended atoll could be readily occupied and an airfield hastily built to help fend off a Japanese counteroffensive.

Military geography, available resources, and the experience at Tarawa shaped the final plan. The 2nd Battalion of the Army's 106th Infantry would seize Majuro Atoll. The 7th Infantry Division, veterans of fighting in the Aleutians, would capture Kwajalein Island at the southern end of the atoll of the same name. The untested 4th Marine Division would attack the paired islands of Roi and Namur,

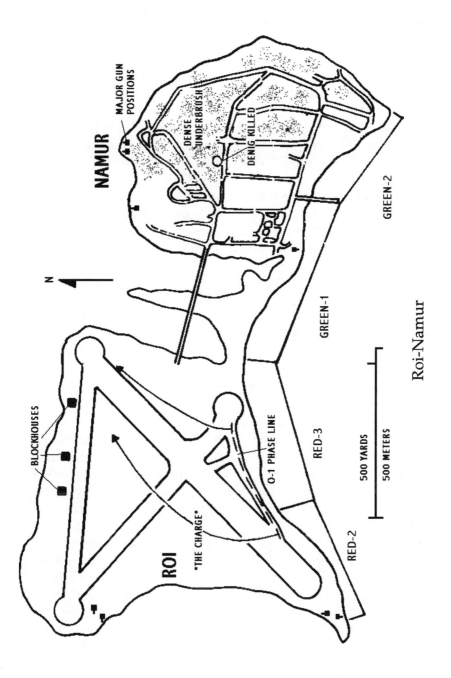

Roi-Namur

site of the biggest air base at the extreme north of Kwajalein Atoll, some 44 miles from Kwajalein itself. The two small islands were connected by a sand spit and a manmade causeway, and together were so small that one held the airfield, the other the support facilities and barracks. Prior to the landings the Marines would seize several nearby islands and emplace howitzers to provide detailed fire support.

The 4th Marine Division was the most intensively trained division yet fielded. The new Jacques Farm facility near San Diego, under the supervision of Major William R. "Rip" Collins, provided the first specially-trained tank crews. In mid-1943 the 1st Tank Battalion on Guadalcanal had received instructions to transfer an experienced captain to the new tank school, and "... being as I didn't have a damned thing to do . . ." Bob Neiman was chosen. He thought he was getting a tank company, but went instead to Jacques Farm, where he was put in charge of field training.

Neiman still wanted a company command: "I made it very clear that I was very disappointed in that ... I was told that I would get command of the first company of tanks for the tank battalion of the 4th Marine Division, but that would be about five months away."

When Ed Hutchinson was transferred stateside after the Cape Gloucester operation, he was also assigned to Jacques Farm as a driving instructor. Trainees advanced through three course segments.[1] "The third section, they could drive all gears, and they just went out in the valley, and you just let them go. You rode in the assistant driver's seat, and just let them do what they wanted to do. We had liberty every night, but there was no place to go." The pragmatic curriculum also included situations that many of the original tankers had faced for the first time under fire. "You would have to stick the tank in a hole, and let the students decide how to get it out. Put a track back on, and so on."

Charles "Chilly" Newman, a student at Jacques Farm: "There were 134 of us, and we got there in six-by-sixes. [Captain Olin L. Beal] said to us 'Which one of you people can type?' and I said 'I can, sir.' He says 'All right boy, you're Company Clerk.' I was Company Clerk when Captain Neiman came in, and I got him first as a captain."

The new 4th Tank Battalion would have only one company of medium tanks, and Neiman was given the command. Pfc. C. B. Ash, another driving instructor at Jacques Farm: "Neiman, and I don't know how in the hell this was worked, hand picked every guy in the company. He really put a lot of thought into this ... He hand-picked the best out of Jacques Farm."

Neiman said: "I made my disappointment known vociferously, and I was given a sort of sweetener. Frankly, I don't know of anybody else in the Marine Corps, or perhaps even the Army or the Navy, who ever had this opportunity. I was given the opportunity to select 100 percent of the personnel for my company-to-be from among the students and the instructors of the tank school." Neiman could hold students by making them instructors, so Newman helped him comb through records to select his crews.[2] "In May of 1943, when my company was finally authorized to be formed, I had been compiling lists for five months or so of the people I wanted in my outfit."

Neiman also campaigned successfully for a commission for Max English.

The massive assault force that would assail the Marshalls was based on the premise that the Japanese, given 20 years to prepare defenses, would have fortified these islands far more heavily than the Gilberts. Max English: "This was right after Tarawa, and we were told that they have strong pillboxes, and we *were* going to get knocked out."

By this time the effects of the Type 99 magnetic mines were well documented, so C Company added a layer of two-by-twelve inch oak planks over the vertical sponson armor. Vertical sections of U-shaped steel channel were welded to the hull sides, planks bolted to the channels. The channel held the planks away from the armor and formed a dead-air space between them. Some tanks also added planks over the slope plate on the front of the tank.

Paradoxically, both the toughness of the defenses, and the overall number and quality of the defending troops, were far below those encountered at Tarawa. The Roi-Namur facility was a communications and administrative center defended by 600 men of the *61st Guard Force*, about 2,000 aviation and support personnel, and 1,000 or so miscellaneous troops. Only ten pillboxes with 7.7mm machine guns, two 13mm machine guns, two 20mm cannon, one 37mm anti-tank gun, and a turret with twin Type 89 127mm naval guns comprised the fixed defenses. The defenses were poorly planned. None of the machine guns were placed on promontories to provide enfilade fire on the beaches. Reinforced concrete bomb shelters and ammunition bunkers would actually prove to be more formidable defenses than the gun positions.

The assault began at 0650 hours on 31 January 1944. The initial stage of the complex operation was the seizure of two small islands that dominated the deep-water channel leading into the lagoon. Despite confusion caused by unexpectedly high wind and surf, uncharted reefs, and poor coordination with the naval force, by 1915 hours control of the channel was secured, and four small islands had been captured to serve as artillery bases.

The landings on the main objectives were scheduled for the morning of 1 February, but were delayed because of a shortage of LVTs. On D-day evening many LSTs (Landing Ship, Tank) did not display the color-coded signal lights that would allow their own LVTs to locate them in the darkness, then refused to take aboard lost LVTs. They also refused to refuel the orphaned LVTs, and precious tractors sank when their fuel was exhausted and their bilge pumps failed. Then on D+1 the inexperienced LST captains launched the surviving tractors from a position five miles too far north.

At 0630 the 10th Amphibian Tractor Battalion was still 48 tractors short of the number needed to transport the assault waves of the 23rd and 24th Marines. As the coordinators scrambled to find extra LCVPs, the landings were delayed until 1130 hours. While the battalion commanders were still trying to sort out this mess the control ship unexpectedly signaled to land the assault force at 1112 hours.

On Red-2 the western attack group of LVT(A)-1 armored amphibians supporting 1/23 did not stop and form an offshore gun line as expected, but surged on ahead to land at 1130, ahead of the rifle companies. The LVT(A)-1s veered left and clattered off unsupported to attack Wendy Point, the southwest tip of Roi. The LVT(A)-1s easily outdistanced the riflemen, a recipe for potential disaster, and only the disorganization of the Japanese defenders saved the amphibians.

On Red-3 the LVT-2s of the assault wave landed 20 minutes after those on adjacent Red-2. Despite a desperate counterattack the riflemen of E and F Companies were well inshore and crossing the south runway at 1205, 15 minutes after the first LVTs grounded on the beach.

Bob Neiman's C Company tanks landed at 1145 on Red-2, and at 1200 on Red-3 and overtook the rifle companies on the south runway. Despite more intensive training than any other division had ever received, communications with the infantry were poor, and coordination depended upon reaching Phase Lines, indicated on maps, at specified times.

C. B. Ash was assigned to Max English's 3rd Platoon as bow gunner in *Kickapoo*. Preparation had been simple. "Each crewman had to memorize the beach area, and at the last briefing they gave you a test. If you flunked, you had to walk ashore with the infantry. The Navy delivery was very good. We didn't even get the tracks wet. The entire island was a huge bomber strip, and the infantry was along the edge of the runway. The Jap infantry were hiding in the storm drains, using them for foxholes. At this point in time, in this outfit, tank-infantry tactics were non-existent."

One of the hard-learned lessons of fighting against the Japanese was the necessity for a systematic, if slow, reduction of their defenses. Bypassed Japanese troops would fall upon support units, and with friendly and enemy units intermixed the rifle companies could not call down artillery or naval gunfire. The green troops of the 4th Division had no experience against the Japanese, but now their blood was up.

The riflemen of the 23rd Marines tore into the scattered opposition, surging ahead in an irregular line that did not guarantee a coherent front against enemy counterattacks. Worst of all were the tanks and the LVT(A)-1s.

"The company moved through the infantry," said Ash, "passing between the aircraft revetments, which were designed to shield parked aircraft from nearby bomb bursts. We didn't pick up any infantry, just formed up into assault formation and moved out."

Bob Neiman at first held his vehicles at the O-1 Phase Line, exposed on the south runway. He called for permission to advance past the Phase Line, but received no instructions through the confused jumble of speech on the tank-infantry radio net.

Rationalizing that it was more dangerous to remain stationary, Neiman ordered his tanks forward[3]:

> One of the basic principles of tank tactics is you don't stop tanks out in the open. They become sitting ducks. You have to keep moving toward the enemy, or get under some kind of cover. Roi was absolutely barren of any vegetation. It was one huge airfield, the largest Japanese field in the Marshall Islands.
>
> The advance was to stop when it reached the O-1, which was more or less the center of the airfield. We got there real quickly. There was an infantry battalion right with us. The battalion commander had his orders to stop there. We could see huge blockhouses, perhaps seven or

800 yards, maybe a thousand yards from the center of the airfield. They were on the opposite end, facing the ocean. But I didn't know what was in them. They could have had all kinds of antitank weapons, and I wasn't about to stop eighteen tanks out there in the open, with those big blockhouses facing me.

I told the battalion commander of the infantry battalion ... that I didn't think we should stop, we should just keep going. There was no reason to stop. The Japanese weren't holding us up, let's go get 'em.

Ash: "The company set up between two map points in a bent line at the edge of runway Charlie overlooking Jap gun emplacements, trenches, et cetera. Our platoon sergeant, Joe Bruno, blew up a Jap fighter plane ... and got chewed up for blowing up a usable Zero that the brass desperately wanted to inspect. He always figured that if he got five, that would make him an ace. Japs were running all over the place, and we fired at anything that moved. In *Kickapoo* [the] crew, Joe Ramos, TC; McCue, gunner; Krauland, loader; Pete, driver; and myself, Ash, BOG were on the far left of the company line . . ."[4]

Unknown to Neiman the rifle regiment commander, Lieutenant Colonel Louis R. Jones, was asking for permission to press the attack, signaling to the division commander, "This is a pip X No opposition ..."[5]

Neiman: "He (Jones) wouldn't do it. He had his orders to stay there, and he wanted me to stay. He was a lieutenant colonel and I was a captain at the time, but he wasn't my commanding officer. I didn't obey him. I took my tanks and went to the end of the island."

"There wasn't anything out there," agreed C. B. Ash. "The infantry didn't follow us."

Unseen by Ash and others, many of the infantry actually did follow. Able Company of 1/23 reported that the tanks just "barged through," and the infantry, faithful to their instructions to support the tanks, followed along.

The tanks shrugged off rifle and light machine-gun fire that rattled against their sides. The errant platoon of LVT(A)-1s from Wendy Point joined in this impromptu raid, ranging up the west coast in tandem with the tanks. Ash wrote that "Burt Nave, in tank 3-2 *Knave*, hit a mine and blew a track. T. J. Taylor, driver in the command tank, ran the CO's tank into a huge shell hole, and Sergeant Owens in *Kapu* had to pull them out. Then we got into a half-assed line, and started a charge for the north end of the island. Along the way we machine-gunned the Japs in the storm drains, which they were using for communications trenches."[6]

The Japanese had razed the island's vegetation, and on the open terrain the tanks could roam like predatory dinosaurs. Neiman repeatedly tried to raise Colonel Jones through the confusion on the radio net—but kept moving forward.[7] In turn, Jones had been repeatedly instructed to halt and reorganize his regiment.

Bob Neiman: "We fired at them [the blockhouses] and our 75 shells just bounced off of them. Apparently there was no one in those blockhouses, but there was an antitank trench completely around the northern end of the island, and in it were all the remaining Japanese troops. Several hundred, I would estimate ... If we had flamethrower tanks in those days, we could easily have cooked them all. But we didn't, and we couldn't depress our guns sufficiently to do anything but force them to keep their heads down. The only man I had killed on that operation was a tank commander looking out of the turret, and a Japanese rifleman in the trench shot him right between the eyes."

Max English had repeatedly emphasized the dangers of open hatches to the tank commanders in his platoon: "I lost a tank commander, name was Ramos. Nice fella. He had his turret open and his head out, looking. We would always emphasize in training that the turret hatch was to be kept closed. You had a periscope to look out. Ramos didn't do it, and we lost Ramos." Ash recounted Ramos's death:

> I thought I heard water running. I looked at the water cans strapped down on the right sponson and neither was leaking, nor had I pissed myself. Looking over at the driver, I saw a sheet of blood running down the turret from the TC hatch between us!
>
> The turret was turned 90 degrees to the right (sic) and the blood was pouring from Ramos's head. "Head for the beach," I yelled at Pete, and he asked "Where is it?"
>
> "You're the driver, you're supposed to keep up with shit," I yelled back. I finally got him moving in the right direction, and moments later, we homed in on the tank retriever and the aid station.
>
> McCue and I pulled Joe out of the turret, and everybody was yelling "Easy, take it easy." With half a bullet sticking out of his head, you could tell he wasn't feeling anything. We laid him next to a growing line of dead Marines and said our goodbyes. Nobody had seen us leave the company line, and we needed to get back. After a bit of back and

forth, I elected myself TC, grabbed a somewhat reluctant live body off the retriever, and we took of into the wild blue.[8]

Ash's combat career was half an hour old.

The tanks eventually fetched up against an obstacle that not even they could overrun when they reached the ocean shore on the northeast corner of the island, nearly a thousand yards to the northeast of the start line.

Major General Harry Schmidt was monitoring this situation through airborne observers, and sent a pointed message to Colonel Jones. "Can you control tanks and bring them back to O-1 Line for coordinated attack?"[9]

Neiman radioed back to the infantry battalion: "… saying 'We've got all the Japanese on the island cornered right here in this antitank ditch. Bring your troops up and you can kill them all.' I was told to pull back, and I said, 'If I pull back, they're all gonna swim over to Namur and shoot at the Marines that are fighting there,' and that's a terrible thing to do." The Japanese were indeed filtering across to more defensible Namur.

It was made clear to Neiman that he was under the command of the rifle regiment.[10] "I was finally told I was being court-martialed, and had to pull back, and I did."

The tanks and infantry filtered back to the O-1 Line about an hour after leaving. The brief rampage was as close as Marine tankers would ever get to the fast-charging armor attacks that were the popular misconception of tank combat in World War II.

C. B. Ash: "The infantry wanted him [Neiman] out of there, because the Navy wanted to shoot in that area. Hell, we'd cleared everything out going there. We had to come back to the beach after doin' a little shootin' there."

Once the tanks were back in the fold, Colonel Jones could start his set-piece attack, which began with a heavy naval bombardment of the area around the aircraft turning circle on the northeast corner of the island—the area just vacated by the tanks. At 1530 the attack stepped off, with 2/23 and tanks sweeping quickly north toward the turning circle. Ash: "The second time 1st Platoon took the right side of the island, and 2nd Platoon in the center, and the 3rd Platoon, English, was over on the left side. Somewhere along the line, and I don't know where in the hell it came from, and I don't even know what company it was, but we did have an M5A1 with a flamethrower in it with us. I haven't the foggiest idea whether it was A Company or B Company.* It fired its little fire machine off. Whether he did any good or not, I doubt it."

On the left 1/23 supported this advance by fire, then moved off in its own attack. The Japanese defense was uncoordinated, and by 1600 the attackers had reached the northeast corner of the island for the second time.

The medium tanks were withdrawn and dispatched south and across the sandspit to Namur. "We got all the way across the island, came back to the beach and drank some sake, and headed for Namur," recalled Ash. "We were told they were having problems over there." Only a thousand yards away things were not going nearly so well.

The two assault battalions of the 24th Marines—3/24 landed on Green-1, on the west, and 2/24 on Green-2—were critically short of troop-carrying LVT-2s. The LVT(A)-1s were to move onto the beach ahead of the troop carriers and support their attack until the lodgement was 100 yards deep, but chance was on the side of the Japanese on Namur. They had, at the last moment, begun belated efforts to fortify the lagoon side of the island, and the LVT(A)-1s were blocked by a new antitank ditch and debris.

The Japanese had not cleared away the underbrush on Namur, so the riflemen were slowed more by natural caution than by enemy action. As they drove inland they began to encounter increasingly stiff resistance.

At 1300 hours three light tanks from B Company landed on Green-1. Two immediately bogged in the soft sand. The third raced inland through the drifting smoke, crashed into a shell crater, and threw a track. At 1400 hours one additional light tank came ashore and used tow cables to extricate its bogged brethren after the infantry drove off two enemy attacks on the stalled tanks. Shortly after 1500 hours the light tanks were ready for action.

In the eastern zone 2/24 fought its way inland, and at 1305 assault engineers blew mouseholes through the south side of an immense concrete blockhouse. Rushing forward, the assault team hurled charges into the interior. Seconds later the building disintegrated in a titanic explosion. Troops all over the nearby islands looked on as a huge mushroom cloud rose into the sky, then scrambled for cover

---

* It was an M3A1 flame tank from A Company.

from a rain of concrete chunks, trees, unexploded torpedo warheads, and other debris. Two monstrous secondary explosions followed.[11] No one knew whether the satchel charges set off the contents of the torpedo magazine, or the enemy had rigged the magazine to explode.

On the left 3/24 pushed slowly ahead until light tanks and SPMs could be brought forward. At 1630 hours 3/24 was still struggling through the dense thickets near the center of the island.

At 1730 hours 2/24 was sufficiently recovered to continue the attack, reinforced by the light tanks of the Headquarters Section and the 1st Platoon of B Company. In the afternoon the light tanks were the heavy punch of attacks by both 2/24 and 3/24, as the rifle squads found it too costly in blood to push blindly into the dense foliage.

The tanks could crash through, and were impervious to the small arms fire, but the infantry sometimes lost sight of the tanks in the thick cover, leaving them vulnerable to assault. The intense heat and fumes inside the tanks forced the crews to open hatches to avoid asphyxiation,[12] and vehicle commanders had to stick their heads out the open hatches to maneuver in the close quarters, further increasing their vulnerability.

Captain James L. Denig, the commander of B Company, led his unit into the attack. His M5A1, although equipped with radios, retained the turret flag port, a small round hatch that was a vestigial feature of the days when tanks communicated with flags.

C. B. Ash speculated that "He [Denig] says, 'It's getting hot in here, I'm gonna open the flag port.' On the M5 there's a little hole up on top [of the turret] just about the size of a hand grenade, with maybe a quarter inch or less to spare." His command tank, *Hunter*, pulled out of a thicket onto a gravel road, and six Japanese swarmed up the sides of the vehicle.

Corporal Howard E. Smith, a member of the squad covering the tank, emptied two magazines from his BAR at the enemy, killing four, and a rifleman got the fifth. One, however, shoved a grenade through the open flag port and into Denig's lap.[13*] The explosion set the tank afire, and the stored ammunition began to cook off in the intense heat. Smith ran forward through enemy fire and leapt onto the burning tank, dragged Captain Denig out the turret and into the concealment

---

* This is the official version, but the tank may have been hit by an antitank gun. Seldom-seen photographs of the left side of the vehicle show evidence of penetration of the sponson by some sort of projectile.

of the underbrush. Running around to the more exposed front he pulled out the assistant driver, Corporal William Taylor, and dragged him to safety. Then Smith climbed back onto the burning tank, still under enemy fire, and dragged the gunner, Corporal Ben Smith, out of the turret.[14]

The driver was trapped, and could not get his hatch open. Ash noted that from photographs "... you'll see the turret is turned where it's right over the driver's hatch. When I went up there to get Denig's ring and wallet, the driver was still in there. He was pretty well cooked." Captain Denig, who had taken most of the blast from the grenade, also died.

The tanks fired canister rounds from their 37mm cannon into the underbrush, shredding the foliage and killing any concealed enemy. The tanks advanced in two waves. Enemy troops would burst out of the underbrush and clamber onto the lead tanks, only to be swept off by shotgun-pellet blasts of canister.

At 1700 the medium tanks of C Company and elements of 3/23 came over from Roi and joined the attack up the western side of the island. The tanks were now under the clear control of the infantry, and elements of 2/24 drove to within yards of the north coast before being forced to pull back. At 1930 all units dug in along a line across the island from northwest to southeast.

All night the infantry suffered minor harassment, but the medium tanks were in logistical trouble. At this stage of the war all supplies were carried ashore in LVTs or LCVPs, and unloaded by work parties on the beach, establishing supply and ammunition dumps. The dump for the medium tanks was back on Red-3. To keep some tanks in action Neiman's company collected the remaining ammunition and redistributed it among the four vehicles with the most fuel remaining in their tanks.

The race to prepare the tanks for the next day's action was completed just in time. A strong enemy counterattack struck the boundary between Item and L Companies of 3/24, and lasted several hours under the washed-out light of naval star shells. The two companies were driven back, but at dawn the medium tanks *Jezebel*, *Jenny Lee*, *Joker*, and *Juarez* were called up, and helped restore the dent made in the line.[15]

By 0900 the situation was stable and the tanks supported 3/24's final attack. The medium tanks fired armor-piercing rounds to punch holes in the concrete structures, then followed up with several high-explosive rounds. Communication problems continued to plague Neiman as the air support coordinator's powerful radio overrode the signal for the tank company radio net.

The powerful medium tanks could easily bull through the dense vegetation, but were at risk when the Japanese tried to rush them. One of Bob Neiman's tank commanders was Corporal Mike Giba in *Jenny Lee*. Neiman: "He was very good ... but he was very excitable. The Japanese were swarming all over his tank. The infantry was supposed to protect the tank from that type of thing, but the vegetation being as heavy as it was, the infantry was not right there.

"The tanks' machine guns would protect each other. In fact it was great to have the Japanese swarm all over a tank, and the other tanks could just shoot them off with their machine guns. I remember hearing Giba yelling through his radio to his platoon leader, Henry Bellmon ... He [Bellmon] was very calm and cool, and he said to Mike, 'Mike, don't be excited. We're killing 'em as fast as they show up.'"

Giba's agitation was excusable. His tank unexpectedly encountered a crater, and lurched to a stop to avoid tumbling in. Enemy soldiers rushed out of the hole and swarmed over the tank, seeking a weak spot. Giba described the scene: "I looked out the periscope. A Jap lay down on the turret and looked me right in the eye. He seemed kind of puzzled about just what to do. Then he rose to a squatting position, removed a grenade from his pocket, held it against the periscope, pulled the pin, and lay down on top of it. The periscope was broken but none of us was hurt. The Jap was killed. Then another tank opened up with its machine gun and cleared the turret of the remaining Japs."[16]

The final enemy stronghold was in an antitank ditch near Natalie Point, the northernmost cape on the island. Two light tanks flanked the ditch and raked the length of it with machine-gun fire and canister. None of the defenders chose to surrender. The gruesome affair spelled the end of organized resistance, and the island was declared secure at 1215.

The disciplinary consequences promised to Neiman did not come to pass. "My battalion commander's father was the division commander, General Schmidt; Dick Schmidt, his son, was the 4th Tank Battalion commander. He was very pleased that I had gone up there. Louis Jones, who later became a close friend of mine but who was really pissed off at me at that point, was the regimental commander.

Louis Jones wanted me court-martialled, and I think that Dick Schmidt wanted me to get a medal. He got his father to intervene, and it all got ironed out."

Charles Newman said that the worst part of Roi-Namur came after the battle, when the Marines buried 3,472 enemy bodies on the tiny island: "We buried their dead. We would take a Cat and dig big ditches, and we'd just throw them in there and cover them up. I've never forgotten that. We had little bottles of brandy, to help us erase the memory, I guess. Of course there's nothing else you could do."

OPERATION CATCHPOLE:
REDUCTION OF THE LESSER MARSHALLS

Taking advantage of maps and documents captured on Kwajalein Island, the American forces elected to seize Eniwetok Atoll and bypass the remainder of the Marshalls. The forces employed were a scratch group of reserve units that had not been previously committed. They had never worked together, and all were relatively inexperienced.

Tactical Group 1 included the 22nd Marines, 2nd Separate Pack Howitzer Battalion, V Amphibious Corps Reconnaissance Company, Company D (Scouts)/4th Marine Tank Battalion, 2nd Separate Tank Company (now equipped with M4A2s), 106th Infantry (less the 2nd Battalion), 104th Field Artillery Battalion, and 708th Provisional Amphibious Tractor Battalion. Training for these units, in particular the 106th, had been slighted, and landing rehearsals had been totally inadequate. The worst problems were an overly optimistic schedule and an ill-defined command structure.

Three major objectives—Engebi, Eniwetok, and the Parry Islands— were to be reduced in succession, with only two days allotted to secure each one. Units used in one assault would form the reserve for the next operation, and units would shuttle from one objective to another on a tight schedule. Operations would utilize a mix of Army and Marine rifle battalions with different training and doctrine.

Engebi was home to about 700 combat troops, 540 support troops, *Ha-Go* light tanks, and mortars. Battleships began pounding the objective islands in the predawn darkness of 17 February.

At 0845 on 18 February the 1st and 2nd Battalions, 22nd Marines went ashore, supported by Army LVT(A)-1s, medium tanks of the 2nd Separate Tank Company, and two M7B1 self-propelled 105mm howitzers detached from the Cannon Company of the 106th Infantry.

Things soon began to go amiss. One LCM inadvertently dropped its ramp and flooded while still 500 yards offshore. It capsized, and four of the tank crewmen drowned, trapped in their vehicle.[17] Fallen trees and debris broke tracks and stalled the LVT(A)-1s that were supposed to go ashore with the troops, and only the presence of the more rugged M4A2s of the 2nd Separate Tank Company saved the day.

The riflemen were soon pinned by withering fire from Japanese tanks dug in as pillboxes until the Marine tanks blasted apart the exposed turrets. The strongest positions were on Skunk Point, where two large concrete pillboxes defied all attacks by the relatively inexperienced troops of C/1/22. Finally two of the loaned M7B1 self-propelled guns on their sturdy Sherman chassis were brought up and blasted apart the pillboxes with indirect fire. The island was declared secure at 1450, but the vehicles of the 2nd Separate Tank Company had already begun to load onto 12 LCMs for the trip to the next objective, Eniwetok Island, 25 miles away across the lagoon.

The 106th Infantry fell upon the 800 defenders of this small island on 19 February. The landings were delayed until 0900 because the LCMs carrying the supporting tanks of the 2nd Separate Tank Company and their weary crews across the lagoon were late arriving. The LVT(A)-1s that were to accompany the assault battalions were stopped by an undiscovered beach terrace with steep banks up to nine feet high. The lack of training and experience began to tell as the inexperienced infantrymen were tangled and pinned in the maze of spiderholes* and only 3/106 managed to struggle ahead.

The delay allowed a respite for the Japanese, and by noon the island commander had organized a powerful counterattack. About half the garrison hit 1/106 in a swirling *banzai* charge, and inflicted heavy casualties on the Army infantry. By 1245 hours the battalion was clearly in trouble.

At the height of the *banzai* the decision was made to commit the operational reserve, 3/22. At 1515 the Marines attacked west toward the last centers of resistance, and although slowed by a series of bunkers, pulled steadily ahead of 1/106, opening a gap on the flank of the Marine line. This galled the 106th's commander, Colonel Russell G. Ayers, and set the stage for another of the tragic episodes that were to poison Army-Marine relations.

---

* Spiderhole complexes were numerous one-man fighting holes connected by tunnels. One or more snipers could move from place to place below ground.

Rather than advance blindly into the thick underbrush Major Shisler, the commander of 3/22, ordered his men to dig in for the night, standard doctrine for experienced Army and Marine units. The tanks, extremely vulnerable in the darkness and thick underbrush, withdrew.

Colonel Ayers, frustrated at the slow advance of his soldiers, was determined to keep up the pressure on what he felt must be a spent foe, and ordered the two battalions of the 106th to continue the advance in the darkness. They passed the unseen flank of the entrenched Marines at about 1945 hours. This passing movement opened up a 100-yard-wide gap between the two battalions.

The Japanese quickly seized upon this opportunity. A sizable force infiltrated the undefended gap, hooked around and into the rear of the Marine battalion, and attacked the battalion CP. Clerks, communicators, and support troops fought off the Japanese attack, narrowly averting what might have been the worst setback of the campaign.

Hashida had expended the last of his reserves in the attack and following a brief pause to reorganize, the soldiers and Marines pressed forward. At 1445 hours the west end of the island was secured.

The most heavily defended objective was held for last. Parry Island was scheduled for attack on 21 February to allow the two assault battalions—1/22 and 2/22—two days rest after the attack on Engebi. This schedule also allowed the heaviest possible bombardment.

The 2nd Separate Tank Company, V Amphibious Corps Recon Company, the 4th Division Scout Company, and a light tank company attached to the 106th Infantry were alerted to act as an additional operational reserve. The delay at Eniwetok Island forced a delay until 22 February, as 3/22 was to form the main reserve for the operation. This delay, and the extra day of shelling, exacerbated a shortage of artillery ammunition.

The final shelling began at 0600 on 22 February. The smoke and dust obscured the navigation landmarks, and the landing was very confused, but at 0900 boats carrying the two assault battalions grounded on the island. By 1400 hours 2/22 had secured the eastern end of the island.

The smoke caused the landing control parties to put 1/22 ashore near the Valentine Pier, not a smaller pier that marked the actual landing beach. A complex of tall dunes towered over the narrow beach, and the enemy counterattacked at the water's edge. For a short while there was hand-to-hand fighting in the dunes, but by 1000 hours a firm beachhead was established and the 2nd Separate Tank Company came ashore to deal with Japanese tanks revealed by air reconnaissance.

Three light tanks emerged to attack the advancing American tanks and infantry. Lt. Colonel Wilfried H. Fromhold, the CO of 1/22, called for naval gunfire and artillery, and the consequences of the mislocated landing began to play out. Marine aerial artillery observers overhead could see the true location of the troops below, and quickly called a check fire to the Army and Marine artillerymen. A naval shore fire control party on another radio net called down five-inch gunfire, which fell on both Japanese and Americans.

The Marine tanks took the brunt of the beating, and several were destroyed or crippled. Total American casualties were one killed and three wounded among the tank crews, and ten riflemen wounded. The Marines recovered more quickly and the surviving Shermans quickly dispatched their opponents. By noon the tanks and 1/22 had pushed across the island, penning the surviving enemy on the western end.

At 1330 hours the worn-out 1st and 3rd Battalions attacked abreast, supported by the 2nd Separate Tank Company. Enemy resistance was particularly tenacious, so that by midafternoon the attack had to be temporarily halted because the tanks had expended their entire load of cannon ammunition. Army DUKWs quickly brought more ashore.

At 1930 the attack was halted 450 yards short of the south cape, and the island declared secure. By 0900 on 23 February all organized resistance was ended, the Marines began to load out, and 3/106 came ashore to search out the scattered enemy survivors.

Captain Henry Calcutt's 2nd Separate Tank Company had set a record for combat mobility that was not likely to be soon equaled. In five days of continuous combat they participated in three beach assaults and covered 28 miles between objectives, fighting by day and traveling and repairing their tanks at night aboard boats. One evaluation stated that "no other unit ... performed as efficiently for as long a period as did this tank company."[18]

Against all expectation, the Marshalls had proven to be the cheapest victories of the Pacific War. The low cost had to be credited more to the poorly organized Japanese defense than to any particular merit of the attackers. The confusion exhibited by the inexperienced units involved, both Army and Marine Corps, demonstrated a clear need for more realistic training, and particularly more intensive rehearsals of tank-infantry tactics.

CHAPTER 8

THE BLOODIEST BATTLE YOU NEVER HEARD OF: SAIPAN

THE BATTLES for control of the Mariana Islands remain some of the lesser-known triumphs of American arms. Less well-known than either the preceding battles for the Solomons and Gilberts, or the subsequent bloodbaths at Iwo Jima and Okinawa, the capture of these large islands was far more strategically significant. American bases in the Marianas would bring Japanese maritime communications under direct attack, and bring metropolitan Japan within range of strategic bombers. The southernmost Marianas also sat squarely across the communications lines between the Japanese homeland and the enormous bastion at Truk, in the Caroline Islands.

Operation Forager would be executed in three stages. The capture of Saipan would eliminate the main Japanese stronghold, and provide interim bases for stage two, the capture of nearby Tinian. The third and final phase would be the capture of Guam. Rota, between Tinian and Guam, would be isolated.

The Japanese never attempted to fortify the islands until it was too late, relying instead upon their fleet. The defenders of Saipan included two infantry regiments and a mixed brigade, four companies of the *9th Tank Regiment*, *5th Special Base Force*, *55th Guard Force*, and the *1st Yokosuka Special Naval Landing Force*. The tank regiment was equipped with Type 95 *Ha-Go* light tanks and Type 97-*kai Shinhoto Chi-Ha* medium tanks. According to Japanese records, the *1st SNLF* had nine *Ha-Go* and five *Ka-Mi* amphibious light tanks.[1]

Beach defenses would fix the Americans and buy time for a massive counterattack led by the *9th Tank Regiment*. At the same time a force built around the super battleships *Yamato* and *Musashi*, as well as the remaining fleet air power, would sortie for a *yogaki*.

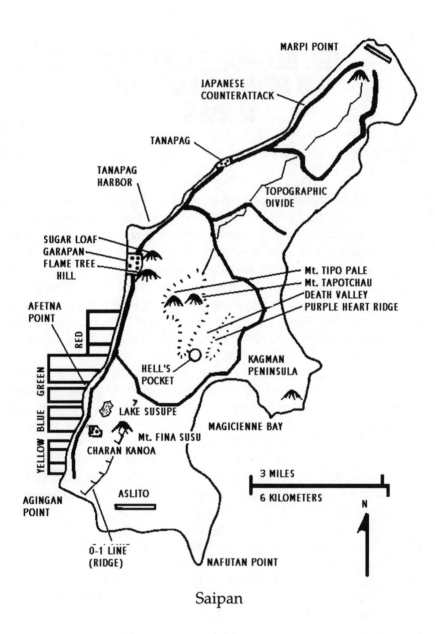

Saipan

The Northern Troops and Landing Forces under Holland Smith consisted of the 2nd and 4th Marine Divisions and the Army's 27th Infantry Division. Two 155 gun battalions and two 155mm howitzer battalions of the Army's XXIV Corps artillery and two howitzer battalions from V Amphibious Corps gave Holland Smith the equivalent of an Army corps.

The Navy could not yet provide the bottoms necessary to carry increasingly larger invasion forces, and the Normandy landings had further depleted resources. The shortfall in shipping would be felt in the Marine divisions as a shortage of motor transport.[2] Each tank company was allowed a single radio jeep, and would for a time have to rely upon division motor transport.

Each of the Marine divisions was significantly more powerful than before. The tank battalions each had 46 new medium tanks. When the IMAC Tank Battalion was disbanded Ed Bale became CO of A Company, 2nd Tank Battalion. "I thought at the time, and nothing has ever changed my mind, that the best-trained Marine division I have ever seen was the 2nd Division when it left to go to Saipan. That was a crack outfit."

Bale attributes this to "... the training the division went through, the fact that it was up on that Parker Ranch [Hawaii], and that it had such a hard time at Tarawa. All the leaders were very conscious of the difference between Guadalcanal and Tarawa. They were really interested in training and preparing. It was a hell of a lot better than anything else I've ever seen. I think that there was a sense [of urgency] throughout the division." Training was heavy, six days a week, with about five days in the field each week[3]:

> There was a great effort to take tanks over to the infantry battalions and educate the infantrymen, to train them how to spot and call for fire, and how to protect the tanks from Japanese trying to swarm them and place mines on them. It was a mutual support proposition. We had good training areas, and good live-firing areas.
>
> The 2nd Division had a rehearsal up on Parker Ranch ... They laid out the landing beaches, and marked off that airstrip the Japanese were building just inland from the beaches. The assault troops walked through the thing, and the tanks came along behind them. We went through the whole landing plan that way. Almost all the small unit commanders had experienced Tarawa, and everybody was damn conscious what could happen to you.

Melvin Swango was back in a tank crew in *Amapola*: "After Tarawa they discontinued our reconnaissance group. I don't think anyone would have volunteered for it anyhow."

The tank crews of C Company, 4th Tank added even more supplementary armor to their tanks before the campaign. Bob Neiman: "We got a number of antitank projectiles that came right through the lumber and the tank in our first campaign. Before we went to Saipan we did the same thing, except in addition we studded the side of the tank with little short pieces of reinforcing steel bar. Then we bolted the two-by-twelves to the sides and put a one-by-three and nailed it to the bottom. We had a perfect concrete form, and we poured concrete in. Now we had two inches of lumber, [and] two inches of reinforced concrete that a projectile would have to hit and go through before it even reached the armor plate. We were the only ones who did it, but we did it to all of our tanks. We figured the little added weight was going to bother us as much as that extra protection was gonna help us."

Even with all this protection, antitank rounds would occasionally penetrate the sponson armor of the Sherman. Neiman: "With the wood and concrete that we put on our tanks we had many of them that went through the side and got stuck. The nose would be inside the tank, but nothing else. The Seabees helped us do a lot of things. They had the equipment—more equipment than we did—and they also had the material. We didn't have all that lumber, but they provided it. They helped us do a number of things. We modified the interior of the tanks to carry a great deal more ammunition than they originally came with, particularly the 75mm ammunition." This additional stowage consisted of racks welded around the inside of the rotating turret cage to hold the extra ammunition.

The tank battalions were also equipped with flame tanks, surplus M3A1s mounting the Canadian Ronson flame gun, with a range of 60 to 80 yards. The crew was reduced to the minimum of two men, a driver and commander/gunner. The projection unit was mounted in place of the main gun, with a stubby section of steel pipe added to act as armor. The pipe couplings that connected the flame gun to the hull-mounted fuel tanks limited turret traverse to 170 degrees.

The coaxial machine gun in the turret was retained for defense, but the restricted turret traverse limited the single machine gun's potential for close defense. The usual practice was for a flame tank to operate with an M5A1 gun tank to protect it from infantry attack. The flame tanks, called Satans by the Marines, were organized as D Company in the 2nd and 4th Tank Battalions.[4]

Invasion day, 15 June, commenced with a noisy feint off Tanapag, on the northwest coast. LSTs moved in to drop over 700 Army- and Marine-crewed LVTs into calm seas off the real invasion beaches about 5,500 yards south of Garapan. The size of the landing force reflected growing American supremacy in the Pacific. The first wave at Saipan was larger than the entire attack force, including the operational reserve, at Tarawa.

Shells from Japanese artillery started to fall on the LVTs at the edge of the reef. High-angle howitzer and mortar fire punished the amtracs. Direct hits flipped tractors end over end, or slaughtered the crew and passengers. Others were holed by shrapnel, and sank in the tidal pools behind the reef edge, leaving the wounded survivors to swim for safety. At 0843 the first LVTs hit the beach under intense mortar and artillery fire.

On Yellow Beach the 25th Marines were particularly hard-hit. On Yellow-2, 1/25 was raked by a deadly crossfire from Agingan Point on the right and artillery to its front. The beach was soon dotted with burning tractors. Some pulled off the beach before unloading vital communications gear, heavy machine guns, or mortars.

On Blue-1 eight LVTs and three armored amphibians pushed inland toward Mount Fina Susu, and on Blue-2 another three troop carriers with five supporting LVT(A)-1s made it well inland. Neither group could be supported by follow-on units, and both had to be called back.

Back of the Blue beaches a pair of LVT(A)-4s penetrated far inland, and into the first tank battle ever fought by the amphibians. Three enemy tanks confronted the amphibians, and were pummeled to destruction by their 75mm howitzers.[5] On the whole though, efforts to utilize the amphibians as tanks failed.

On the northern flank tractors carrying the 6th and 8th Marines were driven north by a strong current and punishing fire from Afetna Point and onto beaches backed by high ground. On the Red beaches tractors were forced to halt less than a hundred yards inland. Confusion was worst on the Green beaches, where 2/8 and 3/8 landed on the same beach. The troops were hopelessly intermingled, a problem compounded when both battalion commanders were wounded. The training and initiative of the NCOs and junior officers came to the fore as the two battalions reorganized themselves under fire. Troops of both divisions began to battle their way inland against both the terrain and the enemy, under artillery fire directed by observation posts on Mount Tapotchau.

The Japanese armored counterthrust never developed, only a series of piecemeal assaults. Just after 1200 hours two Type 95 *Ha-Go* light tanks moved south along the coastal road from the direction of Garapan. The crews of the two tanks appeared to be lost, halted inside the Marine lines, and were immediately blown to flaming shreds by dozens of bazooka rounds. At 1300 three *Ha-Go* tanks attacked the 8th Marines north of Afetna Point. Two were killed in the front lines, the third roamed into the rear areas before also being dispatched by the ubiquitous bazooka teams.

The fighting was primarily an infantry struggle, aided by the amphibian tanks of the Army's 708th Amphibian Tank Battalion. A and B Companies of Major Charles W. McCoy's 2nd Tank Battalion landed between 1300 and 1530 after being diverted from Green-3 to Green-1 because of the storm of fire still coming from Afetna Point. Two platoons of C Company were held in reserve, and 14 of the Shermans were sent south to assist 8th Marines in the attempt to subdue Afetna. Ed Bale:

> We landed with the 8th Marines, and one platoon from C Company. McMillian (who was now a lieutenant) ... had that platoon. We didn't have much difficulty getting ashore. We were waterproofed, and because of our experience on Tarawa we were very careful when we waterproofed those tanks. I had a couple of them that fell into what somebody might call bomb craters . . .
>
> There was an awful lot of confusion, because both divisions landed farther north than was planned ... The Japanese still had the practice of trying to defend the beaches. There were good beach emplacements, but of course naval gunfire and air had done a good job. There were some trench lines between the beach and the airstrip that was under construction ... and there was a lot of mortar fire."

McMillian lost one of his tanks in a shell hole.[6]

B Company 2nd Tank landed in an area not yet secured by the infantry. "I landed in the first wave of tanks," said Robert Thompson. "Fiegeth was the guinea pig again. He ran into some bad luck. He got ashore before the infantry got there. His turret had jammed due to some water[proofing] tape that we had on it. He couldn't rotate his turret, and they got pretty hot on him, so they went back out to the water. They went a little bit too far, and his tank drowned out on him. I got ashore 50 to a 100 yards behind the amtracs."

Once ashore Frederick was put in charge of a platoon, and moved off up the beach. His driver, Jim Carter, said, "We screwed up, got ahead of the infantry, and didn't know it ..."

"A bunch of Japs came out of the brush," said Frederick, "[from] holes they had there, and swarmed all over my tank. My buddy behind me was shooting them off my tank with a .30-caliber machine gun. Knocking them off. We ran out of ammunition, and all of a sudden there was a big explosion, and inside that tank, why, all our ears and heads just went to hell. It's like inside a 50-gallon drum or something that was hit with a sledge hammer."

Bobby Thompson: "I was driving the tank behind him, got a good view of the planting of the mines. Our gunner used the wrong trigger on one that was going to put one of the mines on and hit him with a 75 HE shell. Think that (the blast) also shook up Carter. The man was about ten feet from the tank. When a man is hit with a 75 HE shell, all you see of him is his helmet go up. While that was going on we took three hits from an antitank gun. Shook us up fairly good and knocked out all of our lights. The gun was behind us, luck was with us and a half-track had been watching for the gun, and when they turned to fire on us they saw him and knocked him out."

Frederick's tank returned to the assembly area, but "when they seen my tank come in, they chased me out of there. They didn't want me to park it there. They put me out in the open . . . One of the magnetic mines was still hanging on the tank ... I forget who it was got behind a tree with a rifle and shot that other one off the tank. It caved the side of the tank in ... Both sides of my tank were pushed in. Didn't tear it up or anything. Didn't stop the motor."

Carter said that "they scared the shit out of us. Didn't particularly hurt you, but knocked out your lights and communications."

Major Richard K. Schmidt's 4th Tank Battalion suffered primarily from high waves. Able Company landed successfully on Blue-1 after losing three vehicles to the breaking waves, but only four of B Company's fourteen Shermans made it ashore on Blue-2, in part because six were mistakenly landed on the Green beaches. Of these six only one made it onto the beach, where it was commandeered to make up for 2nd Battalion's losses. Only C Company made it ashore without loss on Yellow-2, and played a key role in smothering counterattacks against the beachhead's right flank. Eight of the light flame tanks of D Company never made it ashore, and the surviving 10 were held in reserve.[7]

Max English, of C Company, 4th Tank, said that "they were supposed to blow a hole into the coral reef, about 500 yards from the beach, but they failed to do it. The tank lighters came to the reef ... and we had to go on in. You were all right if you didn't run into a shell hole. We hit a shell hole, and we had water that came bubbling in. It hit the batteries, and started forming [chlorine gas]. We had to open our hatches. We had seawater coming in, but we had to have some way of getting that gas out. We couldn't breathe."

Bob Neiman attributed the absence of loss in C Company to measures taken to guide the tanks:

> There was a long pier that the Japanese had built from the sugar mill at Charan Kanoa, where we were supposed to land, out to the edge of the reef. They had blasted a channel alongside of the pier so that their freighters could come in and tie up to the pier. The channel was probably 150 feet wide, and the whole depth of the reef. There was a concrete ramp at the beach end of it.
>
> Somebody at division headquarters had decided that would be an ideal place for the tanks to land, and they could run right up that concrete ramp. We were very skeptical. We figured the Japanese would certainly have the whole channel, and especially that ramp, zeroed in with their heavy weapons. Sure enough, the first vehicles that tried it were amphibious tanks, and they got blasted.
>
> We gave up on that idea, but we sent a reconnaissance crew, three tank personnel from our company, ashore to try and find a good spot for us to land. While we were circling in our landing craft off the reef, a landing craft, a speedboat, is coming back from the beach. About a half a dozen underwater demolition men in there ... I hailed them and he pulled his boat over to my craft, and I jumped into his boat. I asked him if he knew a good spot where we could be sure there were no underwater obstacles or mines.
>
> Just at that point there's a big explosion, near the beach, inland. He says, "See all that smoke? Head for that and you won't have any trouble at all." So that's what we did.

The Recon Guides located submerged potholes and craters. Neiman: "We found a solution, called toilet paper ... We took two tank people—we had lots of additional personnel in the tank company besides the crews ... We put one man in the water with goggles and swim fins and a roll of toilet paper, swimming face down in front of each tank. We put another man on the slope plate of each tank to give hand signals to the driver through his periscope. The guy swimming ... if he came across a pothole, which they did periodically, they would just swim around it and uncoil the toilet paper as they went. The water over the reef was very smooth, so the toilet paper would just provide a perfect pathway around the pothole.."

Max English: "They waited until we got on the beach. They were throwing harassing fire out there, but nothing heavy until we got on the beach. A lot of them got pinned down real close to the waterline, but we went inland."

C. B. Ash: "[The plan was to] hit the beach, the infantry would stay in their amtracs until the tanks got there. We would head right to the O-1, through the O-1 to the O-2 which was about 2,000 yards inland. It didn't happen that way. The O-2 was at the Aslito Airfield."

Once ashore the tank crews had to dismount and prepare their tanks to fight. Charles Newman was helping to secure an assembly when he bent over to look under the porch of a native hut, and came face to face with an enemy soldier: "Needless to say, I froze, because I was scared. I'm staring at him, and he's staring at me. But I didn't know he was dead ... What happened that got me off the hook was a fly crawled over his mouth, and around his nose and over his eye. When they did that I realized he was dead. I took my 45 and went 'Hoop,' and he didn't move. And then I damn near fainted."

Getting organized under heavy fire was a major problem, and Ed Bale's company had to endure a particularly galling fire: "We knew that that smokestack of the sugar mill obviously had an observer up in it, because the mortar fire was so damned accurate. Every time you'd move, the mortar fire would move with you." Infantry units also complained bitterly about this observer.

Bale: "You had to get those (wading) stacks off. As I learned, when you land tanks, when you've got to marry up with the infantry, first you've got to find the infantry. It's not only finding a rifle company. You've got to find some command post. Other than McMillian getting shot through the skin under his jaw, I don't think I took any casualties that day. I told him to get the hell off the beach, and get out on ship and get taken care of. He hid in the tank from me for several days. I was dealing with his platoon sergeant. That was common with Mac. He always wanted to be in the middle of the fight."

McMillian said, "Really it was a mortar round that hit in front of me. I still have pieces of steel next to my jawbone." He recalled the incident differently, and said that he did not disregard Bale's order. He just thought "'... Oh, hell, I'll be all right,' and went back about my business."

Bale recalled Saipan as not being particularly bad in comparison to Tarawa, but for others it was an emotional trauma. "I did have one tank commander—in those days you called it battle fatigue. He got scared and got out of the tank and started digging a hole. We had to find a landing craft and ship him back to some hospital ship ..." Such psychiatric casualties apparently were not nearly as common in tank crews as among other troops. "That's the only one I ever saw ... He was a guy that when we were in the States would fight with his fists at the drop of a hat. When he got under gunfire, it was a different story."

By nightfall the beachhead was only 1,300 yards inland at its maximum penetration, and heavy fire—particularly from Agingan Point—hampered resupply and casualty evacuation.

Nocturnal Japanese counterattacks were no better coordinated than the daytime actions. In the extreme north, in front of the sector held by the 6th Marines, observers could see and hear the prelude to a counterattack building up in Garapan. Flag wavers and speakers exhorted a growing crowd, and there was drinking and loud music.

This celebration of impending death preceded the first major counterattack, led by a few tanks of the *9th Regiment*, a battalion from the *136th Infantry Regiment*, and other units. About 2,000 troops hit the Marines at 2200 hours. This assault was driven off.

The main attack at 0545, directed south along the coastal road, was led by three *Ha-Go* tanks of the *9th Tank Regiment*. Although the 6th Marines' listening posts could hear the clanking of the tanks, singing, and shouting, the clearest indication of the oncoming attack came when the commander of one of the tanks sounded the Japanese charge on a bugle. For his trouble, the bugler was one of the first to die.

An hour of hand-to-hand fighting pushed the Marines back, but a counterattack led by five Sherman tanks restored the line. The *Ha-Go* tanks proved no match for the bigger Sherman tanks. Inexperienced at fighting Japanese tanks, the American gunners fired armor-piercing rounds that shattered the armor of the lighter tanks like glass, then passed completely through, sliding them sideways with the impact.

A counterlanding by the *1st Yokosuka SNLF*, spearheaded by Type 2 *Ka-mi* amphibious tanks, succeeded in reaching as far as the landing beaches, where they were fought off by Army and Marine beach parties. It was obvious that most of these enemy attacks were forming up in Garapan, and the Navy flattened the town with gunfire.

Once the night attacks were beaten off, 16 June was a day of preparation for the drive to clear the southern end of the island. By 0950 the 8th and 23rd Marines had eliminated the last enemy positions back of Afetna Point, tying together the two Marine division fronts. The reserve 2nd Marines took over the extreme left of the beachhead, putting a fresh rifle regiment astride the coastal road between Garapan and the landing beaches.

The heaviest fighting was in the far south where tanks of A Company, 4th Tank Battalion, supporting 2/25, pounded away at a troublesome rear-slope defense built around four deadly Type 88 guns.

The 75mm Anti-Aircraft Gun Type 88 was patterned after a British design that also inspired the famous German 88mm guns, and the two guns were superficially similar.[8] It was Japan's most powerful long-range tank-killer.*

Efforts to cross the ridge crest silhouetted the tanks against the skyline and exposed the vulnerable lower fronts of the tanks. Infantry attacks fared no better.

This ridge was the O-1 Phase Line. For Neiman's C Company, 4th Tank, "it was our main obstacle. It was a ridge line that paralleled the beach, a couple of thousand yards inland. The entire area from the beach to the ridge line was wide open. There was no cover. It had been sugarcane fields that had been harvested, and there was absolutely nothing. The Marine infantry had to cross two thousand yards of wide-open space.

"It was decided that we would launch an armored attack up the road that went through Charan Kanoa straight to the ridge line. There was a cut through the ridge ... about 20 feet below the top of the

---

* Many accounts refer to German 88mm guns shipped to Japan and used against American tanks. The Japanese captured several German 88m guns in China, but the captured guns were retained in Japan for antiaircraft defense.[9] The Germans neither shipped 88mm guns to Japan nor licensed them for Japanese production.

ridge. It went down the other side, across another wide open area of perhaps a mile to Aslito Airfield."

C Company lined up in the van of a column described by Ash:

> We got lined up on a road ... *Ill Wind* [Neiman's tank] was out front of this thing. Bob Neiman called back to Hank Bellmon [later a U. S. senator and governor of Oklahoma]. Bellmon turned around and looked back and says "We've got armored amphibs, we got halftracks, we got amtracs loaded with troops. Okay, let's go."
>
> When we got to the O-1 it was a cut in the top of the ridge, just a little wider than the tank. There was a railroad track running along the right side going in, and some caves there. Right up above it at one place there was a .55 [caliber] antiaircraft machine gun.
>
> As I pulled up, I looked out the left side of the tank, and there's a Jap staring at me from some brush alongside the road. He's up even with my eyes. I let my foot off the throttle, and then I went back on it. Neiman says, "What's wrong?" It rattled me a little that the guy was that close, throwing hand grenades at me.

Neiman saw another Japanese setting up a tripod-mounted weapon on the side of the cut. "I thought to myself 'My God, he's not going to fire something at us that isn't gonna hurt us. He wouldn't expose himself like that unless he had some sort of antitank rocket or something.' I'm just anxious as hell to get him, and my gunner is very much absorbed in firing on a group of Japanese on the left. He doesn't see this of course, and the noise is horrendous. Finally I just kicked him as hard as I could right in the ribs and did get his attention."

The Japanese was mounting a heavy machine gun, which he began to fire at the exposed tank crewmen. Ash:

> He was having a hell of a time with this thing. It wouldn't feed good I guess. He would get off two or three rounds and have to jack another round into it. I could see tracers going into him, but hell, he was still shooting. Finally somebody hit him with a 75, and he ceased to exist.
>
> We went on down the road, and got down to where a railroad spur was going across the road. We were still roadbound. I pulled off onto this railroad spur, to the right. Neiman called back to Bellmon again, and says, "How we doin' back there?"

Bellmon says, "There's nobody back here." They had all disappeared. They were getting too damn much fire back there. I said to Neiman, "I think this is a good place to turn around."

[Instead] We went up that railroad to the right, and it took us right to Aslito Airfield, which was abandoned. There were wrecked airplanes all over it, but nothing else.

The effort to get the column turned around resulted in a tremendous snarl on the narrow road. Ash turned the lead tank around, and the vehicle immediately behind also turned around, but two others passed the lead tank and just kept going.[10] "The Japanese had artillery firing indirect fire over the ridge ... and they turned some of those guns on us. They got one of our tanks, and the tank commander ... a corporal, was killed." The stricken tank was stalled in the narrow road, partially blocking the escape route.

Ash was getting a close-up look at artillery fire as the tank ahead rammed its way past the immobilized vehicle. "To get around him he had to hit it and bounce it off to one side ... As I'm starting around ... there's three-inch antiaircraft/antitank rounds hitting on the road in front of me. I'm shifting up gears, and I look off to the left and I could see a burning tank right on the skyline ... But I couldn't see the guns. The guns were no doubt in pits, but they didn't have any AT ammunition. That was a good screw-up ... good for us.

"The next tank by, Burt Nave, was hit five or six times. They were leading me like an airplane, but they weren't leading Burt Nave. All those tanks got back with no problems."

From the direction of the fire they were taking, the burning tank up on the ridge seemed to be in the midst of the enemy guns. "I think he was right in amongst about three of them. I should have known the guns were up there, because when we were heading toward the beach, running up and down the O-1 was a torpedo bomber, a TBM Avenger ... He took a shot, and we did see a couple of parachutes open, but no doubt they didn't last too long after they got on the ground."

The burning tank that Ash had seen on the skyline was an A Company vehicle disabled on the rear slope of the ridge. The crew of the trapped tank continued to fight on with cannon and machine guns, but it was obvious that if the tank was not hammered to bits by the guns, it would be blown up or set afire by an assault team.

The tank commander, Gunnery Sergeant Robert H. McCard, ordered his crew to abandon the tank through the escape hatch while he tried to hold off the Japanese. As the other four crewmen scrambled out into the mud, McCard exposed himself in the turret, hurling smoke and fragmentation grenades to keep the enemy at bay and hide the movements of his men.

The wounded McCard threw the last of his grenades, then ducked into the turret and stripped out the .30-caliber coaxial machine gun and ammunition belts. Exposing himself atop the turret, he opened fire against the enemy infantry, killing 16. Alone now, Gunny McCard was finally cut down, but his stand had enabled his crew to scramble back up the muddy slope to safety. McCard was awarded the Medal of Honor.[11]

The abandoned C Company tank was still sitting in the road in enemy-held ground. In the confusion the crew failed to detail-strip it, rendering all the weapons useless by removing critical parts and locking down the hatches. Ash: "We were sent back up there to fire the thing ... Just pulled up on the ridge where we could see it and blasted him with 75 AP."

On 16 June General Saito managed to coordinate the largest tank attack of the Pacific War, but it was overly complex, involving several simultaneous attacks at different points on the Marine perimeter. Saito could not exercise control over the *1st Yokosuka Special Naval Landing Force*, one of the major units in the attack, and in fact Japanese Army and *SNLF* forces would make adjacent but separate attacks.

The plan was for the *Yokosuka SNLF* to attack down the coastal road while Colonel Goto's *9th Tank Regiment* and the *136th Infantry Regiment* would attack from Hill 500, an area of high ground southwest of Mount Tipo Pale. This main thrust would blow a broad hole in the 2nd Marine Division front and sweep down the coastal road. It was a bold but unrealistic plan.

The *9th Tank Regiment* mustered 44 light and medium tanks for the attack,[12] and nearly a thousand infantry. In a tank battle, however, the Shermans were clearly superior vehicles, despite the fact that many of the Japanese tanks were the improved Type 97-*kai Shinhoto Chi-ha*. Marine rifle battalions were now lavishly equipped with the deadly bazookas, and backed by artillery and naval guns. Surprise was lost when American air observers spotted two tanks in front of the 6th Marines, and alerted them for a possible tank attack.

A and B Companies of 1/6, supported by SPMs, were spread in a thin line across uneven brushy ground facing the mountain. At 0330 on 17 June listening posts reported heavy engine noises and called for illumination. The 6th Marines requested immediate tank support, and a platoon from B Company, 2nd Tank Battalion was alerted. Fifteen minutes later a wave of Japanese tanks, with infantry mounted on the tanks and others trotting alongside, surged out of the darkness, passed across the front of 2/2 and struck B/1/6 head-on. The first Marine response was flanking machine-gun fire from F/2/2. A wall of machine-gun and 37mm antitank fire greeted the assault, but enemy tanks were soon on top of the defenders.

Mortars, the 75mm howitzers of 1/10, and the 105mm howitzers of 4/10 rained airbursts on the supporting Japanese infantry. The Japanese carefully preplotted their own counterbattery fire. Mortar and artillery fire began to fall on the Marine artillery crews, an attack to which they could not respond and still support their own hard-pressed infantry. All along the line artillery battalions firing in support of the rifle regiments began to take heavy casualties among the exposed gun crews as they fought to keep the enemy off the riflemen.

The attack by the *Yokosuka SNLF* was beaten off by the 2nd Marines in a desperate hour-long firefight, but the critical threat was against 1/6.

The 1/6 front quickly degenerated into a "… madhouse of noise, tracers, and flashing lights."[13] Pillars of flame from stricken tanks silhouetted other tanks as targets, but blinded riflemen and gun crews to the approach of other tanks. Deadly point blank encounters came as surprises to attacker and defender alike.

Within half an hour the enemy had penetrated deep into the rear of both A and B Companies, and the battle broke down into dozens of small fights. One by one the tanks began to fall victim to stalking bazooka teams.

Pfc. Herbert J. Hodges had been a mechanic in B Company, 2nd Tank, but had been transferred to the 6th Marines. Robert Thompson: "Those tanks went to coming in on them, those infantry guys were about to go haywire. He told his company commander 'I'm from tanks. I'm not scared of tanks. I know what they can do and what they can't do. If you'll give me a bazooka man I'll take care of 'em.' He and that bazooka man shot seven shells and knocked seven tanks out. He got a Navy Cross for it." The other man was PFC Charles Merritt.[14]

Other tanks were blown up by satchel charges and grenades. One rifleman jammed a board into the road wheels of a light tank, then patiently crouched beside it with an armed grenade until the enemy vehicle commander opened his hatch.[15]

Some attackers veered away from the heaviest defensive fire and spilled over and into the flank of 2/2. A few Japanese tanks blundered into spots of low ground bordering the recently-cut cane fields and mired up to their turrets. At dawn the few surviving enemy tanks retreated back into the foothills of Mount Tipo Pale.

Shermans and SPMs finished off the mired Japanese tanks. The smoke from 31 wrecked tanks (and one more in the hills) cast a pall over the small battlefield, covered with the corpses of about 500 enemy infantry. Another 200 or so lay dead in front of the 2nd Marines' positions to the north.

In the aftermath many tanks were claimed as destroyed by several units. Ed Bale: "The argument has never been settled who destroyed the Japanese tanks, whether B Company [2nd] Tank Battalion did or whether the Weapons Company, 6th Marines did. Anybody that's still living is arguing over it."

Holland Smith tried to delay the scheduled morning attack, but the 2nd Division commander, Major General Thomas E. Watson, concluded he could not call off the attack on such short notice. The enemy had expended his total strength in the failed attack, and the 2nd Marines advanced rapidly north along the coastal road while the 6th took Hill 790 at the foot of Mount Tipo Pale.

The attack by the 8th Marines (with 1/29 attached) ground to a stop in the swamps north of Lake Susupe. Any movement brought down a storm of fire from an enemy-held hill that dominated the area, and the battalion commander was wounded. The new commander, Lieutenant Colonel Rathvon Tompkins, and Ed Bale managed to bring up seven tanks along a narrow, muddy trail. Bale: "One tank got hit ... and it blew the track off. I had a corporal who ran over there to try and get on the rear phone, and he got shot in the hip. Kid by the name of Crotts ..."

On Tarawa, Crotts had wanted a pistol rather than a rifle. On Saipan the pistol—the mark of an officer—made him a target and "... damned if they didn't pick me out. Guy took a shot at me. I was doing just what I told you. We were drawing fire across a big open field. I had my rifle down showing them where the fire was coming from, and dadgum if I didn't forget the sonofagun could shoot. All of a sudden the guy just tore my legs up. Went through one leg and seared the other one."

Bale's tank went to the rescue: "I pulled up alongside and had them drop their escape hatch. They crawled out through the bottom and up through ours. Then we turned around. They crawled back out, and hooked the towing cable up and we pulled that tank out." Together the tanks and infantry scrambled up the steep, rocky slopes and blasted the caves on top with cannon fire.

The war was over for Crotts. "They pulled the tank up right over me so I got some protection." The rescuers put Crotts on a jeep ambulance, which dragged him through several aid posts. "They would take me and say 'We can't work on you here,' and put me back on that jeep. Every little bounce tore me up. Then they would take me somewhere else and say 'Can't do it here.' Finally I burst into tears. I said 'You sonofaB, don't you put me back on that jeep! I have had it with the on and off of jeeps!' I just couldn't stand that vibration any more."

The delirious Crotts thought he was being sent back to the lines, but he was flown to Eniwetok, then to Hawaii, and finally stateside.

The 8th's problems also held up the 2nd Marines on their left, and that night McMillian's platoon absorbed a Japanese counterattack. MacMillian:

> One kid says, "Hey, Gunner, I just killed a Marine." I said don't worry about it, he had no business being out there. The next morning it was a Japanese with an NCO sword. They got that close.
>
> I split machine-gun ammunition with them [the infantry] three times that night. It got pretty rough. On my right flank, H. P. Murray's platoon, 3rd Platoon I believe, Murray got all shot up. It was our own artillery, I think. Someone had called for artillery fire.
>
> You're always gonna have tragedies of that kind. It took a little while to get it lifted. Murray got hurt pretty bad, and I saw a tank moving, pulling out. It was one of his tanks taking him back to an aid station. That worried me, because I didn't know what I had left on my right flank.

In the 4th Division zone the 165th Infantry moved in on the right and attacked eastward along the coast. The Japanese counterattacked from the last ridge before the Aslito airfield, and the 165th dug in at the base of the ridge. This was only a spoiling attack, and the enemy slipped away after bloodying the Army infantry. On their left the 25th

Marines had advanced through the hills north of the airfield, and their patrols were roaming across the 165th's front. Despite pointed suggestions from Holland Smith, Colonel Gerard W. Kelley declined to advance into what he considered less defensible ground just before nightfall, and further infuriated Smith.

That night the tanks in the 4th Division sector withdrew to replenish fuel and ammunition, and missed a Japanese counterattack accompanied by two tanks.

For the next two days the action was far to the west in the Philippine Sea. Admiral Ozawa sent his remaining carrier forces blindly into the attack, and launched his planes from beyond round-trip range. He had counted on the support of land-based air from the Marianas, and a reception at bases on Guam.[16] The ensuing battle, nicknamed the "Great Marianas Turkey Shoot," was the last gasp of Japanese naval air power.

On the 20th the Army and Marines executed a giant wheeling movement that reoriented the American line across the island and facing north. The heaviest action was fought by 1/25 and supporting tanks as they sought to reduce a bypassed pocket centered on a cave complex. The heavy guns of the XXIV Corps Artillery opened fire against Tinian.

The two Marine divisions used 21 June to reorganize and integrate replacements before advancing into the nightmarish tangle of ravines, cliffs, and jagged hills that held General Saito's main defensive line.

The Marines also salvaged what equipment they could. McMillian's lost tank was dragged out of the shell hole on the reef, but the immersion in salt water had caused severe damage. "Of course it had no electrical. Nothing power or electrical. We would pull it to start that old diesel engine off. That was Sergeant Larsen's tank. Crank the turret by hand. He did just as good as anybody else."

Saito's line was anchored in some of the most vicious terrain in the Pacific. The crest of Mount Tapotchau rises 1,554 feet above the sea, falling away to jagged ridges on the north and south. A spur runs south and then east in a large L-shape, guarding access to the central plateau of the Kagman Peninsula. On the west, rugged ridges tumble down to the town of Garapan.

The southwestern slopes of these ridges were sheer and jungle covered, with blind valleys, huge limestone pits with steep sides and no down slope opening. The ultimate redoubt was the very crest of the mountain, ringed by sheer 50-foot cliffs like the turreted keep of a medieval castle. Slightly lower Mount Tipo Pale, 1133 feet high, formed a western salient. Garapan was dominated by artillery in the hills above.

The deadliest ground, however, lay in a seemingly innocuous spot. East of Tapotchau lay a broad valley dominated by both the lower slopes of Tapotchau and a much lower parallel ridge to the east. The southern end of the U-shaped valley was a snarl of ravines and deep sinkhole pits where artillery was useless. In the ensuing struggle the valley, the eastern ridge, and the base of the U would acquire new names—Death Valley, Purple Heart Ridge, Hell's Pocket.

At 0600 hours on 22 June the 2nd Division launched an attack that carried 3/6 to the crest of Mount Tipo Pale, but a strong pocket of holdouts remained near the base of the peak. On their right the 8th Marines bogged down in the tangle of ravines on the lower slopes of Tapotchau proper. On the extreme right the 4th Division pushed along the rugged, sharp-spined north-south ridge that formed the easiest approach to the enemy's main line.

The 4th Division would now have to wheel right to clear the large Kagman Peninsula. Holland Smith decided to plug the 27th Division into the gap opening between the two Marine divisions.

On the morning of 23 June the 4th Division had to delay its attack when the 106th and 165th Infantry became snarled in the Marine logistical trains. F/2/106 was attached to 2/8 to attack along the crest of the spur from Tapotchau, cementing what would otherwise be an exploitable boundary between the two divisions. On 25 June the 27th Division pushed slowly forward into the deadly ground to their front.

The 4th Division's advance into the Kagman Peninsula was hampered by difficulty in negotiating the narrow trails and dense vegetation. One infantry platoon leader said of the cane fields that in each one he "... lost a man or two."[17] Max English recalled that "... a Jap got on the back of my tank with a magnetic mine, and it blew out one of my engines. But at that time we had [M4A2s with] twin engines. You just pulled a lever and it threw that engine out, and of course you were working on half-power then. We worked for the rest of the day on one engine."

The heaviest fighting was the attempt by the 8th Marines and the attached 1/29 to scale the wooded cliffs of Mount Tapotchau.

Ed Bale's tanks could provide little in the way of help. "There was only one thing that would even come close to resembling a road that went up over that thing. It was slow going, and nobody knew what the Japanese had left. People moved slowly because they wanted to keep their flanks tied in. Nobody wanted to get attacked in the flanks."

The shortage of trucks was a major handicap. "You had to come all the way off Tapotchau, back down, to pick up fuel, ammunition, and water. I don't know what the powers that be were thinking about."

Claude Culpepper was a truck driver in Bale's company, hauling fuel and ammunition for the tanks and other units as needed. Culpepper:

> The hardest thing I ever hauled was high explosives. I was afraid somebody was going to shoot that sucker.
>
> [The paths up into the hills were] Not what you would call a road. The tanks would tear up the ground as they moved up, and we usually followed along behind the tanks, in their tracks.
>
> When we went up in the high country, we had to walk. One time I had to carry heavy .50-caliber machine-gun bullets. Heaviest durn thing I ever picked up in my life was a belt of those things. I was skinny, and that thing weighed more than I did I guess. They had an anti-aircraft position ... back up on the side of a cliff, and you couldn't get trucks or anything to get there to take ammo. Put it around your neck and go chugging as best you could.
>
> [Culpepper was only 17 years old.] The men there looked after me. Anything got too dangerous, they would tell me what to do. In no uncertain terms.

Bale's tanks mostly supported troops clearing the lower slopes. Ed Bale: "One day we ran into a strange rock formation that was full of Japanese in holes. A tank commander got shot in the leg, and we took a bunch of casualties. Finally we decided to make a night attack. I took eight or ten tanks with spotlights on them, and turned the spotlights on. We just pounded that thing for several hours. Then the infantry moved in. I guess when we started pounding, the Japanese moved out."

At 1000 hours on 25 June a patrol from E/2/8 slipped up and over the cliffs on the east end of the mountain. By nightfall two companies of 1/29 had bypassed the enemy defenses and held the crest. The 27th Division also tried to bypass the low, tangled ground now known as Death Valley, but again failed to restore the integrity of the corps line.

While their sister units were embroiled in the struggle for Tapotchau and holding south of Garapan, the 6th Marines pushed across the spine of the ridge and onto the rolling ground in back of Tapotchau on 26 June. They had help from tanks brought up along narrow bulldozed trails along which all movement was constantly plagued by snipers and infiltrators. As the 6th began to wheel toward the sea to outflank Garapan, they found themselves in a random tangle of ravines. Tanks were little help as the Marines pushed into dark, shadowy ravines.

The 26th was marked by heavy infantry combat as 2/106 and 3/106 clawed their way along the slopes of Purple Heart. The seemingly cursed 1/106 was again repulsed.

On 27 June the 106th Infantry encircled the last persistent pocket of resistance, the thicketed tangle of ravines known as Hell's Pocket. Over the course of the next three days the 27th Division slowly compressed and then eliminated the tough little pockets still facing them, which had proven to be the toughest defensive terrain on the island. On the 30th the Army formations cleared Purple Heart Ridge and the last pockets in Death Valley, prompting Holland Smith to remark that "No one had any tougher job to do" than the 27th Division.[18] Meanwhile the Japanese quietly slipped away to set up another line of resistance.

On the extreme left the 2nd Marines had been slogging for days to capture the low hills overlooking Garapan from the south, and on 24 June received instructions to go into the town, much of which had been flattened by naval gunfire. The 2nd Marines, supported by the SPMs of their regimental Weapons Company and C Company of the 2nd Tank Battalion started to move into the ruins of Garapan on 28 June.

Mac McMillian's platoon was supporting 1/2 when that battalion was raked by rockets fired by an American plane.[19] "Colonel (W. B.) Kyle's battalion had the assault on Garapan. We called in an air strike from Navy Task Force 69. I was with Colonel Kyle at his OP overlooking this town of Garapan. In came this series, a Navy formation. The lead man led in. He veered off, and they came in right on top of us. Colonel Kyle says 'I'll never call for another air strike as long as I live!' We hauled them [the wounded] out of there. Got quite a few of the guys."

On 1 July the tanks led the infantry into the ruins of the main part of the town. Visibility from inside the tank was much improved over the old light tanks, but it was hard to locate carefully hidden enemy positions from atop the turret. Tank commanders like McMillian often dismounted and guided their tanks using the external telephone. "We jumped off and I led him. We were not like these big tanks nowadays, we couldn't go crushing through things. We had to pick our way and be careful. Go around. It was quite difficult. Of course we didn't mind crushing something when we could. In the street business you don't know what you're going to run into. A gun in a hut or something. We did not run into any in Garapan."

At 1600 hours 3/2 and another platoon of tanks were drawn up along an east-west boulevard that divided the ruined town. The Japanese struck back in a rare daylight counterattack spearheaded by seven tanks.

The Japanese tanks never had a real chance against the Shermans, and were blasted apart. By nightfall the attacks petered out, leaving the broad streets strewn with enemy dead and burning *Ha-Go* and *Chi-Ha* tanks.

North of the town stood the next barrier, a pair of steep-sided rock masses known as Sugar Loaf and Observatory Hill.

On 1 July the 8th Marines with 1/29 and 2/2 attached fought their way down the northern slopes of Tapotchau. They and the 6th Marines, supported by tanks brought over the tortuous trails, wheeled across and to the north of Garapan for the attack that would isolate the town. At this point the Marines of these two battered regiments were physically and emotionally shot and fueled only by pride.

Charles Frederick's section was waiting in a clearing when they "ran into a Japanese patrol," said Jim Carter. "We were lost. We were supposed to contact some infantry up there, and we got way ahead of the infantry and ran into a bunch of Japanese ... He [Frederick] would get out and look at anything that was around, and he ran into a Japanese patrol."

Frederick found a cache of Japanese food:

> I went back to the tank and got my tommy gun. I told my buddy "I'm going to go in and take a look at that." When we walked in there, that's when some Jap hit me. Killed my buddy that was next to me.
>
> Got me right through the right hip, and it spun me around. I don't know what happened to my tommy gun. I hit the ground. I tried to get up to run, and I couldn't because I was just paralyzed.

There was shooting all over, shooting around my head, and the dirt was just pecking up around my head. I couldn't move. The shots just quit, and somebody just drug me out of there. I passed out and they got me out in the open.

Turned me on my stomach, because I looked back and half my body was hanging out behind me. I said, "Goddamn it, do something else! I'm burning in front, burning like fire!"

They turned me over and found out where the … shot went in. I passed out again.

"They killed a kid by the name of Milan," said Jim Carter. "They broke off the engagement. We didn't realize we were up against that many people until after they pulled out. We just thought there were two or three stragglers, but there were probably 30 or 40 … We didn't get Milan out. We got Fred out, packed him out and shot him full of morphine. Milan was killed there, and it was one of the worst things that happened to me. I was senior man there and had to pronounce him dead. We were beginning to realize we were outnumbered considerably."

Unable to raise the company headquarters on the radio, Carter decided to leave the exposed position. "We pulled back, we're not talking maybe over a hundred yards, into the trees. We went back and got Milan's body later on. When you're scared shitless you're not sure your judgment is too good. I don't know if other people got as scared as I did, but sometimes it got pretty scary." Frederick:

The next thing I know I was on a jeep on a stretcher, heading toward the beach, I guess. That was a rough ride going down there.

[He was taken to a field hospital, and] When I woke up I was naked. [They] handed me an envelope with papers in it, and said "Hang onto these." They took me down to the beach and put me on one of the DUKWs, and hauled me out to a troopship.

We sat there for three weeks, out there in the bay. Put me on a damn canvas cot. I just laid there, and some swabbie gave me a pair of socks and a pair of his jeans. That's the only clothes I had.

Finally we hit Hawaii there, going to the hospital. Somebody handed me a crutch. I walked off of that damn ship with one leg and one crutch.

At 0830 on 2 July the Marines began their final encircling movement north of Garapan amid stifling heat, and the 8th Marines on the
right were almost immediately driven down by heavy fire. The tanks
were the key to maintaining the advance by the exhausted riflemen,
since no one not behind armor could long survive in the crossfires
that swept the narrow valleys.

Meanwhile the 2nd Marines captured Flame Tree Hill, a wooded
rise east of the town. SPMs of the regimental Weapons Company
moved up onto the hill, and began to pepper the sides of Sugar Loaf,
an enormous lump of soft limestone that the enemy had hollowed out
into a fortress. The Marines clawed their way up steep cliffs, grenading the caves, and dying not only from enemy fire but falls onto the
jagged rocks.

The remainder of 1/6 and 3/6 went around and onto the gentler
slopes of Observatory Hill, blasting the defenders out of the massive
concrete structure—a lighthouse, not an observatory—on the crest.
Down below, 3/2 pushed on north through the ruins of the town, digging snipers out from beneath thousands of sheets of corrugated
metal roofing that littered the ground for two miles.

On 3 July the weary Marines staggered into the attack that would
close against the sea north of the town. Losses had been so heavy that
each of the three regiments was sustaining the attack with only a battalion each. The Sherman tanks of C Company helped drive the
Japanese survivors into the closing trap. North of town the 8th
Marines, with 2/2 and 1/29 still attached, paused at noon near the
base of the hills. At 1630 hours all began the final push to the sea.

The countryside seemed suddenly alive with Japanese troops fleeing northward, and the Marines delighted in the slaughter of a
trapped and very visible enemy. Riflemen and tanks fired into the
milling masses in the fields and drainage ditches, and the tanks rolled
into the fields, cutting down the occasional knot of defenders who
chose to make one last futile stand.

The carnage in the fields meant that darkness caught the 8th
Marines short of the sea. On the morning of 4 July the last battalion of
the 2nd Division reached the water.

North of Garapan the island narrows, so 2nd Division passed into
corps reserve. The 2nd Marines, not quite so severely punished as its
sister regiments, along with artillery, a tank company, and a platoon
of flame tanks, were attached to the 4th Division for the drive to the

north. The 4th Division had the easier terrain, but the fighting was no less deadly.

On the morning of 5 July the 165th Infantry immediately ran into a strong position they nicknamed Hirakiri Gulch. In this broad, deep ravine men attacking either slope were exposed to fire from the opposite wall. This position held the 165th for two days until Army tanks could be brought up. Similarly 2/105 on the west coast was delayed by enemy sheltering in a large antitank ditch until tanks reduced the position. The 25th Marines, with supporting tanks, pushed onward and reached Mount Petosukara on the northeast coast on 6 July.

The heaviest fighting, and the action that broke the back of the defense, took place on the extreme west, in the 105th Infantry's zone. On 6 July Holland Smith visited the command post of the 27th Division to warn of the potential for a counterattack along the coastal plain, guiding along a natural path formed by the rail line and the coastal road.

On the broad coastal plain 1/105 and 2/105 were drawn up in defensive perimeters with gaps on either flank, and a 500-yard-wide gap between the perimeters. The Army troops intended to deny the gaps with fire, but had not planned on an attack by over 4,000 enemy, supported by tanks.

At 0400 hours the first wave poured around the open flanks. Major Edward McCarthy of 2/105 said that "they just kept coming and coming, I didn't think they would ever stop. It was like a cattle stampede."[20] The soldiers fought valiantly, but by 0630 the two Army battalions were overwhelmed. The attackers poured south down the coastal plain.

At 0515 the leading waves of the attack were washing against the scattered battery positions of 3/10, well to the rear of the broken line. Caught unaware, some of the gunners were killed in their hammocks and sleeping bags. H Battery was the most exposed, and masked the direct fire of the other batteries.

The enemy recoiled from H Battery's stand and swept around to its rear, overrunning Headquarters Battery. Three tanks turned inland behind H Battery. One *Ka-mi* peeled off from this envelopment and plunged into the rear of H Battery, but the gunners manhandled a howitzer around and blasted the tank apart. The gunners fought their guns into the ground.[21] The Fire Direction Center and medical aid post were overwhelmed with heavy casualties. The nearby 165th Infantry inexplicably chose to stand in place rather than aid the gunners or their sister regiment.[22] Farther to the rear, Item Battery fought until its ammunition was exhausted, then fell back into G Battery's position to continue the fight.

The strength of the attack was drained by late morning. When the 106th Infantry and tanks of the 762nd Tank Battalion moved into the counterattack they were able to relieve the isolated battery positions and rescue two pockets of H Battery survivors. Losses among the 105th Infantry were unusually heavy.

While the 105th was being overrun, the 23rd Marines turned westward to reach the coast behind the Japanese and fought their way up the gentle landward slope of a large hill they called Prudential Rock. Unable to bring direct fire on the cliffs below, the Marines hooked chains to the rocket launcher trucks, then used tanks to lower the trucks down the cliff face into firing positions below.

On the morning of 8 July Holland Smith pulled the 27th Division out of the line and replaced it with the 2nd Marine Division. B Company, 2nd Tank was put back into the line after only one day of rest, joining the vehicles of 4th Tank.

Bale's A Company was also back in action. The tanks would move forward, blasting any suspicious positions, halt while the infantry came up, and repeat the process. Sometimes the tanks were too far ahead of the infantry for safety. One night the company found itself in an entirely unwelcome situation, ahead of the 2nd Marines' infantry line. Ed Bale: "Didn't realize it until darkness set in. We spent a night out there. We killed a lot of Japanese. They were as surprised to find us there as we were to find ourselves there."

Melvin Swango's tank ran over a 250-pound bomb rigged as a mine:

> It just blew the track and suspension and everything off our tank, and just dumped it into the crater.
>
> The explosion lifted us, kind of like a giant hand. None of us were injured … We thought we were hit by an artillery shell. It tipped us over to one side, in that bomb crater, and we tried to look out our periscopes. We couldn't, because we were lying at such an angle, so we evacuated the tank. Took the armament out, and started walking back to the lines. The infantry was drawn up about a mile behind us, I guess.
>
> As it turned out there was a little shed about 50 yards from where we were. We looked around but we didn't pay much attention to that shed. In the short while we were disarming the tank, an advance jeep

Quickly I Climbed
on the tk pulled the badly
injured gunner out of the
tank I helped him down to
the ground four of us
carried Haddin several hundred
yds away to our side

patrol came up there. There were maybe four or five jeeps came racing up there when we radioed back and said we'd been knocked out.

One of the fellows with a Browning Automatic Rifle went over and kicked the door to that little shed open, and started firing. He motioned us to come over there. We went over and looked. Inside there were five dead Japanese soldiers, all fully-armed. Why they didn't come out and kill us, we don't know. He surprised them I guess when he kicked in that door.

The enemy was still full of fight, and still deadly. B Company tanks were supporting the riflemen of 2/6 in an attack upon several pill-boxes. Sergeant Grant Timmerman pulled his tank to the front of the rifle line, hosing the enemy positions with fire from his roof-mounted machine gun. Robert Thompson:

Timmerman never operated with a tank commander's hatch closed. He didn't care how hot it was, he had his head out. He said he needed to see. He was quite a remarkable fellow.

We had a .30-caliber machine-gun mount on a ring that you could rotate it all around. He fired it quite a bit. He just [rode] with about his chin up, looking. He had gotten some little nips, but not hurt very bad.

He was not too far from where we were at, and they gave us orders to turn around and head back. They didn't need us anymore. We went back and waited, and in a little while here came the tank with him on it. So far as I know, it was a wounded Jap. He tossed a hand grenade, and made a ringer. It started into the tank, and Timmerman grabbed it in the chest, and smothered it.

Timmerman had been Jim Carter's first tank commander, and Carter was particularly fond of him:

Brownie [Danny Brown, the gunner in a nearby tank] said he was looking right at it when it happened. This guy, the Japanese, was under a piece of tin out there. He came out and threw this grenade up there. Danny saw it going, and he killed him, but that grenade had already been thrown.

I was talking to Timm the night before, and he had suffered a minor wound to the arm. It looked to me like it was starting to get red streaks all up and down it [a symptom of blood poisoning] ... I talked to him, and tried to get him to pull himself off the line and go to first aid. He refused to do it. I don't know this, but I always felt like that arm contributed to the fact that he couldn't get that grenade out of there ..."

"It was in the tank," said Thompson, "and he turned to where he had the hand grenade between the side of the tank and him. I think his gunner got a fragment, but nobody else in the tank was seriously hurt. He just grabbed it, and of course it blew his whole chest area out. It was quite a mess. I had a little thing there that bugged me for years and years ... He had a ring that his girlfriend in China's father was supposed to have made. It was kind of like a college class ring. Not a very big ring, but it had a red set in it with a Marine Corps emblem on it. It always worried me, what happened to his ring, because he was quite proud of it. He had a love affair with this girl over there. If he lived until the end of the war, he was going to get to China and marry her."

As the Marines approached Marpi Point, the Japanese survivors took shelter in the sea caves and cliffs. Melvin Swango:

> I was sitting on top of the tank smoking a cigarette. Joe Wall, who was the gunner in my tank, he and I walked over to the edge of a coral cliff which went down to the ocean. For no particular reason, just killing time.
>
> We peeked over, and there must have been 50 Japanese soldiers down there on a little sandy outcropping. They didn't have any idea we were any place around them. They were just lounging around down there.
>
> We went and told Captain Bale, and he got hold of an interpreter. All of our tank crew members, about 20 of us, lined up around that cliff. The interpreter started calling down to them, told them "You're surrounded! Surrender!" and so forth.
>
> Not a one of them surrendered. We had to kill every one of them, because they just absolutely would not surrender.

The two divisions reached Marpi Point, the most northerly cape, and at 1615 hours Admiral Turner declared the island secure. Marpi Point was the scene of one of the most distressing episodes of the Pacific war. Swango:

> I've never forgiven the Japanese for this. I didn't care how many of them we killed, but they poisoned the minds of those poor natives to

where they were terrified of us. Some of them would sooner kill themselves than be taken captive.

Once when we were out ahead of the lines, I was sitting there on top of my tank ... I saw this woman break from a cave, and start running for the edge of a cliff. She had two little kids with her, a little boy and a little girl.

I knew what she was gonna do. I started running after her and yelling the memorized Japanese ... "Do not be afraid!" and that sort of thing.

She had such a head start I couldn't catch up with her. She got to the edge of the cliff, and threw one of the little kids over, then the other, looked back at me, and jumped herself.

The saddest thing I ever saw. I've never forgiven the Japanese for lying to those people like that.

Ed Bale explained that "We were told not to move in and try to do anything with those Japanese civilians ... You feel bad about it looking back on it, but it was just one of those things. Of course you knew that there were Japanese soldiers in there among them that were causing it. But if you had gone in there to try and do anything, hell, more of them would have jumped than did."

American efforts to stop this last senseless carnage were generally unsuccessful, although the interpreters saved some and amphibian tractors managed to rescue others who had survived the plunge into the sea.

CHAPTER 9

"THE MOST PERFECT AMPHIBIOUS OPERATION": TINIAN

SAIPAN was invaded to break the enemy hold on the Marianas, but Tinian was a true prize, nature's own gigantic aircraft carrier. Tinian is a flat topped plateau rising from the Pacific, ringed by low cliffs that rise sheer from the sea. There were only three potential landing sites. The best was on the southwest coast, where four separate beaches offered the easiest approaches. Two of the beaches, code-named Red Beach and Green Beach by Marine planners, were dominated by Tinian Town. Two other isolated beaches, Orange and Blue, were located north and south, respectively, of the town. Fortified promontories flanked Yellow Beach, an isolated strip of sand on the northeast coast.

The White Beaches, on the northwestern coast and closest to the American staging areas on Saipan, were very narrow; White-1 was only 60 yards wide, White-2 160 yards wide. The only thing that favored the White Beaches was that the Japanese did not take them seriously as potential landing sites.

The backbone of the defense was the *50th Infantry Regiment*, the *1st Battalion, 135th Infantry*, a light tank company of the *18th Infantry Regiment*, with 12 light tanks, the *56th Keibitai (Naval Guard Force)*. The *82nd Air Defense Group*, and the *83rd Air Defense Group*, with six Type 88 antiaircraft guns.

Admiral Richmond Kelly Turner favored the Tinian Town beaches, but Holland Smith preferred the narrow but undefended White beaches.[1] There were vastly fewer mines and obstacles, and the reef was negotiable by men on foot.

Tinian was subjected to a thorough bombardment by 13 battalions of Army and Marine Corps artillery. Unit commanders also had the

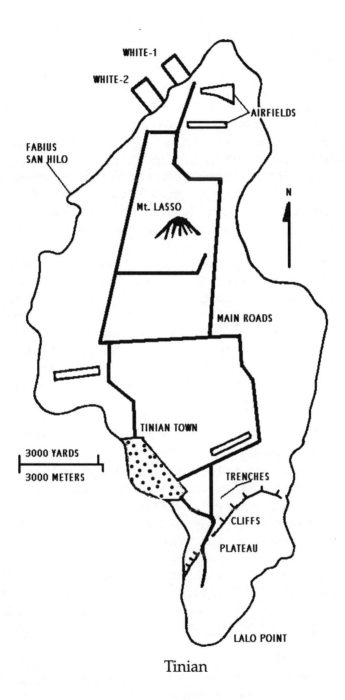

Tinian

unparalleled luxury of detailed personal reconnaissance. Bob Neiman: "All regimental commanders, all battalion commanders, and in the case of tanks, all company commanders, had an opportunity for an aerial reconnaissance of Tinian." Groups of officers were taken up in a Navy TBM Avenger, with a fighter escort.[2] "I was lying face down, the bomb bay was open, and I had an aerial photograph on a map board with a clear plastic overlay and a grease pencil. We slowly circled the entire island twice, and I was able to determine where tanks could go and where they couldn't go."

The two assault divisions were badly depleted by the Saipan fighting, so the two divisions were reorganized for the upcoming fight.[3] The 2nd Tank Battalion, 1st Provisional Rocket Detachment, the 1st and 2nd Battalions of the 10th Marines artillery, and the Army 1341st Engineer Battalion were all attached to the 4th Division for the landings.

The 18 medium tanks supporting the first landing waves were preloaded in LCMs aboard LSDs *Belle Grove* and *Ashland*. Five more LCTs carried 20 additional medium tanks, and 41 more tanks would be shuttled from Saipan.

An elaborate diversionary operation was launched to convince the Japanese that the assault would be directed at the Tinian Town beaches. On Jig-Day, 24 July, seven transports escorted by the battleship *Colorado*, a light cruiser, and four destroyers slipped into the harbor. Just after 0600 the transport *Calvert* lowered her boats and Marines began to scramble down boarding nets. Planes strafed and bombed the beaches and town, and ships, gunboats, and the artillery on southern Saipan joined in.

The *Calvert*'s LCVPs began their fake assault run into the beach. At 0720 hours two undetected six-inch naval guns near the town opened fire on the *Colorado* and the old battleship took 22 direct hits. The destroyer *Norman Scott* took six direct hits. The *Calvert* retrieved her landing boats, and an elated Colonel Kiyochi Ogata signaled Tokyo that he had repulsed a landing attempt.

The UDT assigned to clear submerged mines from the White beaches was scattered and their equipment lost in a rain squall. Ships shelled the reef in an unsuccessful attempt to detonate the mines as air strikes and artillery from Saipan raked the areas in back of the narrow beaches.

On White-1 the 24th Marines landed in a column of companies. Within an hour the 1st and 2nd Battalions were ashore and pushing toward their objectives against light resistance.

Colonel Ogata had prepared better defenses at White-2, where two pillboxes faced two battalions, 2/25 and 3/25, landing in company columns. The initial assault waves went in over the cliffs on either side of the beach, where the troop-carrying LVTs wedged themselves against the cliffs among breaking waves and riflemen scrambled up the coral. The beaches and inland approaches were heavily mined, and three LVTs and a jeep were blown up.

The Marines landed their tanks as mixed groups in order to get a balanced force ashore. The light flamethrower and escort tanks of D Company were split up and attached to the medium tank companies.[4] Each reinforced tank company—eighteen Sherman tanks, four Satan flame tanks, and two light gun tanks—would support a specific regiment throughout the operation.

The tanks of B Company and its attachments landed over the narrow White-1 beach opposed only by the enemy. Off White-2 the foot guides found deep, unmapped clefts in the reef surface, big enough to swallow a tank. The LVTs carrying the assault troops had paddled happily across them, but they formed a potentially deadly maze that tanks were forced to negotiate under fire. A few tanks wandered in confusion, taking a nerve-racking 45 minutes to cross the reef, only to encounter more mines on the beach. Finally some of A Company's vehicles were diverted to White-1, and from there through 1,600 yards of enemy-held ground and into their assigned zone behind White-2.

The 2nd Battalion of the 24th Marines advanced directly inland, occupying the edge of Airfield Number Three, but on their left the 1st Battalion ran up against a tenacious defense around a number of caves. Satan flame tanks attached to B Company were unable to burn the enemy out of the deep caves and dense, wet underbrush.[5]

Colonel Ogata had assigned only a company of infantry, one Type 01 47mm and a 37mm Type 94 antitank gun, and two heavy machine guns to defend the area behind White-2. Though badly outnumbered, these units put up a tenacious defense, and the pillboxes housing the two antitank guns had to be bypassed.

Landing the tanks was delayed to allow the rifle companies of the 23rd Marines to land, but by 1700 hours all vehicles of the 4th Tank Battalion, as well as an additional platoon of Satan flame tanks from the 2nd Battalion, were ashore. The small beachhead held 15,600 troops, four battalions of artillery, 24 SPMs, and 63 tanks. In late afternoon the 4th Division commanding officer, General Clifton B. Cates, ordered his men to prepare for an anticipated counterattack.

Ogata hoped that a counterattack by his mobile reserve could cope with any force that the Americans could push across the White beaches. On their own initiative several Japanese commanders started their troops toward a nocturnal counterattack. The largest formation in motion was the *1/135th Infantry*, moving crosscountry and taking advantage of the forest cover to avoid air and gunfire attacks.

As darkness fell, the C Company, 4th Tank Battalion vehicles were given an unusual mission—flattening sugarcane. In the densely planted cane the Japanese could approach within a few yards before launching an attack. C. B. Ash:

> They sent our platoon out in front of the infantry to clear a cane field … We went out in a column two or three hundred yards, made a right turn, and came back parallel to our lines, and then peeled off in a line to knock down as much cane as we could. The infantry were all in foxholes, and I could see Japs not seven yards from the infantry. Whether they were alive or not, at that point I didn't really know.
>
> Our tank was a little farther back. Two tanks were in front of me. There was a Jap lying there slinging magnetic mines on this thing. We couldn't shoot at him because we would be almost shooting our own people. They would go up and hit those two by twelves [wooden armor] and slide down to the deck and go off. Finally, after a couple of them, he jumped up, went up to the tank quickly, and held one against the wood. His hand disappeared, then his arm disappeared, then his head disappeared. This tank wasn't knocked out. It did split a fuel tank, but it went on through our lines.
>
> I could see that some of these guys were still alive, so I sped it up a little, and did figure eights on these guys … Then we went right back behind the infantry, swung into a line, and set up for the night. [Max] English had found two deck chairs somewhere, and had them sitting on the goddamn engine compartment. He and the infantry company commander were sitting up there riding behind the turret on those damn things.

Late in the evening the *56th Naval Guard Force* bumbled into the blocking positions established by A/1/24 on the far northern flank of the beachhead. The main enemy attack struck A Company at 0200, and continued for nearly three hours. The Japanese were systematically slaughtered by machine guns and 37mm cannon. By early morning the Marine rifle company was badly battered, reduced to less than 30 effectives, but still held an intact line. At dawn the tanks of B Company helped fight off a final, halfhearted attack.

Counterattacks against the eastern and southern flanks were launched by veteran troops of the Japanese Army, and far better coordinated. At 0230 hours a small force supported by light tanks struck 3/24 on the east side of the perimeter, just south of Airfield Number Three. The main blow fell when about 1,500 men of the *1st* and *2nd Battalions, 50th Infantry* punched through farther south. Another part of this force broke into the rear of the 25th Marines, and some made it as far as the beach, where they were annihilated by a hastily organized force of service troops.

At 0330 another attack by these same units, supported by five or six Type 95 light tanks,[6] hit 2/23 on the south flank. A primary target was the night laager for the Marine tanks. The Japanese tanks led the attack down the coastal road but ran into an antitank ambush. The lead tank was quickly set afire by bazookas, and careened into the roadside ditch. The second penetrated about a hundred yards, then ground to a stop in the middle of the road, belching flames. Three other tanks tried to turn around in the narrow road to flee, but were blown apart by concentrated bazooka fire. A sixth tank (if there was one) never penetrated very far into the Marine positions, and was able to withdraw to the north. Subsequent waves of Japanese pressed the attack until just before dawn.

At first light the tanks of B Company were sent in to sweep the killing ground north of the perimeter, while the tanks of C Company and a company from 1/8, the operational reserve, swept the ground to the south. Resistance to the morning attack was sporadic, since the survivors of the Japanese units that had launched the night counterattacks were scattered and disorganized, except for occupants of caves and pillboxes in the small hills below 390-foot Mount Maga.

The 25th Marines tried to encircle the mountain, sending the 1st and 3rd Battalions respectively left and right of the mountain, while the 2nd Battalion pinned the defenders in place. Resistance was heaviest on the left, and the 1st Battalion climbed the spur ridge below the mountain, only to be twice driven off by fire from above. Finally, with the help of A Company tanks, both battalions were able to push around the mountain by dusk. The infantry swept the dense underbrush ahead of the tanks, destroying three more 47mm guns.

With the loss of the Mount Maga position, Colonel Ogata abandoned the positions on higher (564-foot) Mount Lasso immediately to the south. Marines occupied the heights before nightfall on 26 July.

The emphasis was on a slow and steady advance, frugal in lives. With Japanese air and sea power rendered impotent, the need to get the ships away was not pressing. Moreover, the troops were exhausted and equipment worn out from the fight on Saipan.

The 2nd Marine Division came ashore in the morning hours, and by the end of the day had moved across the breadth of the island to establish a south-facing line on the left of the 4th Division. The 8th Marines were given the task of sweeping north to clear out enemy remnants that had survived the failed counterattacks.

In the early morning of 27 July the two Marine divisions commenced the systematic push along the island. To allow maximum concentration of artillery and air support, the two divisions alternated their advances. The 2nd Division led off, following a dawn shelling by XXIV Corps artillery firing from Saipan, and the division advanced 4,000 yards against minimal opposition. On the right the 4th Division advanced about half as far, halting at noon.

On 28 July, it was the turn of the 4th Division to carry the advance. The 2nd Division advanced only a few hundred yards, but this was the day that McMillian's luck finally ran out.

"I got out on the ground, and I was on the telephone. There was a burst from a little ol' Nambu machine gun. There was an infantry kid right beside me. He got it right across the waist. They got me across the legs. I couldn't walk … We got the two Japs that had the machine gun. Before I gave up, we killed them. I hopped around there, and they evacuated me." That was his third official wound, so McMillian was sent back to the States.

4th Division Marines mounted on tanks and SPMs overran the airfield at Gurguan Point, then pushed on past the airfield.

The tank units in particular suffered from the lack of truck transport, but Ed Bale managed a partial solution. "I saw some Athey Bomb Trailers … I guess the 4th Marine Division had landed fuel and ammunition in them because of those narrow beaches, and moved them inland. There were a bunch of empty ones there, and I latched onto them. We loaded them with tank ammunition and fuel, and hooked 'em onto the backs of tanks."

The weather impeded operations more than the enemy. In the late afternoon waves from a passing typhoon struck the exposed landing beaches, and landing operations were suspended. C-47s of the Army Air Force's 9th Troop Carrier Squadron hauled critical supplies from bases on Saipan to the airfields on Tinian.

On 29 July General Schmidt abandoned the systematic advance and ordered a rapid general advance without artillery preparation. Resistance was spotty but deadly as snipers, mines, and booby-traps waited in the dense growths of sugarcane.

"Those cane fields were treacherous," said Melvin Swango, "because you never knew what you were going to run into. A friend of mine, Herschel Fulmer ... was a radioman in one of the tanks. His tank commander was killed. They were in a cane field. He had his hatch open for some reason, and got shot and killed."

No place was safe, even after the riflemen had swept the area. Jim Carter was driving for a new tank commander after Charles Frederick was evacuated from Saipan, and his section was in reserve awaiting orders. "Believe it or not I was reading a book when they hit us the first time. We had orders to hold up, and were just sitting there. It was a nice, beautiful day. I had my feet propped up ... All of a sudden, Ka-Wham! Like idiots, we had been sitting there for quite a while and hadn't moved because we weren't getting any fire. They hit us on the first round. Don't ever let anybody tell you those Japanese couldn't run their equipment, 'cause they never gave us any warning at all. They just hit us."

Fortunately the tank was struck by explosive rounds, not armor-piercing fire, and no one was wounded. "We got hit a couple of more times, but outside of superficial damage, they weren't really hurting us. But we didn't know that."

The large hill that forms the core of Masalog Point on the eastern coast was heavily defended, but fell to the 2nd Marines by midafternoon. One of the light tanks supporting the 25th Marines was destroyed by a mine.

The Japanese used their standard tactic of fire tunnels cut into the lower story of the dense vegetation, but antitank ambushes by the smaller guns were ineffective. C. B. Ash's platoon stumbled into one, and didn't even realize it: "This 37mm, if you can imagine, was so close that I don't think the guys in the turret could see it. I don't know how much vegetation was around it. It shot at the turret of the first guy, and it made a pinhole in the turret. You could clean out the slag in there, and you could see through the hole. Burt Nave was next. He pulls up, and didn't see it. The guy had lowered the damn thing down just below the sponson. We had put into the turret a two-row ready rack of 75 [ammunition]. This [round] came in, knocked off two HE fuses ... and kept going. The loader's sitting there with an HE in his hand. It knocked the fuse off of that, went over underneath the tank commander's ass, and hit a junction box. They drove off. Nobody got hurt, nobody got a Purple Heart. The next tank finally saw it, and done him in. Jeez, that's close, man."

For the infantry, accustomed to fighting a short-range war, an unfamiliar hazard was open terrain that lent itself to defense by long-range fire. Artillery and heavy machine guns dug into deep caves in the hills could rake the Marines at will. "The infantry, at places, took quite a beating," said Jim Carter. "We were crossing this one field going into a kind of ridge line with heavy timber. They were shooting the living hell out of that infantry, and it got so hot they couldn't stay with us. We had to pull back . . ."

Charles Newman of C Company, 4th Tank, recalled: "We were in a valley, and they had several guns that came out of a certain area on the side of some hills that were looking over this valley. The valley was real long and real peaceful looking, but as we approached it—the infantry and tanks—they would come out and fire these guns."

Along the western coast 1/24 encountered a stubborn bunker complex that was overrun by the tanks of B Company, 4th Tank Battalion. After the tanks and infantry had passed, the bunkers came back to life, and the tanks had to be called back to burn and blast the positions again. The tanks devoted four hours to destroying this one small band of defenders.

At nightfall the two divisions stood on a line running from just north of Tinian Town to the big hill on Masalog Point. Enemy resistance began to stiffen, and a soaking rain from the typhoon lasted all night. Probing attacks were directed against the 25th Marines north of Airfield Number Four.

On 30 July the main objective was Tinian Town. Artillery and naval guns shelled the town. The main center of resistance proved to be in coastal caves north of the town, from which several guns, including one Type 88, raked the advancing Marines. Armored amphibians moved along the coast to take the caves under fire while Satan flame tanks of the 4th Tank Battalion moved in to burn them out.

At 1420 the 24th Marines entered the town, and found it abandoned except for one unfortunate straggler and numerous mines. On their left the 25th Marines took Airfield Number Four. The 2nd

Division engaged in several relatively small actions, but suffered its heaviest casualties when a heavy mortar barrage struck 3/2. Patrols from 1/2 bumped up against the foothills that bounded the southern part of the island, were pinned down, and had to be rescued by Ed Bale's tanks.[7]

At 1830 hours on 30 July over 80 percent of the island was firmly under Marine control. Unfortunately the southern tip of the island was the best defensive terrain on the island, and the spot Ogata had chosen for his last stand. He had skillfully extricated nearly two thirds of his troops and retreated into this southern redoubt.

The terrain was the key to the defense. The southern tip of the island is a rugged plateau separated from the island's lowlands by a jungle-covered escarpment that extends from the coast south of Tinian Town, and wraps around the eastern end of the plateau. The escarpment presents a formidable military barrier, with 100-foot cliff faces of rotten limestone. Steep slopes of loose scree and mud offer tortuous ascent routes dominated by local promontories of the cliffs and by the dense jungle that crowns the slopes. Atop the cliffs the plateau itself was a maze of tangled ravines and limestone crags, with numerous caves and a cover of thick underbrush.

In 1944 a narrow dirt road ran south from Airfield Number Four, skirted the cliffs in a series of switchbacks, and deadended above an enormous ravine near the south end of the plateau. A talkative prisoner reported that this road was heavily mined, and sweeping the mines under fire from the cliffs above would be suicidal.

At 0200 on 31 July about a company of enemy infantry, accompanied by three light tanks that could not be withdrawn onto the plateau, attacked the 25th Marines south of the town and were driven off. Throughout the night, division and XXIV Corps artillery rained fire on the wooded cliffs. At dawn battleships and cruisers dumped tons of shells onto the cliffs, interrupted for a 40-minute air strike.

At 0830 five regiments jumped off in the attack against the plateau. The 2nd Marines swept across the base of the escarpment along the east coast, securing the low ground, and 3/24 attacked into the densely wooded low ground along the west coast. The 6th, 8th, and 23rd Marines attempted to scale the edge of the plateau. The 24th immediately ran into underbrush nearly impenetrable to the tanks, and the single road along the low ground was heavily mined.

To their left 2/23 and the supporting tank platoon ran into an extensive minefield blocking the approaches to the cliff, and when engineers attempted to lift the mines they were fired upon by Japanese infantry in a trench line. When tanks attempted to outflank the trench line one struck a buried bomb. The explosion broke the tracks, wrecked the suspension, and wounded the driver, assistant driver, and vehicle commander. The infantry moved on past the minefield while the tanks stayed behind to invest the stubborn hold-outs in the trench. The enemy occupied the abandoned tank and turned its weapons on its companions, so the tank platoon leader ordered his surviving tanks to shell the abandoned vehicle until it was wrecked by internal explosions.[8]

Farther inland 1/23 was attacking through the thick underbrush when the accompanying tank platoon from Neiman's C Company, 4th Tank stumbled into a carefully prepared ambush. Within a matter of seconds six antitank shells struck the leftmost tank. One round penetrated the side of the turret, but the driver was able to reverse the tank and withdraw. The crew fired smoke grenades, and called for suppressive artillery and mortar fire on the area from which the fire apparently had come. The tanks formed up again for a cautious advance, with the damaged vehicle in a trailing position. Six rounds hit the vehicle on the left flank in quick succession. Three rounds penetrated the side armor and disabled the tank, but this time the tanks and infantry located the source of the fire.

The enemy gun was a 47mm in a concrete pillbox, protected by infantry, and placed to fire across the likely axis of any approach toward the base of the cliff. One tank smothered the pillbox with smoke shells while another worked its way into the rear of the enemy position. Armor-piercing and high-explosive rounds smashed the pillbox, and the tank and its accompanying riflemen killed the fleeing enemy.

The main assault on the plateau was the responsibility of the 8th Marines, and Ed Bale said that this is where the resistance really stiffened: "There was a hell of a fight up there ... It [the road] was narrow but it was negotiable. The regimental commander, old Colonel (Clarence R.) Wallace, didn't want us to try to go up it at all until the infantry got on top."

The two assault battalions came under a withering fire from the cliffs as they crossed the open ground below, and suicide squads rushed out to attack Bale's tanks. The 1st Battalion pushed up the narrow road, with infantry struggling to clear the thick underbrush above and below the twisting path.

Engineers gingerly lifted the mines that littered the road, under the protection of tanks advancing in single file. The tanks not only fired into the underbrush, but also served as magnets to draw enemy fire away from the exposed engineers. The engineers were exposed not only to small arms fire but grenades that the enemy simply rolled down the slopes and into the road.

The 3rd Battalion drew the more vicious task, an attack up the cliffs. Marines on the slopes were raked by fire from the cliffs. Suppressive fire from tanks, SPMs, and the arcing tongues of flame from the Satan flame tanks blasted and seared the underbrush and cliff crests, but repeated rushes by the rifle companies were bloodily repulsed.

A few feet at a time the 1st Battalion hammered their way up the switchbacks and through the tangled brush. At 1700 hours the battalion established a small perimeter atop the escarpment. Knowing that the Japanese would be frantic to reduce this pocket, the regiment pushed G Company from the 2nd Battalion, two 37mm guns, and truckloads of ammunition up the fire-swept road. There was no time to set up proper positions or barbed wire, or to establish clear fields of fire.

At 0100 hours on 1 August about a hundred Japanese slipped around the flank of 1/8 and cut the road halfway down the slope. Ambushing traffic moving down the narrow road, they blocked it by setting fire to two ambulances. A hastily assembled force from the 2nd Battalion reopened the road, then set up a strongpoint near the most vulnerable point, but the road remained dangerous for vehicles other than tanks.

On the plateau probing attacks began soon after nightfall and built steadily in intensity. Just after 0315 hours a large enemy force rushed the Marine positions, with the heaviest attack directed against the sector held by G Company and one of the 37mm guns. With the dawn the attack slowly melted away, and with it the last hopes of the Japanese defenders.

By 0800 hours the Marines had three battalions atop the cliffs, with 2/6 held at the base of the slope as a reserve. The surviving enemy had gone to ground in hundreds of small caves that dotted the tangled wilderness.

With the collapse of the cliff top defense, the Japanese elsewhere began to lose heart. Down below, 2/23 and the tanks finally subdued the stubborn handful of defenders in the trench and the tanks were released to join the action on the plateau.

The Marines witnessed more civilian suicides by grenades and leaps from the cliffs. Jim Carter: "I think there was actually more of that on Tinian than there was on Saipan. It didn't get as much coverage … but we were right up there when they were trying to keep them from doing it. The Navy had patrol boats out trying to talk them out of it. We held up, we didn't go ahead and push on in, trying to get them to where they would surrender and let us take care of them. Didn't have much effect. The propaganda had been put out so much that they were scared to death of us."

Despite such senseless carnage, both civilians and enemy troops surrendered in greater numbers than on Saipan or in any other prior battle.[9] Again, this success was in large part the result of the Army Nisei interpreters attached to the Marine units. Ed Bale: "We always had trouble with Japanese stragglers on Saipan, but very, very few on Tinian. Tinian was so safe at night that, on my camp, I didn't even have guards."

Light tanks amid the confusion of the landing on Namur. An LCM is just backing away from the beach. One of the tanks still has its single wading stack affixed, while the near tank has jettisoned its stack. (*National Archives*)

Hunter, Captain Denig's command tank, lies burned out and abandoned. Although official records state that the tank was destroyed by a grenade, a hole left by some sort of antitank projectile is clearly visible just above the track. (*National Archives*)

M4A2 tanks of C Company, 4th Tank Battalion, moving up to support the attack on Namur. This operation marked the first use of wading stacks and wooden supplementary armor by Marine tanks. (*National Archives*)

Platoon Leader Max English's tank *King Kong* bogged in the sand on the Namur beach. Note the covering on the slope plate, and the very effective camouflage on the turret and gun tube of the tank. (*National Archives*)

Jungle Jim attacking Japanese positions on Namur. This vehicle is unusual in that the slope plate is covered by an almost random pattern of oak planks, and it is fitted with the older style of cleated track. (*National Archives*)

The C Company VTR, *Lulubelle*, being used to salvage wrecked Japanese tanks from Namur. One captured vehicle is loaded on the back of an American tank for transport, and another is barely visible between the two bigger American vehicles. (*National Archives*)

A Japanese tank loaded onto the deck of Platoon Sergeant Joe Bruno's tank *Killer*. Bruno is the man with cutoff trousers and open shirt. These captured tanks were shipped to Hawaii for training and display. (*National Archives*)

LCM-3s land tanks of Ed Bale's C Company, 2nd Tank Battalion, at Charan Kanoa, Saipan. The 20mm gunners are sheltering behind the thinly armored superstructure. Note the tall smokestack that served as an enemy observation post. (*National Archives*)

Infantry sheltering behind the 4th Battalion tank *Cavalier* on the beach at Saipan. Rifle company casualties were extremely heavy; the man in the foreground has been shot in the right thigh. (*National Archives*)

The 75mm Type 88 antiaircraft gun was a deadly tank killer, like the more famous German 88mm gun. A battery of these guns created considerable havoc among the tanks of 2nd and 4th Tank Battalions when they attacked the high ridge in back of the landing beaches. (*National Archives*)

This improvised pole mine captured on Saipan is a Type 93 "tape measure" mine, 10 inches in diameter, strapped to a bamboo pole. The user would hide in a roadside ditch or hole and try to shove the mine under the tracks of a passing tank. (*National Archives*)

A tank provides cover while a rifleman dashes past a stretch of road exposed to machine-gun fire. The men in the background are in defilade. The pattern painted on the turret indicates that this is likely Max English's tank. (*National Archives*)

The Marianas operations marked the appearance of specialized tanks with the M1 dozer blade kit. This example from C Company, 2nd Tank Battalion, demolishes a building. Note the three plates of supplementary armor welded to the sides. (*National Archives*)

The SPM, an obsolete 75mm cannon mounted on a half-track, was the heavy antitank weapon of the Marine rifle regiments. These guns were instrumental in smashing the large Japanese counterattack against the beachhead. (*National Archives*)

Observers help a tank target enemy positions below Mount Tapotchau.
The man speaking through the open pistol port is a tank crewman, as
he wears no 782 gear (web gear) and has a .45 pistol in his hip pocket.
(*National Archives*)

Visibility was poor from inside the tanks, so Platoon Leader Mac
McMillian walks beside his tank, C-21, to spot targets on the outskirts
of Garapan. Note the infantrymen sheltered in holes. The vehicle in the
foreground is a Satan flame tank from D Company. (*National Archives*)

An unidentified tank from McMillian's 2nd Platoon, C Company, 2nd Tank Battalion, protects stretcherbearers as they rescue a wounded Marine near Garapan, Saipan, 4 July 1944. (*National Archives*)

The light flame tanks, called Satans by the Marines, had two-man crews, and were armed with a single light machine gun for defense. The plumbing that connected the flame gun to the fuel tanks inside limited the turret traverse to 170 degrees. (*National Archives*)

A Satan flame tank of D Company, 4th Tank Battalion, burns out a Japanese position on Saipan. The short range was a major tactical limitation of the light flame tanks. (*Marine Corps Historical Center*)

Tanks of Ed Bale's A Company and Satan flame tanks of D Company, 2nd Tank Battalion, support infantry in the advance down into the rough ground north of Mount Tapotchau on Saipan, 7 July 1944. (*National Archives*)

A jeep ambulance on Saipan. Wounded men like Doug Crotts faced a long, rough ride down mountain roads in one of these contraptions. (*National Archives*)

A rifle squad warily follows Max English's *King Kong* into the rough terrain of northern Saipan, 8 July 1944. Note the camouflaged turret, the water tank visible above the wading stack, and the squad leader talking on the phone attached to the left rear of the tank. (*National Archives*)

A Satan flame tank and two M5A1 light tanks of D Company, 4th Tank Battalion, near Marpi Point on northern Saipan. The Satans were very vulnerable to attack by infantry, and the obsolete M5A1s were assigned to protect them. (*National Archives*)

Tanks of C Company, 2nd Tank Battalion, landing over the narrow White Beaches on Tinian. (*National Archives*)

In the thick cane fields the infantry was forced to stick close to the tanks to protect them from suicidal attackers. The markings on this tank, C-22 and *Comet*, indicate the platoon sergeant of Mac McMillian's 2nd Platoon, C Company, 2nd Tank Battalion. (*Marine Corps Historical Center*)

Ill Wind, Bob Neiman's command tank for C Company, 4th Tank Battalion, advances through a Tinian cane field on 23 July 1944. Note the wooden armor on the sides, a layer of concrete over the slope plate, and the sponson antenna. (*National Archives*)

A rear view of *Ill Wind* shows the water tank on the rear deck, and an air-recognition panel draped over the turret. The tow cable attached to the wading trunk is very unusual. (*National Archives*)

An unusual overhead view of 2nd Tank Battalion vehicles. The cart towed by the jeep is being used to carry ammunition. (*National Archives*)

Caesar, from C Company, 2nd Tank Battalion, leads a column of SPMs and Satans. On the very open terrain of Tinian the tanks and infantry were exposed to long-range artillery, mortar, and machine-gun fire. (*National Archives*)

An infantry assault squad hugs the cover of a C Company, 2nd Tank Battalion, vehicle during the attack against the cliffs that ring the southern plateau of Tinian. (*National Archives*)

Goldbrick Jr. from the 4th Tank Battalion below the cliffs of southern Tinian. (*National Archives*)

The crew of *Goldbrick Jr.* displays the results of a hit by a Japanese anti-tank gun on the lower corner of the gun mantlet. Note the effect of the "splash" around the penetration. (*National Archives*)

CHAPTER 10

A POINT OF HONOR: GUAM

T HE MARIANAS are one of the most strategically located island groups in the Pacific, and the big southernmost island of Guam is the most strategically located of all. For the United States naval services the third objective in the Marianas also had emotional significance. It had been the first piece of United States territory to fall to the Japanese, the largest part of America ever to be occupied by an enemy, and held the largest captive population of American citizens.

Forty-two years of American rule had been relatively benevolent, especially as compared to the isolation and forced population relocation that characterized the German and later the Japanese occupation of the rest of the island chain. The American military presence was always small, and even after the escalation of tensions in the Pacific, and clear indications of impending Japanese aggression, an isolationist Congress had refused to "antagonize" Japan by improving military positions on the island. In December 1941 the defensive capability was vested in 125 officers and men at the Marine Barracks on the Orote Peninsula south of Apra Harbor, 28 Marines of the Insular Patrol, and 80 native policemen. This small force was no match for the 6,000 veteran soldiers of the attack force that swooped down from Saipan on 8 December. The Governor, Navy Captain George McMillan, ordered the garrison to submit to spare civilian lives.

The Japanese never bothered to fortify Guam, or indeed to occupy the island in force until the fall of the Marshalls in late 1943. The Japanese high command transferred the *18th* and *38th Regiments*, and two companies of the *9th Tank Regiment* to the island, followed by the reorganized *48th Independent Mixed Brigade* (four battalions) and the *10th Independent Mixed Regiment* (three battalions). In addition to the infantry's antitank guns, the *52nd Field Anti-Aircraft Battalion* con-

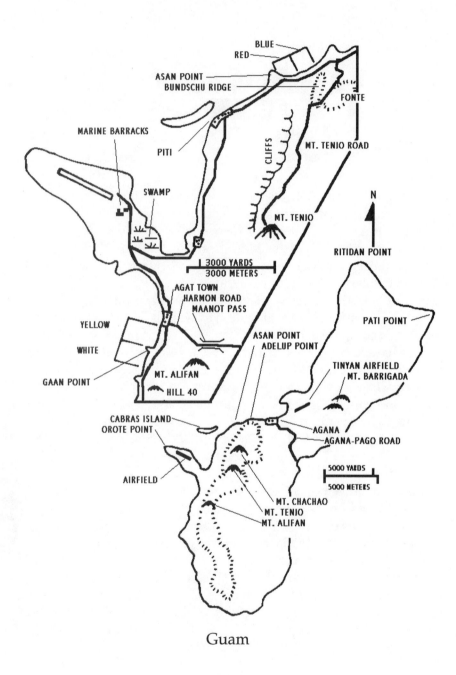

Guam

trolled eight Type 88 guns. Naval troops included about 5,000 men of the *54th Keibitai* with 30 more antitank guns and artillery, and another 2,000 naval aviation personnel hastily trained and armed to defend the now-useless airfields. The *1st Company* (15 light tanks), and *2nd Company* (14 medium tanks) of the *9th Tank Regiment* were both attached to the *48th Independent Mixed Brigade*, and the independent *24th Tank Company* controlled nine light tanks.

All forces were under the tactical command of Lieutenant General Takeshi Takashina, commander of the *29th Division*. Takashina's superior, Lieutenant General Hideyoshi Obata, commander of the *31st Army* was also on Guam, but left routine conduct of the battle to Takashina.

Numerous reefs restricted the number of potential landing sites. The Guam beaches were also one of the few places where the Japanese constructed heavy vehicle obstacles, four-foot cubic cribs of coral rubble, linked by steel cables.[1] The areas between the cribs were seeded with mines. Both sides knew that the landings would have to be made somewhere between Agana Bay and Facpi Point on the western coast. The Japanese gambled on Agat Bay, and placed the *1st Company* of the *9th Tank Regiment*, two battalions of the *38th Regiment*, and a company from the *10th Independent Mixed Regiment* in back of the beaches. The *3rd Battalion, 18th Regiment* and several other mixed units would defend the area north of Apra Harbor. The balance of the tank forces were stationed inland, where they could move along the road net to counterattack landings.

From the high, cliff-ringed Orote Peninsula, site of the old Marine barracks, the *Keibitai* could use their artillery to dominate the beaches in Agat Bay, and completely deny the use of Apra Harbor to the Americans. The peninsula was also the site of the better of the two airfields on Guam.

The strongest defenses were on the southern landing beaches—Yellow-1 and -2, and White-1 and -2—in Agat Bay. Gaan Point was perfectly positioned to enfilade the landing beaches, protruding into the boundary between the Yellow and White beaches. Undetected positions on the Point housed two 75mm guns and a 37mm antitank gun under a heavy concrete roof. Detachments on the small islands along the southern boundary of the beaches could fire into the rear of the assault waves. The beaches themselves were heavily seeded with mines and backed by a deep antitank ditch.

The American attack was originally set for 18 June, but when the 27th Division was committed to the fighting on Saipan the attack was delayed until late July. Major General Roy S. Geiger, USMC commanded the III Amphibious Corps, made up of the 3rd Marine Division, the 1st Provisional Marine Brigade, and the Army's 77th Infantry Division.

The 1st Provisional Marine Brigade was formed on Guadalcanal in March 1944. The rifle regiments were the 22nd Marines, who fought on Eniwetok in the Marshalls, and the 4th Marines. The original 4th Marines, formed in 1911, had been surrendered at Corregidor, and the new 4th was built around a tough core of battle-hardened infantry from the disbanded Raider Battalions. Able Company was excised from the 3rd Tank Battalion to become Tank Company, 9th Marines, and then transferred again to become Tank Company, 4th Marines.[2]

The American onslaught began in early May with attacks by the Army Air Force, and the first carrier raid struck the island on 11 June, followed on 16 June by the first naval shelling. On 8 July the bombardment quickened in tempo.

At 0530 hours on W-day, 21 July, the liberation of Guam began with a two-hour shelling. All this bombardment was not as effective as its executors had hoped. The size of the island diluted the effort, and the defenders had prepared well, if belatedly.

The 4th Marines were assigned the two right-hand beaches, with the 22nd Marines on their left. When the LVTs crawled across the exposed reef, the enemy artillery revealed itself with a telling fire. The guns on Gaan Point raked the troop carriers of the 22nd Marines, blasting apart 24 of the heavily loaded tractors in the first wave. Crossfire from Gaan Point and Yono Island punished the 4th Marines.

The worst problem for the tanks was the deep water. Phil Morell, commander of Tank Company, 4th Marines, recalled that the pre-invasion intelligence had failed to recognize a saucer-reef, with a raised lip and deeper water between the reef edge and shore: "I had a lieutenant, six-foot six-inch Jim Williams, who was also a competitive swimmer in college. He got out of the tank, and jumped up and down with his hand held up so that the tanks wouldn't dip into a big shell crater or something like that. The only tank that conked out on the way in was my own tank."

Harry Harrison, one of Morell's men: "The biggest casualties were among the troop-carrying amphibious tractors ... They were really clobbered." For the most part the tanks were able to shrug off the fire that devastated the tractors, but the enormous improvised mines were more deadly. "One tank got hit with a big 200-pound bomb that was set down inside a well with just the detonator sticking out. It turned it upside down and killed everybody inside. A two hundred-pound bomb right under a tank is just awful, because that's the most vulnerable part of the tank. It's got no armor."

The landing plan called for the troop carriers to move a thousand yards inland before disembarking the Marines, but the LVTs stalled on the beach, unable to cross the tank ditch. Long-range machine-gun and mortar fire raked the troops as they dismounted. The 22nd Marines in particular were inundated with fire from the town of Agat and the high ground below Mount Alifan, with very heavy casualties. On the extreme left 1/22 pushed inland, and by 1030 had secured the ruins of the town. On their right 2/22 was halted short of the Mount Alifan foothills, and anticipating a quick and powerful enemy armored counterattack, established strong blocking positions astride the Old Agat Road leading north out of the town.

One of the first items of business for the tanks was elimination of the deadly guns that raked White-1. Fifty years later Phil Morell toured the landing beaches, which were little changed:

A little row of rocks went out at the southern edge of our beach. It extended out about 50 yards or so. There was a machine gun in there that was raking the landing craft when they came in.

When we got the tanks onto the beach so we could traverse the turrets, we knocked that out and then went inland. I kept getting a call from Colonel Shapley, the commanding officer of the 4th Marines, to get a gun that was up on top of Mount Alifan that was picking off the landing craft ... It was in a cave. Mount Alifan was a kind of red clay mountain. They had some doors on that cave, and the doors were plastered with that same red clay. These doors would open, and the gun would come out, fire about three rounds, and go back in.

I got so damned frustrated. I couldn't see it through the periscopes, so I got out of my tank, inland maybe a couple of hundred yards. I'm out there with just a shoulder-holstered pistol, and here came about 30 Japs over this little grass ridge right in front of me. I thought "Oh, shit! Here I am with a 45 pistol in my hand." The tank saw them right away, and they just took them out.

Then a very strange thing happened. A corporal from the 22nd Marines that was to our left ... came up to me and said, "Hey, Phil." He was a kid that sat next to me in a U. S. History class in Virginia High School, Virginia, Minnesota … Here he comes up and says, "I know where that gun is."

[Morell had his tank fire a white phosphorus round onto the mountainside, and the rifleman talked the gun onto the target. Morell radioed the other tanks to stand by.] Sure enough the cave door opened, and out comes this gun. All 18 tanks cut loose, and it was something else. There were boots with legs in them flying out, and pieces of the gun, helmets, and everything else. We slaughtered that thing, and that's what really saved the beachhead that day.

Tank Company, 22nd Marines had landed in the 4th Marines' zone and moved along the beach to join its parent unit. As an unexpected benefit, it moved behind Gaan Point, and by 1330 that position had been eliminated by an attack from the landward side. On the south the 4th Marines cleared Bangi Point, and an unexpected seesaw struggle for a position known as Hill 40 began. This isolated knob overlooked the beaches and was studded with machine guns. The position was finally subdued with the support of the 4th's reserve battalion and tanks. The 4th Marines also blocked the Harmon Road, leading southeast from the town, where it snaked through a pass on the north flank of Mount Alifan.

The two assault regiments dug in for the night along a 6,000-yard front, and Morell's three platoons separated to cover the most likely routes for enemy counterattacks. One went to the south end near the beachhead, another inland in the center, and one to the Harmon Road blocking position.[3] The beachhead was perilously small, and Bob Botts remembers that they were dug in so close to the beach that "when the tide came in we had water in the bottom of the foxhole."

Takashina's command post was in a cave overlooking Asan Town, and the 3rd Marine Division's landings distracted Takashina's attention. The landing beaches were, from left to right, Red-1 and Red-2 (3rd Marines), Green (21st Marines), and Blue (9th Marines). It was obvious that the 3rd Marines had the toughest task, since the Chonito Cliffs dominated the Red beaches. The 21st Marines were faced with lower but still formidable bluffs farther back from the beaches.

The 3rd Division's landings were at first a textbook operation, and troops were ashore on all beaches by 0833 hours. The 21st Marines pushed rapidly ahead, and in an incredible stroke of fortune discovered two broad, undefended ravines that led to the top of the bluffs.

On the Red beaches things began to go terribly wrong for the 3rd Marines. The supporting Shermans of C Company, 3rd Tank were the first tanks ashore at about 0900 hours. On the exposed reef edge the LCMs carrying the tanks had to be held in place by LVTs connected to the LCMs by cables.[4] Vehicular and foot traffic snarled on the narrow beaches under a deluge of observed mortar fire from the Chonito Cliffs and the positions on Adelup Point. The first task for C Company tanks was to eliminate these positions.

The Japanese garrison of a small rock pile that protruded into the sea between Red-1 and Red-2 held out throughout the day, and split the 3rd Marines' front. The 3rd Battalion, supported by C Company tanks and armored amphibians, moved along the beach, fought their way up and onto the cliffs that connected the bluffs to Adelup Point, and by midafternoon were on the point.

Despite this local success the left flank was teetering on the edge of disaster. By midafternoon medical supplies were running short, and there were not even enough stretchers to drag away the wounded.

The beaches exposed to fire from above are fixed in the minds of the men who landed there. As a company first sergeant, G. G. Sweet split his time between the front lines and the company command post. "What really stuck in my mind ... we had just a little narrow beach ... We had no place to go but on this beach, and there were cliffs on three sides and ocean on the other side. The cliffs were full of snipers, and people in the CP had it worse than the tanks out in combat the first couple of days. We were losing more people at the CP due to these snipers in these little cave holes."

The deadliest enemy positions were on a small rocky spur that extended from highlands behind the Chonito Cliffs. Able Company, 1/3 seized a position near the crest of the spur early in the day, but was so badly mauled that the commander requested permission to withdraw. Unwilling to give up this tiny parcel of high ground, Regiment ordered an afternoon attack in coordination with E Company, 2nd Battalion. The attack reached the crest but was driven back with heavy losses. This small ridge became known as Bundschu Ridge, for a dead infantry company commander, and would be a critical focus of the fighting for several more days.

The inability of the 3rd Marines to clear the heights exposed the 21st to an enfilade fire, preventing them from fully exploiting their position atop the bluffs. Only on the extreme right were things going well, as the 9th Marines and accompanying tanks pushed rapidly along the coast toward Apra Harbor. At nightfall the division held a sizable beachhead, but one in which enemy-held salients reached perilously close to the beaches.

The main counterattack against the 1st Brigade beachhead beach was launched by Colonel Tsunetaro Suenaga's *38th Regiment*. Suenaga had badgered General Takashina into approving the counterattack against his better judgment.[5] It was a typically Japanese counterstroke, undertaken by three essentially independent groups. Suenaga would personally lead one battalion, supported by five Type 95 tanks, down the Harmon Road against a roadblock set up by B/1/4.

The *3/38th* tried to recapture Hill 40 in the darkness. The enemy attacked K/3/4 at 2130 hours without the usual preliminary probes, and broke through the Marine perimeter on the low ground east of the hill. Some drove for the beaches while the main force turned to attack the hill from the rear, setting off an all night struggle for the hill.

Bypassed Japanese also emerged from hiding, and there were attacks everywhere that night, like the one that fell upon Harold Harrison's platoon in the south:

> We weren't combat experienced, and they were in a hidden cave … A little over a dozen of them came out. They were small guys, wrapped in gauze. You really had to put 'em down. I remember them being so small, because we had to carry them down to graves registration, where they bulldozed them [into a mass grave]. They were wrapped in gauze, so they were sort of a suicidal thing.
>
> They tried to get into the tanks, but they didn't have any tank-destroying stuff on 'em, like on Okinawa … This group just had small arms and Nambus, automatic weapons. They were just sent there to cause trouble … because there was no other reason than getting killed. That's all they could have done. They could have wreaked a lot of havoc, but they started right at dawn. As soon as it got light, they were all put down. It sort of scared me, I can tell you that.

Bob Botts: "The next morning we got up there were 37 dead Japs in there, 28 dead soldiers, and we lost two guys. They set three tanks on fire." Company commander Phil Morell, with the central platoon:

> The line on a map looks like "Oh, yea. We can hold that with a regiment," but with the up and down of the hills there were gaps in the lines.

There was a little mound with grass on it, and a few tiny little trees, right in front of us. A platoon of Japs came down that night. It was not a natural mound, but a whole bunch of ammunition with sod put on top. We thought maybe they were 4th Marines going back for ammunition. They didn't know the password, but we still said hold your fire.

That was my call ... I guess I should have just blasted when we saw movement out there, but we had just had some people come down, almost the identical pathway, maybe over 15 or 20 yards, to go back and get ammunition from the 4th Marines. We withheld our fire.

They set a magnetic mine on my tank—it did no damage—and threw a Molotov Cocktail on another tank that started a fire. These were diesel tanks, and the crew put it out with their utility coats. We started firing, and when daylight came up, we just had one tank there. We took the machine gun and sprayed it, so we wiped them out.

Along the Harmon Road preliminary probes began about 2130 hours, and at 2330 Suenaga's main force attacked the roadblock. Phil Morell: "About two in the morning, they heard—coming up Harmon Road—mechanized noises ... it was blackout, and it's very difficult to move tanks at night, particularly with those periscopes. They didn't have the direct vision cupolas then. He [the tall Lieutenant, James R. Williams] held up his radium dial wristwatch and led this one tank up to sort of a junction, sort of a trail."

The enemy tanks rattled blindly down the road into the infantry lines, and into the sights of PFC Bruno Orbiletti's bazooka. Orbiletti hit two of the tanks before being killed.[6] In the pitch-black night the opposing tanks could not see each other. "The gunner was firing [the coaxial machine gun] at the noise," said Morell, "and the tracers started to go straight up," ricocheting off the enemy tank. "He had a 75 shell in, so he let that go. It sounds like a big deal, but it blew the turret off the first Jap tank, and set it afire. It lit up four more Jap tanks following. He got the next three tanks. Shorty Whitcombe his name was, knocked out four tanks. The last tank in column—there was kind of a little bump there—he turned around and started down into this valley. [He] went across the valley and up the other side. At daylight, Shorty got that tank. That was 2,240 yards, because I paced it off the next day."

On the left the remaining enemy battalion attacked the hill line east of Agat Town, briefly breaking through to threaten a battalion command post and artillery positions. Suenaga was killed, and the *38th* essentially destroyed as a tactical unit. Counterattacks against the 3rd Division failed to drive the Marines off the high ground.

Starting at 1150 hours on 22 July the 3rd Marines hammered at Bundschu Ridge, committing another rifle company to the attack. By 1900 hours E/3/3 was on the ridge crest to stay, but the rock pile had cost the regiment 615 casualties. Even as the Japanese resisted attacks up the face of the cliffs, they continued to pound the exposed flank of the 21st Marines, forcing the relief of the leftmost battalion.

The 9th Marines pushed south to link up with the 1st Brigade, finding most of the enemy coastal positions abandoned, and entered the old American naval yard at Piti. The 3rd Battalion launched an assault to seize Cabras Island, the low sandbar that forms the northern side of Apra Harbor. That night a small Japanese attack was directed against 1/21 in the center of the expanding perimeter, but the absence of any significant enemy reaction to the 3rd Division's advance was both puzzling and disturbing.

On 23 July the 3rd Marines pushed farther up onto the high ground above Bundschu Ridge, only to find that the enemy had withdrawn into the tangle of brushy ravines on the high ground of the Fonte Plateau.

The 1st Brigade established a perimeter extending along the crest of the ridge north and south of Mount Alifan, and controlled Maanot Pass, where the Harmon Road crosses the crest. Their main effort was to extend the perimeter north toward the 9th Marines, pushing Japanese stragglers into Orote Peninsula as the freshly-arrived 305th Infantry moved north along the ridge from Maanot Pass.

Efforts by the 22nd Marines to close off the Orote Peninsula were blocked by strong positions on the far side of broad rice paddies impassable to the tanks, and two tanks were immobilized in the mud and then disabled by enemy fire. At 0900 on 25 July 1/22 attacked up the Agat-Sumay Road that skirted the south coast of the peninsula, where a counterattack by five Japanese tanks was driven off by Tank Company, 22nd Marines.

Patrols from the 3rd and 22nd Marines established tenuous contact in the hills behind the neck of the Orote Peninsula. Casualties in the rifle battalions had been enormous, and the Marines and soldiers were stretched too thin to adequately defend the expanding perimeter. Even after 2/4 moved into the line after dark the defensive line across the neck of the peninsula was in actuality a series of company perimeters separated by broad gaps.

Rather than fritter away his resources, Takashina was avoiding contact while he assembled a large striking force. By 25 July he had assembled nearly 5,000 men in the hills along the Mount Tenjo Road. Because of the rugged western slope of the hills, this dead-end road branched off the coastal road east of Adelup Point, climbed the Fonte Plateau from the north, and snaked along the topographic divide parallel to the coast for some 6,000 yards to the crest of Mount Tenjo. The Japanese could use the road for quick lateral movement, while the Americans struggled in the tangle of brushy cliffs below. Takashina also took care to coordinate his attack with the trapped defenders on the Orote Peninsula. This time there was no Suenaga to goad him into premature action.

This caution did not preclude well-executed spoiling attacks. An early morning counterattack, led by eight Japanese tanks, was driven back by bazookas and the Shermans of Tank Company, 22nd Marines.

Unaware of Takashina's plan, the 3rd Division was struggling to expand the northern perimeter, and 2/9 was attached to the depleted 3rd Marines for a renewed attack on the Fonte highlands. At 1900 hours 2/9 cut the road where it climbed the northern slope of the Fonte Plateau, but the battalion was exposed on both flanks and critically short of ammunition. F Company, on the left, pulled back to a more defensible position, followed by G Company at 2200 hours. Four tanks from C Company, 3rd Tank Battalion scrabbled up the steep slopes, engine decks loaded with crates of small arms ammunition. The commander of one of the rifle companies used the powerful tank radios to call in naval gunfire, and arranged for artillery and naval gunfire to register on the areas to his front.

South of Asan town the 21st Marines, with tanks from B Company in support, fought their way through a series of enemy cave defenses, and the 2/21 also cut the Mount Tenjo Road. The supporting tanks worked their way up a twisting footpath to a position above a steep ravine. On the far right the other two battalions of the 9th Marines had pushed farther than expected down the coast, and without its 2nd Battalion that regiment was badly overextended. To meet Takashina's offensive the Marines were thinly spread and stood with their backs to a cliff. Isolated outposts made up long sectors of the line.

As casualties among the tank crews mounted G. G. Sweet took the place of a wounded tank commander in C Company: "When my Gunnery Sergeant (C. C. Churchill) was shot at Fonte Ridge, I replaced him. We were every other day in the CP or in the tanks. It's the way this Julius Octave Lemke ran the company; everybody had to get a little bit. When he was shot, I stayed with the tanks." In the late afternoon sun Sweet was forward of the lines on the western end of Fonte Ridge: "I sat with binoculars, in a tank, and watched the Japs get ready, in the late afternoon, to attack us in the morning. They were all drunker'n hell, and singing songs, and hollering 'banzai' and everything. Way across the ridge, they were under a big water tower." Artillery fire was called down to break up the party.

The usual practice for the tank crews at night was to dig a hole, drive the tank over the hole, and drop open the escape hatch on the bottom of the tank. The crew could sleep safely in the hole, and if attacked in the night, quickly scramble up into the tank. That night "we just tied right in to the friendly lines. We would dig right in under the tank, set up two machine guns, and sleep there with one man awake, the guy manning the turret."

The 77th Infantry Division had relieved the 1st Brigade in the defense of the hill line above Agat Bay, and the Brigade marched north to help close off the neck of the Orote Peninsula. Phil Morell said that before they moved out "the Navy flyboys came down, and kept bombing the tank that was out in front of the lines, all day long … I got on the channel, which I was not supposed to do, and I said 'Hey, you birds. That was knocked out long before you started over.'"

The night of 25-26 July was rainy and unusually dark. Artillery and mortar observers reported enemy movement along the fronts of the 9th and 21st Marines, and soon artillery and mortar fire began to fall along the 3rd Division front. The enemy probed the front with small attacks, and there was especially heavy activity along the boundary between the 9th and 21st Marines. No one thought much of such pin-pricks, but they represented the Japanese tactic of reconnaissance by attack. The probes against 2/9 grew in violence, and by 0100 the battalion was under full-scale attack.

At 0400 seven Japanese battalions struck in one of the most concerted counterattacks of the Pacific war, and by 0430 the 3rd Division was fully engaged along its entire overextended front. The heaviest blow fell on the boundary between the 21st and 9th Marines.

The most severe rupture occurred when B/1/21 was overwhelmed, leaving only 18 survivors. On either flank of the penetration A and C Companies drew back and the enemy poured in, only to encounter the crest of the cliffs behind. Caught with the enemy in this three-sided deathtrap were the tanks of the 1st and 2nd Platoons of B

Company. Moving in through their own artillery fire to attack the tanks, the frenzied enemy for some reason did not use the magnetic mines and satchel charges they had brought with them.

Louis Spiller had taken over as tank commander when Lieutenant Warden was wounded by mortar fire earlier in the afternoon:[7]

As often happens in the tropics, night came upon us suddenly and it became too dark to negotiate the narrow twisting road back down to our company command post. The tank crew, made up of PFC Smith, assistant driver; Cpl. Herbert Parmenter, radio man; PFC Schaeffer, gunner; and myself, a sergeant and now tank commander assigned to Lt. Charlie Kirkham's 2nd Platoon. This made a total of seven tanks, which we formed into a semi-circle with our backs to the ridge.

It was a new experience for us as tankers to get stuck out by ourselves in enemy territory without infantry dug in around us. It's the nature of tanks to not be very good at defending themselves from an enemy that is positioned too close. The enemy has a nasty habit of throwing gasoline fire bombs at them. Realizing this, we were prepared for a long night. Things were quiet for the first few hours but then about 2330 some Jap flares started to fall in between our own flares that had been fired intermittently. We began to see Japs silhouetted against the skyline.

I checked with the platoon leader to see what our next move would be and he radioed to commence firing. We fired our .30-caliber machine guns and 75mm cannon at anything that moved, knowing that our own Marines would not be out moving around in this situation. Some Japs slipped around our flanks and came up from our rear. Two of them set up a machine-gun nest right under the rear of our tank. We could hear them talking in Japanese and firing their machine gun in short bursts.

About this time I was wondering what to do about these two fellows as I looked out the driver's periscope at the unbelievable sight of some Japs charging the tanks with drawn sabers. All of this was illuminated by flares and star shells of different colors, fired by the Japs to signal their attack. Suddenly it got quiet and I saw a high explosive artillery shell explode about a foot from my periscope on the front slope plate. In rapid succession, another round hit. The explosion shattered my periscope and left me temporarily blinded from the flash. The shock of the explosion jarred the escape hatch loose and it fell down on the ground behind where the assistant driver sat.

And so there I sat in the driver's seat, not able to see, with two Japs under the tank that I had to eliminate before they decided to throw a hand grenade through our open escape hatch or to throw us a fire bomb or demolition charge. I knew that moving the tank in the dark would be dangerous as I wasn't sure how much distance lay between the rear of our tank and the edge of the cliff that dropped several hundred feet off to the gully below. Knowing that something had to be done quickly, I pulled the tank forward a few yards, then put it in reverse with one track locked. The tank spun halfway around, crushing the two Japs and their machine gun.

All night long the Japs came at us but we held our positions. When daylight finally came, we picked our way back through hundreds of dead Japs, back to our company headquarters to refuel and replenish our dwindling ammunition supply. Thus ended the longest night of my life.[8]

Marine rifle company positions held, some under repeated and continuous attacks that lasted well into the morning hours, but small positions and outposts were simply overwhelmed. Dozens of attack parties flowed around the isolated company perimeters. Once through the front the attack lost coherency. One large party recoiled from the defenders of the division hospital. The command posts of the division and 21st Marines were similarly assailed. Other attackers made for supply and ammunition dumps, and all night long the defensive parties from the Pioneer Battalion and shore party personnel fought dozens of small battles in the wet darkness.

On the neck of the Orote Peninsula the first attack came at 1030 hours from behind a mangrove swamp and along the Piti-Sumay Road that led toward the old Marine Barracks. The attack included a bizarre procession with a color guard in full dress uniform. Drunken Japanese officers charged American tanks brandishing swords, but more stealthy attacks killed Marines in their holes before they were aware of the attack. The Marines laid down a barrage that swept to and fro across their front, smashing this and subsequent attacks.

At first light on 26 July the Marines moved out to take advantage of the debilitation and disorganization that plagued the Japanese after their all-out night attacks. The two surviving companies of the 21st sealed off the breach atop the cliffs, and 3rd Division reserve and service troops hunted down isolated parties of the enemy throughout the division rear.

The 1st Brigade's primary goal was to secure the Orote Peninsula, freeing the beachheads from artillery harassment and securing the use of the harbor. Support was provided by both regimental tank companies and by the Army's 706th Tank Battalion.

The 26 July attack against the peninsula was immediately rocked back by heavy small arms and artillery fire, but by 0830 the Marines were again moving forward. The north and south coast roads converged about 1,250 yards forward of the start line, passing along a 200-yard long causeway between the mangrove swamp and an open marsh. North of the road the advance by the 22nd Marines was blocked by tangled mangrove swamp bristling with defenders. As 1/22 veered left onto the roadway, it came under terrific flanking fire from the swamp. The tanks carefully edged along a narrow strip of passable ground north of the road, drawing the bulk of the enemy fire and blasting any positions they could locate.

Both regimental tank companies were tied to this road, with Phil Morell's Tank Company, 4th Marines in trail. "The Tank Company 22nd was moving out ahead of us. They met five Jap tanks, and same thing—knocked them all out."

Terrain in the 4th Marines' sector on the left was more amenable, but the regiment held back to stay aligned with the 22nd, and because the tanks were blocked by a minefield. At nightfall both units dug in along a new line, but in all-around company defenses. There were too many bypassed enemy positions in the swamps and marshes.

The 3rd Division concentrated on rooting out the survivors of the nocturnal attack, and securing better defensive ground on the Fonte highlands and ridges. In the rough, brush-covered ridges there were unnumbered small attacks and counterattacks. G. G. Sweet: "I was in a tank that a Jap officer put a sword through the crack in the top of the tank, and broke it off. I had about eight inches of blade in there, the rest of it went with the Jap, because everybody in my platoon shot him off my tank with .30 calibers. Whenever we would get in a scrap and people would be coming in to put these different types of bombs that they would stick on the sides of your tanks on long sticks,* we just would spray each other. We would call the platoon and tell them 'Boy, scratch my back.' They would just spray the hell out of us, but watching out that they didn't knock our periscopes out. We never did [lose any tanks to the suicide charges], but there were a lot lost."

---

* Satchel charges were used to attack the thinner armor around hatches and the engine deck. The Japanese learned that an attacker would often be shot down while trying to climb aboard the tank. One tactic was to attach the charge to a pole, and place the charge from ground level.[9]

On 27 and 28 July, the 1st Brigade pushed toward the old Marine Barracks. The tanks supporting the 4th Marines advanced along the tops of the cliffs that made up the south coast, and on the north, the 22nd breached the minefield and cleared the back side of the mangrove swamp. Both regiments halted along an overgrown road short of the old rifle range.

Inland two battalions of the 9th Marines pushed slowly up the steep slopes of Mount Chachao, in a struggle that would continue until 29 July. The terrain objectives had been modified, and the 77th Division moved up and onto the slopes of Mount Tenjo at the insistence of Major General Andrew D. Bruce. Bruce wanted to avoid committing his division piecemeal. On 29 July 1/9 made contact with Army troops in the saddle between the mountains.

Takashina was trying to deal with the consequences of his big counterattack. Among the dead were 96 percent of his officers, including the commander of the *48th Independent Mixed Brigade.* He tried to extricate his forces from the Fonte high ground, hard-pressed by 2/9. Takashina was killed by a C Company tank as he tried to manage the withdrawal from Fonte. By 1500 hours the Marines had stopped along a power line right-of-way, and the enemy was allowed to break contact.

General Obata assumed tactical command, but destruction of so many units, and leadership casualties, spelled the end of serious Japanese resistance. Obata had managed to extricate his remaining force only because General Geiger had decided to rest his troops and await the destruction of the enemy on the Orote Peninsula.

In the predawn hours of 28 July all available American artillery and naval guns relentlessly shelled the remainder of the Orote Peninsula, and the infantry advance began at 0830. Japanese survivors staged a hopeless defense in the thick underbrush and buildings.

The Marines asked for and received a platoon of Army tank destroyers and another of light tanks to support the afternoon advance. At 1530 the brigade was again stopped by the Japanese defense along a line through the old barracks complex and down to Sumay town. Mines were still the deadliest threat, and in the ruins of Sumay Town one Sherman and its crew were lost to a mine augmented by a 1,000-pound bomb.

On 29 July the Army and Marines laid on another stunning bombardment, and surged forward through a suddenly demoralized defense. Morell's tank company had the central role:

We were attacking toward the old Marine Barracks, which was just the frame, a couple of steel pieces stuck up there, and the airport. We had quite a battle moving up to the airport.

There were a series of bunkers, coconut logs with dirt piled on top and so on. An airplane flying over would not see these things, because they had mud on the top, but they were very easy to spot. They didn't have little apertures to look out. Visualize a hot dog stand at a football game. They had a big window in front, open, maybe a foot and a half high and six or eight feet long. There were several Japanese in [each of] them, six to eight maybe ... There were several of these in a pattern designed to defend the airfield.

We fought through those bunkers and got up to the tip of the airstrip ... Colonel Shapley ... got in one of my tanks and said, "Drive me down to the tip." I said, "What about mines?" But he said, "Just go!" We whipped down to the end of the airfield.

He got on his radio and called back to one of the battalions. He [the battalion commander] said, "Oh, we're meeting resistance up here." He [Shapley] says, "Goddamnit, I'm at the tip of the airfield, and you're at the other end of it. Just get your men up and run down here!" They raced down there like they were running a track meet.

Shapley then ordered Morell on what the official history called a combat reconnaissance:

He sent me on a little trail to the very tip of Orote Peninsula. Just as I'm ready to go out in the attack, I had my plans all laid that each platoon to go down a little trail peeling off as the main trail went down to the tip, I get a call from Shapley. He says, "Phil, I'm giving you 34 Army tanks." I don't know where they came from. I didn't even know they were in our sector. They were light tanks, not mediums. I just hooked them onto our tanks, and we went to the tip of the Peninsula.

There were a handful of Japs out there, 20 or less. They had an anti-aircraft gun, and I hooked on to that—it was on a sled—and we pulled it back.

All the way back I'm getting calls from Colonel Shapley. When I get my tank back to where my radio jeep was, my jeep driver says, "You gotta talk to him right away."

The company's only support vehicle was Morell's jeep, equipped with a red light and siren.[10] "Shapley had run over to where my jeep was. He hopped in the jeep and says 'Drive over there.' I drove over there and there was a little formation of General Shepherd, Colonel 'Red Dog' Snyder, and Colonel Shapley. Suddenly a spotter plane came in and landed on the airport, and out came Admiral Spruance and 'Howling Mad' Smith ... They raised the flag, on a flagpole strapped to one of the beams of the old Marine Barracks."

Despite the fall of Orote only about a quarter of the enemy strength had been eliminated. Obata continued the withdrawal into the mountainous northern reaches of the island. Patrols from the 77th Division scoured the southern part of the island, finding only Japanese stragglers who plagued the long-suffering civilian population.

Obata organized a series of delaying lines, blocking roads at critical points. The American drive to the north was organized with the 3rd Division on the left and the 77th Division on the right. This plan placed the only north-south road in the 3rd Division zone.

The final sweep to the north began at 0630 on 31 July, and by day's end the soldiers and Marines had reached the narrow neck of the island. When 3/3 secured the territorial capital of Agana they found a handful of Obata's stay-behinds in the rubble.

The paved Agana-Pago Road led east from the town, crossed the mountainous spine of the island, and descended the valley of the Pago River to the eastern coast. The 1st and 2nd Battalions, 3rd Marines advanced up the road from the town, and by late afternoon controlled the road east to the topographic divide, forcing their way past snipers and tanks left behind to delay the advance.

One encounter with an isolated tank was surreal, as if a Japanese tank crew had decided to commit collective suicide. The Japanese tank, with the wounded and bloody commander standing high in the turret hatch, roared down the road, through the surprised rifle line of the 21st Marines, and past a platoon of idling American tanks. The crew of platoon leader Lieutenant George Cavender's tank ran to their Sherman and gave chase, slowly overtaking the speeding enemy. The crew of the Sherman was reluctant to fire at the fleeing tank for fear of hitting hundreds of riflemen either resting or walking along the verge.

The Japanese tank raced past the files of gawking infantry without paying them the slightest attention, then suddenly veered off onto a secondary road and hid somewhere behind a line of underbrush on either side of a T intersection. The enemy tank apparently expected his pursuer to come through the gap at the upright of the T. Instead, Cavender took advantage of the relatively quiet sound of his M4A2 to creep around the end of the tree line, and surprised the would-be ambusher from the rear. Two HE rounds from the American tank racked the smaller tank, which throughout the action had never fired a single round.[11]

At nightfall the 77th Division lagged behind the 3rd Division, the corps line staggered back in a big Z-shaped curve. East of the mountains the rugged, trackless terrain hindered the advance of the 77th Division. Establishing complete control of the Agana-Pago Road was critical to resupply the 77th and evacuate their casualties.

On 1 August the 77th Division crossed the Pago River unopposed, and both divisions secured the remainder of the road. A backed-up torrent of artillery, tanks, and logistical vehicles poured over the pass into the 77th's zone, and the division quickly straightened the corps front.

Rumors circulating among the civilians suggested that the defenders had decamped for a new line of resistance extending from the town of Finegayan near the west coast, across the crest of Mount Barrigada, south through the town of the same name, then east to the coast. This line was anchored in high ground overlooking a valley that connects the two coasts.

While the 1st Brigade was hunting stragglers in the south, drenching rains came, and an odd and unexpected hazard. Phil Morell: "They had big frogs. I don't know where the hell they came from, but they would come out at night when all this rain came. They would plop in your foxhole, make a big 'Plop,' and you would get a little gun happy when you hear a bunch of those. There were so many of them that after a big rain they crossed the road and vehicles would run over them, and they would be slippery. Vehicles would slide and everything else."

The rains made life particularly miserable for the infantry. Bob Botts:

> When we would go up to the front in the morning, we would throw a couple of five gallon water cans and dump a box of rations back there in that exhaust manifold. By the time we got up there we had hot water and hot beans.

My platoon bought five cases of cigarettes on Guadalcanal, before we went up to Guam. You would see those poor devils trying to get a dry cigarette out of a pack and it had been raining most of the night. We would say "Hey, Mac. Where's your squad leader?"

He'd come over, and we'd say "How would you like a dry cigarette?" We would throw them a carton.

We'd give him the cigarettes, and say "Would you guys like to have a cup of coffee?"

"You shittin' us, Mac?"

"Nope. Get your canteens and your instant coffee. There's hot water in the back. There also a can of hot beans." They took pretty good care of us.

Late each afternoon patrols from the division Reconnaissance Company, mounted in radio jeeps, SPMs, and tanks advanced up to 6,000 yards into enemy territory, mapping possible axes of advance and centers of enemy resistance. Late on 1 August one such patrol pushed forward as far as the north end of the airfield at Tinyan, east of Agat Bay.

The American advance struck the Finegayan-Barriaga line on 2 August. In the early morning 12 tanks of the Army's 706th Tank Battalion led the 307th Regimental Combat Team into Barrigada town, and into a hornet's nest of enemy fire. Efforts by the 305th RCT to outflank the town proved fruitless. For two days the 77th pounded the town flat with artillery, air attacks, and repeated tank attacks, but not until nightfall on 4 August did the division control the town and the crest of the mountain behind. This savage resistance was prompted by control of the town well, one of the few sources of water left in Japanese hands.

In a bizarre repetition of the Agano–Pago Road incident, a Japanese tank broke through and raced past the command post of 1/3, the tank commander firing wildly with a pistol. The speeding tank overturned in a ditch, and the crew abandoned the tank before it was blown apart by an American tank.

On 3 August the 3rd and 9th Marines swept past the undefended Tinyan Airfield and bumped into the main defensive line at a road junction south of Finegayan. This enemy position turned out to be a platoon strongpoint, an outpost of the main line, which B/1/9 overran with the aid of two tanks. The main enemy positions commanded the crossroads west of the town and it took 1/9 and tanks until midafternoon to batter their way into the town.

Division ordered a strong motorized reconnaissance column to advance as far as possible toward the north cape of the island. This column included the Recon Company, Item/3/21, SPMs, and A Company and parts of HQ Company, 3rd Tank Battalion. The advance party consisted of two radio jeeps, a pair of SPMs, and a platoon of tanks, all under the command of Lieutenant Colonel Hartnoll Withers, the CO of the 3rd Tank Battalion. The patrol barely made it out of the Finegayan perimeter before it was ambushed by a battalion of enemy infantry, supported by 75mm guns and light tanks.

The enemy guns raked the road, destroying one SPM and damaging a tank and a truck. The patrol extricated itself under the cover of fire from artillery and tanks, and sensibly abandoned the mission. The Marines dug in along a line controlling the road junction, but they had not seen the last of the enemy tanks.

At 2130 hours two Type 97 tanks came clattering down the road from the northwest and one ran over a 37mm antitank gun positioned to defend the crossroads against just such a sortie. The two tanks milled about in the darkness, spraying machine-gun fire at random and without effect, then rumbled away to the northeast, unharmed. This impromptu raid may have been a premature foray by two tank commanders who just hadn't gotten the word, as it foretold an attack by other tanks and infantry that was broken up by artillery.

On 5 August the Army and Marines advanced against a demoralized and ineffective enemy. The following day 3rd Division paused to allow the 77th Division to come on line following the nasty struggle for Barrigada. The 3rd Division shifted to the right, and the 1st Brigade moved into the line to advance along the west coast.

Phil Morell: "We encountered a few guns along the road, which we easily knocked out. They were 37s and a few 57s.* The fighting was mostly gone and many of the Japs jumped off the cliffs to the left, or western side of Guam, to be killed down below in the surf."

Marching men could not keep pace, and detachments of riflemen were mounted on the tanks. "If we hit something, they would jump off and flank both sides. We wouldn't have them on the lead [tank].

---

* The Japanese 57mm was an obsolete low-velocity tank gun. Many World War II Marine tankers referred to the 47mm Type 01 as a 57mm, perhaps because of its similarity to the US 57mm gun.

I'd have a section of tanks, then I'd be the next tank, and then a platoon or two or three tanks behind that. Then a platoon—there were
five in a platoon then—with infantry loaded. The rest of the infantry
would come behind.

"I had all eighteen tanks with me, going in this little column. This
was a dirt road, but a pretty good road. Not an open maneuver place
generally . . ."

By contrast, the jungle inland was so dense that tanks supporting
the 9th Marines passed within 15 feet without being able to see each
other.

The 77th Division bore the brunt of the heavy fighting, particularly around Mount Santa Rosa, so they were given priority on artillery
fire. By noon of 7 August the 77th Division was in position to begin
the assault on the final enemy stronghold, built around the village of
Yigo and Mount Santa Rosa behind. By 1300 hours on 8 August the
77th Division had cleared the slopes of the mountain, and the 306th
Infantry swept through the rugged terrain west and north of the
mountain. Many Japanese slipped away toward Mount Mataguac,
along the boundary between the 3rd and 77th Division zones. An
effort by the 306th Infantry to pursue the enemy into this area was
repulsed by Japanese armor.

Enemy survivors began to infiltrate into the area faced by the 3rd
Division, where Obata had planned to make his final defense. Most
were killed or driven northward by the advance of the 9th Marines,
who advanced steadily toward Pati Point, the most northeasterly tip
of the island. The largest remaining enemy force chose to defend the
Savana Grande, a broad area covered with tall grass and scattered
copses of trees. Rather than face an enormous enemy force in this
nightmarish tangle, the 9th Marines called in an artillery barrage that
swept over the small plateau for hours.

At dusk on 8 August the 3rd Marines were in night defense on the
plateau about 2,000 yards inland from the coast, facing the last enemy
pocket. Obata launched a final anticlimactic counterattack in which a
half-dozen or so Type 97 tanks attacked 2/3 under cover of a heavy
mortar barrage. Marine bazooka rockets were ineffective, apparently
damaged by the continuous rains, and the Japanese tanks seemed
reluctant to close with the Marines. Both sides blazed away for about
half an hour, until the tanks withdrew with no loss on either side.
Such attacks provided evidence that many enemy troops, and an

uncomfortably large number of their tanks, remained unaccounted for in the wilderness areas.

The American command was eager to put an end to enemy resistance because dispirited as they might be, the enemy still found energy enough to punish the civilian population. On 7 August a patrol from the 21st Marines found the bodies of 30 civilians, all beheaded.

Harold Harrison remembered that in the dense underbrush these clearing operations presented their own hazards: "We never operated alone. We had infantry back of us. We never did lose radio contact. In that kind of operation, you had to have fire control, because you'd fire into somebody if you didn't. You had to know where everybody was at. We were the number one tank, and had good radios. The tank commander was usually a lieutenant.

"It was a good tank-infantry operation. We had the telephones on the back. If we saw some jungle there, you'd put canister in and just eliminate the jungle, just strip it. The infantry then could move forward."

The Brigade found only scattered stragglers on the northernmost part of the island, so at 1800 on 9 August, General Shepherd declared that part of the island secure.

At 0730 on the morning of 10 August 2/3, with a platoon of tanks in support, was ordered to eliminate the tank force that had attacked the infantry the night before. The narrow, twisting trails were better suited to the smaller enemy tanks, but the Shermans encountered two Type 97 tanks, and in a short and violent exchange of fire destroyed both. The enemy fled down the cliffs, and abandoned seven more Type 97 tanks in running order. When Geiger learned of the destruction of this last sizable force, he declared the end of organized resistance at 1131 hours.

He was barely ahead of the arrival of the cruiser *Indianapolis*, carrying Admiral Chester Nimitz and the Commandant of the Marine Corps, Lieutenant General Alexander Vandegrift. Nimitz intended to establish his forward headquarters on Guam, from where he would direct the final assault on Japan.

On the morning of 11 August the 306th Infantry, supported by Army tanks and engineer demolition squads, moved in on Mount Mataguac. By midafternoon the mountain was in American hands, Obata was dead, and the battle for Guam truly over.

The Americans had underestimated the number of disorganized enemy still at large, perhaps 10,000 in all. For weeks individuals and small bands continued to snipe at patrols and raid the civilians, but with most civilians in protective camps, their food situation became increasingly desperate. Many turned to raiding military dumps or wandered aimlessly. Over 8,500 such stragglers were killed, captured, or found dead of starvation, disease, or suicide.

CHAPTER 11

IN THE GORY OVEN:
PELELIU

P ELELIU is at once one of the least known and most controversial
battles of the Pacific war, fought at a time when the attention of
the America public was riveted on the advance of Eisenhower's
armies across western Europe and MacArthur's much-publicized
return to the Philippines. The small island was also the first major test
of a new Japanese defensive stratagem.

Capture of the Palaus had long been part of the naval strategy to
isolate the big Japanese base at Truk in the Carolines. MacArthur now
planned to invade the large southern island of Mindanao as the first
step in his return to the Philippines, and in 1944 began to clamor for
positions to protect his eastern flank. In Japanese hands the western
end of the Palau Island group would be a gun pointed at the back of
the Philippines invasion force.

The Japanese were convinced that the main American blow would
fall upon Babelthuap, their biggest base in the Palaus. The original
American plan did indeed call for capture of the entire Palau chain, but
Allied manpower was inadequate for such an ambitious undertaking.

In July 1944 Nimitz and MacArthur met with President Roosevelt
in Hawaii. The three agreed upon a coordinated plan that involved a
15 September landing in the Palaus. From the Palaus, land-based
American aircraft could neutralize Japanese naval efforts launched
against MacArthur across the vast Philippine Sea. The big enemy
base at Babelthuap would be isolated.

X-Ray Provisional Amphibious Corps, consisting of the 1st Marine
Division and the 81st Infantry Division, would take Peleliu and
Angaur in the western Palaus, while the XXIV Army Corps would
take Yap and Ulithi in the Carolines. This new version of the plan was
codenamed Stalemate II.

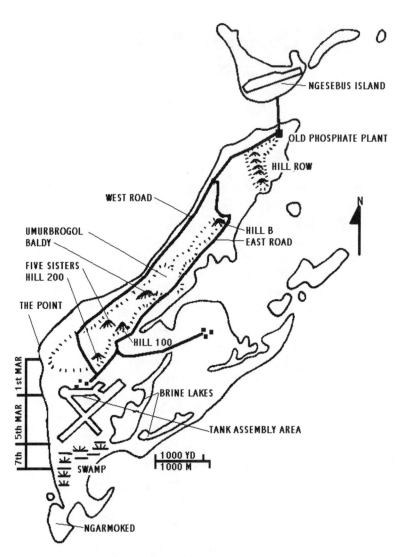

NGESEBUS ISLAND

OLD PHOSPHATE PLANT

HILL ROW

WEST ROAD

N

UMURBROGOL
BALDY

HILL B
EAST ROAD

FIVE SISTERS
HILL 200

THE POINT

HILL 100

BRINE LAKES

TANK ASSEMBLY AREA

1st MAR

5th MAR

7th

1000 YD
1000 M

SWAMP

NGARMOKED

Peleliu

The operation would suffer from manpower problems, limited resources, and technical failings. The Army's 81st Infantry Division was new and untested. The 1st Marine Division was a mixture of worn-out and often sickly veterans of two Solomons campaigns, and inadequately-trained replacements.

Following the Cape Gloucester operation, the 1st Division was sent to a rat-infested base on Pavuvu in the Solomons to recuperate. The rest of the island was impassable swamp.

For the tanks it was the same old story. The 1st Tank Battalion was re-equipped with new M4A2s, and the light tanks were completely phased out, but there was no place to fire the tank cannons. All efforts to conduct maneuvers on the island evolved into practice in dodging trees and extricating bogged vehicles. Training consisted of maintenance, hikes, and close-order drill.

Many veterans remember Pavuvu more vividly than Cape Gloucester, although Bob Boardman viewed it more benignly than most:

> Most guys talking about Pavuvu hated it, but I thought it was a great place. I think the camaraderie on Pavuvu was just outstanding. We had to build our own tent city under and among the coconut palms. There were lots of land crabs, rats, and jungle.
>
> We trained on a part of Pavuvu called Hooper's Peninsula. There were six or seven hundred acres of coconut palms there ... These palm trees were planted in symmetrical rows, so you had to stay within those rows. Every so often a tanker would hit a coconut palm. They were tall ... Some would fall right over, but others were very very rigid, no give at all, and would stop that 30-ton Sherman tank dead. If the drivers or any other crew member's teeth were level with the steel hatch, he would lose his teeth.
>
> Herman Serubin from New York [had] the most beautiful set of teeth in C Company. He lost them in that manner.

Staff planning was equally hamstrung. There was no direct communication between the division headquarters and CINCPAC headquarters in Hawaii. Even the most urgent radio messages were relayed by hand-carrying a text of the message to a small naval base on Banika Island—two hours by fast boat—where it was radioed to Hawaii.[1]

Major General William H. Rupertus was in Washington during most of the operational planning, and his role was assumed by Brigadier General Oliver P. Smith, his deputy commander. High-level decision making was snarled by the protracted Marianas operations, which absorbed the attentions of Spruance, Roy Geiger, Kelly Turner, and Holland Smith. With the attentions of virtually every high-level officer in the chain of command riveted upon the Marianas, the Palaus planning staff lost course.[2]

Ultimately the most serious problem was a failure of reconnaissance. No American had set foot in the Palaus since a Navy medical corpsman went to Koror to retrieve Pete Ellis's body in 1923. No American had ever set foot on Peleliu.

The unexpected protraction of the Marianas campaigns drained resources. Air reconnaissance made it clear that the enemy had for all practical purposes abandoned the Carolines, withdrawing surface fleet elements and most aircraft. The big base at Truk was in communication with the rest of the Empire only by radio and the occasional submarine.

Despite the changed circumstances, the Palau operation took on a strange life of its own. While the ships carrying the soldiers and Marines plodded toward the Palaus, Admiral Halsey's 3rd Fleet raided Iwo Jima, the Palaus, and the central and southern Philippines. The raid drew a halfhearted response from the Japanese. On 13 September Halsey dispatched an urgent message to MacArthur and Nimitz recommending that the upcoming Palau operations be canceled in favor of a more ambitious plan to jump farther to the north in the Philippines. The message triggered a bureaucratic tragedy of errors.

Nimitz believed that Peleliu was lightly defended, and that he did not have the authority to cancel the operation. He bumped the decision up to the Joint Chiefs of Staff without endorsement, and some historians lay the blame for the ensuing tragedy at Nimitz's door.[3]

MacArthur was onboard ship en route to the first Philippines landing and observing radio silence. His controversial Chief of Staff, Lieutenant General Richard Sutherland, informed the Joint Chiefs that Halsey was in error, declined to approve cancellation of the Palaus landings, but approved the great leap in the Philippines. The Joint Chiefs endorsed the decision.

Thus two divisions sailed on toward objectives that no longer had any strategic significance. Worse, the assessment of enemy defenses was seriously in error.

A radio relay station was Peleliu's only military facility until late 1943, but by early 1944 the island was the most heavily defended island in the group. Colonel Kunio Nakagawa's garrison included the *2nd Infantry Regiment*, the *3rd Battalion* of the *15th Infantry*, the *346th Infantry Battalion* of the *53rd Independent Mixed Brigade*, a tank company, the *45th Naval Guard Force Detachment*, as well as field and antiaircraft artillery, naval air personnel, and a combat-trained labor force. There were two dozen artillery pieces, 30 Type 88 antiaircraft guns, over 100 heavy machine guns, and 19 tanks. The senior officer on Peleliu was Major General Kenijiro.

Peleliu was a hybrid of the worst features of Tarawa and Saipan, with a few other hellish features thrown in. The relatively small island, six miles long by two miles wide, is shaped like the northeast-facing skull of a gigantic crocodile. The main airfield was located on low ground at the back of the skull, the western end, with a smaller satellite field on Ngesebus Island. The jaw of the crocodile is marshy ground, broken by saline lagoons and scattered hillocks of coral shot through with caves.

The final Japanese redoubt would be in the upper skull and snout, high craggy ridges of volcanic rock and coral limestone. Air photos suggested to American analysts that this area was low hills covered with trees. In reality, it is extremely jagged terrain, with tall trees growing in the better-watered low spots, and ridges and pinnacles covered with scrubby brush. The effect of this vegetation pattern was to smooth out the topography as seen from the air. The largest and most rugged mass is the Umurbrogol, a 550-foot-high, three dimensional maze of ridges, caves, blind ravines and sinkholes that dominates the flat ground near the main airfield.

The climate in the southern Palaus is brutal. Late summer temperatures routinely soar above 100 degrees F, sometimes reaching 120 degrees. Black volcanic rock baking in the tropical sun can blister flesh. In late 1944 Peleliu held only one source of potable water, a small pond nestled in a broad ravine in the southern Umurbrogol.

After two years of watching their generals squander resources in futile displays of offensive vigor, the Japanese general staff had instructed field commanders to implement a new defensive strategy. Beaches would be defended only as resources allowed. The defenders of Peleliu were instead to burrow into the coral hills, and extract the maximum price in blood for their little patch of the Empire. There would be no more of the hopeless *banzai* charges.

Nakagawa's men took advantage of the caves and soft rock to create a warren of tunnels. Some caves were equipped with steel doors, and held artillery pieces mounted on rails. The doors could be opened, the gun slid out and fired, and the gun returned to safety in under a minute. Numerous openings assured that attackers would be caught in a vicious three-dimensional crossfire, with automatic weapons firing along and across the ravines and from the heights above. All these positions were in deep ravines protected from naval gunfire by the steep ridges. Natural chimneys in the limestone served as 20-feet deep mortar pits. No American artillery piece or naval gun could provide the vertical plunging fire necessary to penetrate these pits.

There was only one potential landing beach, and it was protected by over 500 horned mines and manmade obstacles. Concrete pillboxes and caves hid naval guns, 37mm and 47mm antitank guns, 75mm Type 88 guns, and field guns. Range-poles were implanted in the coral of the reef, and fields of fire surveyed to the yard.

General Geiger asked for four days of shelling. The Navy offered two days, and both parties compromised on three. Then the battleships *Tennessee* and *California* collided, and the latter limped away toward the Solomons. The Navy was short of ammunition for the big guns. Worst of all, the three days of precious gunfire were wasted on old-fashioned area suppression fire rather than against specific targets. On the evening of 14 September Rear Admiral Jesse Oldendorf, commander of the bombardment group, reported that they had "… run out of targets."[4]

Bill Henahan remembered being told that "… Army Air Force [planes] were returning to base with their bombs because all the targets had been destroyed. Rupertus made the comment that if the 2nd Marine Division took Tarawa in 76 hours, the 1st Marine Division was gonna take Peleliu in 48 … They were dead wrong on that place."

The Marianas operations had absorbed most of the Navy's transport capability. Only four LSDs were available, and the two assigned to the 1st Division could carry only 30 tanks to Peleliu. Sixteen tanks were left behind on Pavuvu, but all the battalion personnel went along. There were shortages of trucks and heavy engineer equipment.[5]

The three rifle regiments would land abreast, with the 1st, 5th, and 7th Marines from left to right. Five landing beaches, White-1 and -2, and Orange-1, -2, and -3 covered a distance of over a mile from north to south.

The tanks would land as soon as possible, in six columns of five tanks, each column led by a single amphibian tractor. The amphibians were to scout paths around unmapped potholes and fissures, and the unpredictable shell craters. Each tractor was equipped with a radio on the tank frequency, and an officer could signal to halt the tanks if the driver felt the LVT begin to float.

The scout amphibians also served as the only logistics vehicles for the tank companies, carrying a small assortment of ammunition, tools, and a few spare parts.[6] The limited ammunition would have to suffice until the beach parties had established dumps ashore, and major repairs would have to be made by cannibalizing vehicles.

Lieutenant Colonel Arthur "Jeb" Stuart instituted a change in the tactical utilization of his tank battalion. The usual practice was for a company to consistently support each rifle regiment. This scheme would be used in the assault phase, where confusion would most likely reign. Tank companies A, B, and C would support the 1st, 5th and 7th Regiments, respectively. Once ashore, tank company commanders and liaison personnel would remain with the rifle regiments, but individual tank platoons would be shifted about as needed.[7]

Dog-Day at Peleliu began at 0530 hours with two hours of shelling by the old battleships. When the tractors were about a half-mile from the beach, the hidden Japanese artillery and mortars opened up, their muzzle flashes clearly visible to the embarrassed Admiral Oldendorf and his sailors.

When the tractors clambered up over the edge of the reef flat trajectory fire began to rip into the unarmored hulls, and the aerial observer radioed to the command ship that numerous amtracs were in flames. Within the first 10 minutes smoke from the pyres of 26 tractors obscured the beach from observation. Nevertheless, the first wave of armored amphibians was on the beach at 0832 hours, the first troop carriers at 0833.

The worst punishment originated from The Point, the 30-foot high coral mound at the water's edge on the extreme left, from which four heavy machine guns and a 47mm gun raked the length of the White beaches. Colonel Lewis Puller of the 1st Marines narrowly escaped death when the tractor carrying the bulk of his command group, and his radios, was hit seconds after beaching. All along the beaches pieces of men and vehicles were blown into the air by direct hits.

Fire from The Point was devastating, and Puller assigned K Company of his 3rd Battalion, supported by a handful of A Company tanks, to take the position, setting off a savage struggle for possession of the little knob. Forty-five minutes later Marines had circled behind the hill and were on the crest, grenading and blasting five concrete positions and their protecting trenches and spider holes. To their right, Item Company advanced inland, but the bulk of the 1st Marines were mired in a stinking waist-deep tidal swamp.

The 7th Marines were raked by three 75mm guns. The intense fire caused many of the tractor drivers to shy away to the left, and elements of the 7th became hopelessly snarled with the 5th. Confusion was compounded by the error of deploying 3/5 and 3/7 on adjacent beaches so that similarly designated companies were intermingled. Once ashore, the Marines of the 7th found that their beaches, and particularly the southernmost Orange-3, were covered with Type 98 horned mines and aircraft bombs rigged as mines.

The big Type 98 (1938) Anti-Boat Mine had a cast-iron body, and the 21kg explosive charge would cripple or destroy American tanks. The smaller Single-Horn Anti-Boat Mine, or tea-kettle mine, was of welded sheet metal with a single detonator horn protruding from the top.[8]

Fortunately many of the mines were laid on top of the ground or poorly concealed, while others were either unfused or had corroded beyond function. One tank commander dismounted and picked a path through the mines, guiding his tank by paying out a roll of toilet paper.[9]

Across the front of the 5th Marines on Orange-1 and -2, an eight-foot deep antitank ditch blocked the amphibians. The troops disembarked into raking small arms and mortar fire, but began to struggle inland toward the airfield. By 1000 hours 60 LVTs were out of action, and troops were wading ashore through the carnage.

As the columns of tanks started across the reef, the enemy singled them out for special attention. The greatest threat was the heavy mortars that dropped plunging fire onto the vulnerable engine decks. Fifteen tanks were hit, and three disabled, but the balance were on the beach by H plus 30 minutes.

Six more succumbed to the rain of mortar and artillery shells. In the zone of 3/1 tanks were called up to help deal with a series of positions in a low coral ridge that covered a tank ditch. As soon as they appeared the enemy laid down such a torrent of mortar and artillery fire that they were forced to withdraw to spare the nearby infantry.

By midafternoon the Marines had clawed their way inland to establish a precarious beachhead. The most serious problems were water and communications. Planners had concluded that it would be much more efficient to bring water ashore in 55-gallon fuel drums rather than in the usual 5-gallon cans but most of the water brought ashore in barrels was tainted by fuel residue or brown with rust. The desperate men choked it down and promptly vomited it up again, and were stricken by crippling cramps. In the brain-frying heat desperate Marines were drinking polluted, brackish water from puddles and craters.[10]

The tanks were already running short of cannon ammunition. As on Tarawa, the crews began to scavenge back along their trail of disabled tanks.

Rupertus, with a broken ankle, sent Oliver Smith ashore to set up a forward command post. With Puller's radios gone, neither senior officer had any idea of the desperate situation on the left. The 5th Marines, along with elements of the 1st Marines, had pushed inland as far as the edge of the airfield, but on the extreme left the 1st Marines were pinned by fire from the high ground of the Umurbrogol.

On the right 1/7 was snarled in a mangrove swamp and 3/7 was still having problems sorting out their boundary with 3/5. When Item/3/7 called for tanks to help reduce a bunker complex the tanks trundled forward and found some riflemen who identified themselves as Item Company. Nobody thought to inquire further, so the tanks happily attached themselves to Item/3/5.

Well behind schedule for the advance across the island, and hamstrung by the inability of the 1st Marines to make progress against the unexpected resistance, the division paused at the edge of the open airfield. If the enemy planned to launch a counterattack, this was the place to receive it; 1/5 emplaced four 37mm antitank guns and called up three tanks from B Company. Unable to dig fighting holes in the stony ground, Marines stacked rubble and chunks of loose coral to make improvised walls.

At 1515 hours observers reported movement and a cloud of dust along the northern edge of the airfield. A few minutes later a large group of Type 95 tanks clattered out onto the open runways. This attack, by the *Tank Company* of the *14th Infantry Division*, was the second largest Japanese tank attack of the Pacific war.

The ensuing fight was so chaotic that it is difficult to sort fact from myth, and even the time of the attack is disputed. Official records state that the attack came at 1615 hours, although some reports place it as late as 1730 hours.[11] The axis of the attack took it across the front of 2/1 and into 1/5 on their right.

Unlike the usual *banzai* charge, this was a deliberate attack, with the enemy infantry dodging from cover to cover. Between 13 and 19 tanks raced across the open ground, outdistancing the infantry company supporting them. The small gaggle of tanks and infantry were taking on two battalions of Marine infantry.

According to various accounts the Japanese tanks had either ten to fifteen infantrymen tied to each tank by ropes, carried one or two infantrymen in upright oil drums fastened to the rear decks, or were accompanied by trucks carrying more infantry. Lieutenant Colonel Stuart later reported that he had seen pipe frames, and an upended oil drum on the back of one wrecked tank. The infantry were adamant that there were enemy infantrymen riding the tanks. What is certain is that the riders did not long survive.

The counterattack charged into a classic L-shaped ambush, with a crushing fire from their front and right flank. Three Sherman tanks clattered up to the edge of the airfield just as the enemy attack fell, adding their firepower to that of another Sherman already lying in wait with 2/1.

The little *Ha-Go* tanks were hit repeatedly. The bazookas of the Marine rifle companies easily pierced the light armor, setting off secondary ammunition explosions that ripped the tanks apart. Two tanks veered away from the main axis and charged the front of 2/1, only to mire up in soft ground at the edge of the airfield.

The armor-piercing rounds from the 75mm cannons on the Shermans ripped through the enemy tanks. Loaders switched to delayed action high-explosive rounds, only to see these rounds pass right through the enemy tanks and explode in the air. The loaders switched to quick-fused HE rounds, which shredded the light tanks, blasting them apart and flinging the turrets high into the air. One

Sherman, hit in the drive sprocket and the track broken, limped to and fro over its broken track to acquire targets.

The battle was not entirely one-sided. Bill Finley: "I knew one of the guys, he was a professional wrestler, who was tank commander of one of the tanks. Of course those Japanese tanks were no match at all for the Sherman tanks. This guy was named Quinlan. 'Beast' Quinlan was what we called him.

"He was riding about from his waist up out of the turret. One of those [rounds],what would be comparable to our 37, one of those took the whole top of his head off. That was the only casualty in A Company that I know of in that deal."

The 75mm pack howitzers and mortars poured fire onto the Japanese infantry. Men of the 5th Marines doused the surviving enemy tanks with flamethrowers and hammered them with heavy machine-gun fire and rifle grenades. A few tanks penetrated the American line, and two men were crushed under the tracks. One rifleman stopped a tank with a rifle grenade, then leapt atop the tank as it shuddered to a stop. When the enemy tank commander threw open his hatch, the Marine grabbed the tank commander by the scruff of the neck and threw him off onto the ground below, then dropped two grenades into the smoking hulk.[12]

Another tank bore down on a machine-gun pit, and a desperate gunner stood up with the heavy gun and sprayed the oncoming tank. It burst into flames but kept coming, crushing the gun pit as the Marines scrambled from its path. The tank rolled on another 10 or so yards and exploded. Survivors in some tanks tried to surrender or at least escape, but the Marines tossed grenades into the open hatches, and gunned down any who tried to evacuate the burning hulks. One tank managed to penetrate almost to the division command post, about a hundred yards to the rear, before it was stopped by a round from a 75mm pack howitzer. In the chaos three bazooka rounds struck one Sherman.

Four more Shermans came out of the 2/5 area on the far right and charged into the flank of the Japanese attack, adding to the carnage. In the melee one of the Japanese tanks loosed several rounds into the rear of a Sherman. Infantry officer Bruce Watkins watched fascinated as the Sherman slowly traversed its turret and blew the turret off the enemy tank, which lurched away "… like a beheaded chicken."[13]

Two enemy tanks retreated across the fire-swept airfield, concealed by the clouds of dust and the dense black smoke from their burning comrades. Several American guns or tanks had fired upon each of the enemy tanks, and after the action 110 tanks were claimed as destroyed. In the rush of events following this deadly battle no one bothered to make an official count, and today the precise number of tanks destroyed remains unknown. The best guess is 13, although the official history cites 11 as destroyed.[14]

The Japanese were nothing if not persistent. More infantry, and two surviving tanks, tried another counterattack at 1750 hours. Mortar and artillery fire stopped this attack on the other side of the open ground.

The following morning the 5th Marines, aided by tanks, attacked across the airfield at 0800. The advance across the barren surface in the face of artillery, mortar, and machine-gun fire was ghastly. Heavy machine guns and a pair of 20mm antiaircraft guns raked the open field taking a heavy toll of the riflemen. The tanks finally silenced some of the machine-gun fire emanating from the underbrush of a swamp in the 2/5 zone on the right of the airfield, but much of the fire was coming out of the highlands of the Umurbrogol to their left rear.

Finally the tanks had to pull back to spare the rifle companies the rain of artillery fire they always attracted, and were used in rescue work. The tanks would interpose their bulk between the Japanese guns and the LVTs sent out to recover the wounded, absorbing punishing 20mm automatic cannon fire that would have been fatal to the tractors.

On the right the 7th Marines drove small Japanese formations into the southern tip of the island. By noon the 7th had reached the east shore.

On the second day the extreme heat—105 degrees—began to claim a heavy toll. Men began to strip away all unnecessary clothing, discarding leggings and underwear, and hacking off the legs and sleeves of their utilities. The rear flaps of helmet covers, normally tucked between the steel helmet and the plastic liner, were pulled out and left to hang down to shade the neck and ears. Critically short of water, they scraped holes and drank the brown water that seeped in.

The tank crews were not exposed to the sun, and could carry more water, but the heat inside the tanks was hellish. The ventilator systems were designed to slowly circulate air and remove fumes, not to provide a cooling breeze. With ambient air temperatures that eventually reached 120 degrees in the shade, and the tropical sun beating down upon the dark vehicles, no one knows for sure how hot it got inside.

The tanks also generated their own additional heat. Bill Finley: "The heat off the spent brass that comes out of the 75 and the machine gun would heat it up a lot more. We had those deals in our ears to hear, and a band around our throat, an elastic band, to talk." The band held an induction microphone tight against the larynx. "Even though it was real soft rubber I've had my ears so sore I could hardly touch them, just from having them in there so long at a time."

The most terrible ordeal was on the left, where the 1st Marines were butting their heads against the lower slopes of the Umurbrogol. All day the enemy counterattacked K Company atop The Point. Two tanks supported an attack by 1/1 that finally relieved K Company.

That night the enemy began another series of violent counterattacks. At dawn the Marines still held the crest, but only 78 of the 235 men who came ashore had survived two days and nights on The Point.

The following day was equally violent, bleeding the 1st Marines dry as they continued to hammer at the flanks of the main hill mass. The 3rd Battalion could make progress along the coast, but had to hold back to maintain contact with the 1st Battalion. The 1st Marines were experiencing a terrible battering, despite destroying 48 fortified positions.

The 1st Marines tried to push into the high ground by dispatching a tank and two LVTs to escort an infantry force onto Hill 200, a ridge that dominated the junction of the East and West Roads. The enemy allowed the small force to advance into the killing ground, then opened a maelstrom of fire. The tank suffered a broken track after repeated hits, and the two tractors were wrecked. The infantry clawed their way up the rugged slopes, and by afternoon controlled the crest, though the enemy held out in caves beneath their feet. They found their new position dominated by Hill 210, a fact not clear from the inadequate maps.

There were more crews than tanks, and this enabled the crews to emerge from the fierce heat inside the tank while a spare crew rearmed the tank and took it out on another foray. The tanks were using an open area on the airfield as a logistical site, but it was exposed to enemy observation from the hills to the north, a fact which made this rear area as dangerous as the front lines.

Bill Henahan: "They were dropping those 150mm mortars in there until it reached the point where when you were back there you got underneath the tank. One [round] landed on top of the engine compartment of this one tank, and blew both engine compartment doors right down into the engine compartment onto the engines. Smashed the engines. They got on your nerves after a while."

This is where Bob Boardman was first wounded:

> We would make our runs up against the caves on Bloody Nose Ridge. We would come back to rearm and refuel on the edge of the airstrip, using the old bombed out hangars for our fuel and ammo.
>
> When we were refueling and re-ammoing I walked out onto the airstrip, among the bombed out planes. Fortunately, just at that moment it was quiet. I was out on the edge of the airstrip and heard an artillery shell go through the air—shew-shew-shew-shew—just like that, directly over my head. I hit the deck simultaneously with the shell exploding. It hit about 10 yards away, and I was covered with coral dust. Shrapnel and pieces of coral went whistling all around, zinging through the old airplane engines.
>
> While lying there and praying a piece of either shrapnel or coral raked me hard. It wasn't serious enough to be evacuated, so I went back to my tank. Those who were back there knew I was out near where the shell hit. They thought I was dead. I came up all covered with coral dust. I'm sure they thought they were seeing a ghost. The corpsman just wrapped up my arm, and I went back into combat.

The advance stretched the logistical system to the limit. Without adequate trucks, LVTs drove across the beach and straight into the front lines, offloading fuel and ammunition for the tanks under fire.

On the far right 1/7 and 3/7 cleared two small extensions of Peleliu that were connected to the mainland by sandbars at low tide. At 1000 hours two tanks and a platoon from L/3/7 crossed onto the unnamed southeastern promontory, and the peninsula was secured by 1315 hours.

From the southern island, Ngarmoked, another 75mm gun continued to rake the landing beaches with deadly effect, and had resisted all efforts to destroy it with naval gunfire or air strikes. Additional tanks, SPMs, LVT(A)-4s, and 37mm guns were brought up to lay a curtain of fire on the defenders, allowing A Company and tanks onto the tiny island.

The sandbar was heavily mined, and the advance slowed while they were lifted. One platoon from B Company, escorted by two tanks, crossed the sandbar, only to be pinned by very heavy fire. Giant boulders blocked the movement of the tanks. As two additional infantry companies were brought into the line, two of the precious tankdozers were dispatched to laboriously carve a path. With the aid of the tanks the riflemen quickly secured about half the island and destroyed the stubborn 75mm gun.

On 18 September temperatures soared to 112 degrees. The 5th Marines secured the eastern part of the island, but now their left flank faced the jagged ridges that had stalled the 1st Marines. On Ngarmoked 1/7 and Item/3/7 were fighting to retake some of the same ground they had secured the day before, where bypassed Japanese kept emerging from caves and attacking the Marines from the rear. Only the tanks could negotiate the rugged terrain, and when they were forced to pull back to replenish, the attack bogged down. Then, inexplicably, the enemy began to commit suicide in large numbers, and the little island was secured by midafternoon.

Men were wounded by stone splinters as shells exploded on the rocky ground among men who could not dig into the stony soil for shelter. Heat prostration was taking a heavy toll, and the first men were starting to fall victim to dysentery. On 19 September the temperature climbed to 115 degrees.

Flame tanks could have rooted the enemy out of the caves, but only a few C Company Shermans were fitted with the E4-5 bow-mounted flamethrower. Bill Finley: "You could take the machine gun out of its bracket, and put the flamethrower in there. There wasn't very much fuel; it [the tanks] had to sit up on the bulkhead [in the sponson next to the bow gunner]. It would shoot flame out for a while. I can't remember how much we used it, but we did use it some."

In the morning 2/7, attached to the 1st Marines, seized Hills 200 and 260. Tanks and a long-range flame gun mounted on an LVT attacked a line of stone pinnacles called the Five Sisters. The thinly armored, open-topped flame vehicle was frightfully vulnerable, and bound to attract plenty of fire when it appeared. The usual tactic was for two tanks to move ahead and try to suppress enemy fire with their cannon. The LVT would then move in between the armored bulk of two tanks, sheltering between them while it brought its flame gun to bear. Even with this aid, 2/7's attack withered away under intense fire. The Five Sisters would hold out for two more months.

That same day C/1/1 was attached to the 2nd Battalion for the assault on Hill 100, one of the minor knobs on the southern margin of the Umurbrogol. Two tanks that supported the attack were put out of action when they slipped off the road and bogged down where the road embankment crossed a large, brine-filled sinkhole. The riflemen somehow reached the top of the hill, only to find that it was overlooked by another higher knob. Repeated night attacks reduced C Company to eight survivors, fighting with knives, rocks, and empty ammunition cans. At daybreak enemy artillery forced a retreat.

By 20 September the casualties in the 1st Marines were so heavy that the regiment could muster only the equivalent strength of a single rifle battalion. Men who remained functional were now literally in foul condition. Sunburned, slashed by rock splinters, their tattered clothing was stained by urine and the uncontrolled diarrhea induced by food contaminated by the flies that shuttled between unburied human waste, the unburied dead, and what little food the men could stomach. Again 1/1 and 2/1 fought their way to the top of the ridge overlooking the East Road again, and again were driven off.

The two remaining battalions of the 7th Marines were brought up to take over part of the front held by the 1st Marines. The only answer to the tough defenses was sheer volume of fire. In one foray Bill Henahan, this time riding as a bow gunner, forgot how quickly machine guns could overheat:

> There were two pillboxes we were engaging and the main gun was shooting at this one pillbox. I'm turning the periscope around, and I see this one off to the right. I pushed the gun over and fired a few tracers, and when I got them going into the gun slit, I just held it down and put the whole belt through there—a 250 round belt. Then I loaded another belt in and did the same thing, and then I loaded another belt and did the same thing again ...
>
> Near the end of the third belt I was looking out the periscope, watching the tracers, and they were corkscrewing, going up in the air in all directions, hitting the ground in front of the tank. I looked at the barrel, and it was white-hot. You could see shadows passing through it. I dragged some cartridges out of the belt, and let it go. It was firing by itself, cooking off.
>
> When it hit the place where there were no more cartridges, it quit. I got a hot-shell glove and pulled the gun out and I stuck another one in. We had five spare machine guns stacked behind the assistant driver's

seat. I started shooting again, and did the same thing with this one. I was into my third belt, almost finished with it, when the gun got overheated, so I pulled it out and stuck another one in there.

I set this pillbox on fire with the tracers, and nine Japs ran out the back. The infantry were waiting for them, and mowed them all down. After we neutralized both pillboxes we were sitting there, and we had opened up to let in some fresh air in that thing, because it was stifling in there with the gun smoke and all ... [An] infantryman comes up to me and says, "Hey, Mac ... How about gettin' me one of those special machine-guns."

I said, "Special machine-guns?" and he said, "Yea. One of those suckers that'll shoot all week." He didn't know I was changing machine guns. They were pinned down, and all he knew was there was one hell of a lot of machine-gun fire.

The fighting in the ravines and ridges took place at ranges that the tank designers had never dreamed of. The gunsights, designed for ranges of hundreds of yards, were useless at ranges measured in yards. Bill Finley: "... we would commence firing with the [coaxial] machine gun, and when it was on target, we would fire the 75."

In this armored version of hand-to-hand combat, tank commanders often guided their tanks standing in open hatches to direct fire. By the end of the battle eight were dead, fifteen badly wounded.

Inside the baking-hot tanks, human endurance was limited. "A tank would go out with a full load of ammunition and fuel," said Bill Henahan. "They would go out and shoot up this load of ammunition. They would come back with the tank, and an entire new crew would get in it, load it up with ammunition, check the fuel, make sure everything was okay, and they would go out. They would shoot up their load, and they would come back, and another crew would get in.

"One time you might go out as a bow gunner, another time you might go out as a tank commander, sometimes as a driver or gunner, or a loader. They kept all the C Company guys together in a tank crew. You'd go together when you got in a tank."

The tank crews did not notice the debilitating effects of the heat until it was too late, but heat casualties had to fend for themselves. Henahan:

> I went out as a loader, and as fast as I could load this 75, this guy was shooting. It was just boom, boom, boom, boom. The tank was designed

to carry 90 rounds of 75. I loaded between 50 and 60. There was a little round seat in the turret where the loader was. I was just perched on that, and I couldn't move my arms and I couldn't move my legs.

They got the assistant driver to come up, and they pushed me down into the assistant driver's seat. I went in there head first. My head and shoulders were on the floor in front of the seat, and my knees were on the seat.

They continued shooting until they shot up all the ammunition. They went back, and I'm still down there that way. I couldn't move my arms or legs. When they got back, the driver reached over and unlocked the hatch, and they pulled me out feet first. I had heat exhaustion. It was like my arms and legs were asleep.

Anyway, they filled me up with salt tablets, and everything was okay. The next time I went out as a bow gunner.

This grim struggle for useless rocks was already being forgotten. Civilian correspondents and photographers abandoned Peleliu. MacArthur was bound for Leyte, so the grinding hell on this obscure island was no longer newsworthy. Sacrifice was getting to be boring.

On 21 September Roy Geiger visited the command post of the 1st Marines and found Colonel Puller physically and emotionally exhausted, his regiment devastated. Geiger overruled Rupertus and ordered Puller's regiment replaced by fresh Army troops. That afternoon A and C Companies of 1/7 infiltrated up the East Road, past the disabled tanks in the sinkhole, and joined up with tanks that moved through the swamps. The effort was in vain, and another attack on the ridge was driven off.

The 22nd was another day of futile attacks. Efforts to move tanks into the floor of Death Valley, one of the few broad gorges, were stymied by mines, and riflemen of 1/7 were blocked by cliffs and pinned by heavy fire from the heights. At 0830 they were finally able to withdraw under the cover of C Company's tanks.

On 23 September the 321st Infantry Regiment relieved the remnants of the 1st Marines. With the Army infantry came an engineer battalion, and A Company, 710th Tank Battalion, equipped with the latest model M4 tanks. The 1st Marines had suffered the heaviest losses of any regiment in the history of the Corps. The 3rd Battalion was in the best shape with only 55 percent casualties. The 1st Battalion had suffered 71 percent losses; every single platoon leader was a casualty. The same day the 323rd RCT landed unopposed on the scattered islands of Ulithi Atoll. The anchorage was a grand strategic prize, taken without loss while soldiers and Marines were dying for rock that no one wanted any more.

The 321st, with 3/7 and the Army tanks, was assigned the task of advancing along the west coast of Peleliu to block the route of enemy reinforcements infiltrating from Babelthuap. By 24 September this force had advanced nearly to the northern cape. They had also pushed patrols onto the northern slopes of the Umurbrogol, and almost to the eastern coast along a trail that crossed the island north of the hill mass.

The aggressive but inexperienced 321st Infantry was pushing too fast. The regiment had dropped off its 2nd and 3rd Battalions to secure the area where the coastal strip narrowed down and low hills dominated the road. The two battalions withdrew in the face of enemy fire, and followed in the wake of the lead battalion. Now the enemy was flowing back into the gap to cut off an entire regiment. Marines had to retake the hill, with heavy losses.

On 25 September the 5th Marines moved up the West Road and passed through the lines of the 321st Infantry. The northern part of Peleliu was ideal tank country, and by late afternoon the tanks and infantry had advanced as far as the junction of the East and West Roads, where they halted for the night.

On 26 September the 7th Marines battered at the eastern slope of the Umurbrogol, and all attempts to get tanks into the hill mass itself were defeated by the terrain. Trails bulldozed up the ridges were precarious, and rotten coral cliffs crumbled away under the weight of the tanks. The tanks could not move through the more tortuous ravines, and even in the broader ravines they were vulnerable to suicide attacks. For Bob Boardman the worst feeling was "… seeing the infantry going up the ridge, where we of course could not go in our tanks. It was a terrible experience to see the casualties in the infantry. We would do what we could to help. Many wounded infantry were taken out on the backs of tanks. [We] rescued them in certain places. But on the ridge, it was helpless feeling to see them up there, taking such tremendous casualties."

A smaller hill mass called the Amiangal forms the core of the northern cape of Peleliu, and it contained some of the most elaborate cave defenses on the island. An assault by 2/5 and elements of the 321st Infantry was stalled by a secondary ridge that the Marines called Hill Row. The north branch ran parallel to the west coast overlooking the road, and the east-west branch, which blocked access to the north of the island, was capped by four pimple-like hills that gave the ridge its name.

Approaches to Hill Row were blocked by a tank ditch that fronted the ridge. Four of 1/5's supporting tanks were lost in an attempt to bypass the ridge along the West Road, where the gap between the ridge and the sea limited the tanks to advancing in single file.[15] They were further blocked by another deep ditch fronting the wreckage of the old Japanese phosphate refinery. The refinery buildings were total wrecks, but the basements and concrete foundations had been converted into a subterranean fortress.

An attack on Hill B, the last Japanese position blocking the East Road, was more successful. A force of seven tanks and riflemen in LVTs moved south along the road, and by 1700 hours Hill B was in American hands. The Umurbrogol was completely encircled.

The next day at 0830 the last surviving tankdozer filled gaps in the ditch in front of the phosphate plant, and the flame-gun LVT moved up to finish off the fortress. Two rifle companies gained the crest of the north arm of the ridge, but heavy fire still interdicted the road parallel to the beach.

A single Long Tom from the 8th 155mm Gun Battalion spent most of the day firing at the Hill Row positions over open sights. To avoid fragments and debris from the explosion of their own shells the gunners would dive for cover as the number one pulled the firing lanyard.[16] Late in the afternoon the tankdozer constructed ramps across the ditch and Army and Marine infantry overran the hill complex.

The troops found that the tunnels resisted even the 75mm cannon of the tanks, and 100-pound explosive charges failed to collapse the larger tunnel mouths. The tankdozer began to systematically seal the defenders into their self-dug graves.

On the morning of the 28th, 3/5 launched a shore-to-shore landing that quickly secured Ngesebus. Sixteen of the nineteen operable Marine tanks were mustered for the attack, and formed the first wave, followed by LVTs carrying the riflemen of 3/5. Army LVT(A)-4s formed wings to protect the flanks. As the tanks picked their way across the reef the LVTs and amphibian tanks quickly left them behind.

Bill Finley: "They lost one tank. It drove off in where a bomb had hit ... Everybody got out all right, but they lost the tank. That trip over there was something. We had deals [wading stacks] on the back of our tank ... and it [the water] was up just about as high as it could get without coming in the driver's hatch. We had to go over when the tide was out. We followed an amphibious tractor. We went over there, and it was snap. I never did see anything more than a rifleman. I heard they had a 77mm howitzer over there, but I never did see it."

The infantry fight on Ngesebus was bitter, although losses were light compared to the carnage elsewhere on Peleliu. The little island was secured within two days, but the airfield proved useless. The Japanese had surfaced it with sand too soft to support the weight of a plane.

On 29 September 1/5 captured the crest of Radar Hill, the last and easternmost pinnacle of Hill Row, although the enemy held out for days in the caves below.

One of the paradoxes of Peleliu was that for the tankers, the safest place to be was inside the tank, fighting. Like Boardman, Henahan was wounded by random fire while in a rest area:

> We were sitting in a shell hole back in the bivouac area. There were eight of us in there, and I was sitting on a water can. One minute we were talking, and the next minute I was laying flat on my face on the ground. All these guys were on top of me. Never heard an explosion or anything.
>
> I reached down and grabbed my ankles and started running my hands up my legs, right on up. When I got on my right side, I felt something sticking out of my side. These guys started moaning, and when they got up, everybody was wounded. We found out later ... about 40 yards away from us, behind us, there was a pile of bangalore torpedoes. They were stacked there, a stack about six feet high ... A 150mm mortar [round] landed right smack on top of it. There were 85 guys wounded in that area. I helped dig out four that were buried alive.
>
> Then I went over to see the corpsman, and I said "Hey, what's this stickin' out of my side?" He pulled out a piece of shrapnel that was wedged between my ribs. It was three-quarters to an inch long, and about the size of a wooden pencil in diameter. When it hit me it was way hot, and it just cauterized where it hit me. It never bled. They just put a BandAid on it.
>
> In Charlie Company tanks ... until we got to Okinawa, we never had a man killed inside the tank. Everybody that was killed was killed outside the tank by snipers or shrapnel.

One of the KIAs was the commander of C Company, Captain John Heath. Heath had acquired some Winchester M1912 Trench Guns, pump-action 12-gauge shotguns that fired a brass-cased buckshot round, and armed himself and a team of four enlisted men with these weapons.[17] Henahan: "On Peleliu when a tank would go up, he—the company commander—would walk behind the tank. When the tank engaged a pillbox and shot it up, they would run in with these shotguns and wipe out everybody who was still alive in there ....

"On the way back, these guys would ride on the back of the tanks. I heard two different versions. I heard that he got shot between his eyes, and I heard that he got shot right in the throat. I don't know which is true, but he was killed. We had another sergeant who was killed the same way. He was standing on the back of the tank and a sniper shot him off. There were two or three enlisted men that got sniped and killed."

By the end of September the defenders were compressed into a pocket of the Umurbrogol about 900 by 400 yards in extent. The island was declared secure on 30 September, although the bloody struggle would continue for nearly two more months.

The battered 1st Marines were evacuated on 1 October. Inexplicably, General Rupertus also ordered the 1st Tank Battalion—by now reduced to 12 operational tanks—back to Pavuvu. In the final struggle for the Umurbrogol the Marines would be supported by the Army's 710th Tank Battalion. The 710th was a good unit but less experienced, and Oliver P. Smith later questioned the decision to remove the Marine tanks rather than bring forward the extra tanks sitting idle on Pavuvu.[18]

On 4 October Army tanks participated in an action that demonstrated the near-helplessness of tanks in this terrain, a desperate attempt to save a rifle platoon cut off by the Japanese. Just after 1400 hours the 48 survivors of L/3/7 started up the slopes below a feature called Baldy Ridge. One rifle platoon advanced hand over hand, pulling themselves up the rocky, precipitous slopes by grasping roots and boulders. By 1630 hours the platoon had reached the upper slopes, only to find that they were in a deadly trap, overlooked by caves on nearby knobs.

When the Japanese opened fire the platoon was isolated atop a low cliff above a broad ravine. Men were hit repeatedly. The survivors retreated to a position with their backs to the cliff, and the platoon leader was hit and fell to his death as he tried to scout a way down the cliff. The company commander, Captain James V. Shanley, ordered an Army tank into the ravine, but the lip of the cliff blocked the vehicle from firing on the slopes above.

Pounded by automatic weapons fire, the handful of surviving Marines and a Navy medical corpsman took a desperate chance. They dropped their wounded over the edge of the cliff, and jumped after them. More were killed or wounded as they dropped onto the rocks, or ran for the scant shelter offered by the bulk of the tank. The frantic Captain Shanley left his cover at the rear of the tank to help two wounded men. He succeeded in carrying one to safety, but was killed when he returned for the other. The executive officer was killed when he went for his captain.

Company L had only 11 survivors. Rupertus reluctantly declared the 7th unfit for further combat, and the 5th Marines relieved them on 6 October.

All through the rest of early October, the 5th Marines slowly crushed the boundaries of the enemy pocket, pushing into the blind ravines and up the cliffs. Army tanks fought along the floors of the ravines, pumping shells into suspected cave positions.

On 12 October assault operations were declared over, and by 19 October all Marines were out of ground combat. On 27 November the 81st Division closed in on the final stubborn pocket of resistance, but nobody told the last Japanese survivors the battle was over. Twenty-six surrendered as a group on 21 April 1947.[19]

In this battle the tanks, too few in number to start with, had been in constant demand. Rifle battalions and regiments were rotated out of the line but the tanks never went into reserve. The tanks had played a pivotal factor in reducing casualties, not only by providing fire support, but by providing a steel shield to protect Navy medical corpsmen as they rescued the wounded. For their part, the riflemen had repaid the debt by offering unparalleled protection. There was not a single successful Japanese close assault on a tank at Peleliu.[20]

Tank unit casualties were heavy. Most of the recon guides who went ashore with the first waves of infantry became casualties. In the smoke and dust the vision devices on the Sherman tank were totally inadequate, forcing the crewmen to stick their heads out of hatches to navigate. Casualties among experienced tank commanders were particularly severe.

The maintenance crews also suffered mightily. There was only one VTR available on Peleliu, and it had often been impossible to recover damaged tanks in a timely fashion. With only the spare parts carried ashore on D-day, the repair crews had to scavenge parts from wrecked vehicles.[21] Unfortunately most of the tanks available for scavenging were exactly where they had been wrecked—under the enemy's guns—and had to be disassembled under fire. Despite all these difficulties the same tanks were returned to service again and again, so that the battalion averaged 20 tanks per day in operation. Only one tank emerged unscathed. Nine were left on the island as total losses.[22]

Gun tanks and a dozer tank from 3rd Tank Battalion move across the beach near Adelup Point, Guam, H+90. The congestion on the beach includes several disabled LVTs, and a medical aid station in the foreground. (*Marine Corps Historical Center*)

Infantry and tanks of C Company, 3rd Tank Battalion, assemble behind Adelup Point shortly after the landings on Guam. (*National Archives*)

A gun tank of Phil Morell's Tank Company, 4th Marines, 1st Provisional Marine Brigade, fires in support of infantry. The charging rhinoceros symbol of this company is visible on the side of the tank. (*National Archives*)

BOTTOM LEFT: Tank Company, 22nd Marines, 1st Provisional Marine Brigade, fight their way up the road toward the old Marine Barracks on the Orote Peninsula. (*National Archives*)

BOTTOM RIGHT: Vehicles of Tank Company, 4th Marines, move up a trail through some of the typical mountainous terrain of Guam. (*National Archives*)

Blood and Guts II, Tank Company 4th Marines, clears away a wrecked Japanese tank blocking a trail. The shamrock symbol on the turret indicates the Headquarters Platoon. The charging rhinoceros is in gray, with white puffs of dust from his feet. (*National Archives*)

Almighty, an M32B2 VTR of 3rd Tank Battalion, hauls away one of several Type 95 light tanks captured intact on Guam. The elephant symbol is the same used by C Company, IMAC Tank Battalion at Tarawa. (*National Archives*)

Tanks of the 1st Tank Battalion advance across the reef toward the shell-torn beach at Peleliu. At the center of the photograph is one of the LVTs that served as guides and logistical vehicles. (*National Archives*)

A tank from A Company, 1st Tank Battalion, and infantry of "Chesty" Puller's 1st Marines fight their way inland and into the dense vegetation at the base of the Umurbrogol on Peleliu. (*National Archives*)

Another A Company tank on the main airfield, site of the large Japanese armored counterattack on the first day of battle. (*National Archives*)

Marine riflemen watch fighting on the other side of the open airfield from the shelter of Japanese tanks wrecked in the Japanese counterattack. (*Marine Corps Historical Center*)

C-14, the dozer tank of C Company, fires at Japanese positions amid the rugged terrain at the base of the Umurbrogol on Peleliu. (*National Archives*)

Riflemen return fire against Japanese positions in the Umurbrogol from the shelter of a B Company tank. (*Marine Corps Historical Center*)

A crewman on the ground flinches as a dozer tank fires upon enemy positions hidden in the thick underbrush. (*National Archives*)

An infantryman follows behind a tank from C Company. Apparently the ground phone handset cable has been severed, as a wire can be seen hanging down behind the right track. (*National Archives*)

This shot of Marines following a late-model M4 of the Army's A Company, 710th Tank Battalion, gives some idea of the forbidding terrain that limited tank operations on Peleliu. Tanks of this unit are frequently misidentified as Marine Corps tanks. (*National Archives*)

Army tanks and an LVT mounting a long-range flame gun pick their way into the central valley of the Umurbrogol on Peleliu. The ponds were one of the few sources of drinkable water, and the Japanese fought tenaciously to retain control of them. (*Marine Corps Historical Center*)

CHAPTER 12

HELL BOILS OVER: IWO JIMA

OPERATION DETACHMENT was the archetypal Marine Corps battle of the war, and the largest struggle ever fought in its entirety by Marine Corps ground forces.The fighting on Iwo Jima was also the most dramatic illustration of the disparity between myth and fact about the Marines. Marines cultivated a public image as fast moving assault troops. In reality many of their battles were systematic slogs, frontal attacks repeated day after day against the most formidable defenses in the world. Iwo Jima was the ultimate example of this prolonged savagery, and no account of the battle can ever capture the sheer day to day sameness of intense terror.

The Japanese radar station on Iwo Jima gave the mainland air defenses two hours warning of inbound raids, and fighters based there regularly picked off crippled B-29s.[1] Operating near the extreme limit of their range, other damaged bombers that slipped past Iwo were lost when they ran out of fuel on the 700-mile leg back to the American bases.

In American hands Iwo would provide emergency landing strips for the B-29s, and bases for air-sea rescue planes. Long-range P-51 and P-47 fighters based there could accompany the bombers over parts of the Japanese mainland, while attack aircraft could suppress enemy activities on the other islands of the Nanpo Shoto island chain that extends from Iwo Jima nearly to the mouth of Tokyo Bay.

Bases in the Marianas were by no means safe from Iwo's depredations. In December 1944 Claude Culpepper was still on Saipan. "I was on guard post up above the camp. Bob Hope was down near the rec area putting on a show. [The] Japanese came over and bombed us. That thing came up, Bob went one way and I went up under my 55-gallon drum. We had three 55-gallon drums in a triangle shape, with

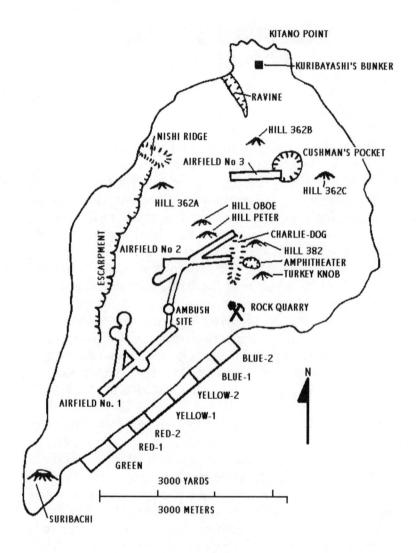

KITANO POINT

KURIBAYASHI'S BUNKER

RAVINE

NISHI RIDGE

HILL 362B

CUSHMAN'S POCKET

AIRFIELD No 3

HILL 362C

HILL 362A

HILL OBOE
HILL PETER

CHARLIE-DOG

AIRFIELD No 2

HILL 382
AMPHITHEATER
TURKEY KNOB

ESCARPMENT

AMBUSH
SITE

ROCK QUARRY

BLUE-2

BLUE-1

N

YELLOW-2

AIRFIELD No. 1

YELLOW-1

RED-2
RED-1

GREEN

3000 YARDS

3000 METERS

SURIBACHI

Iwo Jima

sandbags on top of them. When you were on guard post, that was your air raid shelter. While I was there the island had thirteen bomb attacks, the bombers coming off Iwo Jima. One night antiaircraft fire hit a bomber ... and I thought that durn island was going to sink. For a seventeen year old kid, that's scary."

Iwo Jima is less than eight square miles of barren, vile-smelling red and black volcanic stone. The island is dominated by Mount Suribachi, a dormant volcano. North of a low-lying waist is the Motoyama Plateau. In early 1945 there were two Japanese airfields on the waist of the island, and a third under construction near the center of the plateau.

The beaches are loose black volcanic ash so soft that a man on foot sinks in up to his shins and vehicles belly up. The beaches are backed by 30-foot high terraces of black sand thrown up by enormous winter storm waves. There is little fresh ground water, and in 1945 the handful of wells had to be supplemented by cisterns that trapped rainwater.

In June 1944 the garrison commander was replaced by Lieutenant General Tadamichi Kuribayashi, who was under no illusions about either the industrial might or the fighting abilities of Americans. Kuribayashi knew that he could never successfully defend the island, and seriously investigated the possibility of splitting it in half with a gigantic trench.[2] Accepting his fate, he set out to make the cost of capturing Iwo Jima as dreadful as possible.

By early 1945 the garrison numbered over 23,000 men, with 434 pillboxes and blockhouses, and tanks. The presence of five independent antitank battalions attested to the importance the Japanese placed on countering the increasing numbers of Marine tanks. The Independent Anti-Tank Companies were organized as either three or four platoons of two guns each, with an ammunition platoon in support. An Independent Anti-Tank Battalion was three such companies grouped together.[3]

The backbone of the defense was the artillery, including two independent artillery battalions and five mortar battalions. The small island boasted 33 coastal guns, 361 field guns, a dozen giant 320mm spigot mortars, 65 heavy mortars, and 70 rocket launcher platforms. Anti-aircraft defenses included 94 heavy antiaircraft guns of 75mm or larger caliber, and 200 light guns. The antitank defense would be built around the five independent antitank battalions, augmented by the heavy antiaircraft guns. Lieutenant Colonel Baron Takeichi Nishi's

26th Tank Regiment lost its entire complement of tanks when its transport was sunk by a marauding submarine, but received 22 light replacements.

The physical structures alone made Iwo Jima one of the most effectively defended places on earth, with bands of mutually-supporting positions arrayed hundreds of yards in depth. Kuribayashi declined to defend the beaches, knowing that beach positions were most vulnerable to naval gunfire. Artillery was preregistered. Antitank guns and field guns up to 150mm caliber were sited to covered ditches, stone walls, and natural ravines that would channel the American tanks.

Broad belts of mines subdivided the island. Included were buried aircraft bombs and torpedo warheads with small antitank mines rigged as detonators. The explosion of one of these mammoths would literally toss a 30-ton tank into the air. The situation was made worse because the volcanic soil was opaque to the American magnetic mine detectors. The only way to locate mines was by hand-probing the stony soil with bayonets and sharpened sticks.[4]

Most fighting positions were linked by tunnels, and work was underway to knit together the whole island with 17 miles of tunnels. Positions would not inevitably be held to the death. When advantageous, the defenders would abandon doomed positions. To dispirit the Americans, Japanese dead would be carried away to be burned or concealed in catacombs. There would be no futile suicide charges. The only defenders allowed on the surface would be special tank-hunter teams and night infiltrators.

Unlike most Japanese commanders, Kuribayashi deployed his artillery under a central command, and Colonel Chosaku Kaido directed all guns from a bunker under a hill the Marines would call Turkey Knob.[5] The Americans would be allowed to land with minor resistance, but once on the beach they would be inundated with artillery and mortar fire. Kuribayashi did not believe that he could drive the determined Americans back into the water, and he had drawn up plans for systematic withdrawals to successive defensive barriers.

The best American hope for neutralizing Kuribayashi's efforts was a heavy pre-invasion bombardment, but delays in MacArthur's seizure of Leyte, Mindoro, and Luzon delayed the release of the fleet carriers and battleships supporting operations there. The Joint Chiefs declined to authorize a delay in the Iwo Jima operation because that would in turn delay the planned invasion of Okinawa. The delay would have to be absorbed in the Iwo operation.[6]

A proposal for 10 days of shelling by the fast battleships was vetoed by the Navy, who wanted the battleships to protect the carriers during a raid on the Japanese main island of Honshu. The Honshu raid had been planned to divert enemy attention from Operation Detachment, but took on a perverse life of its own and drained resources from the operation it was intended to support. Historian Ronald Spector has conjectured that the Navy wanted to demonstrate its capability for strategic bombardment by attacking aircraft factories, at the expense of support for the Marines.[7]

The efficacy of what shelling did take place was further reduced by some of Kuribayashi's ruses. Marines later discovered dummy gun emplacements and fake tanks carved from soft stone in the midst of crater fields left by naval gunfire.[8]

The firepower in the reorganized rifle companies was staggering by early-war standards. Each platoon included a demolition squad with a flamethrower team and a demolition team. These teams trained intensively both in their specialties and in cooperation with their assigned tank unit. In the assault landing phase the tank companies would be committed at the discretion of the rifle regiment commanders, and not according to a fixed schedule.[9]

The 3rd and 4th Tank Battalions were seasoned units. Iwo would be the first action for the new 5th Tank Battalion, but it was leavened with combat veterans. The rest of the men were graduates of the tank training facility at Jacques Farm.

Many problems still afflicted the tank battalions. Only eight of the new POA-CWS flame tanks that mounted a long-range flame gun in place of the cannon had been converted by the Army Chemical Warfare Service workshops in Hawaii, and four each were assigned to the 4th and 5th Tank Battalions.[10] Most tanks were equipped with E4-5 flamethrowers that could be fitted in place of the bow machine gun, but these were hampered by short range and a limited arc of fire, were easily damaged, and were not very popular with the crews. The 3rd Tank Battalion got their new tankdozers at the last moment, and never got any POA-CWS flame tanks.[11]

The improved gasoline-powered M4A3 gun tanks were also finding their way into Marine service, but this placed an even heavier training burden on the units, and the 5th Tank Battalion was not considered fully trained on the new vehicles.[12] The M4A3 was powered by a gasoline-fueled Ford engine. Bob Swackhammer, senior company maintenance officer in the 5th Tank Battalion: "Colonel [William R.] Collins called me in and said he was going to Washington, and there were two things they would want to know. Did we want rubber or steel treads, and did we want gasoline or diesel?* There is more abundant gasoline than there is diesel. Diesels are a little bit temperamental when it comes to fuel. It's got to be clean and it's not always available, but there's always gasoline on somebody's truck or jeep. We took the rubber tread ... some of the steel tread, they seemed to have difficulty getting them back together [when damaged]."

External telephones for use by the infantry were now standard, and radio communication between vehicles was improved by new FM radios and multiple radio nets.

Swackhammer designed a modification for the escape hatch on his vehicles to allow the tank crews to more easily recover wounded men lying on the ground. A pin welded to one corner allowed the hatch to drop down several inches without falling free, and pivot to clear the opening. The hatch could be lifted and locked back into place.[13]

Long-term logistics and repair were problems that had bedeviled the Marines throughout the war, and improvements to the support system would be a critical success factor in the battle for Iwo. The tank battalions had bigger motor transport and repair components, and repair sections at both company and battalion level.

Charles Burt, a tank repairman in Headquarters Company, 5th Tank Battalion: "What we did with the retriever was to change engines, change turrets, change the front ends of the tanks when the line company didn't have time to do it, or didn't have the proper tools. We always said we were the elite of the maintenance people, but the line companies I'm sure would disagree with that."

The maintenance sections were equipped with M32B2 and M32B3 VTRs, based on the diesel-fueled M4A2 or gasoline-fueled M4A3, respectively. These vehicles had the turret replaced with a fixed superstructure that mimicked the shape of the normal turret. The VTRs could recover vehicles with broken tracks or damaged suspen-

---

* Ken Estes has researched the issue of conversion to the gasoline-fueled vehicles. He concluded that the changeover was driven by the Army's decision to withdraw logistical support for the M4A2, despite protests by units in the field. Collins was a known partisan of the gasoline-fueled vehicle. (Ken Estes, personal communica-

sions, right overturned tanks, and carried repair equipment and spare parts.

Gunnery Sergeant Sam Johnson of C Company, 4th Tank designed and built a one-of-a-kind flail tank to clear mines. The battalion was equipped with M4A3s, but the flail was based on a redundant M4A2.

Johnson's design added two pulleys onto the drive shaft behind the transmission. The pulleys powered belts that in turn drove a jeep drive shaft that went over the top of the transmission. This shaft went out a hole cut in the front of the hull to the differential and drive shaft from a truck mounted across the front of the tank on a tankdozer blade mount. On the ends of the axle were 18-inch diameter drums with a staggered pattern of replaceable screw mounts. Each mount held a section of one-inch steel cable, and a two-foot length of heavy chain. The rotating drums would cause the chains to beat against the ground with enough force to detonate most mines.[14]

Johnson celebrated his accomplishment prematurely, as described by C. B. Ash: "When the General showed up to see this, Sam had been out the night before and was still smashed out of his mind. He was at the tank park, but he was blind [drunk], and they hid him."

"Sam, he got the full credit for it," said Bob Neiman.

Ash: "It worked, but it was underpowered. They couldn't get a new tank, and used a worn-out M4A2. When they finally blew the damn thing apart setting off mines, they gave the M4A2 to the 3rd Tank Battalion, because they were the only ones [on Iwo] with M4A2s." Bob Neiman believed that the main problem was that the underpowered, worn-out tank tended to bog down in the soft volcanic soil.[15]

In addition to better training, the tank units also drew upon hard-won experience from previous campaigns, and Iwo Jima would see the first really widespread use of supplementary armor to provide protection against suicide attackers. The 4th and 5th Tank Battalions both added wooden plank armor to the sides of some of their tanks.

All three battalions also added a variety of protective cages over the driver's and hull gunner's hatch covers and rotating periscopes on the turret roof. Satchel charges thrown onto the hatch covers could cave in the hatch, with fatal results to the crewman below. The 3rd and 4th Battalions welded cages of steel rods over the hatch covers and periscopes to hold a satchel charge away from the vulnerable hatches and fittings, so that the charge detonated with a dead air space between it and the tank. The 5th Marine Tank Battalion used three-inch long nails welded to the hatch covers and rims, periscope covers, and ventilators, making each a porcupine with steel quills.

Tank crews stacked sandbags over the rear decks to prevent plunging mortar rounds from penetrating the thinner armor over the engine and fuel tanks, and loaded the slope plate with sandbags, spare wheels, track shoes, stowage boxes, coils of wire, or anything else that might absorb an explosion.

The beach parties could never provide enough water to replenish the two quarts each infantryman carried ashore in his personal canteens, and heat exhaustion and heat stroke were major causes of casualties and loss of combat efficiency. Tanks of C Company, 4th Tank carried water drums mounted over the engine deck. A pipe extended down to a rear corner of the tank, with a spigot on the end for refilling canteens.[16]

The new M4A3 Shermans were wider and heavier than the old M4A2s, and the lighter LCMs could neither carry them nor be expected to survive in Iwo's heavy surf.[17] Most of the tanks of the 4th and 5th Tank Battalions were loaded into LSMs. The seagoing Landing Ship, Medium could embark five Sherman tanks (the usual load was three) and did not require an LSD as a mother ship. The 3rd Tank Battalion was loaded aboard three of the precious LSTs.

At 0830 hours on the morning of D-day, 19 February, a wave of 68 LVT(A)-4s escorted by gunboats moved in on the beaches under cover of a rolling naval barrage. The LVT(A)-4s kept up a steady if unaimed fire on the run toward the beach. Behind the armored amphibians came eight waves of 482 LVTs carrying the 9,000 men of eight rifle battalions, strung out over nearly two miles of beach frontage. From left to right the assault battalions were 1/28 with 2/28 behind (Green Beach), 2/27 (Red-1), 1/27 (Red-2), 1/23 (Yellow-1), 2/23 (Yellow-2), and 1/25 and 3/25 abreast on Blue-1. Beach Blue-2 was not used.

Kuribayashi had issued strict orders that the artillery was to wait until the Americans were most vulnerable, packed cheek by jowl on the tiny beaches. The limited volume of return fire seemed to justify the pre-invasion scuttlebutt. Jim Carroll, a 19-year-old corporal and a tank gunner with C Company, 5th Tank, was told that "… because of the heavy naval and air bombardment of the island, probably the tanks would not be called upon to land. The Japanese defenders would be wounded or dazed. The infantry would go in there and mop up in three or four days, and wouldn't need any armor. That didn't prove to be true."

The key to the operation was momentum, to penetrate deep into the Japanese defenses while they were still stunned and disorganized by the shelling. Momentum was lost because the wet volcanic sand was firm enough to support a moving tractor, but above the wave line it was like dry quicksand. Any vehicle that stopped in the wave zone slowly sank into the wet sand.

The first waves of infantry managed to push 300 yards inland, but the follow-on waves bogged on the beach as vehicles broached in the surf, wheeled vehicles sank into the sand, and supplies began to pile up in chaotic heaps. As the advance slowed to a crawl, the naval barrage rolled forward and the Japanese began to recover. By 0935 all beaches were under heavy artillery and mortar bombardment. Reserve units and shore parties, and particularly the cargo-handlers, were caught in Kuribayashi's fire sack and suffered heavier casualties than the assault companies.[18]

Advance parties from the tank battalions went ashore with the first rifle battalion. These tiny units usually consisted of men who were knowledgeable of tank capabilities, but not immediately needed in action. Charles Burt went in with the 5th Tank Battalion maintenance officer and a JASCO (Joint Assault Signal Company) officer:[19] "The three of us went in at H plus 55 … and determined where to bring the tanks in, and when to bring them in. Hooh! It was scary! Anybody who said he wasn't scared was a damned liar. There was still fire coming in … They [the infantry] were off of the beachhead of course, up on the second or third level, but there was still artillery fire from Mount Suribachi coming down onto the beach. It was scary. I was scared as hell, I'll admit it."

The rifle regiments were already filling the airwaves with desperate calls for tanks, so the LSMs were among the first boats that tried to utilize the beaches. Their sufferings were a preview of things to come. The LSM was designed to drop a kedge anchor and pay out a cable on the run-in that would both hold it bow-on to the beach and help it retract after unloading.

The anchors refused to hold in the light, soft volcanic sand. The LSMs buried their noses in the soft sand and wallowed violently from side to side in the surf. Complicating the task was the milling mass of infantry, service troops, and wounded among the wrecked equipment.

On the extreme left the 28th Marines pushed across the island, and a small patrol from B/1/28 reached the western shore. Able Company and the following 2/28 built up a bedraggled defensive line facing the foot of Suribachi.

A full-strength tank company landed on Iwo Jima with fourteen gun tanks, two flame tanks (limited to two companies each in the 4th and 5th Tank), a dozer tank, and a VTR.[20] The 18 vehicles of A Company, 5th Tank Battalion were among the first ashore, at 1005 hours. One tank moved out of the LSM, backed into the water, and drowned out. The tank commander radioed the succinct report, "*Horrible Hank* sank."[21] Four other tanks broke tracks on the rocky ground above the beach and the engine failed on a fifth.

The survivors moved up to support the advance of 1/27 across the southern end of Airfield Number One. Enemy fire raked the flat, open ground at the south end of the airfield, and the riflemen were savaged by airbursts from Japanese antiaircraft guns firing down the runways. Even with the support of the tanks the rifle companies were driven back.

B Company came ashore on Red-1 at about 1300 hours, and also moved up to support the 27th Marines. The 18 vehicles of C Company, 5th Tank Battalion, assigned to support the 28th Marines in the attack on Suribachi, suffered the worst ordeal of any tank company after they came ashore at 1145 on Red-1.

Jim Carroll's tank was the first off its vessel:

> When we first rolled off the LSM the only thing I could see was through my periscope. All I could see was down into the surf. First thing I saw was an antitank gun, one of ours, hitched onto the back of a jeep. But there was nobody in the jeep, and the gun was sitting in the surf with the waves washing up around the wheels. I don't know where the driver was, whether he was dead or run off, or the jeep had stalled.
>
> Hanging onto the muzzle of the 37mm gun was a Marine. He was facing out to the ocean, and he'd lost control of his bowels. He was emptying them right there in the surf. He couldn't be concerned about all the other stuff that was going on around him. I guess he had the nervous drops, or whatever. Then we began to see wounded and dead Marines on the beach, and we knew it wasn't a John Wayne movie. It was for real.

Charles Burt met another boat: "The first tank that came aboard threw its track, and myself being a maintenance man, the Captain told me to make sure we got it running. The tank crew and myself jumped in and got the track back on. The captain and the JASCO man took the rest of the company up to the front lines, where the line commander was calling for them."

Breaking and repairing hundreds of pounds of track with cables and hand tools is vicious, backbreaking labor. Under shellfire, it is unimaginable. Burt: "You had to take the connector off of it, get it back on top of the rollers and the gears. We had a tool called a track jack ... All it was was a threaded tool that hooked onto the two track ends, and you just screwed it together, and kept screwing it until you got the two ends back together close enough to where you could put the connector back on and bolt it in place. I would guess that the total track would weigh seven or eight hundred pounds. Of course all we were doing was just lifting it and getting it up onto the rollers, and then you could roll it on so two or three people could work on it."

Burt's perception was that the volcanic sand that "stank like sulfur" seemed to be more troublesome than the shelling. "We were trained to do something, and we went ahead and done it. Do the best damn thing you can with whatever you've got."

One tank bogged in the deep ash, defying the VTR's attempts to extricate it, and another's engine failed. Engineers probed for mines, and found that the Japanese were also using new ceramic mines. The Type 3 Model A Pottery Mine consisted of a ceramic body, held three kilograms of explosive,[22] and was invisible to mine detectors. The lead tank, following two white tapes that marked a lane cleared of mines, strayed out of the lane and hit a big two-horned anti-boat mine. The massive transmission absorbed most of the blast, but the mine blew the front off the tank and seriously injured the driver.

Jim Carroll's tank was second in line as C Company struggled up the berm:

> The Japanese had bulldozed a trail to get their equipment down to the beach ... When we left our LSMs we fell in in a column of tanks, one behind the other. The lead tank in our column was the executive officer of C Company, Melvin Hazaleus. He was a reserve officer, older than most of our other officers. I remember because I had never heard of animal husbandry, and he was a professor of animal husbandry at Colorado.

The Japs, being very defensive-minded, had an antitank gun at the very top. When he topped the rise, they popped him. The column stopped because he took a round right where the turret meets the hull, and it not only jammed the turret but also wounded him and his gunner. The tank column was effectively disabled because no one could get around him.

Over the radio they asked for a volunteer to get out of one of the tanks and see if they could find a way to get around his disabled tank, and not expose ourselves to the fire of that antitank gun. I volunteered. I don't know why. Don't ask me. To this day I have no idea why I volunteered.

I got out through the loader's hatch, and dropped out on the deck. Being inside the tank was noisy, but we had no idea of the volume of the small arms fire that was going on. Not only small arms, but everything else. As soon as I got out of the tank I realized that we were in an extremely dangerous zone.

I crawled up beside the column of tanks. I could see that on either side of the trail that we had been following there were big tank traps that had been bulldozed or dug by hand. If we had ventured off to the left or right of the trail, either the tank would have tipped over or been bellied up in the sand, and we wouldn't have been able to move.

Even though the Japs had constructed those tank traps, I could see that if we were careful we could maneuver around the disabled tank and move on up to our objective. I got back in the tank and told my tank commander, Dutch Madsen, we could get around if they took it real easy ...

Four more tanks threw tracks maneuvering on the rough ground. Eventually the column made its way off the beach at the extreme right of Red-1, then cut across the front of Red-1 and Green beaches to join the 28th Marines. As the column advanced the tanks stumbled into one of the carefully prepared fire lanes, and the two lead tanks were disabled, with six men wounded. At 1400 hours the tank company hooked up with their infantry, having suffered 60 percent losses getting off the beach.[23]

Jim Carroll: "We were able to spread out in line, and move up with the infantry, and take the bunkers and such at the base of Suribachi under fire."

The tanks of C Company aided the infantry in several attempts to seize the lower slopes of Suribachi. In the final attempt the tanks found themselves in the unusual position of fighting a rearguard action to cover the withdrawal of infantry. One tank tumbled into a shell crater and had to be abandoned. The crew set fire to the vehicle to keep the enemy from either occupying it as a pillbox or getting the weapons and radios.

The fighting at the base of Suribachi was brutal, but it was worse on the extreme right. The 4th Division landed closer to the main enemy defensive lines where over 50 unscathed pillboxes overlooked the beach. The three LSMs carrying 16 tanks of A Company, 4th Tank Battalion were all hit, but at 1005 hours the first tanks were ashore and immediately plowed into a mine field.

C Company was the hardest hit while trying to land in support of the 23rd Marines on the Yellow beaches. The rifle companies of the 23rd were in desperate need, trapped under the fire of two huge blockhouses untouched by the shelling.

Like other tank company commanders, Bob Neiman was concerned about the soft volcanic ash:

> We had two teams of reconnaissance people, a corporal and two privates in each team. Each corporal had a walkie-talkie radio on my tank radio command frequency. They went in with the first wave of the infantry, and we were supposed to go in right after the third wave and ahead of the fourth. But we didn't know where to go. We had a place assigned, but we didn't know whether we could navigate the volcanic ash there.
>
> I only got one report, and it was very hurried and somewhat garbled. It was right after the first wave hit. All it said was something like "For Christ's sake don't try to land here. You'll bog down. Wait 'til you hear from us." We waited and waited, but we never did hear again. As it turned out, five of the six men were killed very early on D-day.
>
> Much later than planned we had to just go into the beach and try it.

LSM-216 carried three tanks and a command car of Neiman's command element.[24]

C. B. Ash drove Neiman's command tank ashore: "I'm the first tank out. The ramp went down, and off I went. I got just a little bit wet, and started up, but it was too steep. This volcanic ash was piling up in the tracks, between the bogeys and the tracks." Neiman, Gunnery Sergeant Sam Johnson, and the rest of the crew dug frantically while Ash tried to pull and rock the tank out of the sand. Finally a track snapped.

"The ship is catching hell," said Neiman, "and the only thing that saved it from being sunk—it was eventually sunk—it was so thin-skinned that the Japanese shells would go in one side and out the other before they would explode. It was a very frustrating experience. Tanks were needed ashore, but we couldn't get ashore."

Ash: "They made us get out and back aboard the boat. They pulled off, but while we're sitting there we're taking on wounded by the dozens. When we got back to [the] control [boat] we went on by, and the skipper says 'We're dumping these wounded off.' They had a floating dock tied up to either a hospital ship or an APA.* We took off altogether over 250 people, and never lost a man. And we had some bad ones. We came back in and they moved us down a little bit. The ramp went down, and we took eight rounds of 47mm."

Neiman and Sam Johnson jumped off the ship. Neiman: "We had bayonets, and we were probing the sand, but it was obvious to us right away that this was an identical situation … The one surviving member of the reconnaissance people ran over to me, a corporal by the name of Jewel. He said he had a spot where we could land." Jewel said he had also found a place to get over the beach terraces, and "it was like money from home."

Ash was still aboard the LSM which was again catching hell: "The holes in the side of the ship were three feet in diameter. The first two hit right below the con, in the radio room. There's two guys sitting in this room and they both hit the deck. The next round was lower, and the next round just took all the radios. They went aft and shot up a couple of life rafts, then they went down and were just about five inches above the water line. Two rounds into the engine room. They had a chief on there that ran the engine room. He had spent, up until that point in time, the whole war on some little island down in the Caribbean. He was gung-ho. Man, he wanted to hit the beach with us. He looked up and saw these two holes, and fainted dead away."

Without a tank, Ash and his buddies were scrambling for cover. "We're hiding behind 55-gallon drums of napalm. Now that's the best place to hide."

The crippled landing ship managed to back off the beach, again loaded with wounded. "We made five landings before we got the tanks all off. The last tank off, they shot the goddamned ramp down."

---

* Several transport ships were designated as floating hospitals.

Charles Newman's tank *Cyclops* was next in line behind Neiman's in the LSM. "Sam Johnson kicked me out of the commander's thing, and I took over the gun."

By that time the beaches were a madhouse of wounded men, piles of supplies and ammunition, flaming vehicles, and overturned tractors. A horrendous flotsam of dead men and the remains of over 100 splintered boats sloshed to and fro in the surf under a steady rain of mortar fire. With no tank support, the advance of the 23rd Marines lurched to a halt in the maze of pillboxes between the beaches and Airfield Number One.

The landing was an ordeal for Neiman's other platoons as well. "Oh my God, we got our ass tore up," said Max English. "We got to about the fourth terrace that first day. The Japs had everything marked … They knew where to drop it. They would wait 'til a shell hole or bomb hole filled up with Marines, and they would drop something in it." Tankdozers helped bulldozers build ramps through the steep beach terraces.

Three of English's tanks were immediately disabled by mines.[25] "It was raining just a little bit. I worked my way up to the third terrace, and I hit a magnetic mine. It blew the track off, but thank God the 300 or 500 pound bomb that it was sitting on top of didn't blow.

"My track was blown. I had to sit there all day in the position I was in and fire. When it became dark, our company maintenance came to me and broke my track. My track was broken, but you see, to repair it, you still have to break more and pull the tank off of that part and put it back together again."

The repair crews played a heroic role in the struggle for Iwo. The fearsome attrition of tanks by mines, artillery, and antitank guns, as well as the usual mishaps like thrown tracks, made rapid recovery and repair imperative.

The remaining C Company tanks struggled through the congestion on the beaches to reach 1/23 by late afternoon. The tanks assigned to 2/23 were blocked by yet another of the ubiquitous mine fields, as were the tanks of A Company. Other vehicles were stuck in soft sand, and the rain of mortar shells that the tanks attracted hindered the activities of the repair crews.

Once the tanks joined the rifle companies of 1/23, "it changed from frustrating to very satisfying," said Neiman. "Not more than 200 yards in front of us, very low to the ground and hard to see, was a row of pillboxes with machine guns. They couldn't depress the machine guns enough to get Marines who were on the ground, but any Marine who would try to stand up or run would be immediately cut down.

"This was a tank commander's dream. The tank directly behind me was one of our flamethrower tanks, and we had the whole damn company following up in a line behind. We immediately opened up on these pillboxes, which only had machine guns and couldn't hurt us at all. Had a very satisfying afternoon destroying them."

One of the gun tanks was equipped with a movie camera that shot through the seldom-used loader's periscope,[26] and it captured dramatic footage of a flame attack on a pillbox. The film showed "… the flame going right in the aperture. Then two Japanese crawling out of the pillbox with their shirts on fire and running … as our machine guns dug up the sand in back of them, and finally dropped them."

More attempts to push onto the runways of Airfield Number One were driven back by heavy machine-gun and antitank fire. A small group of Marines were trapped in a shell crater, unable to escape. Sergeant James Haddix's tank lumbered up and positioned itself above the trapped men, shielding them from machine-gun and mortar fire with its armored bulk. For four hours the tank and its crew squatted amid the heavy fire, systematically eliminating enemy positions as they were located. The tank pulled back only when the infantrymen dashed to safety.[27]

In the 5th Battalion area the tank maintenance units were scheduled to come in with the last assault wave. They were at first waved off because of the incredible congestion and high surf on the beaches, but the need for their service was too pressing. "Captain Jones put in an emergency call for us," said Bob Swackhammer. "We went aboard the rear end of an LST which was nosed up against the beach, late in the PM."

The heavily-burdened men had to leap from bobbing boats to grab for dangling rope ladders, climb up the high stern of the LST, then move forward and down through the tank deck to the beach. "How these young lads carried their tool box, which weighed about 50 pounds, and their own gear … how they did it, I don't know. In my backpack I had the reserve supply of morphine for the battalion … Just as we were going out the bow they sounded an air attack. We had no place to go, so I ordered my men back aboard ship. The ship got hit by a bomb … Pieces of shrapnel were ricocheting around in that well deck."

By the time Swackhammer and his maintenance crews made it ashore only six of A Company's tanks were functional. The tank stuck on the beach proved a total loss. "It was gone. It sank down in the sand. Each time the tide came in it sank a little deeper. The last I saw of it, it was clear up above the tracks. So far as I know, no attempt was made to get it out."

The maintenance crews worked around the clock. "Everybody pitched in. They saw what needed to be done, and they did it. I only recall issuing one order. We had to do a lot of track work."

The maintenance teams made repairs that would normally have been done in well-equipped repair depots far back of the lines. Repairs were rough-and-ready, performed in a light-proof shelter made of tarps stretched over a crater:

> We even cut the barrel off of one tank. I don't know what it had been hit by. Leo Mason was the tank commander … It dented the barrel to the extent that it was dangerous to fire it. We took a torch and cut it off, then borrowed a [go-no go] gauge from the artillery people … We test fired it, so he finished out the campaign there on Iwo with a 'howitzer.'
>
> We had one [tank] hit right square in the bow gun, on the front slope plate … Again, we took a torch, cut out the damaged part, and welded in another one. [Parts were scavenged from anywhere.] I got put on report by the 3rd Division. We were up there doing some scavenging.
>
> That first day ashore some of the guys took time out to dig themselves a foxhole. For some reason or other I didn't, and when it came dark, I just fell in on top of them. I tell you, nobody moved. The rest of the time my foxhole was under a burned-out tank. There was nothing left but the hull.

Night came and the beleaguered Marines dug in for the expected counterattack. No counterattack came, only suicidal infiltrators with explosive charges seeking tanks, artillery positions, and command posts. Colonel Kaido's gunners doubled, then trebled their rate of fire onto the exposed beaches, playing havoc with the casualty evacuation stations, supply dumps, and crews laboring to repair tanks on the blacked-out beaches.

In the morning the enemy brought down an accurate early morning shelling that concentrated on the rifle battalion command posts. Among the casualties was the commander of B Company, 4th Tank

Battalion, wounded as he was conferring with the commander of 2/25.[28]

Symptomatic of the problems caused by enemy observation from Suribachi was the continual harassment of the 5th Tank Battalion. After expending all their fuel and ammunition, and with the beachhead in a hopeless snarl, the tankers were scavenging parts and ammunition from the trail of dead and disabled tanks.[29] Tanks had to be laboriously refueled from cans, five gallons at a time, and it took 33 cans per tank. Each time the tank crews tried to assemble to transfer fuel and ammo they were harried by a rain of mortar fire.[30]

Not until 1100 hours on the second day could the 5th Battalion assemble a force adequate to support the advance against Suribachi. All afternoon the tanks blasted away at caves and concrete pillboxes, covering the approach of the infantry assault squads. By nightfall only five tanks remained in action, and the hard-pressed maintenance crews began another of their nocturnal repair marathons.

At 0830 the 4th Division and the right flank units of the 5th Division turned north for the slow, methodical, and bloody reduction of the bulk of the island. The Japanese had leveled a broad area for the main airfield, and the flat ground was covered by crisscrossing fields of fire from multiple antitank guns and liberally seeded with bombs rigged as antitank mines.

The effects of the mines could be freakish and horrifying. Max English: "Mines were awful, awful bad. Hank Baughman's platoon sergeant's tank ran over a mine. It blew in the escape hatch and killed the whole crew in place. Sad tank to look at. Look in there and here's these fellows sitting there doing the last things. They're dead. They're sitting there, burnt up. The flash fire killed them."

Jim Carroll saw another tank that struck a huge mine: "It had blown the turret right of the tank. All the spare rounds for the 75mm gun were stored under the deck of the turret; there were about a hundred rounds under there. If they all go off at once, it's a considerable explosion. It blew that turret 40 or 50 feet, and killed everybody but the driver."

A and B Companies of the 5th Tank Battalion managed to work their way around the western edge of the main airfield. Between them the two tank companies mustered 26 vehicles, but as always the number dwindled steadily under the onslaught of artillery fire and suicide troops. True to their orders the Japanese tank-hunters singled out command tanks, marked by multiple radio antennae. One team disabled a command tank by tossing a satchel charge under the rear, rupturing a fuel tank and setting the tank aflame. The crew bailed out into the midst of a swarm of enemy infantry and managed to fight their way clear.[31]

The 4th Tank Battalion moved out onto the deadly space around Airfield Number One, with A Company supporting the advance of the 24th Marines. B Company supported the 25th Marines, while C Company supported the 23rd Marines. The tanks found themselves hopelessly entangled in a maze of gullies and minefields, and B Company was on the receiving end of an unusually heavy mortar barrage.

The handful of survivors from C Company, 5th Tank were still chipping away at the lower slopes of Suribachi. Jim Carroll's tank lost a track to a mine and could not be recovered under the intense fire so the crew was sent back to help out the maintenance and logistics people.

Fuel was now being brought ashore in drums, rather than heaps of five-gallon cans. The drums caused problems because there were too few of the special rotary hand pumps that fitted into the drums. Jim Carroll:

> They had a big pit bulldozed ... Down in this pit there were a whole bunch of 55-gallon drums of gasoline. As our guys would need to be refueled, they would pull up beside this pit. We would manhandle—if you can imagine this—these 55-gallon drums up the side of this hole dug in the sand. We would all get under the damned thing and lift it up.
>
> It was the only day it rained on the island, so it was doubly miserable. We would manhandle it up onto the tank, and we would put a donkey-dick (a flexible, screw-in spout) into the bung of the drum, open it up, and refuel the thing right there. Very primitive. We didn't use a pump or anything, just let it run down in there. We were lucky the damn thing didn't catch on fire.

Another night brought no protection from the incessant shelling. The tank unit command posts were located near the beaches and were hard hit. The 5th Tank Battalion command post was almost destroyed when a DUKW loaded with howitzer ammunition was struck by artillery fire as it passed nearby.

After another dark, wet night 21 February dawned with a 19-knot wind pushing heavy waves onto the beaches. C Company, 5th Tank Battalion, with only five tanks in action[32] was still suffering from a shortage of fuel and ammunition, and the three battalions of the 28th Marines began the attack on Suribachi without them. Their efforts were futile until the handful of surviving tanks finally arrived at about 1100 hours. The tanks were stalled in a minefield until Corporal Wallace Johnson dismounted and scouted a path through the mine-field under machine-gun fire.[33] Supported by long-range fire from the tanks, the 2nd and 3rd Battalions were able to push up and onto the slopes of the mountain by 1400 hours. The tanks were sent to the rear to replenish fuel and ammo, having lost three more vehicles—one to a mine, another to an antitank gun, the third temporarily abandoned with a broken track.

In the north A Company, 4th Tank Battalion supported continuing attacks by the 25th Marines east of the airfield near the Rock Quarry, while B Company supported the efforts of 1/24 to root out stubborn defenders from areas already bypassed by the front-line battalions.

The smallest mistake or inattention could have disastrous consequences. Inside the tanks the roar of the engine and weapons overpowered the intercom. "We had hand signals," said Charles Newman. "If you were going to fire three rounds, which I was, you held up three fingers. And then I was firing high explosive; that's a clenched fist. So I did three, clenched fist. I was shooting at a little ol' hole. I squeezed one off. I got my crosshairs lined up, and squeezed off another one, and then I squeezed off the third. I got ready to turn my turret … Monk Masterson, the driver, yells 'Chicky's been hit!' I look over underneath the gun, and he's laying on the deck of the tank."

The loader had bent over into the recoil path of the massive breech just as Newman fired the last round. "It hit him right above the eye, and split it open. He had blood all over himself, on the deck of the tank, and the worst thing, he was trying to draw his 45. He thought the enemy had hit him. I locked the gun … I had to put my legs around his body, and my head around his arms to keep him from drawing his damned old 45. He was spitting blood. We finally got him out of there, but Sam [Johnson] actually had to cuff him a couple of times upside the head to get him aware of what was wrong."

The injured Wells was relieved of the two perks of a tank NCO, his 45 and his government-issue Hamilton watch. His crew got the pistol, and the Navy relieved him of the watch aboard the evacuation ship.[34]

The big Japanese mines were thickly strewn, and the 4th Battalion lost two more tanks. One belonged to Max English's platoon. "My platoon sergeant ... hit a 500 pound bomb that took his tank. His turret—it flew like a clay pigeon. It took the tank upside down. The driver and assistant driver were killed immediately. The gunner [was pinned under the turret]. Joe Bruno, my platoon sergeant, and his loader rode that turret out and neither one of them [was killed]. It's a miracle."

Bruno had been blown completely clear of the turret, and fell onto the rocky surface about 20 feet away. Riflemen rescued the smashed Bruno, who had a broken back and head injuries, and his gunner, but could not free the man whose leg was pinned under the massive turret. C. B. Ash: "They're gonna send up a patrol from the tanks that night to get this guy out, because they know he's still alive. They get a little corpsman, a doctor, and a guy named Dever [a platoon leader]. These guys go up with two or three others. They get in there, and the doctor can't get in to cut this guy's leg off. With the help of a flashlight this little corpsman got down in a spot where he could work, and took this guy's leg off. The doctor gives him instructions. They got him out and took off. Just when they got to the edge of the airstrip, either a mortar or a round of some type landed and wounded all of them. Along with their patient, they all ended up in sickbay."

Another tank was disabled when it hit a mine that broke a track on the airstrip. Ash: "... Jimmy Parker, he hit one. The ten-pound AT mine went off. They all came out through the escape hatch. The dust was thicker than hell. They got off the strip and came back down to the company. The next day they came up to get their tank with the retriever ... Jimmy crawled underneath that tank, and here's this uncovered 500-pound bomb. He about shit his pants."

Sanitary arrangements inside the tanks were not at all improved over those in the old light tanks. Ash:

Right in front of the assistant driver there was four-inch steel pipe, with a cap on it. You ate enough cheese that you didn't have any problem about that, but you might have to pee. You would piss in a brass [shell casing], hand it over to Baughman, and he'd drop 'em out. That was the sanitation.

On Iwo, in our bivouac area, we had somewhere close by—maybe 500 yards away—a sniper, but he wasn't too good. We had dug into the ground a 55-gallon drum with a little hole cut in top of it. I don't know how deep they went, 'cause I didn't have the pleasure of digging it.

You would get on this, and boy, don't spend too much time. That sonofabitch, he could hit the drum. You always faced away from him, so he had a small [target]—just your ass. He never did hit anybody, but that was interesting. Sanitation was otherwise nonexistent.

Charles "Chilly" Newman said that when his tank was hit by artillery on 21 February, "We had all our gear, and our toothbrushes and shorts, and all that stuff tied outside the tank ... It tore everything up. I went for the first 31 or 32 days on Iwo wearing the same pair of shorts, just like quite a few of them did."

The progress of the 4th Division was slow, held back by the open airfield on one flank and rugged terrain on the other. On the left 1/26 and 3/27 were able to take advantage of the support offered by the other two companies of the 5th Tank. They advanced nearly a thousand yards along the western shore, until they were brought to a halt by the 4th Division's inability to make headway.

The 21st Marines of the 3rd Division landed at 1345 and suffered their first casualties when they were hit by heavy artillery while crossing the open areas south of the airfield. The 3rd Tank Battalion had already suffered its first casualties. The battalion's tanks and soft-skinned vehicles were loaded aboard three LSTs.

For *LST-477*, carrying A Company and parts of Headquarters Company, it was a hard-luck voyage. On 19 February the ship developed steering trouble and fell astern of the small convoy. Then on the morning of 21 February two of the ship's crew were working with an IFF transmitter when the self-destruct detonator exploded in one of the men's hands, killing him and wounding his companion.[35]

LST-477 had almost caught up with the convoy when five enemy aircraft appeared. One *kamikaze* hit the AKN *Keokuk*, and another plowed into the starboard side of *LST-477* at 1720 hours.[36] Flaming gasoline engulfed the enclosed tank deck. The wounded sailor, five other sailors, and three Marines were killed, and fourteen Marines wounded.

Other *kamikaze* bored in as the tank crewmen joined the sailors in manning the antiaircraft guns and tossing blistering-hot ammunition over the side. A sailor, Blaine Heinze, crawled over cooking ammunition in the burning tank deck, and wriggled into a small space below the tank deck to restore power to the emergency fire fighting pumps. He remained there as the crew fought the fire that raged over his head.[37]

Through another dreary night and cold drizzling rain the Marines suffered under steady shelling. Wet volcanic ash turned into a gluey, abrasive paste the consistency of cookie dough. It stuck to men and equipment, wrecked and jammed weapons, mechanical equipment and radios, and turned the tracks of tanks into enormous mudballs. Topographic depressions turned into deadly quicksand pits into which tanks sank up to their turrets. By a herculean overnight recovery and repair effort C Company, 5th Tank managed to put seven tanks back on the line for the 22 February attack on Suribachi. Three tanks pushed into ravines below the western foot of the mountain, but a driving rain blinded the tanks, and they had to be led into action by men on foot. At day's end the 28th Marines had completely encircled Suribachi.

Up north the front-line rifle regiments were relieved by their sister regiments in the predawn hours, but even with the help of tanks the replacements could make little in the way of tangible advances. The 26th Marines advanced about 400 yards along the west coast, but the fresh 3rd Division was bogged down. Any movement along the low ground drew withering blasts of heavy machine-gun fire from the high ground in the 3rd Division sector, and the 26th was forced to relinquish its gains.

Although C Company, 5th Tank was in the worst condition, all the tank companies were taking a severe battering. At day's end the 5th Tank had 13 tanks written off as losses and four under repair. The 4th Tank had eleven destroyed and eight in the shop.

In the cold, wet morning light of 23 February a small patrol from F/2/28 reached the nearly abandoned crest of Suribachi. Another patrol was given a very specific mission, and at 1020 hours raised a small flag on the lip of the crater. Some time later a runner arrived with a larger flag from *LST-779*, and civilian photographer Joe Rosenthal snapped his famous photo.

Russell W. Lippert, whom Chilly Newman described as "... looking like a regular Marine ought to look" was acting First Sergeant for Neiman's company when he was killed. "Joe Rosenthal ... lost his helmet aboard a small craft coming in. He needed a helmet ... and some guy said 'There's a whole stack of them over there.' He got a helmet. It was Russell W. Lippert's, because the name was inside the damn helmet. Mister Rosenthal kept that particular helmet, and only last year did he go through *Leatherneck* magazine … to find the relatives of Russell W. Lippert."

The flag was more of a symbol than any achievement of immediate tactical significance. For modern Americans the flag raising is a symbol of the fall of Iwo Jima, but in reality most of the killing and dying still lay ahead.

The Marines of the 4th Division, and the attached 21st Marines, couldn't spare the time to watch the flag raising. At 0730 they had started into another assault across the airfield and into intense fire. A particular problem was a battery of 47mm antitank guns sited to fire down the long axis of the main runway. Tanks that tried to pick their way through the mines and buried bombs were sitting ducks for these guns. The mudcaked engineers who crawled forward to deal with the mines were sliced apart by airbursts from 75mm antiaircraft guns and fire from Type 92 7.7mm machine guns that the Marines called "the woodpecker" because of its distinctive sound. The 21st and 26th Marines made repeated assaults, and were repeatedly driven back with crushing losses.

At 1730 hours *LST 646* beached with the first of 3rd Tank's vehicles, but *LST 741* was hit by gunfire and forced off. The long-suffering *LST 477* got a cable tangled in its screws and was immobilized for the entire day.[38]

On 24 February 25 tanks of the 3rd Tank Battalion came forward to bolster the depleted ranks of the other two units. The big push of the day was an effort to capture Airfield Number Two. At 0910 hours three rifle regiments, the 26th, 21st, and 24th from left to right, attacked along the high ground that formed a topographic divide connecting Airfield Numbers One and Two.

Frustrated by the jumbled ground south of the airfield, and with their ranks badly depleted, the tanks of all three battalions were consolidated into a single powerful force under the command of Rip Collins of the 5th Tank Battalion.[39] The 5th and 3rd Battalion tanks would advance in an assault column along a broad taxiway that connected Airfield Number One to Airfield Number Two.

The lead unit, A Company of the 5th Tank, quickly ran into a storm of fire from guns firing head-on at them down the long, straight approach. The lead tank, the command tank of Lieutenant Henry Morgan, struck a mine that blew off a track and damaged the suspension. The second tank in line, another platoon command tank belonging to Lieutenant Obert Richardson, veered out to bypass the crippled tank, and ran over another mine. The powerful explosion blew in the belly, and hurled the turret high into the air. The blast killed four crewmen, and the fifth was thrown out of the wrecked tank. PFC John Currie dismounted and dashed out into the machine-gun fire to rescue the wounded survivor, PFC Dale Plummer.[40]

Salvaging useful parts from wrecks was a gruesome task. "The driver had thick black hair," said Bob Swackhammer. "About the biggest piece left of him was a patch of his head.

"This must have been an aerial torpedo ... We salvaged part of that tank. One lad was telling me years later that 'I went up there to get the radio out of there, and there was brains all over it.' You just can't let those things get to you."

The stalled column, clearly visible from Turkey Knob, was immediately deluged by enemy artillery. Four more tanks were stricken and fifteen more men killed or wounded.[41] The survivors withdrew back down the taxiway.

On the west 2/27 made good gains across the open coastal plain but advanced into a huge ambush. Once F Company had advanced into the killing zone, the enemy opened fire from well-hidden pill-boxes and dug-in tanks, pinning the Marines in place. A rescue attempt was racked by a mortar barrage, and also pinned down with heavy losses. Only the arrival of four tanks saved the two companies. The tanks moved forward through the pinned infantry, and for once their tendency to draw enemy fire was a blessing. Shielded by their armored bulk, the stunned riflemen slowly withdrew to the start line, dragging their dead and wounded.

The main effort in the 4th Division zone, an attempt to cross the air-field, was to be made by the 21st Marines, and their attack was delayed while the tanks worked their way past mines. Under a heavy exchange of fire between the tanks and the Japanese north of the run-way, K/3/21 managed to gain a foothold on the far side.

The tanks crossed the main runway, and from the base of the ridge pounded away at any enemy positions they could find as the infantry clawed its way onto the crest. K/3/21 captured the top of the ridge, only to be driven off by friendly artillery fire. The company scaled the hill a second time, but were driven back in heavy hand-to-hand fight-ing. Faced with the alternative of capturing the ridge or braving the terrors of another passage across the runway, the Marines went up the ridge a third time. Both sides fought with knives, clubbed rifles, and bayonets, but this time the Marines held a foothold atop the ridge.

The heaviest losses occurred when the 24th Marines and 2/25 slowly fought their way across the east end of the main runway and onto the crest of a low ridge known as "Charlie-Dog." The depleted Marines could not dig in on the crest of the stony ridge and were driven off by 1600 hours. Charlie-Dog concealed numerous antitank guns.

Charles Newman: "We were the fifth tank in a line. I don't remember how far apart we were—we were staggered. I saw something wink. I turned my gun over there, and I squeezed one off. The wink was an antitank gun of some type, and he hit a boy by the name of 'Polly' Parrot, whose tank was right in front of ours, maybe 20 or 30 yards. It didn't hit any of the other tanks, but it noticed that we had seen it, and it turned on us. He fired on us five times, and hit us all five times … Needless to say, we had a lot of things going on in those last few moments."

The loader was a maintenance man who had replaced the wounded loader, R. D. Wells, and was inexperienced at the task. Newman:

Niles [Darling] would pick up and throw an HE in there. That's the prescribed shell for this kind of combat. I would fire that, and he would pick up the next thing on the deck of the tank, [which] was a smoke I'd say, and he'd throw that in. That has less range the HE. Then he'd pick up an armor-piercing, and that has longer range, and so I wasn't able to bracket it.

To be honest with you, I wasn't trying to bracket it at that particular time, because he was shooting pretty accurately. We backed the tank up, X number of feet, but apparently not far enough. I figured I fired eight or nine rounds at him, and I know he fired at least five at me, because we found five [hits].

We had blue smoke, we had dust going through that sucker, and it was rocking back and forth [with each hit].

The front slope plate of the medium tank is about three inches thick. It was just like it was wet sand, and you'd scoop out a handful. We had bogey wheels and some track welded on there—the Seabees did that for us before we went into combat—and it stripped off that, of course, but it didn't penetrate our tank.

Apparently what I did, I scared him off. We went up here a day or so later, and that particular gun was on a ledge, above the … airfield. It was a pretty scary thing. I don't think we ever hit him ... but he stopped firing, and the whole column, including us, we got our butt out of there.

Communications were vastly improved, but tank commanders sometimes dismounted to confer with the men on the ground. Max English:

> I had the shit scared out of me. I remember coming out of my tank. You know the top of that tank is 18 feet from ... the ground. I would open my hatch, and grab my hands out there [on the hatch rim] and I would jump. I'm falling 18 feet. Coming behind me is a steel helmet. I had already taken my tank helmet off, so I'm coming out bareheaded. A steel helmet comes down and I grab it and slap it on my head. Behind that comes a sawed-off shotgun, and I grab that. I run like a son-of-a-gun to where I know I'm supposed to go, because I've already talked to 'em on the radio.
>
> I'm running to where they are, so that they can tell me [what they wanted me to do] ... I liked to get out and get on the ground, talk to them. They would point out to me what they needed done. I would run back and get in my tank. They [the crew] would see me running. They'd open up the top hatch, and I'd come in, feet first, and then close that hatch. Things were popping all the time. You'd hear the little Jap bullets hitting that tank, coming after me, saying "We'll get him." But they didn't get him.

At day's end the Americans held an irregular line across the main runway of Airfield Number Two, but bent back along the base of Charlie-Dog almost to the north end of the landing beaches.

Between the taxiway massacre and the crossfire on the runway the combined tank force had lost 32 tanks in one day. Unknown to the Marines, they had thus far been struggling against Kuribayashi's secondary defenses. Only in the east had they impinged upon the main cross-island defense line that ran across the edge of the central Motoyama Plateau.

Most enemy positions were linked to Turkey Knob by buried telephone cables. Nearby Hill 382 was crowned by the island's wrecked radar station. The peripheral defenses of the two hills included twenty pillboxes, three of the deadly Type 88 antiaircraft guns sited as dedicated tank-killers, a dozen heavy dual machine cannon, and scores of machine guns. Four of Baron Nishi's tanks were dug in up to their turrets. The Knob and Hill 382 overlooked The Amphitheater, a topographic depression that itself held three successive defensive lines. These three unimpressive topographic features, collectively known as The Meatgrinder, became the costliest real estate in Marine Corps history.

As tank losses soared, the repair crews spent more time in the front lines. Swackhammer and his repair crews from A Company, 5th Tank were hard-pressed, as they had come ashore without their VTR and had to perform all front-line recoveries with jeeps and hand tools.[42] Swackhammer:

> Actually, most of the type of work we did it (the VTR) wouldn't have been a real valuable piece of equipment anyway. We did a lot of scavenging from disabled tanks.
>
> There was a place up there they called the Bowling Alley. The Japanese artillery had an area there where they were really blowing things apart. They even hit ambulances going out. They passed word to get out of there as quick as you can, any way you can. We had a jeep with our tools in it ... Everybody in that area was scrambling out of there, because we got word they were going to saturate that area with artillery fire.
>
> I certainly didn't want to lose our tools, so I told my gunnery sergeant, "You can go out with me or get out the best way you can." He jumped in the jeep and laid down. They were firing at every other vehicle that went out of there. Later they hit one of our tanks and burst the seam of the gasoline tank; it caught on fire.
>
> We waited until he fired a round, and I put that little ol' jeep in low gear and floorboarded it. I didn't want to let up until we got clear back to the bivouac area.
>
> [The maintenance crews also suffered from the mines.] There was a flamethrower tank—one of ours—coming out to get another load of napalm. The engineers had marked the supposedly mine-free area. I was guiding this tank out, and he hit a mine ... I don't remember the name of this lad who was with me. What he was doing standing there beside me I don't know ...
>
> I can see it to this day. That tank just raised up and settled back down. A piece of something hit this chap who was with me in the thigh, and they evacuated him.

Amid the carnage, small comforts could seem incredibly important. Charles Newman: "One thing the old man (Neiman) did for us that was so great, he had two six-by-six trucks screened, like an old covered wagon over the top. He had screen wire to keep out the bugs and stuff. He had two or three stoves bolted to the deck of these six-by-sixes. He threw cases and cases of corned beef hash, and all that kind of good stuff in there. When we got ashore far enough where we could use them, Goony-Bird Campbell and some of these other cooks would bring these things ashore, and we had hot meals on Iwo Jima."

At 1305 hours the battered *LST 477* at last beached on Green-1, and by 1415 hours the last 3rd Battalion tanks were on shore.

The inability of the 9th Marines to push farther into the interior of the plateau meant that the right flank of the 5th Division was dominated by high ground along the rim of the plateau. Although the 5th Division was relatively lightly opposed, any movement on the low ground was severely punished by fire from positions hidden in the ravines.

Nosing up into the ravines, the 5th Battalion tanks were essentially blind. Jim Carroll: "We were getting our target designations through the tank-infantry phones that were mounted on the back end of the tank. It was just a telephone handset on a reel of cord that reeled out of a box on the rear right of the tank. Infantry would get up there and pull that thing down into their hole and say fire to your left or to your right, and they would adjust our fire."

On a few occasions infantry rode inside the tanks, but "… most of them were very claustrophobic. They'd ride in there for a little bit, and they'd say 'Let me get out of this damn thing.' They would realize what our limitations were as far as visibility. While it might seem obvious to them where the fire was coming from, we might not be able to see that hole because there were so damn many holes."

On the morning of 25 February it fell to the 9th Marines of the 3rd Division to relieve the badly mauled 21st and begin to batter themselves senseless against some of the strongest positions in the Motoyama defensive line. The 3rd Division had not yet gained a foothold on the north side of Airfield Number Two. The fate that awaited the 3rd Battalion tanks trying to support another attack across the main runway was all too clear. The four antitank guns that had mauled the 4th Battalion tanks still fired down the runway into the flank of the attack, adding to the destruction wrought by the mortars and artillery called down by Turkey Knob. Nevertheless, the tanks of A and B Companies led the way out onto the open runway. The leading tanks were hit immediately, two knocked out of action and a third immobilized. The trapped crew of the stalled tank continued to fight on. The infantry suffered heavy losses but made it across the runway to the base of the low but rugged ridge on the far side. Eventually nine of the 23 tanks that started across the runway were put out of action.[43]

The slow headway of the 9th still exceeded the gains scored by the 23rd Marines on their right, in the 4th Division zone. The terrain east of the airfield was impassable to tanks, so C Company, 4th Tank moved over into the 9th Marines' zone until an armored bulldozer was able to scrape a trail into the area. The 24th Marines made similarly limited progress against The Amphitheater.

The short combat ranges made the Type 01 47mm gun a deadly tank killer. Max English: "The Japanese had a 57* that *would* penetrate. I saw my driver [Whisenant] get his left arm shot off. I looked down, and saw his arm just hanging by the coat sleeve. We were trying to back the tank into a shell hole to get away from them, and I was looking at the antitank gun. My gunner was shooting at that antitank gun ... And we were backing at the same time. I'm sitting there looking at three or four shells coming—you can see them coming, actually see them coming to you, and hitting you."

The two assault battalions of the 9th Marines spent all day on 26 February in another futile effort to batter their way onto hills Oboe and Peter, north of the main runway. At 0700 hours 1/9 and 2/9 moved out onto the relatively open ground supported by A and B Companies, 3rd Tank.

The tanks moved in a textbook attack formation in advance of the infantry and into the deadly crossfire of several 47mm guns. Machine guns drove the riflemen to ground. One tank was struck in the side of the turret and four crewmen wounded, then a second was hit and four more men wounded, one fatally. When a third tank moved in to evacuate the wounded, it was hit and three more men wounded.[44]

Six A Company tanks also moved out onto the open ground. Two were immediately wrecked by antitank fire, and another crippled

---

* The Japanese 57mm gun was an obsolete, low velocity tank gun suited to fire only high-explosive rounds. At the time—and today—many Marines referred to the 47mm Type 01 antitank gun as a 57mm.

and stalled. A wounded Marine, a tourniquet knotted about his thigh, crawled up to the front of the stalled tank, *Ateball*, and waved to attract attention. He pointed out the position of the antitank gun and four machine-gun positions for the tank gunner, then hugged the ground while the tank crew fought off two suicidal attacks by Japanese infantry. When the driver eventually got the tank running again, the crew dragged the wounded man up through the belly hatch, and the tank limped away to safety.[45]

All day long the tanks and infantry butted at the mutually supporting pillboxes and low hills north of the ridge. By dark, the infantry had taken severe losses, and Major Holly Evans of the 3rd Tank Battalion reported that he had lost nine of his remaining 20 tanks.[46]

Able Company, 5th Tank Battalion and 3/26 were still working their way along the western rim of the plateau, digging the enemy out of one ravine at a time. Artillery could not reach targets in the deep, narrow gullies, and the tank-infantry teams had to venture into these clefts. The walls on both sides were shot through with caves, so men and tanks attacking one opening were exposed to a vicious crossfire. When one cave mouth was blasted shut by the demolition teams the defenders would simply filter through the underground maze to a new position. The deadly process would continue until all six or eight openings of a cave complex had been sealed, and the team would move on to the next.

The ultimate solution to the interconnected caves were the handful of specialized tanks. Max English: "On Iwo the best vehicle we had was the dozer. He would go and close up the caves."

The flame tanks were a godsend, but presented unique logistical problems. The thickened fuel had to be mixed in 55-gallon drums, then pumped into pressurized tanks inside the hull of the tank. Bob Swackhammer: "You had a pump that you screwed into the barrel, and turned a rotary crank. That stuff didn't pour ... Essentially it was a hand operation."

The thickened fuel was hand-mixed, a dangerous task that fell to the maintenance men like Charles Burt:

> What we did when we weren't busy operating with the retriever was to mix the 'glop' as we called it, the stuff that they used for the flamethrower tanks ... We fixed that stuff by the 55-gallon barrel, several of them every day.

[Preparing the napalm required mixing aviation gasoline with a thickening agent.] We would open those cans, as I remember they were about a gallon, a square or rectangular container. We would open that, and dump it into the drum of gasoline. We started out with just a stick, stirring it. We couldn't even keep up with them. It would take about two hours to mix a 55-gallon drum of napalm ... We had a gentleman, he was an old guy—he must have been about 25-or 28-years old—with all us young kids. He was an inventor, a very ingenious type of person. He rounded up an air compressor, put a hose on it, took a piece of pipe and drilled a bunch of holes in it, and capped the pipe off. We'd start the air compressor, stick that thing down in that barrel of gasoline, and in a few minutes we'd have a barrel of napalm. Then we were able to keep up with the crews. Two people could do what 20 could do before that.

[This dangerous work was done close to the fighting.] We were behind the lines of course, but behind the lines on Iwo was not very far from the front lines any time. It wasn't that big an island.

No place was safe from artillery and snipers. Anthony J. Monico was a maintenance man in B Company, 4th Tank, who had killed 20 enemy soldiers on Roi-Namur.[47] Charles Newman: "On Iwo Jima—he went that far—he was in the back area where a maintenance man should be. He was stepping out of a hole with a canteen of coffee in his hand, and one of them got him through the chest."

B Company, 5th Tank supported F/2/26 in their advance along the western coastal slope. This day's advance captured the last water well available to the Japanese, prompting a rare daylight counterattack.

The 4th Division was still attacking The Meatgrinder. Three battalions of the 25th Marines pushed into The Amphitheater under a torrent of heavy mortar fire. When A Company, 4th Tank tried to assist they lost two tanks and were forced to retire because they were drawing fire onto the infantry they were supporting. Three more A Company vehicles tried to assist C/1/25 in an effort to bypass Turkey Knob, but were driven back by heavy mortar fire. The only unqualified success for the 4th Division came on the extreme right, where Item/3/25, assisted by two tanks, finally managed to destroy a long-lived enemy pocket above the East Boat Basin.

In the morning hours of 27 February the 23rd and 25th Marines resumed their grinding assaults on Hill 382—Turkey Knob line. Repeated attacks against Hill 382 by the 23rd failed to gain a foothold on the slopes, until at noon 3/23 followed a rolling barrage up and onto the crest of the smoldering hill.

In the early afternoon 1/23, supported by tanks, drove a wedge into the rough ground west of Hill 382 and moved up onto the rear slopes. The glacial pace of the advance was regulated by the rate at which a lone tankdozer could carve a trail around house-sized boulders and into steep ravines. As the dozer worked, other tanks followed along the narrow, tortuous trail while riflemen bled and died to protect the tanks.

Atop Hill 382 the 3rd Battalion found that the Japanese were determined to hold the hill, and sent reinforcements through tunnels that connected the hill to other positions. All afternoon the 3rd Battalion fought with grenades, knives, and bayonets in the rubble of the old radar station.

While the defenders were occupied with the bitter struggle atop Hill 382, 1/25 and three A Company tanks tried to force their way into the ground between the two hills and attack the western slopes of Turkey Knob. The Marines still did not realize that this small hill was the central fire direction center for the Japanese, and they were again on the receiving end of fire from every mortar and artillery tube the enemy could muster. Within minutes two tanks were destroyed, a third damaged, and the infantry retreated in disarray.

The Marines knew that they could never hope to provide 3/23 atop Hill 382 with enough ammunition and water to allow them to hold through the night. At 1700 hours the surviving riflemen began to filter back down the rocky slopes.

Before daylight on 27 February the 27th Marines relieved the 26th on the west coast sector, and continued the advance through the broken terrain and seaside cliffs. Useless knobs of barren rock changed hands again and again amid showers of grenades. A flame tank laboriously inched forward, only to be immediately disabled by mortar fire.

In the center the primary effort was made by 2/9. In the early morning hours 2/9's attack against hill Oboe was bloodily repulsed. Following an artillery bombardment in the early afternoon 1/9 and 2/9 were committed, supported by B Company, 3rd Tank. Charlie Company had been ordered to stand down, as several tanks were in positions where they were unrecoverable. Despite heroic repair efforts, that evening C Company could still muster only 11 tanks.[48]

At 1300 hours the two battalions secured hill Peter, then Oboe, but at heavy cost. The rifle companies were decimated, and another 11 disabled tanks littered the small battlefield north of Airfield Number Two. The enemy had lost the last positions overlooking the airfield, but still held positions that dominated the open plain. Attempts to recover the abandoned tanks were driven off by machine-gun and mortar fire.

On 28 February the 23rd and 25th Marines were again in action against the barren hills east of the airfield. All efforts to move into The Amphitheater resulted in prohibitive casualties. Enemy positions in the shallow dish of boulders did not prevent the Americans from working on the nearby airfield, so the decision was made to bypass the stubbornly-held depression. The 1st and 2nd Battalions of the 23rd picked their way through rugged, heavily mined ground that blocked the advance of the tanks below Hill 382, and by noon had encircled the hill.

Wallace Johnson again dismounted and led the tanks on foot, directing their fire from the telephone on the back of a tank. The fighting was at such close range that Johnson picked up enemy hand grenades and hurled them back.[49]

Two battalions of the 25th tried to encircle Turkey Knob, without success. The 1st Battalion, supported by two tanks, moved into the gap to the west, where one tank was damaged by a mine and abandoned. Long-range tank fire proved ineffective, and the 2nd Battalion's attack around the eastern slope ground to a stop without tank support.

Before dawn on 28 February, the 9th Marines, depleted by the struggle for the hills north of the airfield, were relieved by the 21st Marines. At 0900 the 1st and 3rd Battalions, covered by the handful of operational tanks, commenced a slow slog through the heavy defenses on the plateau.

Item/3/21 was advancing across open ground when several small knolls suddenly crumbled apart and five Type 95 tanks bore down on the Marines. The tanks had been completely buried, turrets and all. At first the startled Marines began to fall back, but quickly rallied. Three of the light tanks were wrecked by bazooka fire, and the others escaped to the north.

On the western coast the 27th Marines fetched up against the enemy bastion at Hill 362A, the highest terrain on western Iwo and one of the toughest positions on the island. The hill is a rounded mass on the edge of the plateau that extends a steep, rocky spine westward to the coast. The southern slope of the hill is cut by ravines impassable to tanks. This whole mass dominates several hundred yards of open terrain to the south. On the north side the ridge drops off an 80-foot cliff into a broad, deep ravine. This ravine is overlooked by yet another parallel spine to the north, Nishi Ridge. Hill 362A was honeycombed with caves, including positions in the north cliff that formed a reverse-slope defense.

The 1st Battalion attacked the western ridge while the 3rd took on the hill itself. In the early afternoon a small patrol from Item Company actually made it to the crest of Hill 362A, but had to withdraw. All efforts to drive a wedge onto the crest were met with fierce counterattacks.

On the left, the tanks were able to move forward, and in the afternoon blasted out several stubborn caves and pillboxes. One tank plunged into a ravine and overturned as it maneuvered to escape a suicidal attack. The crew abandoned it and ran to the safety of nearby tanks.[50] At nightfall the Marines dug in at the base of the hill.

The veterans of the fight for Suribachi moved north in the darkness, relieving the 27th Marines, and at 0900 on 1 March the 28th launched its deliberate attacks on Hill 362A. All three battalions attacked the ridges east and west of the peak. A dozen tanks of C Company, 5th Tank supported the 2nd Battalion's assault on the ridge just west of Hill 362A, but access was blocked by an antitank ditch.

Every effort to get tanks up and onto the ridge was unsuccessful, and one tank became stuck in the soft ash. When the tank bogged down over 40 Japanese rushed out of the caves and crannies in the surrounding rocks, and set upon the tank with demolition charges and fire bombs. The crew abandoned the tank and fought their way out on foot. Nevertheless, at day's end the 28th held an almost continuous line along the crest of the ridge on either flank of the hill.

Up on the plateau the 3rd Division at last pushed forward across the open ground and broke through another defensive line. To their east the 4th Division was still blocked by hills near The Amphitheater. The battered 23rd Marines were relieved by the 24th, which immediately went against Hill 382. At nightfall G/2/24 held a precarious foothold on the crest of Hill 382, while C/1/24 and two lone tanks from the 4th Tank Battalion held the low ridge that connected the hill to Turkey Knob.

On 2 March the 4th Division launched another major effort against both Hill 382 and Turkey Knob. At 0630 hours three battalions supported by eight tanks executed a surprise attack without artillery preparation in an attempt to encircle Turkey Knob. The enemy artillery command center on the small hill promptly called down all its resources on the two battalions, and despite a steady drumbeat of Marine artillery on the hill, at nightfall the battalions were still short of their goal.

All three battalions of the 24th Marines were now committed against Hill 382. There were two main efforts, by the 1st Battalion from the south, and the 2nd Battalion from the north, the latter supported by four tanks and rocket launcher trucks. Again the vehicles were withdrawn because the rain of artillery fire they attracted made conditions too hazardous for the infantry. By noon E/2/24 fought its way through to the rubble of the old radar station in savage close-quarter fighting, only to be relentlessly whittled away by repeated counterattacks. In the early afternoon elements of F Company joined the survivors on the crest and the beleaguered rifle companies managed to hold the crest through the night. The hill would remain under Marine control, although for several days the enemy would continue to reinforce the positions within by sending men through tunnels.

In the center 3/9, attached to the 21st Marines, fought its way onto the slopes of Hill 362B but stalled in the face of shelling by the enemy's heaviest artillery.

On the western coast the entire remaining strength of 5th Tank was committed to aid the 28th Marines in the assault on Hill 362A. An armored bulldozer finally scratched a trail up the slopes of the ridge west of the hill, and the tanks of B Company joined the attack into the ravine behind the ridge. As the tanks advanced toward Nishi Ridge, they were under fire both from the ridge to their front and from the holdout caves in the north slopes of Hill 362A in their rear. The armored dozer built a trail down the forward slope and filled a crossing of yet another antitank ditch, and the rifle companies lugged .50-caliber machine guns into the ravine and hammered away at the caves to their rear.

The tanks advanced into the broken ground on Nishi Ridge proper, where they were frightfully vulnerable—sometimes operating in ravines too close to traverse the big overhanging cannon to the side—and dependent upon the riflemen for protection. The defenders of this maze launched repeated suicide attacks, all unsuccessful. In the intense fighting the tanks blasted out one cave after another, and by noon were running low on ammunition.

At 1400 hours C Company's tanks came forward to shell and burn the northern slopes of Hill 362A, and then were ordered up to relieve their sister company. The 26th Marines had already moved in on the right to help plug a gap caused by the advance of the 3rd Division, and the tanks of A Company moved in to support them. At 1700 hours the Marines secured the advance for the day and dug in along the lower slopes of Nishi Ridge.

In this fighting along the coast west of the airstrip, Jim Carroll's TC was killed:

> We were sitting in a column, nothing going on particularly ... We were waiting for a fire mission, a couple of tanks behind us and a couple in front. We were buttoned up. We didn't operate on the island unbuttoned at all ... All of a sudden we heard a terrific explosion on top of the tank commander's hatch, and the hatch actually popped open. It had blown the latch off of the hatch.
>
> I looked back, up over my shoulder, and my tank commander whose name was Duane Madsen, was bleeding through the nostrils, dazed, and slumped, but he was conscious. I said, "Dutch are you okay?" What the hell do you say in a deal like that? Obviously he was hurt.
>
> We didn't know what had caused the explosion ... We backed out of the column and evacuated him. Nobody else took any more fire. That was the strange part of it. They put another tank commander into the tank.

Dutch died aboard a hospital ship. Months later a gunner from another platoon told Carroll he thought he had killed Madsen. His TC told him to fire over the top of Madsen's tank, but the gunner argued that there wasn't enough clearance. Ordered to fire, the gunner saw a flash and smoke, and was convinced that he had hit Madsen's tank. Carroll: "I said 'Well, what can we do now?'"

On the morning of 3 March the attack by the 28th Marines was supported by tanks, SPMs, 37mm guns, and armored dozers. At 0945 the Marines were dug in on the crest of Nishi Ridge, and already moving down the northern slope.

In the center the 3rd Division encountered unusually strong positions in Motoyama Village, and the 9th Marines were again stalled.

Two battalions of the 26th Marines, with B Company, 5th Tank in support, were ordered to eliminate the salient sticking into the Marine line, then attack northeast along the western edge of the Motoyama Plateau to take over positions from the 3rd Division near Hill 362B.

The lead battalion, 3/26, relieved 3/9 at about 1600 hours and immediately attacked Hill 362B. In the rough terrain the B Company tanks could no longer move forward to assist, but two rifle companies fought their way onto the crest by nightfall. In the effort to get tanks forward three of C Company's tanks were damaged; the company dozer tank suffered a broken track, and two were hit by a 47mm guns. The tank with the broken sprocket was quickly recovered.[51]

The 4th Division was similarly overextended where the 23rd Marines had relieved the 25th at 0500 for yet another grisly attack against Turkey Knob. Throughout the day engineers worked steadily at lifting mines that blocked the approach to the top of the hill, suffering heavy losses from incessant sniper fire. At 1400 hours the demolition teams of 1/23 and supporting flame tanks from Neiman's C Company rushed in for the kill, but at nightfall the Japanese were still firmly in control of Turkey Knob.

The 3rd Battalion drew the unenviable task of making another attack on The Amphitheater, and spent the day slowly and relentlessly blasting an opening into the southwest corner of the topographic depression, aided by A Company tanks and SPMs.

Although past Hill 382, the 24th Marines found themselves in yet another deep defensive belt. The tanks of B Company, 4th Tank found the terrain too rough and the rifle companies, by now exhausted both mentally and physically, bore the brunt of the fight. In another day of routine fighting losses were twelve tanks knocked out of action, eight damaged.

The fourth of March was the day the cost of Iwo Jima began to be redeemed. A B-29 named *Dinah Might*, with its fuel transfer system damaged in a raid over Tokyo, staggered down for a landing on the half-repaired Airfield Number One.

General Kuribayashi's force had been whittled down to about 10 percent of his original strength, but the struggle had turned into the grinding battle of attrition that he wanted.

On the right the 25th Marines held their positions along the coast, while the 23rd and 24th wheeled into the enemy defenses. The brunt of the struggle was again borne by the 24th in the broken ground to the north. It was a slow, deliberate struggle, with flame tanks and demolition teams blasting one cave mouth at a time.

The day's attack by the 21st Marines in the center was badly cut up by enfilade fire coming from the 5th Division sector. One tank was destroyed and the tank commander killed, and the infantry driven to ground. The 5th Division was still locked in a deadly struggle in a three-dimensional maze. The Marines sealed one cave entrance at a time while the Japanese scuttled through subterranean passages to pop out from the next entrance.

The crew of *Dude*, the VTR for C Company, 3rd Tank was sent to recover the company dozer tank abandoned the previous day. The broken track had spooled off and lay about 20 feet away, and the tank could not be dragged out through the sand and loose rock.

The crew chose dusk as the best time for their foray. The job had to be done quickly. With the coming of night, enemy infiltrators emerged and the Marine riflemen became increasingly skittish.

The VTR rushed up to the abandoned tank, uncertain whether the infantry had eliminated the gun that had crippled the dozer tank. Hooking the winch cable to the tangled track, they dragged the dead weight back and laboriously threaded it around the wheels. Six track blocks had to be replaced from onboard stores.

As a sweating mechanic drove in the final connector pin, the crew scurried in to reoccupy their tank. The entire process had taken just 23 minutes.[52]

The relentless pressure was punishing the Japanese, a fact brought home when Jim Carroll and his mates moved into one of the small valleys back of the broken Hill 362 line:

> We knew we were doing them some harm, but we didn't see many dead Japanese bodies. They were killed in the caves, or they pulled the bodies back down into the bunkers. We stopped in a column, and got out to take a smoke break.
>
> It was an incredible sight. There were probably four or five hundred Japanese bodies laid out in rows. They had been dragging them back all this way, and I guess they had finally run out of places to put them. These bodies were in a state of four or five days of decomposition, lying in great big rows in this little valley. It was a horrible stench, and a really shocking sight to us. We realized we were really putting the hurt on them at that point.

Swarms of flies were breeding in dead bodies and human waste. Charles Newman: "I had gotten some hash in my little bucket, and dipped in my cup to get some coffee. I turned to walk away, and someone yells 'Plane! Plane!' You always flinch. You always just scrunch up. You don't dive in a hole or anything because it's right on you before you know about it. He went right by. I started looking down, and on the back of my hands were little black, oily specks. All over my coffee cup was oily specks. All over my food. The Marine Corps—or the Navy—was DDTing Iwo Jima."

The planes were torpedo bombers from the carrier *Makin Island*.[53]

After two weeks the attackers were near the end of their endurance. The assault rifle companies had come ashore as highly trained teams. All the men had been experienced at working with their tanks, and knew the strengths and limitations of the powerful, clanking monsters. Most of these men were gone now, covered in temporary graves or lying in hospitals.

Replacements had been fed into the rifle squads as bewildered individuals, untrained for their role in the assault team. Their survival was often measured in hours or even minutes. It also meant more confusion, hesitation, inefficiency, and deaths among the veteran riflemen.

Now the replacement drafts were gone and the divisions were cannibalizing service units. Whole specialist units like the division recon companies were fed into the line. General Harry Schmidt ordered a 5 March stand-down for the entire amphibious corps, a day to rest, integrate replacements, and reorganize for the final effort. Shattered units were merged to form Provisional Battalions. For the tanks, it meant a blessed day of maintenance for the remaining vehicles, a task normally accomplished at the expense of sleep and food.

The next day was business as usual. By now most of the Motoyama Plateau was in American hands, although the 3rd and 5th Divisions were still enmeshed in the grotesque landscape north of Airfield Number Three. Naval guns, aircraft, and 11 battalions of artillery pounded the ravines and crags north of Hill 362B for 90 minutes. The deep caves and steep-sided ravines protected the defenders from all but chance hits. Engineer bulldozers and tankdozers were impeded by mines. Gains were measured in yards and numerous lives.

The 3rd Division in particular was severely battered. It had run up against what would become known as Cushman's Pocket, defended by Baron Nishi's remaining tanks and antitank guns.

The notebook kept by G. G. Sweet, the First Sergeant of C
Company, 3rd Tank, provides a terse account of a typical day on Iwo:

Plt. Sgt. Wehmeyer (WIA)—both hands cut and fractures; air evacuation
Scott (KIA)
MacDonald (KIA)
Bell (WIA)—shell fragments both arms, neck and back; air evacuation
Sgt. Burden (WIA)—gun shot wound right arm
Lt. McPhee (WIA)—shell frag, face; duty status
Cpl. Kline (KIA)[54]

The 4th Division was granted massive artillery support in an effort
to secure the rubble of Higashi Village. The 25th would advance slowly while the 23rd and 24th continued their wheel toward the rugged
coastline. The two assault battalions of the 24th were mired in the
impenetrable ravines, while 1/25, which had tank support, made the
biggest gains.

On 7 March the 4th Division began preparations to squeeze out the
final enemy pockets on the eastern coast. A battalion of the 25th
Marines laid mines and strung barbed wire while the 23rd and 24th
Marines slowly squeezed the enemy pocket. Gains were measured in
yards and tens of yards. The surviving tanks were operating in support of the 1st and Provisional Battalions of the 25th Marines, still battering away at the last holdouts inside Turkey Knob.

The 3rd Division launched a night assault on stubborn Hill 362C.
The 9th Marines caught the Japanese sleeping, but at dawn they
brought down a withering fire on the attackers. At 0730 the 3rd
Battalion reported the capture of the hill, but disoriented Marines
were actually on Hill 331. They moved out onto the fire-swept ground
toward the true objective.

By 0800 the 1st and 2nd Battalions were completely pinned down,
and E and F Companies were fighting for life. F Company was completely surrounded, and repeated attempts to rescue the isolated unit
were dashed against a wall of mortar fire. Although the ground was
a random tangle of ravines unsuitable for armor, Lieutenant Colonel
Cushman sent a desperate request for tank support.

By the time the tanks reached F Company, most of the Marines
were beyond human aid. The tanks pulled four survivors up through
their belly hatches and carried them to safety. E Company fared better. Seven men survived.

With the 2nd Battalion all but destroyed, the 1st was ordered to push forward and try to cut off Hill 362C. The enemy proved too strong, and the battalion fell back.

The morning of 8 March dawned cold and wet, but 3/9 was able to isolate Hill 362C. The maintenance crews had just about used up their bags of miracles, and the tank units were severely depleted. C Company, 3rd Tank was typical, with seven functional tanks out of the fifteen it had brought ashore.[55] The ground north of the hill was yet another maze of flat-topped outcrops of sandy stone, separated by narrow rock-strewn ravines, so every advance had to be led by a tankdozer scraping a narrow track.

The 4th Division launched a predawn attack without the usual artillery preparation. The 24th Marines encountered heavy resistance but the 23rd and tanks made rapid gains toward the coast, though the tanks were blocked by mines. Three tanks were damaged by mines and one splashed by an errant napalm canister.

Here too every move by the tanks had to be led by a tankdozer. C. B. Ash described clearing one road cut of mines: "What I was doing was just skimming off enough dirt to take care of any mines … Once in a while I would have to get up in the turret to see. I couldn't see what was in front of me because that blade really cuts your visibility down. I would slide back down, and go on another chunk."

Ash was stopped to examine a dogleg turn in the road, when a Japanese officer strolled nonchalantly around the corner: "It looked like he had just come out of a showroom window … I'm stunned. The bow gunner can't use his gun, because all it does is shoot into the blade. They didn't pick it up in the turret. This guy turned around quickly and went back around the corner. I moved some more, and as the blade is digging this stuff, it's piling up on each side of the blade, away from the tank tracks. There was a regular ten-pound AT mine sitting on this … and when I went by it tumbled down behind me. The tank behind me set it off with a machine gun. It was sitting right under the radiators. These were M4A3s, Ford engines … It shot the radiators all to hell."

The rugged engine in the damaged tank survived long enough to construct a turn-around, then bypass the column of tanks behind despite all the gauges being red-lined. Once safely behind the infantry line Ash killed the engine, and the loader reached out through the pistol port and opened the radiator cap. "He didn't even get steam out of the thing. The water was gone … I got it started, and went back another two or three hundred yards, and we got out and put five gallons of water in this thing, and headed back to the beach." Despite this mind-boggling abuse the tank was back in action after the radiators were repaired.[56]

The 28th Marines made good gains along the rugged western coastline, but mines blocked the advance of the surviving tanks of C Company, 5th Tank. The 26th Marines were stalled by unusually heavy resistance in the ruins of Kita Village, near the northwestern edge of the Motoyama Plateau. Engineers reported the road approaches to the village as clear of mines, and the tanks of A Company started forward to assist the infantry. Undiscovered mines in the roadway wrecked two tanks, and the attack stumbled to a stop.

Captain Samaji Inouye, the commander of troops in the large pocket isolated by the 4th Division, chose to disobey his orders, and promulgated an ambitious plan. The survivors of the *Naval Guard Force* would break out of the pocket, overrun the airfields and supply dumps along the center of the island, and join the forces which, he assured them, still held out on Suribachi. Many of the Japanese had no weapons and equipped themselves with spears or strapped on explosives to transform themselves into human bombs.

Inouye's men stealthily approached the lines of the 23rd and 24th Marines. At the last minute the Marines called down artillery and mortar fire, but the enemy was already inside their thin defensive line. For hours a savage fight raged with machine guns, grenades, bayonets, knives, rocks, and helmets used as clubs.

At dawn on 9 March Japanese bodies lay scattered over the small battlefield. At 0700 hours all three regiments of the 4th Division carefully advanced into the pocket.

In the center patrols from the 9th Marines reached the north coast. Other units kept squeezing the enemy pocket, but an attack by 3/21 against the eastern side was slapped down by an unusually well-coordinated defense. Japanese artillery fired airbursts that drove the infantry to ground. Suicide attackers bored in through their own artillery fire, hitting the tanks with satchel charges and firebombs.

One tank from C Company was immobilized. When the crew abandoned the crippled tank, Sergeant Chadbourne and PFC Donaho were immediately killed. Corporal Mitchell, disoriented, ran toward the Japanese. When he realized his mistake, he ran back toward friendly lines but was shot as he leapt off a low cliff.[57] Without tank support the infantry attack failed.

The rifle battalions of the 5th Division advancing along the west coast paused overlooking a large, extremely rugged gorge that dropped down to the sea.

During the night the 24th Marines passed into 4th Division reserve. At 0800 on 10 March the 23rd and 25th Marines closed in on the broken remnants of the enemy in the east coast pocket, leaving isolated caves and bunkers to be eliminated by the flame tanks and demolition teams. The situation was far different in the west, where all three regiments of the 5th Division experienced desperate resistance in the broken ground south of Kitano Point.

The final stage of the battle, the elimination of the pockets, began on 11 March. By now all three Marine divisions were on their last legs, and began to cannibalize combat units—the artillery and amphibian tractor battalions—to fill out the ruined rifle companies.

The 4th Division encountered terrain too rough for tanks, and the engineers found it difficult even to build foot trails. The fighting took place at such close quarters that it was too dangerous to call in artillery fire. On the west coast the 5th Division still faced the huge ravine, which had walls so steep that men on foot found it difficult to move down into the upper reaches. While the 28th Marines held the southern rim the 27th Marines and 1/26 looped around the upper, inland end, isolating the pit. The concentrated fire from the artillery regiments of all three divisions, plus the heavy guns of the corps artillery, was poured into the ravine with no visible effect.

The largest enemy pocket faced the 3rd Division in the area between Kitano Point and Hill 362C. The remnants of three rifle battalions, aided by the vehicles of 3rd Tank, commenced to slowly squeeze this remnant; the 1st and 3rd Battalions of the 9th attacked from the east and 3/21 from the southwest. The 1st Battalion was the main benefactor of tank support, and made good gains, but the terrain facing 3/9 was too rough for tanks, and an armored bulldozer had to build a precarious trail up onto the ridges.

C Company, 3rd Tank tested a new type of rocket launcher. The 20-tube M-17 launcher, designed to be mounted on the roof of a tank turret, could put 640 pounds of explosive onto an area target in a single salvo. Through some flaw in the design the four launchers shipped to Iwo would not fit the tanks, so the maintenance personnel improvised a steel sled to be towed by a tank. This awkward device had to be towed forward, fired, then laboriously backed out and reloaded. The M-17 fired 10 salvos into the pocket, but the imprecise fire did little except splinter rock and perhaps temporarily stun some defenders. In the narrow, twisting ravines maps and aerial photos were useless. Once committed, the tanks had no room to turn around and might find themselves facing an antitank gun only a few yards away. To add to the hazard the ravines were sometimes floored with thick deposits of soft ash, turned into a gooey paste by the rains. Any tank that stumbled into such a mire was a sitting duck for the enemy suicide squads.

For both the 4th and 5th Divisions the fighting was largely an infantry struggle, grim little battles fought by small groups of inexperienced replacements. Only the 27th Marines were still fighting on suitable tank ground, around the head of the big ravine.

The carnage went on for days as the Marines sought to destroy some of the most elaborate cave defenses on the island. Close-range flamethrower and bazooka fire, and hand-thrown demolition packs, sealed one opening after another in a grim procession.

Flame tanks on loan from 5th Tank scorched the caves from a reasonably safe range. The Japanese too knew the value of the flame tanks, and in the close confines of the ravines they were vulnerable to weapons that were normally ineffective. A flame tank attached to B Company, 3rd Tank was wrecked and two crewmen wounded by a usually ineffective Type 42 hollow-charge rifle grenade.[58]

Resistance on the east coast was broken on 15 March when the 4th Tank was able to work flame tanks up a road laboriously carved along the coast, and fired up into the ravines from below. At 1030 on 16 March the 4th Division declared its zone secure.

On the same day the 1st and 2nd Battalions of the 21st Marines launched their final attack downhill toward the coast. For the first time groups of the enemy emerged to throw themselves against the tanks. By early afternoon the tanks and riflemen had reached Kitano Point, the northernmost cape of Iwo Jima.

On 15 March, C Company, 3rd Tank Battalion was fighting to eliminate stubborn defenders around Hill 201E when *Dagwood*, the command tank, hit a mine and broke a track.[59] The crew evacuated safely, but the abandoned tank set into motion another harrowing experience for the VTR crew. Recovery was imperative, as the company now had only nine functional tanks.

The next day *Dude* clanked forward to repair the broken track, but sniper fire came from all directions. The crew finally pulled the retriever close beside the crippled tank, and sheltered behind it as they struggled to replace the damaged track.

The big retriever drove the defenders into a frenzy of rifle and mortar fire. The crew of a hapless Weasel passing nearby was pinned down, and an armored engineer bulldozer clearing an escape path tumbled into a crater. As soon as *Dagwood* was functional, the crew moved it over to shield the Weasel, which escaped without further harm.

The VTR commander, Sergeant Rogers, made a run for the dozer but was pinned down. The crew used *Dude's* bulk to shield the sergeant as he hooked up to the dozer. After extricating the tractor the long-suffering wrecker was beating a hasty retreat when it ran over a mine and broke its own track. Corporal Joseph Murphy was shot through the knee as he ran from the crippled vehicle, the only casualty of the entire ordeal.

Because of the intense small arms fire *Dude* sat abandoned until 18 March, when the crew finally managed to recover their own vehicle, scarred by attempts to set it afire with Molotov Cocktails.[60]

On 17 March the 5th Division closed the final ring around the west coast pocket, and Kuribayashi and his diehards were pressed into a 200 by 500 yard area deep inside the fearful ravine. The next day the flame tanks began to sear the ravine, firing across into emplacements on the far wall. Each day 10,000 gallons of napalm were sprayed across the cliffs.

On the 19th the Marines discovered Kuribayashi's enormous command cavern with the bunker on top, located at the upper end of the gorge. Tanks expended round after round at the concrete structure without effect. Forty-pound cratering charges also failed to breach the structure. The frustrated engineers ripped the armored covers off the vents and dropped four tons of explosive down the air shafts. Even the titanic explosion that followed failed to wreck the structure, but no one inside could have possibly survived the concussion and toxic gases.

On 21 March the remnants of two Marine battalions moved into the gorge, with the engineers scratching a tortuous trail down the sides for gun tanks and flame tanks. The Japanese had few antitank weapons left, and Jim Carroll said that backpack mines and satchel charges were "... the only effective device they had. They would come out of these holes while we were sitting still, throw it underneath the tank, and pop this fuse-type thing like a grenade. They're hoping of course to disable the tank or blow the track so that we would have to get out, and then they could pick us off."

On 25 March the staggering survivors of three rifle regiments finally silenced the last position in this hellish pit.

Still the killing continued. On 26 March about 300 Japanese, equipped with scavenged American weapons, surged south and attacked the camps around Airfield Number One. In a three-hour orgy of destruction the marauders shot up tents and men until finally slaughtered by the units they attacked. The survivors were killed by the 5th Pioneer Battalion assisted by Army flame tanks.

After this episode the Army's 147th Infantry assumed occupation duties, but it was not the usual boring garrison assignment. For two more months the soldiers hunted stragglers and raiders, and destroyed the odd position that suddenly came back to life. The Army garrison killed over 1,600 enemy and gathered in 867 POWs after the last Marine had departed.

Over 150 tanks had been used in the battle, and a typical tank battalion, the 3rd, had 15 of its 49 tanks totally destroyed.[61] Losses among distinctive vehicles—tankdozers and command tanks with multiple antennae—were high because the Japanese singled them out for special attack. The small bow-mounted E4-5 flamethrower had proven totally inadequate, but the long-range POA-CWS flame gun was highly effective.[62] Some later writers have stated that the flame tanks had no "substantial impact" on the battle,[63] but the Marines would emphatically disagree.

An M32 VTR comes ashore on Iwo Jima from an LSM in the background as Marines of the assault waves hug the beach. (*Marine Corps Historical Center*)

Maintenance crews of the 5th Tank Battalion labor to salvage a tank amid the wreckage on the Red beaches. The fighting has moved inland, but the carnage of the first day is apparent from the mutilated amphibious tractors. (*National Archives*)

Maintenance crews assisted by a bulldozer try to recover another 5th Battalion tank on the Red beaches. The steep berm that blocked the tanks is apparent in this photograph. (*National Archives*)

The crew of *Davy Jones*, 5th Tank Battalion, replenishes ammunition. The wooden side armor and the nails welded to the hatch rims are clearly visible. One man removes the rounds from their fiberboard shipping tubes while the other stows them in the turret. (*National Archives*)

Lt. Hank Bellmon's tank *Calcutta* exhibits many of the modifications made by C Company, 4th Tank. The infantry phone is inside the cloth bag at left, and the clock reminds the infantry to properly designate targets. (*National Archives*)

The improvised mine flail built by C Company, 4th Tank Battalion, prior to the Iwo Jima operation, using *Joker*, one of the company's redundant M4A2s. Some of the scavenged parts, like the truck differential and axle, are readily identifiable. (Bob Neiman via Ken Estes)

Bed Bug, of B Company, 4th Tank Battalion, shown during the advance toward Airfields One and Two. The camouflage pattern of tan bands was used on many 4th and 5th Battalion tanks. (Still frame from 16mm color movie, *Marine Corps Historical Center*)

40 Coed, a flame tank from C Company, 4th Tank Battalion, sprays a stream of raw fuel toward a Japanese pillbox. The fuel will be allowed to soak into openings, then the tank will ignite it with a burst of flame. (*National Archives*)

The crew of *41 Cairo* examines a track broken by a mine. The track extensions, commonly called duckbills, provided additional flotation in the soft volcanic ash. The track blocks and extra wheels are welded to the front of the tank. (*National Archives*)

Fourth Battalion tanks and infantry of 3/28 move out across the open ground around Airfield Number Two. On open ground long-range fire from Japanese heavy machine guns and 75mm antiaircraft guns was deadly. (*National Archives*)

A column of 3rd Tank Battalion vehicles moves toward the front. This unit, equipped with M4A2s, did not make use of supplementary armor as did the other two battalions on Iwo Jima. The Japanese singled out tanks with multiple radio antennae, like the lead vehicle, for special attack. (*National Archives*)

Dude, the VTR for C Company, 3rd Tank Battalion, prepares to recover a bogged tank on the open ground north of Airfield Number Two. The fighting is still going on nearby, as indicated by the flamethrower man near the rear of the vehicle. (*National Archives*)

Maintenance crews of C Company, 3rd Tank Battalion, repair a tank damaged by a mine. In the background *Dude* is using its lifting boom to remove an engine from another tank. The overhead snarl of telephone lines was a constant hazard to tank crewmen. (*National Archives*)

The crewmen of a 5th Battalion Tank protect their vehicle, *Lucky*, after it has broken through the roof of a Japanese bunker. (*National Archives*)

Infantrymen look on as a tank from the 4th Tank Battalion blasts
Japanese-occupied caves during the fighting on the northeastern part
of Iwo Jima. Combat at ranges measured in tens of yards was charac-
teristic of the Pacific fighting. (*National Archives*)

A Navy chaplain conducts religious services for men of the 3rd Tank
Battalion on 3 March 1945. The slabs of armor welded to the sides of
the tank provided additional protection for the ammunition racks. The
slab welded to the front of the turret protected a thin spot in turret
armor, a design flaw in the Sherman tank. (*National Archives*)

CHAPTER 13

PROCESSING THE ENEMY: OKINAWA

T HE HUGE ISLAND OF OKINAWA was to be the staging ground for the invasion of the Japanese home islands. Its capture was a titanic struggle that would dwarf any prior amphibious campaign.

Okinawa is the largest island of the Ryukyu chain, 60 miles long from northeast to southwest, and 18 miles across at its widest point. The entire coastline is rimmed with reefs, and cliffs and rocky promontories break the coast up into a series of narrow beaches.

The island narrows at the Ishikawa Isthmus. North of the isthmus the island has a mountainous central plateau covered with pines, scrub oak, and tangled underbrush. In 1945 this region was largely unsettled, with coastal villages connected by narrow unpaved roads.

The southern part of the island consists of rolling hills and in 1945 was more densely populated. The hills and ridges were wooded, but the lowlands were covered by small farms and scattered villages. A dense net of single-lane dirt roads generated clouds of dust when dry, and turned to mud pits when the seasonal rains came in the May to September wet season. In 1945 the island had only one improved road, paved with stone blocks, that connected the main town of Naha, on the west coast, with the old capital of Shuri, in the southern highlands.

Burial practices for the unique Okinawan religion incorporated artificial concrete or stone-lined caverns built into hillsides opening into stone walled courtyards with small houses for visitors to the dead. During the battle the Japanese utilized most of the tombs as defensive positions. Housing was of wood-frame and paper construction, and the few concrete structures and stone temples were destined to be magnets for artillery and naval gunfire.

In late 1944 Lieutenant General Mitsuru Ushijima assumed command of the *32nd Army*, subordinate naval commands, and *Boeitai*,

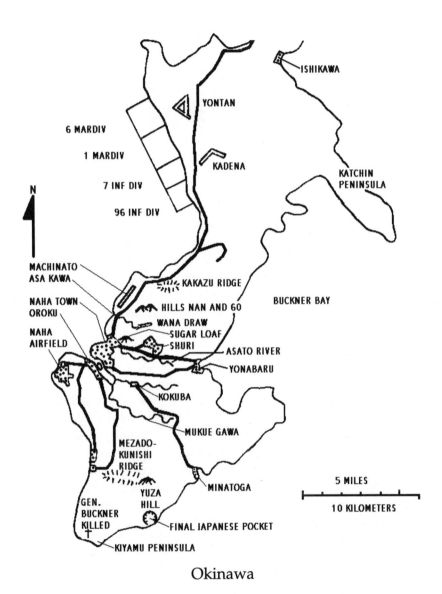

ISHIKAWA

YONTAN

6 MARDIV

1 MARDIV

KADENA

7 INF DIV

KATCHIN
PENINSULA

96 INF DIV

N

MACHINATO
ASA KAWA

KAKAZU RIDGE

NAHA TOWN
OROKU

HILLS NAN AND 60

BUCKNER BAY

WANA DRAW

NAHA
AIRFIELD

SUGAR LOAF
SHURI

ASATO RIVER

YONABARU

KOKUBA

MUKUE GAWA

MEZADO-
KUNISHI
RIDGE

5 MILES

YUZA
HILL

MINATOGA

10 KILOMETERS

GEN.
BUCKNER
KILLED

FINAL JAPANESE POCKET

KIYAMU PENINSULA

Okinawa

about 100,000 men altogether. The primary combatant units were the *24th* and *62nd Infantry Divisions*, the *2nd Infantry Unit* (the reorganized *44th Independent Mixed Brigade*—the names were often used interchangeably), and the *27th Tank Regiment*.

The *2nd Infantry Unit* was inordinately powerful for its size, and included three antitank companies with four 47mm or 37 mm guns each. The *27th Tank Regiment* had 27 tanks, a four-gun battery of powerful 75mm Type 90 Field Guns (the most modern artillery piece in the Japanese inventory), 47mm antitank guns, and heavy machine guns.

Seven regiments of artillery formed the backbone of the defense, and were organized as the *5th Artillery Group*. Great care was taken to plot and preregister artillery impact zones, forming deadly traps for an attacker.

General Ushijima promulgated an order which stated in part that "… the enemy's power lies in his tanks. It has become obvious that our general battle against the American forces is a battle against their … M4 tanks."[1] In addition to the guns organic to the infantry formations, the general could also rely upon three independent antitank battalions and two independent antitank companies. Seven independent antiaircraft battalions contributed 72 of the deadly Type 88 75mm guns.

Ushijima knew that even this huge force could never defend the entire island. The rugged, almost trackless north offered itself as the natural redoubt, but retreating into it would serve no military purpose. A withdrawal into the southern highlands would forfeit control of the main airfields, but from the hills Ushijima could at least maintain a credible threat.[2] He set about a massive fortification program to build beach defenses and successive defensive lines based on the Shuri highlands.

Ushijima's operations officer, Colonel Hiromichi Yahara, analyzed previous American campaigns, and advised against a waterline defense. At the last moment the General heeded Yahara and decided not to contest the landings, withdrawing his troops into the interior.

Three defensive lines were built into transverse ridges that run across the southern part of the island, with heavy emphasis on reverse-slope defenses to thwart the American superiority in tanks and artillery. Each time the Americans seized a ridge or hill they would be inundated with preregistered artillery fire, then counterattacked from rear slope positions. American units often suffered more casualties as the result of being driven from a position than they did in capturing it.[3] The antitank defense would use artillery and heavy mortars to strip the tanks of their infantry protection. Once isolated, the tanks would be attacked by 47mm and 75mm guns deployed singly and in groups. Only as a last resort would a close assault by infantry be utilized as an antitank defense.[4]

The land campaign was a secondary element in the overall defensive plan. Ushijima was not really expected to carry the major burden of battle. His role was to make the task of capturing the island as slow and laborious as possible to buy time for the new *Special Attack Forces.* While the vast, mostly American, naval armada was tied to the support of the landing force, human torpedoes, suicide swimmers, suicide speedboats, and *kamikaze* suicide aircraft would fall upon the fleet and inflict crippling losses.

On the American side the Northern Landing Force, III Amphibious Corps under Marine Corps Major General Roy Geiger, included the 1st and 6th Marine Divisions. The new 6th Division was built around the two rifle regiments that had fought as the 1st Provisional Marine Brigade on Guam. The XXIV Army Corps under Major General John R. Hodge included the 7th, 77th, and 96th Infantry Divisions and the 2nd Marine Division, with the 27th Infantry Division in reserve. The 2nd Marine Division had never been fully reconstituted after its battering in the Marianas, and would be primarily used to make landing feints.

An Army unit that would heavily impact Marine Corps operations was the new 713th Tank Battalion (Provisional Flamethrower), under Lt. Colonel Thomas McCrary. The 713th had 54 POA-CWS-H1 flame tanks,* and would support the entire Tenth Army. B Company was assigned to work with III Amphibious Corps, and sections of three tanks were detached to work with gun tank platoons, controlled by the Marine platoon leader.[5] The integration of the flame tanks was smoother than might have been expected, since Major Sam Littlepage, the Executive Officer of the 713th, had served as an observer on Iwo Jima with the 4th Tank Battalion. "The biggest compliment I guess he could be paid by the guys in our company," said Bob Neiman of the 4th Tank, "was that he should have been a Marine."

The 1st Tank Battalion was equipped with diesel M4A2 tanks,** but the 6th Tank Battalion was issued new M4A3s after the Marianas

---

* The Army flame tanks on Okinawa were converted from late-production M4s with a composite cast and welded hull. Although often misidentified as Marine tanks, even in official histories, they are easily distinguished from the Marine Corps tanks by the rounded corners on the hull fronts.

** The M4A3 was the preferred tank in USMC service, but Art Stuart convinced General Pedro del Valle to obtain permission from Headquarters, Fleet Marine Force Pacific to keep the M4A2 in service for this operation. (Ken Estes, personal communication)

operations. The new tanks were not universally popular. Harold Harrison:

> The diesel was more powerful at low rpm, you could just chug along ... The diesel, you would sometimes have to pull the engine if it got real bad. We had twin clutches in the diesels. Two tachometers, and if they didn't jibe, then the mechanics had to go to work on 'em. There was less maintenance with the M4A3s, battle damage discounted, of course.
>
> The only problem was battle damage. They were set up pretty good, and they were easier to work on than the diesel. They were more familiar to the mechanics.
>
> We had to quit smoking in the tank, and chew Beechnut tobacco. It was sort of ridiculous, because right back of the driver there was a little engine, an auxiliary generator with a gas line going to it. We called that engine Little Joe. We needed it sometimes to build up the batteries or whatever. I remember one time ... I reached back and felt something cold on my hand. That copper tubing that fed it, the vibration ... had broken [it] off. It was gasoline.
>
> I just had to stop the tank, turn it off, and yell, "Gas." There were these little plugs in the bottom. We punched them over on my side, drained the gas out of the tank, and stayed out of the tank until it aired out.

Another complaint was the noise. Bob Botts said that the M4A3s "... were noisy. They sounded like a fleet of B-24s coming. The ones we really liked were the ones we had on Guam. They had those two marine diesels in them. Those were quiet. You couldn't hear nothing but a little track noise until after they got by."

One of the continuing problems was the lack of a true amphibian tank. Most of the tanks would be transported by LCMs and LSMs. Six M4A2 tanks of the 1st and 2nd Platoons, C Company, 1st Tank Battalion were fitted with the experimental T-6 Flotation Device, which would allow a Sherman tank to swim ashore and to fire its guns while afloat. Test platoons from A Company, 6th Tank Battalion were similarly equipped.

The T-6 consisted of six large steel floats attached to the tank, which turned it into a low, turreted raft. Special brackets welded to the front and rear held detachable pontoons, and smaller non-detachable pontoons were welded to the sponsons of the tank.[6]

Bill Henahan was a driver on one of the tanks fitted with the T-6: "Down below where we used to fasten our towing cables and such, they had brackets. They had pins that went in there, and the pins were wired to a switch in the driver's compartment. These pins had an explosive charge in the end, and they would shoot out and the pontoons would fall off. You had to warn people away, because the pins would fly a couple of hundred feet, and they were pretty good size. They were a couple of inches in diameter and six or seven inches long. The side pontoons provided no extra protection, but they were welded directly to the hull. They stuck out close to sixteen, eighteen inches. You couldn't get in and work on the suspension system."

Propulsion was provided by the churning tracks, which were equipped with special track connectors that incorporated cup-like cleats like those on the tracks of LVTs. Top speed in the water was only about half that of the armored amphibians, about two miles per hour. The tank commander stood on the deck behind the turret and pulled on two ropes to control crude rudders.

One major problem with the T-6 was its size, which imposed a serious penalty on transport space. The device was also awkward to jettison. The driver had to blow off the two rear floats, pull forward several yards, blow off the front floats, then back out from among them. The most serious tactical drawback was the front of the hull. If the hull front grounded on a submerged obstacle the tracks were still floating free, preventing the tank from simply scrambling over like an LVT.[7]

Following the capture of several smaller islands as support bases, the invasion of the main island came on the morning of Easter Sunday, 1 April 1945. The big gunfire support ships had shelled the beaches for seven days, and throughout the battle naval gunfire would be lavish, with ships assigned to support specific units.

On the morning of the invasion four divisions landed in the first waves, the 1st Marine Division, 6th Marine Division, 7th Infantry Division, and 96th Infantry Division from left to right.

The handful of tanks with the T-6 Flotation Device were dropped an hour late and 10 miles offshore.[8] As a test of their seaworthiness it was a success. As a tactical measure it was absurd, since it took the tanks five long hours to work their way to the reef edge.

The lead tank of the 1st Tank Battalion detachment, commanded by Sergeant D. I. Bahde, immediately ran afoul of a passing destroyer.

Unable to speed up, slow down, or steer adequately, the tank plowed inexorably toward the ship, which refused to give way. The tank crashed into the side of the ship, achieving the dubious honor of being the only tank ever to ram a ship at sea.[9]

The collision may have damaged the pontoons, for the tank began to take water. The T-6 tanks arrived off the reef at low tide, when the reef edge was hardest to surmount. Just short of the reef Bahde's tank ran out of fuel and the bilge pumps stopped. The crew abandoned ship, pausing only to rescue a bottle of bourbon and a large can of peanuts.

The other tanks chugged to and fro at the reef edge, unable to climb over the steep underwater break. Finally Bill Henahan, a crewman on Lieutenant Jerry Atkinson's tank, swam across the reef and onto the beach, where he persuaded a bulldozer operator to bring his vehicle out onto the reef to help. They dragged out the heavy steel tow cable by hand, then persuaded a passing LCVP to ferry the cable end out to the stranded tank. The dozer winched Atkinson's tank up and over the reef edge, and it waddled ashore. The remaining tanks eventually went ashore miles away on the 6th Division beaches.[10]

The test platoons of the 6th Tank fared better, but an unexpected problem showed up once ashore. The cups that protruded from the track connectors tended to break, and when they did they fractured the entire connector. "The first thing we'd do when we had a chance," said Bob Botts of the 6th Tank, "was to take a cutting torch and cut the things off. They were always breaking. They would break that unit, and we would lose a track."

To the delight of the riflemen the first of seven assault waves went in standing up at 0837, and 16 rifle battalions were ashore by 0900. At 0930 the LCMs and LSMs began to land the tanks, four hours ahead of the T-6 swimming tanks. The only tank casualty was a crewman from the 1st Tank Battalion who died when his tank tumbled into a hole in the reef.

Things continued to go unexpectedly well. At 1030 on 1 April the 7th Infantry Division overran the airfield at Kadena, and the 6th Marine Division seized bigger Yontan Airfield at 1130. By nightfall 50,000 troops held a beachhead nearly a mile deep. Casualties had been gloriously few, with only 158 total killed, wounded, and missing among four divisions.

The next day only the 4th Marines met significant resistance. The 6th Recon Company, mounted on tanks, reached the east coast, and by 1400 the 7th Division was also in position overlooking the east coast. The biggest problems were that not enough trucks had been brought ashore, and the Sherman tanks tended to collapse the small bridges.[11] By 3 April four Army regiments were facing south to begin their task of clearing the southern part of the island. The Marine divisions were facing north to move against the suspected enemy redoubt.

Through early April the Marines pushed north as fast as legs would allow, the advance hampered more by logistical problems than by the enemy. The assumption had been that the Japanese would contest the beaches, and that the fighting for the first two weeks would be close to the landing beaches.[12] No one had planned for a foot race. The want of trucks led to shortages of ammunition and fuel, and the artillery could not keep pace with the advance.

While the Americans ashore punched at an empty bag, the United States Navy began its calvary under the *kikusui*, or floating chrysanthemum blossom, the poetic name for the most relentless onslaught ever directed against a naval force. Waves of *kamikaze* came against the ships, throwing themselves at the combat air patrols and antiaircraft guns.

Detachments from the 6th Reconnaissance Company and 2/22, transported by the 6th Tank Battalion, scouted far ahead of the marching infantry. By 6 April the columns had reached the town of Awa on the south coast of the big Motobu Peninsula, and ran into steadily stiffening resistance.

On 8 April the 29th Marines attacked the heavily forested Motobu Peninsula, where the *Udo Force* turned to fight. Unimproved roads skirted the coast of the peninsula, but the interior is a knot of rugged, forested hills separated by narrow, swampy valleys. Use of tanks was "out of the question."[13]

It was an infantry fight, pure and simple, in terrain so rugged that a standing man could reach out and touch the slope he was climbing. Eventually, on 19 April, the 4th and 29th Marines reduced the last organized resistance around Mount Yae Take.

While the 29th Marines invested the peninsula, the balance of the division advanced along the coasts. "We would take a bulldozer tank," said Bob Botts, "and three regular tanks and all the infantry we could pile on the four of them. We'd just take off down the road until we ran into something." On 13 April A Company, 6th Tank reached the northernmost tip of Okinawa, soon followed by the marching infantry.

While the 6th Division was engaged on northern Okinawa, the 1st Division swept across the island and captured the Katchin Peninsula. When the Japanese did stand and fight, they savaged the rifle companies. With a shortage of artillery for lack of trucks to move the guns forward, Bill Finley's platoon was pressed into service as makeshift artillery. "In order to get the guns up high enough ... we had to have the tank parked in such a way that the front was higher than the back. We had an officer with us that knew all about it.

"These infantry guys got down in there, and walked into a trap. The Japs let them go through. They had 'em circled, and they were shootin' 'em up pretty bad. That's why they had us firing those 75s that way. He got 'em out, so I guessed it worked."

On 5 April, the 96th Division met heavy resistance at Kakazu Ridge on southern Okinawa. The Division lost three tanks, and suffered heavy infantry losses in a maze of minefields and antitank ditches covered by machine guns and antitank guns. The 7th Division was similarly entangled in rough terrain along the eastern coast, losing two more tanks. The two Army divisions settled in for a prolonged struggle. The advent of the seasonal rains slowed the movement of the 27th Infantry Division and III Amphibious Corps artillery assets toward the south.

At 0600 on 19 April, the 27th Division attacked Kakazu Ridge, and its supporting tank battalion suffered the worst destruction of any Allied tank unit in the Pacific war. In front of the ridge was a deep, rugged ravine, with Kakazu Village on the reverse slope of the ridge.

Infantry of 1/105 were to cross the ridge. Thirty Sherman tanks of A Company (Reinforced), 193rd Tank Battalion would swing around the western end of the ridge, through the adjacent 96th Division zone along the only passable road, and link up with the infantry in the village.

The battalion was never able to breach the ridge. Three tanks were immediately lost to mines, and the rest, not in communication with the infantry, rounded the end of the ridge about 0830. They missed the narrow trail that led toward the village, and immediately blundered into an antitank ambush laid by the *22nd Independent Anti-Tank Gun Battalion*.[14]

The 47mm antitank guns destroyed five tanks. The tank company clattered on down the road, became disoriented in the maze of unmapped roads and trails, and lost another tank. The surviving tanks backtracked and found their way into the village.

In three and a half hours of desperate close-quarter combat, eight tanks were wrecked by mines, one bogged down and had to be abandoned, four were destroyed by artillery fire or antitank guns, and another was blown up by a box mine. Many of the crewmen were killed when they were forced out of burning tanks or hatches were pried open and grenades shoved inside.

Unwilling to concede defeat in breaching the ridge, 2/105 attacked on schedule behind the pinned-down 1st Battalion. The enemy allowed G Company to follow the tanks past the ridge. When the lead platoon could actually see the tanks struggling for survival in the village, machine guns and mortars began to rake the exposed soldiers, trapping one platoon. At 1330 the eight surviving tanks started back around the end of the ridge. The senior survivor of the trapped infantry platoon flagged down the tanks, and the riflemen moved out in the lee of the armor. Total casualties for the day were 720 killed, wounded, and missing.[15]

Through 23 April the Army continued to batter away in equally futile attacks. The heavy losses among Army tanks caused XXIV Corps to alert the 1st Marine Tank Battalion and more artillery elements of the 11th Marines to stand by to move south. Roy Geiger lodged strenuous objections, arguing against piecemeal commitment of his divisions.

A major attack on the morning of 24 April stumbled over abandoned positions. After imposing a lengthy delay on the Americans, Ushijima had ordered a withdrawal.

On 30 April and 1 May the 1st Marine Division and the 77th Infantry Division relieved the 27th and 96th Divisions, respectively. The 1st Division took over the attack down the western coastal plain, while the 77th faced the formidable Maeda Escarpment that provided the Japanese with a commanding view of the American positions.

Now it was the turn of the Marines to endure the flail of Japanese artillery. In the very first operation 3/1 and seven tanks from A Company, 1st Tank captured Miyagusuku Village, at the foot of the hills east of the Machinato Airfield, but were immediately driven out by artillery and heavy mortar fire. On 2 May heavy rain interfered with Japanese observation, and a company of 3/1 slipped through the village and into the low hills beyond.

The broad Machinato Airfield was heavily mined, and south of the airfield 1/1 was driven back from its first attack across a deep ravine. Charlie Company, 1st Tank supported the attack across the ravine from the end of the airstrip, sniped at by Japanese heavy artillery. Fired at low angles, huge rounds ricocheted off the hard-packed airfield surface.

Bill Henahan: "Eight-inch artillery shells were cartwheeling down the airfield behind us. We were swerving over to the side and watching them go by, never exploding. I must have seen six or seven of those. One time we were waiting to go up to fire, and there were two M-7s ... and a couple of tanks from another company around there. One of those eight-inch shells landed right in one of the M-7s, and blew it all to hell. Another one, a high-explosive, hit on the front slope on the assistant driver's side [of a tank]. The top part of the tank [hull] was peeled back like by an old-fashioned can-opener. This part of the tank was bent back, and it killed the assistant driver."

Thickly strewn pottery mines and buried bombs dotted the flat ground. Bob Boardman saw

> ... tanks that had been flipped over by that type of mine, and had caught fire ...
>
> Out on Machinato airstrip we were under heavy artillery bombardment on this very flat coral airstrip. We were playing cat and mouse with the Japanese artillery. They would lay in barrage, and we would move our tanks, then they would lay in another barrage, and we would move.
>
> I don't know where this fellow came from, or who he was, but he was badly wounded. Instead of lying there, he was staggering like a drunken man on the airstrip, completely exposed to enemy fire. Jerry Atkinson, who got the Navy Cross later for several actions on Okinawa, unhesitatingly got out of our tank. He went out to this fella, put his arm around him, put the fella's arm around his shoulder, and brought him back to the tank. We got him up on the tank, and took him to safety at the battalion aid station. There were very, very many things like that that Jerry Atkinson did.

In a second attack a rifle battalion crossed the ravine and entered the little village of Jichaku, overlooking the Asa Kawa, a muddy estuary that extends inland from the sea. The enemy fought desperately to hold this lodgement north of the mudflats, and two rifle companies were badly battered in the village and ravine.

Ushijima was being badgered by officers who wanted to drive the Americans into the sea in a display of offensive vigor, and this faction found an able spokesman in his deputy commander, Lieutenant General Isamu Cho. Colonel Yahara countered his arguments, but under Cho's hectoring Ushijima at last agreed to an ambitious counterattack.[16]

On the night of 3-4 May naval troops would infiltrate along the western reef and fall upon the rear of the 1st Marine Division north of the Machinato Airfield. A similar effort on the east coast would envelop the American 7th Infantry Division. A mass of infantry and tanks would smash through the center of the American line, and annihilate them.

The Japanese telegraphed their intent with a heavy shelling of the 7th and 77th Division fronts, and armored amphibians patrolling offshore detected the movements along both coasts. The western amphibious force became disoriented in the darkness, and those not caught by Navy gunboats and LVT(A)-4s landed too far south, right in front of B/1/1.

The Marines virtually annihilated the amphibious attackers. The main tank-infantry attack forced a mile-deep penetration through the boundary between the 7th and 77th Divisions, but wilted away under the fire of 28 battalions of Army artillery.

American reserve units and scout dogs hunted down survivors. Bill Henahan and Joe Alvarez rashly went into the area. Henahan carried a .45 with one seven round clip in his hip pocket. Alvarez was unarmed. Henahan said that they had just crossed a small stream when "he (Alvarez) jumped backward and landed on his back and fanny in the stream. I looked at him and said 'What the hell are you doing?' I thought maybe he had seen a snake. But he said 'Japs! Shoot 'em.'"

Alvarez had stumbled upon two survivors of the counterlanding hiding in the underbrush. Henahan:

> I just fired. The first one, I hit him right dead-center in his chest. He was a little tiny guy. He just stood there and looked at me. Then he said, "Oh," and fell over dead.
>
> The other one started crawling through the bushes. I shot at him four times before he stopped crawling. I went over, and he was still alive. I realized that I had fired five shots, only got two left, and what if there's some more of these guys around? I didn't do any more shooting.
>
> A guy came around with a carbine, with a 15 round clip in it. I said "Hey, we just shot two Japs here. How about covering us in case there's

more of these bastards around here." He looked down and this guy was laying on his stomach on the ground. He was moving, but he wasn't going nowhere. His head was between my feet.

This guy says, "He's alive!", and he emptied that 15-round clip into this Jap's head, right between my feet.

I said, "Gee, great shooting. You got any more ammunition?"

He says, "No."

I said, "Well, what are you gonna do if there's some more of them around here?"

He showed me. He was gone.

The Japanese persisted in their attacks through 5 May. The final effect of Cho's counterattack was 5,000 Japanese dead, and serious attrition of the *5th Artillery Command* by American counterbattery fire. The Japanese pulled back into the Shuri line to await the Americans.

The Americans girded for the attack against the high ground, but several preliminary steps were required including crossing the Asa Kawa. Other preparations included trying to straighten and reorganize lines. On 6 May Able Company, 1st Tank supported the attack of 3/1 against Hill Nan and Hill 60, losing three tanks to 47mm guns. On 7 May heavy rains turned the narrow, unpaved tracks into waist-deep quagmires. The 6th Division crawled southward, and on 8 May took over the positions of the 1st Division overlooking the Asa Kawa.

The Japanese used artillery to snipe at tanks, and the best way to defend against this threat was to increase the weight of metal. The 6th Tank Battalion crews welded extra track shoes to the sides of their tanks, completely covering the sides of the hull from front to rear, as much of the glacis as possible, and with either a single or a double row to completely cover the sides of the turret.

Unlike planks, the track-block armor was a field expedient. Harold Harrison: "We lost so many tanks there right away that the guys were putting track blocks on the front of the slope plate and on the side of the sponson, and then piling sandbags on that. We were a platoon that came in late, and the maintenance had been doing that for 24 hours. They said 'Hey, we're quitting for a while.' Old L. K. [Taylor] had me drive up there where the arc-welder was. He started it up, and he proceeded to have me hold the blocks while he welded them on. Then we got back and had the rest of the crew put sandbags up there."

Through the night and into the early morning hours of 9 May, 6th Division engineers labored quietly to lift mines and build a narrow footbridge across the Asa Kawa. At 0330 the leading company of 3/22 raced across, and by daylight two rifle companies were on the south shore. The division's M7B1 self-propelled guns and 37mm guns fired in support from the north shore. The tanks of B Company, 6th Tank failed to get across upstream, but the infantry of 2/29 waded through the mud flats.

All through the night of 10–11 May the engineers struggled under Japanese flares and through heavy shelling to build a heavy Bailey bridge across the Asa Kawa. At 1000 hours Lieutenant Colonel Robert Denig Jr. led a column of B and C Company tanks across the narrow bridge to attack the fortified tombs and caves that were blocking the infantry.

The 1st Battalion of the 22nd Marines crossed upstream and was halted by Charlie Hill, a cave-riddled mass that overlooked the main east-west road. Repeated attacks were driven back until gun tanks could move forward through the mire to blast out the caves. C/1/22 held the crest through the night, and the following day the gun tanks and Army flame tanks returned to blast and sear the lower slopes. By midafternoon the Marines controlled the entire hill with its three levels of tunnels and galleries.

South of Charlie Hill, a small, rectangular, steep-sided mass of honeycombed limestone that the Marines called Sugar Loaf Hill dominates the terrain to the north and west, and falls away into a pair of deep, broad valleys to the south.

Ushijima's main defensive line was anchored on formidable terrain features like Conical Hill in the 96th Division zone, Shuri Heights facing the 77th Division, and Wana Draw in front of the 1st Marine Division. No American realized what importance the Japanese attached to the seemingly insignificant hill. Sugar Loaf was only about 50 feet high and 300 yards long, but closed the only natural gap in the Shuri Line. South of the Shuri heights a broad belt of lower ground and a good road extends from Naha on the western coast up and over a lower topographic divide to the town of Yonabara on the east coast. Once past the Shuri Ridge the Americans could roll up the main defensive line from the flank and rear. Conversely, until Sugar Loaf fell all other gains were futile, as large formations could not be supplied across the steep, muddy ridge.

Sugar Loaf and all its approaches were overlooked by the Shuri heights, and the tanks and riflemen who attacked it would struggle across a muddy plain like ants on a billiard table. In addition to the 47mm gun positions that speckled Sugar Loaf, there were more strong positions on Half Moon Hill, immediately to the east. Long-range 150mm guns could snipe at tanks from the heights of Shuri. On the west the defense was firmly anchored in the northern edge of Naha Town.

In the late afternoon of 12 May, G/2/22 and 11 tanks of A Company, 6th Tank, pressed toward Sugar Loaf from Charlie Hill. The tanks dodged from cover to cover, sheltering behind rock out-croppings. Only four riflemen survived to reach the crest and were soon driven off by mortar fire.[17]

For the tanks, the 2nd 'Circle' Platoon's experience was typical. Harold Harrison's tank fell victim to a mine:

> We were supporting the infantry, ahead of them maybe 150 yards. Someone got on the phone and says, "We got good news and bad news. It's getting on to four o'clock, and the infantry's gonna fall back into a little ravine there and secure. The bad news is you're sittin' in a mine-field."
>
> The lieutenant asked me what to do, and I said, "Well," this is usin' logic, which you can't use, "I don't want to turn around in a minefield, I'd wanna back up until we get almost out of it. Then I'll give it left brake, and pull on out."
>
> He says, "Okay, Harry. Go ahead."

Of course the possibility of blindly backing the tank out through its own presumably safe tracks was almost nil. Harrison's logic may have been flawed, but sometimes a bad decision has unexpectedly good consequences: "I pulled about two or three yards, and the whole world exploded underneath us. We had hit one of the mines.... It hit the engine compartment, and just blew it up."

The explosion lifted the tank bodily about two feet, but fortunately did not flip it over. Harrison:

> When you get hit in a tank, all you know is afterwards. I don't know how to explain it, but when you're hit it's blank, and if you're lucky, you're still alive. It happens fast. There's no thinking. Either you got away with it, or you didn't. It's a big boom. It's atmospheric concussion.

When I bailed out of the tank, these [other] guys were on the good side. On my side these little rounds kept going "pink pink-pink," and they would hit the dirt. You oughta seen me scat, low to the ground. We had to go about a hundred yards or so back to the infantry and get into that little ravine.

I had a slight arc-burn, so my eyes were running a little bit. My face was sweating and covered with black dirt from this rice paddy. They said get up by the aid station and you can get a truck back to the tank battalion.

Sergeant Jeff Bunting's tank was hit and set afire, but he stayed and raked the hill with machine-gun fire to cover the escape of his crew. Finally sprinting for the protection of another tank, Bunting stumbled across infantryman Ed DeMar lying in a muddy ditch. The badly wounded DeMar had dragged himself down from the crest, but could go no farther.

Bunting scooped up DeMar and tossed him onto the tank with another wounded man, PFC Davis, already placed there by Sergeant Rupe and infantryman Jim Chaisson. As the tank slowly fought its way free with the walking wounded crouched beside it for cover, Corporal Perrault, who had bandaged DeMar, was hit. He too was bundled onto the engine deck as Lieutenant Blair kept up covering fire with the skymount machine gun.

When machine-gun fire raked the tank, the lieutenant was shot through the hip and fell off the tank. When more fire raked the engine deck and the wounded lying behind the turret, Perrault was hit again, splashing DeMar with blood and brain tissue.[18] DeMar desperately held onto the hemorrhaging Perrault until the tank reached the safety of the F/2/22 command post, but Howie Perrault was dead.[19]

When Harrison started to leave the aid station:

The corpsman grabbed me and said, "What's the matter? You get hit in the face?" I said no, so he washed my face off a little bit with water. I wish he had never done it—never stopped me—because I turned around and right by the aid station was row upon row of infantrymen, dead. They were putting something in their mouth.* Boy that was

---

* One of the dead man's metal identification tags was placed in his mouth to assure positive identification during later exhumation and reburial.

awful. But the worst part was the first two guys in the first row. I recognized them.

The first guy was Perrault. I had just cut his hair about a week before, so I knew him real well. The next guy was George Brannick. Brannick was full of holes, and Perrault just had his eye hanging out. You know, I didn't want to see that. Of all the things I've seen there, and I'd seen dead people on Bougainville by the alligator truck-load full, bringing them back through the jungle. But those two guys, and those rows of dead Marines, it kind of shook me.

The tank company had suffered three dead, eleven wounded in their first foray across the open ground, but their casualties were trivial compared to the riflemen. The day was the opening round in an incredible battle of wills and casualties. Bob Botts: "Okinawa was worse than Guam, so far as having the equipment to really create havoc with us. They were dug in. They had heavy artillery pieces. You had to dig 'em out one hole at a time. We put a company of infantry on Sugar Loaf Hill three days in a row. Go out there the next morning and there wouldn't be a living soul."

On 13 May, the 22nd Marines directed a major effort at the hill, and the 2nd Battalion took the crest, only to be driven off by artillery fire. On 14 May, the 22nd and 29th Marines returned; F and G Companies of 2/22 were back on the crest by 1500, and were again driven off by the guns of Shuri. Another attack secured the base of the hill, but at the cost of two-thirds of the riflemen and three of the four supporting tanks.[20] Major Henry Courtney Jr. pressed ammunition carriers into service and went back up the hill. The small party managed to hold out through a night of savage hand-to-hand combat. The commander of 1/22 and executive officer of C Company, 6th Tank were killed, and three rifle company commanders were wounded when the battalion observation post was hit by artillery fire. It had been a rough day for the tanks, with 18 vehicles put out of action in a single day.

For survivors like Harrison, the next few days were another morale-builder. "You ever see tanks that blew up, got hit? God. When we drew tanks—we had to do it twice—they had the graveyard for tanks and trucks down there. Some would get their turret blown off, others had holes punched in them. None of them were in nice shape, but when they got hit, and one 75 [round] would go off, everything in the tank would blow up."

At dawn on 15 May the bedraggled survivors of Courtney's command were driven down again by artillery. Fifteen men staggered back down the slopes, all that remained of two shattered rifle companies. By now the hill was denuded of trees, and the approaches were a shell-churned morass.

That same day 1/29 tried to outflank Sugar Loaf by taking Half Moon Hill, only to bog down in the reverse slope defenses.

On 16 May, 1/29 and its supporting tanks, restricted by the boggy ground and intense fire from Shuri, continued to batter at Half Moon. The tanks swam through mud up to their sponsons, and were slow, wallowing targets for the big enemy guns.

The long-range sniping by 150mm guns on Shuri was not as serious a threat as the mines, but some were unlucky. Harold Harrison and his crewmates had taken out another tank after the first fell victim to the mine. Harrison: "They said over on the other side of Shuri this big gun came out of the side of the hill, doors opened, and they started firing at us. We were guarding the Zippos, the flamethrower Army tanks. This big shell came over. The infantry said they could see it coming. It hit the ground, and bounced up underneath us."

The freakish skip of the cannon shell caused it to explode against the underside below the main crew compartment. Harrison: "That killed Sullivan (the gunner) in the turret. Smashed up the lieutenant's legs. I don't know if the loader lived or not. Me and L. K. Taylor had our hatches unlatched and our hand grenades ready. They [observers] were gonna tell us if these little satchel-charge guys were gonna come out. We were gonna throw a hand-grenade at 'em. It blew us half out of our hatches, and that saved our lives. All you know is after that big Ahoom! Afterwards, you get out. Instinct tells you to bail out of the tank, if you're a tanker, especially if you've bailed out of one already."

Specialists like tankers and artillerymen could not be spared. Harrison:

> L. K. and I came out of it with only minor injuries, bleeding here and there—nose, rear end. I think our urine was red for a couple of days. They were sympathetic. They told us to draw another tank.
>
> We were pretty shook up. They examined us and everything, and they said, "Well, you're still walking, and we're still in the heat here, so you're gonna have to get another tank. We got part of another crew that's gonna join you."

They gave us three bottles of this Legion brandy, little bitty miniature bottles. I tasted mine and didn't like it, so I gave it to L. K., who was a drinker. We went back and were cleaning our gear, and I said, "L. K., I'm not gonna make it."

He says, "Rrr, rrr, rrr," you know, kind of half in the bag, "Why not?"

I says, "Well, this is our third tank in this campaign, right here. I just had my third birthday overseas. This is also my third campaign. I'm not gonna make it." I had this numb feeling that I wasn't gonna make it.

Some people have that and it comes true, and some people it doesn't. It don't mean a thing. But it really was, to me, a real feeling. I got that thousand yard stare, and I didn't think I was gonna make it.

Sullivan had been Harrison's friend: "I came back to camp and had to tell a couple of his good friends. That bothered me also. You can see a lot of bodies, and sort of toughen yourself up to look the other way, but not when your friends get it. You can't do that."

The only solid ground was where a railway track passed through the American-held ridge in a deep cut, then continued south through the gap between Sugar Loaf and Half Moon. B Company's tanks crawled out of the cut in the early afternoon to escort 3/29 across the fire-swept valley, stopping to fire toward their rear to suppress the reverse slope positions blocking 1/29, while A Company tanks fired over their heads to support 3/29. G and Item Companies, 3/29 pushed up and onto the western spur of Half Moon and frantically began to dig in under concealment of a smokescreen.

An early morning attempt by 1/22 to outflank Sugar Loaf from the west was thwarted by heavy fire from the ruins of Naha. At 1500 hours C Company's tanks moved out in support of an Item/3/22 frontal assault on Sugar Loaf. The tanks moved across the front of the ridge trying to find positions from where they could see the enemy positions, but blundered into another minefield. One tank was blown up.

A counterattack drove 3/29 off the northern slope of Half Moon, exposing the backs of the lone company on the slopes of Sugar Loaf. The infantry slogged back through the mud, the tanks loaded down with wounded. The battered 22nd Marines had taken 60 percent losses, and were withdrawn. The suffering 29th Marines assumed the burden of attacking both Half Moon and Sugar Loaf.

On 17 May the 29th attacked with all three battalions. Three times E/2/29 staggered out of the railway cut and up the northeastern slopes of Sugar Loaf and nearby Crescent Hill, and three times they were driven back with heavy losses. The fourth attack held against a savage counterattack, only to be withdrawn when they could not be reinforced. Again the tanks and A/1/29 fought their way onto the front slopes of Half Moon, but were ordered back again when they could not build up a strong defensive position.

Incessant rain, shelling, and repeated attacks and withdrawals had left the terrain a kind of hell with mud. "You can't believe the carnage in that place," said Bob Botts. "A lot of people won't believe it, but you couldn't move any place when you went up there the next morning without running over dead people. Both sides. There wasn't a whole lot you could do about it. We did a pretty good job of getting the wounded out. We hauled a bunch out on tanks."

On 18 May, the 29th Marines and tanks went at Sugar Loaf again. Short-range antitank gun fire, long-range artillery, and the thickly strewn mines disabled six more tanks.[21] The survivors fought their way onto the crest of a spur that extends southeast from Sugar Loaf. From there the tanks of A and C Companies raked the reverse slope with cannon fire that prevented the buildup of another counterattack like those that had repeatedly driven the rifle companies off the crest.

The 47mm guns on the hill had the whole area covered by fire. Bob Botts's tank was disabled, but "I got three of them suckers one day. I sat there all day, though, 'cause they knocked me out pretty early in the morning. We had a good field of view, so I didn't even call for the retriever 'til I almost ran out of ammunition. After sitting there all day long, the retriever came out. I opened my hatch, and stuck my head out. [Something went] 'Weeng'. There's a little sucker sittin' over there in a hole. Just missed my head, and cut a groove right in the hatch on that tank. But that's the last shot he got 'cause we stuck a white phosphorus shell in that hole with him."

The 47mm gun could seldom penetrate the thick slope-plate of the Sherman at long range, but when Botts and his crewmates inspected their tank, they found that "three of them went in the transmission and put us out of commission. None of them penetrated the [crew] compartment. But that three-inch slope plate of the front of the tank, it was knocking a patch of white enamel off on the inside, just about a six or seven inch circle. It was almost penetrating. The Army had those [composite hull M4] tanks with the cast steel hull [front]. Boy, that sucker hit them and it went right on through."

This time D/2/29's assault carried it up and over the crest, and the riflemen began to clear the reverse slope. Under punishing fire from the Horseshoe Hills (a row of rocky knobs behind Sugar Loaf) and artillery from Shuri, D Company dug in on the reverse slope. The Marines had at last cracked Sugar Loaf. The cost had been most of the 22nd and 29th Marines.

Botts and his crew took the crippled tank for repair: "My crew was down welding up all the holes and replacing the final drive unit one night, and an Army general came over there. He was looking our tanks over, and he said 'I can't understand why you get hit with that 47 and it don't go through, and every one penetrates the Army tanks.' This captain says, 'Why, this might have something to do with it, General,' and he pointed to a little bitty Marine Corps emblem, about an inch and a quarter high, right underneath the gun turret. That didn't go over very well."

The 4th Marines relieved the remnants of the 29th after dawn on 19 May, but at nightfall the Japanese launched a series of powerful counterattacks that forced F/2/29 back up the slopes of Sugar Loaf. Dawn found the 29th still firmly in control of the south slope.

On 20 May, the 4th received the support of the complete complement of survivors from 6th Tank. Fearsome resistance made it appear that Half Moon would be another Sugar Loaf, but with the aid of the tanks and Army heavy mortars the Marines took the small hills along the rim of Horseshoe Valley, and Half Moon up to the crest. A savage two-and-one-half-hour counterattack failed to drive 3/4 off Half Moon.

On 21 May, the 6th Division started south toward the Asato River. By midafternoon 3/4, with strong tank support, had pushed into the Horseshoe, the bowl-like valley that harbored the heavy mortars that had punished the Marines in the battle for Sugar Loaf. In slimy, maggot-ridden mud, and under the continued torment of fire from the Shuri heights, advance down the slope was simple. A man or tank simply gave up the struggle to keep from slipping down into the crossfire.

The next phase would carry the 6th Division into urban combat in Naha, that night the rains came back with a vengeance, again turning Okinawa into a vast mud pit.

While the 6th Division was hemorrhaging at Sugar Loaf, the 1st Division was hammering at the Shuri foothills. On 10 May, the 7th Marines and a battalion of the 5th attacked Dakeshi Ridge, and the village of the same name on its reverse slope, but a whirlwind of artillery, mortar, and machine-gun fire drove the Marines back. The 1st Marines tried to cut the road leading west from the village, but could not hold position under the fire plunging from the ridge.

On 11 May, the 7th bored its way through the tangle of torn trees, caves, and pillboxes, and by 1600 held a salient across the crest of the ridge and into the village. The Japanese on Dakeshi Ridge were unusually tenacious, but on 12 May the Marines pushed two tanks and a flame tank into position to attack the rear slope. By 13 May the Marines held a toehold in the village, and the integrity of the Shuri Line was seriously threatened. The worst obstacle still lay ahead.

The attackers had to cross the Wana Ridge and the Wana Draw to the south. Upstream from its mouth the Asa Kawa flows across a broad, poorly drained flood plain. South of Dakeshi the valley narrows and is dominated by Wana Ridge, covered with tombs and caves, and a southern ridge that ends with a rocky knob, Hill 55, on the western end. To the east an even worse feature, 110 Meter Hill, dominated both the 77th Division and 1st Marine Division fronts.

In the early morning hours of 15 May, the 5th Marines were poised for an attack across the Draw. Tanks and M7B1 guns of the regimental weapons company moved in to neutralize some of the positions overlooking the Draw.

Nine tanks moved onto the open ground, blasting away at any positions that revealed themselves. The infantry could protect the tanks by long-range fire, but the appearance of unescorted tanks was a provocation beyond resisting for the Japanese. Suicide attacks were held at bay by mortar fire and artillery airbursts. The battalion lost no tanks to suicidal infantry attacks.[22] Punishing fire from a 47mm gun scored at least 15 hits, though none penetrated the tanks. Eventually this gun was located and the tanks called in naval gunfire to destroy it. The tanks withdrew to replenish, and in midafternoon returned to destroy another 47mm gun.

The next day C/1/7, with 13 C Company tanks and a pair of Army flame tanks, moved across the Draw and occupied the western end of Wana Ridge. Reinforcements were struck by heavy fire from the tombs built into the slopes, and the foothold on Wana Ridge had to be relinquished. Another 30 Army and Marine Corps tanks supported a morning attack by 2/5 into the Draw itself. Mortars and antitank guns disabled two tanks and damaged two others, and the Marines were slowly forced back.

The 1st Battalion tanks were called upon to rescue wounded caught on the barren ground between the ridges. This called for a particular kind of heroism, to stop the tank and dismount to gather in wounded who otherwise faced lingering death in the mud. Bob Boardman witnessed such heroism virtually every day: "Without hesitation, several of our tankers got out of their tanks to help the wounded, both our wounded and the infantry. Place them on the backs of the tanks, to take them to the battalion aid station. We were not told to do that, or assigned to do that. That was the right thing to do."

The Japanese, desperate to keep the Americans away from the final approaches to Shuri, turned the battle into a grim struggle of attrition. On 17 May a single platoon of the 5th Marines attained a tenuous foothold on the top of Hill 55, from which Japanese fire had ripped apart any attempt to cross the Draw. Staked down by enemy fire, the platoon was resupplied by tanks.

Fourteen tanks escorted two companies from 3/7 across the valley and onto the west end of Wana Ridge. The enemy laid a dense smoke screen that blinded the tanks and covered a relentless counterattack that again forced the tanks and infantry back across the valley.

The hard-pressed Japanese used any weapon available, including some that were long obsolete. The basic Japanese infantry battalion antitank weapon in 1941 had been the 20mm Anti-Tank Rifle Type 97. This weapon was a small cannon designed to be carried by four men, but it was heavy, had a beastly recoil, and was ineffective against American medium tanks.[23]

William Finley's tank was ambushed by one of these weapons:

> Just to our left there was a burned-out Sherman tank sitting facing across the direction we were sitting ... All of a sudden something hit that tank, and it sounded like something pretty good size. It didn't hurt anything that I know of. I told the driver to move up, and it hit us again. I guess it hit us about four times ...
>
> Somebody, I don't know if it was an observation post or where, they called me by name, and asked me if I knew what was hitting us. I told them no. I was looking way off, 'cause there wasn't any brush or anything around us where anybody could hide ...

I just happened to turn my head and caught a glimpse of something that moved under that burned-out tank. I told the gunner to put about two rounds of HE under there, and that stopped all that . . .

When we got out of there, we got out and looked at the track. Just one side was holding; it had knocked one side loose [broken a track connector]. He hit the tank beside where the driver was. He couldn't get any higher than the top of the track, or didn't, so I figure being under that tank limited his elevation ...

Exchanges of ground in the valley developed into a grim pattern. American tanks and infantry would move in to destroy and kill all day, then withdraw. The Japanese would filter back under cover of night to repair and reoccupy the positions. The Marines would return in the morning to blast and sear the same positions. This grisly, systematic struggle was a microcosm of the campaign for Okinawa. There was nothing of sophisticated tactics; the only goal was to inflict death in maximum numbers. The tank-infantry teams referred to the ghastly procedure as "processing."

Bill Henahan's tank was coming back out of the Draw after one such foray:

We had shot up everything in the tank except four or five rounds of canister, and I don't know how many rounds of armor-piercing. We didn't have any high explosive. There was a squad of infantry pinned down.

They waved to us and we pulled up by them. They got behind the tank, and got on the phone. They said there was a Japanese machine gun in one of the caves that had them pinned down. This cliff face was full of caves, and we didn't know which one they were talking about.

I had the loader pull out some tracers, and give them to this guy to load in his gun and shoot at the cave that's got the gun in it, so we would know which one he's talking about. He did. The Lieutenant, Jerry Atkinson, said, "Let's see you knock it out."

We loaded armor-piercing. I was estimating that this cave was seven or eight hundred yards [away]. Out to 700 yards, the trajectories of the 75mm and the .30-caliber coaxial were identical except that they were three feet apart. I just fired the machine gun until I got the tracers hitting just to the left of the opening, and I cranked one off. The tracer just went right into that cave.

I saw a machine gun come flying out. These guys were jumping up and down, pounding on the side of the tank. It was strictly luck.

On another day they broke a track in the Draw. Henahan:

You don't know what the heck caused a track to break ... We were somewhere between 500 and 1,000 yards out in front of our infantry when this happened. We had a brand new guy as a bow gunner, Ed Soltinsky. It was his first time ever out in a tank.

They had a little two-inch mortar in the turret used to lay down smoke. Traverse the turret and this thing would shoot shells out and lay a ring of smoke all the way around you. We laid down some smoke, and another tank pulled up next to us.

We started bailing out of that thing, because you're a sitting duck when you can't move. They dropped the escape hatch. The first guy out was Soltinsky, the bow gunner. He didn't crawl toward the back of the tank; he crawled out in front of it, and of course that's where all the machine-gun fire was coming from.

He stood up in the middle of all this machine-gun fire, realized that somebody's shooting. He crawled back under the tank, back through the escape hatch, came out the top of the turret, and over the back end.

As usual, the departing crew took the radios, the machine-gun bolts, and the firing mechanism from the 75mm gun. "We weren't gone five minutes when they blew the turret right off of it."

At noon on 18 May the Marines of 3/7 forced their way back onto the ridge, and were again pushed off. A rifle company from 2/5 actually got into the village of Wana and destroyed fortifications and weapons dumps before withdrawing for the night.

19 May was a dreary repetition of the previous days. The 1st Marines relieved the 7th at midmorning, and supported by overhead fire from the tanks and M-7 guns, started across the Draw. By 1600 hours the fresh battalion had fought its way onto the northern slope of Wana Ridge to stay. Efforts to cross the crest were blocked by strong reverse slope positions, and the battalion dug in under heavy artillery fire.

On 20 May, 3/1 again tried to rush the reverse slope positions and was again driven back. Efforts to get the tanks up the ridge were useless, and the infantry resorted to a Hollywood expedient. They dragged three barrels of napalm provided by the tank unit up the ridge, punched them full of holes, and rolled them down upon the enemy. These unguided missiles were predictably ineffective.

Things were going better on the right where 2/5 flowed around Wana Village and pressed south. By 2000 hours the tanks and infantry had severed the Naha-Shuri road.

The climactic battle for the Wana positions took place on 21 May under drenching rain. Additional forces were moved forward across the Draw while L/3/1, with strong tank support, attacked up the Draw from the lower end. Several tanks were damaged by antitank guns, and more fell victim to antitank mines. Still, the riflemen were able to make significant progress in clearing this persistent enemy hornet's nest. Of the three companies that were supposed to move across the lower end of the valley to assist L Company only one, C/1/1, made it across. The others were pinned by heavy fire that still emanated from the upper end of the draw and from Shuri.

The attack against 110 Meter Hill and the upstream end of Wana Draw was blocked by steep cliffs that precluded tank support. In the night the rain increased steadily into a torrent, under which the Japanese attacked all along the Wana Ridge in a vain attempt to maintain this last position in front of Shuri.

The rains continued for nine days. Unpaved roads and low ground turned into bottomless pits of glutinous red mud that sucked the boots off walking men. Vehicles sank out of sight in lakes of foul brown sludge that stank of excrement and the unburied dead. Only critical cargo and casualties moved in the LVTs and Weasels.

Attacks somehow went on through the rain, and Bill Henahan remembers firing at targets he could not see. Once they were called forward to deal with an antitank gun that had destroyed three Army tanks. The wrecked tanks were on the far side of a low stone wall, and the tankers went forward on foot to formulate a plan.

"We could tell from the holes in the tanks which way this gun was [firing from]. They had a group of five shots in the middle of the white stars on each tank. We went back, and any tanks in our company that had white stars, we painted 'em green."

The next day the platoon went back, but the driving rain blinded the gunners. Lieutenant Atkinson had Henahan fire the coaxial machine gun, and walked the fire onto the source of the enemy fire: "While I'm doing this I can see red tracers coming back toward us, going past us off to the right. When he finally got me on with the machine gun, he says 'Okay, crank one off with that 75.' I had a high explosive in there, and he says 'You got it.' It was one of those 47s. It had knocked out these three Army tanks. When they went out to the Army tanks, there were still crew members in there, dead, still sitting in the driver's and assistant driver's seat and stuff."

Henahan had reason to be wary of the Japanese antitank guns. "That 47mm was hell on wheels. One of our tanks from A Company got hit. They abandoned the tank, and the crew was running for shelter. As they were running, these Japs were shooting at them with the 47. I think it was a Lieutenant Butcher [who] got his arm blown off. I was much more worried about them than mines."

The enormous and unexpected expenditure of tank ammunition created problems. A Sherman tank normally stowed 97 rounds of 75mm ammunition, but the crews would overload the vehicle with another 60 rounds lying on the floor of the turret. "We were going out and shooting that up three and four times a day," recalled Henahan. When ammunition ran critically short because the rains snarled the supply system, the tankers improvised. They collected expended brass from the 75mm tank gun, and cobbled-up rounds by adding a primer and the powder charges from two 75mm howitzer rounds to the used casing, then mating it to the 75mm howitzer projectile.[24]

A jeep led a detachment of flame tanks into the front line. Henahan: "They said the Zippos are goin' down and are gonna fill those caves full of napalm. On the last match they were gonna light 'em off. It was pretty horrible from the Japanese point of view."

This was a common tactic for flame tanks. The normal tongue of flame consumed much of the fuel before reaching the target, so the tank would hose a target with fuel, wait for it to seep into openings, then light it with a burst of flame.

On 23 May, the 4th Marines crossed the flooded Asato River. Supplying the troops south of the flooded Asato became a particularly vexing problem, and men formed bucket brigades standing chest-deep in the rushing water to pass supplies and ammunition across the river. This situation was alleviated on 24 May when Marine engineers completed a pile bridge. At 1840 the first tank crossed onto the south bank.

With the American counterbattery guns blinded by rain, no place was safe from the Japanese artillery. Back of the lines Bob Botts's platoon had rigged a big tarp as protection from the downpour. "That night a big 'Whap' woke me up. An artillery shell had come through the roof of the tent, and it didn't miss my stomach by six inches. It went into the ground. One of the guys had a jungle hammock strung up. That shell turned him over, just tied him up in a knot. But they had graciously forgotten to put a fuse in it."

With the Shuri position outflanked, General Ushijima had to decide whether to be destroyed in place or to fall back into one of two possible redoubts on the south end of the island. The general chose to withdraw into the Kiyamu Peninsula, where pursuit by the dreaded American tanks would be hindered by steep cliffs, ridges, and ravines. The first column departed at midnight on 23 May.

General Simon B. Buckner fretted over the slow progress of American forces, but in the morass and torrential rains the Americans were hardpressed just to sustain themselves in place. The 6th Marine Division and 7th Infantry Division kept up the pressure along the coastlines, with the 4th Marines working their way through the mud to capture the final approaches to Naha town. On 25 May the division Recon Company crossed the flooded river.

Mines remained the worst hazard for the tanks. Along the boundary between the 1st and 6th Divisions, Bill Henahan and his crewmates were watching a 6th Battalion tank back into a defensive position:

> The tank commander was out on the ground, and he was backing the tank up to where he thought it would be protected. The loader and the gunner were up in the turret, halfway out of the hatch. The tank backed over a land mine.
>
> There was a 250 pound bomb underneath the land mine. It blew the tank right up in the air. These two guys popped out of the turret like corks out of a bottle. Neither of them, from what I saw, got hurt. Minor stuff.
>
> The driver and the assistant driver were pinned in there, because the tank went up in the air and came down upside down. The entire engine compartment was blown off. The tank was on fire, and they never got those guys out. They were trying to force open the escape hatch, and they couldn't. They burned to death.

The next day G/2/22 crossed the Asato bridge into Naha against minimal—for the tenacious Japanese—resistance. Inside Naha the tanks of Botts's platoon took shelter from Japanese shelling in a sugar mill. "They busted one of the vats full of syrup, and we waded in syrup about an inch and a half deep. That's kind of a messy thing, particularly with the blowflies around, and there were lots of them. I've seen the time it took two guys to eat a meal; one guy to keep the flies off, the other to eat it."

The 1st Marines, who had taken over the Wana Draw area, made yet another advance into that hellhole, but not until 28 and 29 May were the Marines finally able to enter the Draw and stay there.

The even heavier rains of 27 and 28 May brought all movement to a stop. In nine days almost eighteen inches of rain had fallen.[25] On 29 May the 22nd and 29th Marines advanced through the mud to close off the Naha peninsula by taking the hills commanding the river south of town. The Japanese stubbornly resisted the advance of the 77th Division on the left, but left a clear path for the 5th Marines to slip through and capture Shuri Castle. The commander of the 1st Division, Major General Pedro Del Valle, thought it imperative to seize this unparalleled opportunity, and gave permission for one of his companies to cross the division zone boundary, cutting across the front of the 77th Division. At 1015 hours A/1/5 occupied the ruins of the medieval castle. Notified at the last minute that the Marines would be crossing the zone boundary, the staff of the 77th Division worked frantically to call off an air and artillery strike on the castle.

Improvising at a rapid clip, Del Valle shoved 3/1 in to occupy the crest of the Shuri heights and 1/5 continued its advance down the south slopes. General Buckner pressed for even more rapid advances, and Del Valle sent all available rifle battalions through the gap to encircle the ridge.

The effort was in vain because Ushijima had already executed a skillfully staged escape. Without tank support the rifle companies could make little headway against sacrificial rearguards, and the bulk of the *32nd Army* was safely away by the time the trap closed.

The morning of 31 May dawned bright and clear, and the Marines found that the Japanese rearguards had melted away. By noon the last diehards in the Wana Draw were dead. The only real resistance was around a hill mass west of the twin villages of Kokuba-Shichima two miles southeast of Naha. Tanks took until 1300 to wallow south into firing positions, but repeated attacks directed against the hill were driven back.

With the enemy driven off of Shuri the Americans controlled the main road across the island. Marine divisions were always chronically short of heavy equipment, and the tanks were pressed into service as tractors. The 2nd Platoon of C Company, 1st Tank helped the division engineers deploy a Bailey bridge over the Yonabaru River. It was Henahan's most memorable experience with the Japanese 320mm mortars:

> We were hooked onto the Bailey bridge. On the other end were 20 or 30 of these Marine engineers; they were like a counterbalance to keep it from tilting down into the gap while we're drawing it across. They were shooting these spigot mortars, and they were landing in the river. You could hear them. They made a "Wheet" when they took off, and you could see them coming through the air. They tumbled end over end.
>
> They were landing in the river, and everybody was getting wet. When they would go off the water would go up a couple of hundred feet. They had a 69-caliber machine gun that fired a miniature explosive shell. They started shooting at the bridge, and sprayed it from one end to the other. You could see sparks flying all over the place.
>
> All these guys bailed off, down behind the embankment out of the line of fire. We had got hold of some .50-caliber machine guns. I cranked that up, and where we had seen tracers coming out, I sprayed it with the .50-caliber. We didn't get any more fire from that.

Following a night-long barrage the 22nd and 29th Marines, supported this time by tanks, slogged through the mud to take the hills west of the villages, and the rest of the 6th Division prepared to clear the Oroku Peninsula.

The Oroku Peninsula is separated from Naha by a broad estuary formed by the confluence of two rivers. The island of Ono Yama separates the estuary into two channels between Naha Town and the south shore villages of Kakibana and Oroku. Naha Naval Airfield occupied much of the western tip of the peninsula, and the defenders were formidably armed with heavy machine guns and 20mm cannon stripped from wrecked aircraft.

In the early morning hours of 4 June the 6th Reconnaissance Company and the Army's 708th Amphibious Tank Battalion seized Ono Yama, while 1/4 and 2/4 landed on the north coast of the peninsula. Twenty tanks of A Company, 6th Tank, four M7B1s of the regimental Weapons Company followed at 0650 hours, and at 0800 the tanks of C Company, 6th Tank arrived.

The landings began a 12-day struggle that was for all practical purposes a separate battle. The peninsula was an incongruous mix of soft, poorly drained ground and steep, densely forested hills that restricted the tanks to a few roads cratered and thickly carpeted with mines.

The 4th Marines struggled through the mire along the seaward side of the airfield, but made significant advances only when tanks laboriously picked their way along slightly firmer ground along the coast. The 29th Marines pushed along the south bank of the Kokuba estuary to secure bridge sites, and by nightfall vehicular traffic was moving across the bridges.

On 6 June the two regiments encountered a heavily forested ridge that forms the spine of the peninsula and were rocked back by streams of fire from 20mm automatic cannon. The heaviest resistance was in front of a hill that the men of 1/4 began to call Little Sugar Loaf. B Company's tanks crossed over from the mainland. There was no place to employ them in this world of mines, mud, and wrecked bridges.

No further gains were made until 7 June when the roads were cleared of mines and tanks and M7B1 guns were brought forward. Along the eastern coast the Marines broke through onto drier ground, and the tanks moved forward to assist in the capture of the village of Oroku. Outside the village the tanks were halted by yet another extensive minefield.

While the 4th and 29th Marines attacked into the peninsula the 22nd Marines closed off the escape of the garrison. On 8 June the three rifle regiments and their supporting tanks surrounded the pocket that had developed at the base of the peninsula. On 9 June the tanks and infantry closed in, but tanks were slowed to the crawling pace of engineers lifting mines.

On the south coast a Type 88 gun emplaced in a cave ambushed the tanks. Fortunately for the tanks the position was either not supplied with armor-piercing ammunition, or the gunners panicked. Under a hail of explosions the tanks slithered out of the field of fire.

The riflemen of 2/4 worked their way through the rubble of Gushi Village, southeast of the airfield. Once the village was cleared of suicidal defenders a single tank slowly worked its way along the beach, through the village in defilade behind a low ridge, and into position flanking the cave. As the tank hove into view the gun got away the first shot, which passed over the top of the tank. The tank returned fire, and its first round wrecked the troublesome gun.[26]

By midafternoon the last survivors of Admiral Ota's force were pressed into a pocket in the hills and the rubble of Oroku Town. The converging fires of the Marine regiments were becoming a hazard, so 2/4 was instructed to move in on the last of the dominating hill positions. A thick belt of mines and a flooded antitank ditch blocked the tanks, and the riflemen fell back under heavy fire.

In the predawn hours engineers cleared approaches for the tanks, and at 0945 on 10 June, 2/4 attacked again. With adequate tank support it took the battalion less than an hour to seize the ridge and squeeze the defenders deeper into the trap being forged by the 6th Division.

Resistance now centered on the village of Oroku where 2/29 slowly picked its way through the desperately defended rubble. Army flame tanks were the key to the advance, and the attack faltered when one was obliterated by two direct hits from eight-inch shells. Nevertheless, by day's end the Marines controlled most of the built-up area.

The night of 10–11 June was marked by desperate breakout attempts by the trapped enemy. After dawn 3/4 passed through and attacked the western flank of the Oroku pocket, but was held up by long-range fire from Hill 62 on the south side of the pocket. At the same time 2/22 attacked Hill 62 from the south under cover of heavy fire from seven battalions of artillery. The battalion went against the hill several times, finally gaining the crest just after noon.

Control of this hilltop allowed the Marines to dominate by fire the last stretch of enemy-held shoreline. The tanks were to follow through and support an attack by 3/22 against Hill 53 to the northeast, but movement of the tanks was stalled by a minefield. Engineers worked steadily under enemy fire, and by early afternoon had cleared a route for the tanks.

At 1450 the last high ground fell to L/3/22 and the tanks, and the 6th Division held a complete circle around Admiral Ota's survivors. On 12 June the riflemen of the 6th Division overran the last of the hill positions, and skirmishers swept the muddy fields for stragglers. The fight for the peninsula had cost 30 Marine and Army tanks.[27]

As the 6th Division fought its separate battle, the 1st Division and the Army's 7th and 96th divisions pushed on toward the south as fast as the torrential rains allowed. Men slogged forward, but no vehicle traffic could win across the Kokuba River crossings. The tanks were ordered off the roads, and trucks dragged by engineer tractors churned the roads into sludge. Men on foot carried burdens through sucking thigh-deep mud to supply the division.

Throughout the campaign the native Okinawans suffered innocently and grievously. Bob Boardman, like many others

> ... felt great pity for them. One day we were behind the front lines, and had the day off. My buddy and I, Joe Alvarez, went out. Just looking back on it, it was very foolish, but we went out just looking around at the caves, and hunting for souvenirs.
>
> We were very foolish, because we were only armed with 45s at our hips. We came across one cave and looked inside, and there was a Japanese soldier. We were sure he was a soldier because of his age, and he was dressed in white. No doubt preparing to take his own life by hara-kiri, or as the Americans say, harry carry. He was sitting there cross-legged, and had a mat over his lap. Very possibly had a hand grenade, or a dagger with which to commit hara-kiri.
>
> We motioned to him with our 45s to come out, but he wouldn't move. He just sat there. I'm very glad we didn't shoot him; we just left him. That's what he was going to do, so we just left him ...
>
> We went on to other caves and came across hordes of civilians hiding down deep in the caves. Terrified. Fortunately, we tried to get them to come out. Some wanted to. They were starving. They were defecating in little lacquered bowls. We felt so sorry for them.
>
> We finally found someone who spoke a little Portuguese. Joe is Hispanic, spoke Spanish. When [we found] this Portuguese-speaking Okinawan, Joe, through a few words in Spanish, conveyed to them that we would take them to safety. We managed to get all of them to come out.
>
> Along the way going back to our rear area we came across other caves. We ended up with 250 Okinawan civilians, leading them back to the stockade that had been set up there.
>
> We were, again I say, so foolish. A Japanese sniper could have picked us off so easily.

The 1st Marines delayed their southward movement to root the last defenders out of the Shuri defenses while the 5th advanced and the 7th helped close off the neck of the Oroku. On the afternoon of 4 June, 1/1 was ambushed as it crossed an open valley blocked by a flooded creek. On the right the 7th Marines were completely blocked by the churning waters of a stream in which several men drowned while trying to string lines for assault bridges.

The battle remained primarily a savage infantry dogfight until 10 June, when the floods subsided and tanks could cross the Mukue Gawa. The tanks immediately moved up to support the attack of the 1st Marines against Yuza Hill, the western end of the Yuza Dake escarpment that faced the 96th Division. The line of cliffs was so formidable a barrier that General Ushijima felt confident enough to defend it with a single regiment, freeing up reserves to face the Marine divisions. With tank support 1/1 took Yuza Hill, but suffered under heavy artillery fire as the neighboring Army troops clawed at the high hill mass.

On 11 June the tanks supported an attack by 2/1 through the broad valley that led around the edge of the hills, but moved into a Japanese artillery ambush. Three tanks were lost, but the force gained the next hill line by nightfall.

To the west the 7th Marines faced Kunishi Ridge, the westward extension of the Yuza Dake highlands and another of the most stubborn positions on Okinawa. This high, steep east-west ridge was riddled with caves and trenches, covered with fortified tombs, and dominated an open stretch of pasture land, streams, and rice paddies to the north. Tanks would be restricted to roads. For the depleted American formations it was an obstacle as formidable as the Wana Draw or Sugar Loaf, and the first assault on the afternoon of the 11th was driven back.

A night attack at 0330 on 12 June produced a lodgement by C/1/7 and F/2/7 on the ridge, but heavy fire pinned reinforcing companies in the middle of the valley. Three attempts failed to force a passage through the valley, and the two companies isolated on the ridge were slowly melting away in the face of frantic Japanese counterattacks. Parachute drops placed critical supplies within the small perimeter, but enemy fire killed many of the men who tried to retrieve the containers.

Six tanks were loaded with emergency supplies and reinforcements in preparation for an attempt to break through to the ridge. By leaving behind three of the crewmen each tank could carry six riflemen inside. Critical ammunition and medical supplies were heaped onto the engine decks. The dozer tank and two gun tanks escorted the cargo carriers.

The last tank in the column blundered onto the edge of the narrow road, which caved off, stranding the tank. Another tank moved up under a smoke screen to pick up the riflemen and the column continued on toward the ridge. The tanks were able to traverse the enemy held ground without loss.

Under a steady drumbeat of fire several riflemen were shot as they tried to exit the tanks through the turret hatches. The rest wriggled out through the escape hatches, and other men on the ground risked their lives to scrape the cargo off the decks. Twenty-two of the worst casualties were dragged in through the bottoms of the tanks and carried to safety. In two passages across the valley the tanks carried 54 riflemen to reinforce the trapped companies. The ridge position was at last reasonably secure.

The Japanese held out in the caves and tombs that dotted the slopes below where the Marines were entrenched. Resupply and evacuation of wounded had to pass through enemy controlled ground, so all day on 13 June the tanks shuttled forward carrying supplies and more reinforcements. On the return trips the wounded men who could not fit inside were piled onto the engine decks and buried under sandbags.

All this effort was costly. Antitank guns embedded in the ridge face wrecked or damaged 21 tanks in front of Kunishi Ridge.[28] To the east the Army's 7th and 96th Divisions were smashing apart the final Japanese defensive shell and pouring up onto the plateau.

On the night of 13-14 June, 2/1 put another another company on the ridge in a night attack, but again the riflemen were cut off. The tanks now supplied three rifle companies, ferrying reinforcements forward and evacuating 160 wounded in a single day.

Bill Finley's platoon was sent forward to attack one of the fortified tombs: "We got up within, I'd say, 30 yards of them. I don't know why they didn't hear us ... We let loose with everything we had. One of them . . .came out of there with one of those magnetic explosive devices, and headed for Bahde's tank. He was in the middle, I was on his right, and another tank on his left ... They shot the machine gun first and didn't hit him, so Bahde told the gunner to shoot him with the 75. He hit him with that 75mm, and I mean when the smoke cleared there was nothing left. I guess that explosive device he had with him went off too ..."

Although not an antitank weapon, a basic tool of the Japanese close-assault teams was the Frangible Smoke Grenade, a glass sphere filled with titanium tetrachloride. When the glass broke the chemical produced a dense, choking white smoke that would blind the crew when thrown onto the front of a tank.[29]

"Then they threw smoke grenades out," said Finley. "We got back out of there because I knew in that smoke they'd come up there and disable your tank." Despite Ushijima's orders, they would try this tactic "every chance they got."

On 15 June the two battalions of the 7th Marines labored to expand their foothold on the ridge, but despite close support by both gun and flame tanks they were making little headway. Part of the tank battalion was reassigned to help the 1st Marines.

On 16 June, 1/7 benefited from a three-hour bombardment by 15 artillery battalions and secured much of the ridge. Sister battalion 2/7 made only slight gains, the handful of supporting tanks all lost to antitank guns and mines. On the far left of the line the tanks were again acting as ambulances when 2/5 became entangled in vicious small-arms fire while trying to gain a foothold on that end of the ridge.

On 17 June, Father's Day, the tanks were committed in support of 2/5, churning up the face of Kunishi Ridge and into the rear-slope defenses. Relatively unscathed positions on the south slope savaged the rifle companies as they crossed the skyline, inflicting heavy losses, and the tanks were pressed into service as armored ambulances. By nightfall the 5th Marines held another major chunk of the ridge.

The 7th Marines were already in a position to attack Mezado Ridge, 600 yards south of Kunishi Ridge across an open field of underbrush and old sugarcane fields. The assault would be mounted by 3/7 and supported by the survivors of two platoons of C Company tanks under First Lieutenant Charlie Nelson and Second Lieutenant Jerry Atkinson.

In war, life or death often hinges not upon skill, but random chance. Bill Henahan was the gunner on his fifth tank of the campaign; four others had been shot from under Atkinson and his crew. Henahan:

[On June 16] We went out at four o' clock in the morning. When daylight came, we start operating. We stayed out, except to load up with ammunition and stuff, until dark. When we came back in, they had a crew of maintenance men that would take the tank. They would clean all the guns, replace all the machine guns, and load it up with ammunition and fuel. We came in on the evening of the 16th of June, and these guys took the tank over.

I walked over to where these guys were sitting around drinking coffee. I said, "Where's it at?" and they said, "In that water can over there." I grabbed my canteen cup, and walked over towards it. It was dusk, and the light wasn't too good. I looked at the can and thought "Gee, it looks kinda fat."

[Somehow the lid had gotten jammed, and pressurized steam built up inside.] I just touched the lid and it blew up. All I had time to do was shut my eyes. A huge cloud of steam hit me on the face, and on the arms where my sleeves were rolled up. I ran right over the top of the hill and into the sick bay.

These guys had all hit the deck. It [the exploding can] made a booming noise, and I was gone. [When I came back] This guy Eugene Hoffman, who was killed the next day, said, "You know, I thought you were blown to pieces, 'cause you were gone when the smoke cleared."

In the morning, my eyes were swollen shut. I couldn't see a thing, and my whole face was swollen. They got this guy, Robert M. Bennett, a sergeant that worked in the clerk's office. He wasn't a gunner, but he volunteered to go out as one. They took him, and he went out in my place. It saved my life.

On the morning of 17 June the two tank platoons, reinforced by two company headquarters tanks to make a force of seven vehicles, moved across the open valley. The supporting infantry was soon pinned by mortar and howitzer fire, and the tanks stumbled blindly onward. When artillery fire began to fall around his tanks Atkinson ordered them back up the slope to where the infantry sheltered in a ditch. Unknown to the lieutenant, the Japanese had laid a deadly anti-tank ambush built around a 75mm Type 88 gun.

Sergeant Bud Brenkert's tank was the first struck, and the round tore off an external fitting. The second hit went through the side below the driver's seat, narrowly missing "Pop" Christensen and fouling the gearshift. The shell, deflected upward, struck assistant driver Albert "Scuddly" Hoffman under the arm, and he slumped over, bleeding profusely. Christensen, struggling with the gearshift and the dying Hoffman, cleared the jam, but a third round tore through the sponson armor, ripping open both main fuel cells and drenching the interior and crew with smoking fuel.

The gun shifted fire to Atkinson's tank, and the first round broke the left track. The second nicked the back of driver Bob Boardman's seat, then tore out through the starboard side.

Boardman: "They ambushed us from the side. The armor on the side is not as thick, and perpendicular to the ground, and the rounds would go through more easily. I tried to turn the tank straight on to the fire, so that the front, which is sloped and has thicker armor, would repel those shells. The engine was still running, but I guess they had knocked a track off. I couldn't turn the tank. They put, I don't know, maybe five or six rounds through our side."

A third round went in the left side of the turret, spraying loader K. C. Smith with steel shards. The replacement gunner, Robert Bennett, took the brunt of the hit, and was torn almost in half. The same round ripped through Atkinson's left thigh. A fourth round smashed through a fuel cell and port engine, spraying the interior with smoking fuel. The engine burst into flame.

The survivors abandoned the burning tank, Boardman and Smith carrying the wounded officer by the arms. The inside of Brenkert's tank was filled with smoke and fuel, and Christensen finally threw open his hatch and drove with his head exposed.

Unaware of the other tank in the noise and smoke, the survivors of Atkinson's crew staggered away into the sugarcane, and into the sights of a sniper. A single round tore through Boardman's right hand and throat, through Atkinson's neck, and smashed into Smith's chin. Boardman and Atkinson tumbled to the ground, and the twice-wounded Smith staggered away. Boardman, in shock, with one finger shot away and another shoved into the wound in his throat, crawled away into the cane, leaving the apparently dead Atkinson with a nearly severed leg and a paralyzed right arm.

Brenkert's tank, with fuel sloshing in the floor and the engine compartment smoldering, pulled alongside Atkinson's burning tank to find the crew gone. Christensen began to back his tank toward safety, with rounds from the Japanese gun still tearing past. Smith and Boardman flagged down the crippled tank almost simultaneously, and were unceremoniously thrown onto the engine deck. Rounds from snipers hidden in the cane were snapping past, and Brenkert crawled out of the turret and lay down on top of Boardman to protect him.

The crippled tank, smoking fuel pouring out through the escape hatch, finally gave up the ghost, but another tank came down the ridge and pulled up alongside. The wounded, and Hoffman's body, were thrown onto the back of the other tank for the trip to an aid station.

Nelson's tank moved in to help, and frightened away several Japanese who were stalking the now conscious Atkinson. Atkinson waved his remaining arm to attract the attention of the tank. The gunner mistakenly opened fire on the mud-caked figure with his coaxial machine gun, wounding Atkinson through the left hand. As the tracers closed in, Atkinson desperately waved his last functional limb, his right leg. Charlie Nelson recognized the bright red socks Atkinson was wearing and told his gunner to cease fire. Two anonymous riflemen dashed in, bundled the bloody Atkinson into a poncho, and heaved him onto the engine deck.

Taken to the company CP, Atkinson located the gun for the other tanks before he would be evacuated. Wounded seven times in the Father's Day Massacre, Atkinson had earned a new nickname. "Ack-Ack" Atkinson was now "The Sieve."[30]

The 6th Division had moved into the line and was involved in its own two-battalion attack against the Mezado Ridge line. The 6th Battalion tanks found their ground impassable because the only road through the marshy ground and rice paddies had been mined and cratered.The engineers cleared the mines, and the tanks moved forward to dump bundles of logs into the craters. Beyond the craters they discovered that a small bridge was also mined, and the area swept by machine-gun fire that precluded mine removal by the engineers. The tanks supported the riflemen with long range fire from the road below the bridge.

To the east the 7th and 96th Divisions had breached the formidable Yuza Dake-Yaeju Dake defenses, and enemy resistance suddenly collapsed. In the predawn hours of 18 June the 8th Marines and Ed Bale's A Company, 2nd Tank Battalion moved into the lines, replacing the depleted 7th Marines and C Company's surviving tanks. General Buckner held the 8th Marines in high regard, and had specifically requested them.

Bale's company had supported the 8th in the capture of some offshore islands, and found that "there wasn't anything on there but old men and women. I took 10, 12 tanks. Took a rifle company sitting on top of the tanks, and went from one end of the island to the other and didn't see anything but people 50, 60, 70 years old."

After leading an unopposed landing on another island, Bale rejoined the rest of his tanks at the 1st Tank Battalion CP. "I went up to where the 7th Marines were, and the tank company (C/1st Tank) commander up there, Jerry Jerue, was an old friend. The big thing was that what they needed were some fresh troops. Those people were beat to death, and under strength, in bad shape physically and mentally."

On 18 June, 2/8 moved forward against sporadic fire, and easily gained its objectives. Over the repeated objections of Marine officers, General Buckner insisted upon going forward to personally observe "his" Marines.

"I sat up on a ridge line at the 8th Marines CP," said Bale, "and directed the tanks for a couple of days. On Tinian, the 8th Marines had captured some big binoculars. I mean, they stood on a tripod, and looked like something somebody would stand up on a cliff and look out to sea with. They were presented to the regimental commander. They were bright and shiny (brass).

"We were up in that CP, and those damn binoculars were shining in the sun. Some of us began to worry, and mentioned it to the Old Man (Colonel Wallace), and he just looked at us ... Right after General Buckner showed up, we got these three rounds of direct-fire artillery." The explosions threw shards of stone and metal, but only Buckner was seriously hurt.

"You could have put a beer bottle through his chest," said Bale. Lieutenant General Simon Bolivar Buckner had the unhappy distinction of being the most senior American officer killed in action.[31]

General Buckner had directed his chief of staff that Marine Major General Roy Geiger was to succeed him as commander of Tenth Army. Geiger was spot-promoted to lieutenant general, and became the first and only Marine to command an army.

Elsewhere on the morning of 18 June 1/5 was pinned by heavy fire in their attempt to subdue the last remnants of Japanese still holding out on the eastern end of Kunishi Ridge. After tanks arrived at 1100 hours they secured the lower slopes, but could not advance in the face of heavy fire still coming from the 96th Division zone.

Bill Finley found that even at the bitter end the enemy would still snipe at lone tanks with big guns:

> They told me to get on that road and go south until we got to an intersection. There was supposed to be somebody there to tell us what they wanted us to do.

We parked there a little bit, and nobody came. We had just gotten some new ammunition for the 75 that had a timer fuse. It had a little metal circle on it, and you had a little wrench that you could set it for so many seconds. [This was the variable time fuse, used by the artillery to produce the airbursts that are so deadly to exposed infantry.] I called back to the observation post and asked if it would be all right to do some firing. They told me anywhere ahead of me.

I guess we got somebody's attention, because after we fired a few rounds, we had an artillery piece hit right in front of the tank, then pretty quick after that one right behind us. I told my driver he better back that sucker down in a hurry. I knew where that third one was gonna' hit.

There was a kind of ridge right of us and we pulled around behind that. They landed several pieces awfully close. They called me from the OP and wanted to know if we was hit.

I had my hatch open, and some of the pieces of shrapnel hit that lid and came down on my neck. Didn't hurt me. Burned a little bit, and I shut it after that.

After a while we came on back, because nobody ever showed up to tell us what they wanted.

Bob Botts's tank was trying to get at the enemy on the rugged terrain back of Kiyamu Ridge: "They were throwing hand grenades back and forth over a razor-back ridge. I tried to get my tank up in there where I could get down in the hole, even with the [E4-5] flame thrower, but I just couldn't get down to where I could get in there."

The effort of adding the heavy supplementary armor paid off. Botts:

There was an artillery piece over across the valley, and he hit us three times. It was about a six-inch so near as we could tell.* But it hit that armor, that old track and stuff out there, and blew up. This crap would fly off that tank, and look like it had blown it all to the dickens. It hit hard enough that it knocked the [auxiliary] generator clear out of the sponson and into the turret with us.

Then one of them went under the tank and it broke my radiator, so I had to get out of there before I lost all my coolant. I didn't want to burn my engine up. We went up to where the forward OP was.

---

* Likely one of the 150mm guns extricated from the Shuri position.

We had called for artillery. I was going to spot it for them. This guy said, "Someone just called for some artillery."

I said, "Yea, I did," and he said, "Where were you?"

"Up there in that tank," [replied Botts.]

"The one that got blew up?"

I said, "Well, it wasn't as bad as it looked."

Botts was told to spot and correct the fall of shot from a smoke round:

It puffed up over there, so I said, "Move it in about 50 yards this way and let 'er go."

Then in a little bit it sounded like freight trains coming. It was a battleship out there, with those 16-inch shells. Another one of our tanks took my place up there when I got out of there. When that shell blew up, it took the whole back out of that hill, and his gun was sticking out over the front of it. I said, "Hey! Get that stuff back up where it belongs!"

He said, "Buddy, you better get ahold of your buddy on that tank and tell him to get the hell out of there, because that ship is 22 miles away, and there's two more salvos on the way."

I can't believe the accuracy with which they could pinpoint that stuff in there.

Bob Neiman of 4th Tank had been recuperating from the Iwo Jima battle when word came that Jeb Stuart, CO of the 1st Tank Battalion, had been wounded. Neiman volunteered to take his place, but upon his arrival found that Stuart was suffering from amoebic dysentery, and was by no means willing to give up his battalion in the midst of the fight. Nieman became Stuart's Executive Officer.

A Type 88 gun hidden in thick vegetation was causing considerable havoc among the 1st Battalion tanks. Neiman volunteered to go up in an OY-1 spotter plane to search for it. With a portable radio he could locate and direct artillery onto the gun. Stuart instead sent a junior officer.[32]

Neiman: "He was the battalion intelligence officer, fine young man, and Jeb Stuart said that he felt he, being the intelligence officer should do that." The flight located the troublesome gun, but "machine-gun fire came up through the plane, and right through his knee. They eventually had to amputate it, which was too bad. But he located the gun, and [marked] it with smoke grenades, and we knocked it out. That worked pretty well."

On 19 June Army tanks were blasting away at the cave where General Ushijima was hosting a farewell dinner for his staff. The fresh 8th Marines broke through to the south coast, but elsewhere the Marines were held by stubborn hill positions that neither the tanks nor the M7B1 guns could reduce.

In the 1st Division zone resistance centered about Hills 79 and 81. An attack by 1/5, supported by gun tanks and Army flame tanks, broke onto the crest of Hill 79 but could not hold the ground. When the tanks and M7B1 guns were delayed, an attack on Hill 81 was delayed. When the tanks at last arrived, the riflemen, supported by overhead tank fire, quickly seized the crest of the hill. When the tanks had to break off for lack of ammunition the infantry withdrew back down the slopes.

On 21 June the 4th Marines and the supporting vehicles of 6th Tank overran the last resistance on Hill 72 on the far southwest end of the island. The last pockets were now around two hills in the 1st Division zone, and a larger pocket around the *32nd Army* headquarters in the 96th Division zone.

In the final days of the campaign Harold Harrison, L. K. Taylor, and their new crewmates were assigned to provide security for road clearing operations. "It had rained several times," said Harrison, "and the tips of those mines were sticking out. Looked like a little galvanized thumb sticking up. The engineers would shoot them out.

"Then they would go out with the mine sweepers and sweep the road. Sometimes they would find one, and we would have to wait while they dug it up. Then we would move forward until they told us to stop, and then they would go 'ping … whoop, ping … whoop' and they would blow those [mines] up. Then later on the dozer could come along and sort of smooth the road out. The holes weren't that tremendous."

One Sunday they were granted a holiday. Harrison: "This team went out souvenir hunting. One guy checked out a cave … went in and made sure. His buddies all went in and started carrying out stuff. The corpsman who was with them said 'Hey, you guys better quit that.' They all went into the cave, and it was a treasure trove. It blew. These were professional mine detector guys. We lost all four of 'em. I had got acquainted with them, and that wasn't too thrilling either, to lose all four of those guys. It was horrible, because they knew better."

A final assault by 1/5 carried to the crest of Hill 79, and this time the riflemen stayed. All three rifle companies of 2/5 fought their way onto the crest of Hill 81, and by late afternoon L/3/5 had joined them on the crest. It was the end of effective Japanese resistance in the III Amphibious Corps zone.

The 305th Infantry and the vehicles of the 711th and 713th (Flamethrower) Tank Battalions launched the final attack against Ushijima's headquarters positions in Hill 89. By nightfall the American soldiers were in control of the hill, but General Geiger had already declared the island secure at 1305 hours.

At noon on 22 June Lieutenant General Ushijima and the hotheaded Cho dressed for death. Cho led the way onto a ledge overlooking the sea south of Hill 89. The two knelt. Each thrust a short sword into his abdomen, and ripped it across in the prescribed ritual of *seppuku*, followed in an instant with a merciful decapitation by sword. The bodies were buried nearby, but three days later were disinterred and identified.

On 23 June Lieutenant General Joseph "Vinegar Joe" Stilwell arrived to assume command of Tenth Army. Stilwell ordered a coordinated sweep to eliminate stragglers and pockets of resistance. The 1st Marines and 307th Infantry formed a blocking line across the island. All other combat commands swept north toward this line, eliminating resistance, burying the dead, and scooping up discarded weapons and equipment.

The battle might be officially over, but this 10 day operation resulted in another 8,975 Japanese dead and 3,808 prisoners.[33] The Army units that garrisoned Okinawa and the nearby islands continued to fight pitched battles against stragglers for months.

This late model M4A3 of the 6th Tank Battalion has broken through one of the flimsy bridges on Okinawa. The marking on the back of the turret, a two inside a shamrock, indicates a company Executive Officer's vehicle, probably of C Company. (*National Archives*)

The T-6 Flotation Device during testing on Bougainville, showing the wading stacks, large rudders, the shroud over the gun mantlet, and the enormous overhang at the hull front that kept the tanks from mounting the reef edge at Okinawa. (Official USMC photograph, via Don Gagnon)

An M4A2 of the 1st Tank Battalion bypasses a damaged bridge. This unit made use of strips of ships deck matting hung on the sides of the hull as extra protection. The vehicle on the right is a DUKW amphibious truck. (*National Archives*)

A tank of the 6th Tank Battalion, loaded with infantrymen of the 29th Marines, speeds along a road on northern Okinawa. This unit later welded extra track blocks to the sides of the vehicle hulls as extra protection against Japanese guns. (*National Archives*)

A tank of A Company, 1st Tank Battalion supports infantry from 3/1 in an attack on the Hill 60/Hill Nan positions on Okinawa, 6 May 1945. (*National Archives*)

A tank from C Company, 1st Tank Battalion, in early May 1945. The tank mounts a .30-caliber machine gun fixed to the commander's cupola, rather than the unwieldy .50-caliber antiaircraft weapon usually mounted on the turret roof. (*National Archives*)

An Army flame tank douses a Japanese position, probably on Charlie Hill, Okinawa, 11 May 1945.(*National Archives*)

A tank from the 6th Tank Battalion under artillery fire on Okinawa. In this battle the Japanese made extensive use of artillery in the antitank role. (*Marine Corps Historical Center*)

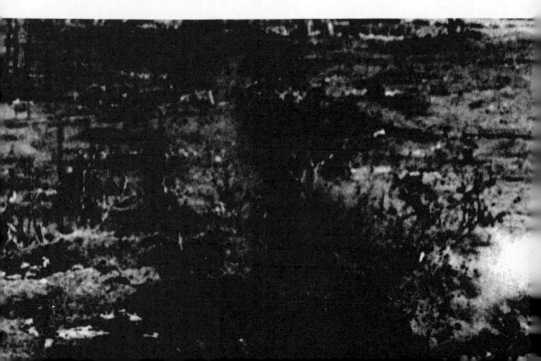

Tanks of A and C Companies, 6th Tank Battalion, support the 29th Marines during an attack on Sugar Loaf, Okinawa, 18 May 1945. The tanks were able to work their way onto the rear slope of the hill, finally unhinging the Japanese defense. (*National Archives*)

Flame tanks from the 713th Tank Battalion working along the front face of Sugar Loaf during the last stages of the battle on Okinawa. A number of cave openings are clearly visible, as is the painted-over white star on the side of the tank. (*Marine Corps Historical Center*)

Death Of A Tank – 1. The platoon sergeant's tank from 1st Platoon, B Company, 6th Tank Battalion, moves across the front of Sugar Loaf. A few seconds later the tank struck a buried aircraft bomb. (Still frame from a 16mm film, *National Archives*)

Death Of A Tank – 2. The explosion blew the 30-ton tank into the air. One crewman was thrown clear, but four others were trapped inside. The man beside the tank is trying to fight the fire with a hand-held extinguisher. (Still frame from a 16mm film, *National Archives*)

Death Of A Tank – 3. The company VTR works to recover the bodies of the crew and salvage useful parts. The 81mm mortar mounted on the front plate of the VTR was used to lay a smokescreen to conceal operations from the enemy. (*National Archives*)

A view of the front slope of Sugar Loaf on Okinawa taken after the battle, showing disabled tanks from 6th Tank Battalion being recovered. (*National Archives*)

View from a Japanese position, looking toward Sugar Loaf, showing the battlefield littered with disabled tanks and other vehicles. (*National Archives*)

A close-up of the catastrophic damage caused by the big Japanese mines. The engine compartment was gutted, and detonation of cannon ammunition stored beneath the turret floor blew the turret off the tank. (*National Archives*)

Lt. Colonel Robert L. Denig of the 6th Tank Battalion poses with dud rounds fired at his tanks by the Japanese guns on Shuri. This photograph also shows the track extensions used to increase traction in the soft mud, and the way in which the extra track shoes were welded to the armor. (*National Archives*)

The Type 95 was the most commonly encountered Japanese tank. This example was trapped when a road collapsed under its weight during the fighting for the Shuri heights. It was captured intact by American troops. (*National Archives*)

The platoon leader's tank of 2nd Platoon, B Company, 6th Tank Battalion, advances across the Naha Airfield after the 4 June landings on the Oroku Peninsula on Okinawa. (*National Archives*)

A dozer tank of the 6th Tank Battalion being used to clear mines from the approaches to Oroku Village, 7 June 1945. Using the dozer tank to skim away the upper part of the soil was the most effective mine clearing tactic for the tank units. (*National Archives*)

Crews from the 4th Platoon of C Company, 6th Tank Battalion, load logs onto the fronts of their tanks. The logs were used to fill craters during the attack on Mezado Ridge on Okinawa, 17 June 1945. Detonation cord (explosive line) was used to sever the ropes that attached the logs to the tanks. (*National Archives*)

A Navy medical corpsman aids a Marine wounded by the explosion of the mine that ripped the track off the 6th Battalion tank in the background. The frames and canvas shrouds over the gun mantlets and the fixtures on the transmission covers indicate tanks that were originally fitted with the T-6 Flotation Device. (*National Archives*)

CHAPTER 14

ANTICLIMAX: THE COLLAPSE OF JAPAN AND OCCUPATION

LONG BEFORE THE FALL OF OKINAWA the Army and Marine Corps were making preparations for what promised to be one of the bloodiest struggles in human history. On 1 November 1945, Allied forces—almost entirely American—would land on Kyushu, and in March 1946 on the Tokyo Plain.

The Marine Corps tank battalions would be equipped with a new flame tank, the POA-CWS-H5. These were converted from late-production M4A3s with improved suspension and wider tracks for better mobility on soft ground. The flame gun was mounted beside the main gun, so that the tank retained its 75mm main gun.

"After Iwo we decided we weren't going to mess with another flail," said C. B. Ash of the 4th Tank. "I guess Sam [Johnson] decided, because he was the builder, designer, and everything else, that maybe two D-8 tractor blades welded together would do a great job. We did that, but [with only] the 500 horsepower in the Ford [M4A3], we needed more. On the back of this tank we put a bumper. All it was was one inch plate steel built out a little bit over a foot, and maybe two feet long, hanging down below. It was welded at the back of the hull, and hung down. It was healthy. You could go down to where you were spinning your tracks or really lugging it, pull another tank into that thing, and hit it with another 500 horsepower. You could go down through a concrete road. It was really hell for power."

Like most potential participants Jim Carroll was "... not looking forward to it. When you go in on your first operation, you're nineteen and you think you're invincible. It's always the other guy who's going to get killed or wounded. But after you've been in a while and seen what goes on, you're not really eager to get right up there and get your nose into it."

Men like Carroll had good reason to worry. The best planes, tanks, and artillery the Japanese military possessed had been hoarded for this apocalypse. The new *Chi-Nu* tank with its 75mm gun, and the *Ho-Ni* III Gun Tank were the most advanced Japanese weapons of their type, never before seen in combat.[1] Japanese civilians were being trained in the use of weapons ranging from spears and knives to anti-tank bombs, and special attention was to be paid to the American flame tanks, which the Japanese military considered the greatest threat.[2]

The Japanese motto was "One Hundred Million Will Die for Emperor and Nation." For the first time in history a major nation stood poised to immolate itself. At the time, casualty estimates ranged from 132,000 to 268,000 American dead and wounded for Operation Olympic alone; General MacArthur's staff provided an almost certainly optimistic estimate of 156,000 casualties for Operation Olympic, and an additional 100,000 for Operation Coronet.[3]

These estimates were almost certainly too low because Allied intelligence was seriously flawed, underestimating the numbers of virtually all types of weapons available to the Japanese.[4] More reasonable estimates placed potential American casualties at 500,000 for the capture of Kyushu, and 2.2 million Japanese civilian casualties through battle, winter cold, disease, and famine.[5] To the toll would be added civilian deaths in occupied China and southeast Asia, and Japanese military leaders planned to execute 400,000 civilian and military prisoners.[6] A carefully planned holocaust was apparently thundering forward under its own momentum.

The atomic bombings of Hiroshima and Nagasaki ended the war by forcing the intervention of Emperor Hirohito. These two attacks have been repeatedly criticized as barbaric, but the destruction inflicted upon those cities may have saved the lives of millions.

The first postwar task for the Marine Corps was to disarm the remnants of the Japanese war machine in the home islands and northern China. The 4th Marines were sent to occupy the big naval base at Yokosuka prior to the formal surrender, and the 2nd and 5th Divisions landed at Sasebo and Nagasaki.

"When we landed in Japan," said Jim Carroll, "we landed with our guns loaded, even though the emperor had declared a ceasefire. We didn't realize what a disciplined bunch of people they were. We never had any incidents whatsoever between our troops and the discharged Japanese military. When the emperor said put the guns down boys, that's what they did." Unknown to the Americans, the Japanese civilian government had narrowly withstood a coup staged by reactionary elements who wanted to "rescue" the emperor and fight on.[7]

Throughout the war the civilian population of Japan had been treated to a steady diet of fairly outrageous propaganda. American fighting men were bestial, and particularly enjoyed crushing wounded prisoners under tanks or wrapping them in barbed wire.[8]

Jim Carroll: "When we landed at Sasebo, they were as scared of us as we were of them. They had had taken all their women and children and moved them out of the city. It's hard to imagine, because Sasebo is a pretty big city. We didn't see any kids or women for probably two weeks until they realized that all the propaganda they had heard was not true, and they started bringing their families back into the town."

As Marines were shipped home for discharge, the two divisions were steadily merged and the remnants of the 5th Tank were absorbed into the 2nd Tank Battalion. In spring 1946, a much-reduced 2nd Division left for home, turning over its occupation duties to the Army.

And then there was China. Throughout the war Communist and Nationalist forces had coexisted in an uneasy peace, each fighting the Japanese with one hand while keeping the other firmly on the throat of their domestic foe. Civil war was inevitable.

The 1st and 6th Divisions (less the 4th Marines) were sent into northern China, where they were to disarm a half-million Japanese troops and keep order until Chiang Kai-shek's Nationalist troops arrived. Instead, Chiang sent his troops into Manchuria in a bid for advantage against the communists, leaving the Marines holding the bag in Hopeh and Shantung provinces.

Demobilization reduced the combined divisions to little more than a rifle regiment by mid-1946. When full-scale civil war erupted in 1947 the Truman administration conceded that its efforts to mediate had failed. The rump force limited its activities to protection of the American naval enclave at Tsingtao, and evacuation of American nationals.[9]

Captain Max English had a reinforced tank platoon—19 vehicles— at Tsingtao. To avoid unwelcome attention, the tanks seldom patrolled the countryside. "At night we would drive the tanks, all night long, around the air base. In daytime we would refuel, work on the tanks, et cetera."

Pappy Cheshier said that the tanks sometimes escorted convoys to Peking. The communists occasionally ambushed these convoys, but as a gesture rather than any serious military effort. In particular, they wanted no part of the tanks. "A couple of times we got pretty involved. We just fired a bunch of rounds at them, and they disappeared when we came up and started shooting."

When the last Marines boarded ship in 1949, few were sad to bid China goodbye. Max English: "We had to get the hell out of there. They were shooting at us, and we, legally, couldn't shoot back at them." All too soon some of the Marines would again meet the very same Chinese, this time in full-scale battle.

But that would be another war.

EPILOGUE

EACH YEAR the active-duty and reserve tank battalions of the Marine Corps select their best crews to compete in the Marine Corps Tank Gunnery Competition at Fort Knox, Kentucky. Powerful M1A1 tanks and crews compete in live-fire exercises simulating offensive and defensive combat, firing machine guns and the big 120mm cannons at long and short ranges, and even fire with limited crews to simulate the effect of casualties. Bob McCard's sacrifice for his crew on Saipan is commemorated when the McCard Trophy is presented to the winner of the competition.

In early July 1994 a small group of veterans went to Emporia, Kansas, to attend a ceremony naming a park in honor of Sergeant Grant Timmerman. For 50 years Bobby Thompson had wondered what became of Timmerman's prized ring.

Timmerman had been one of the "Old Breed," the prewar Marines, and served in northern China until 1941. There he had fallen in love with a Russian refugee remembered only as Bonita, whose father reportedly made the ring. Forbidden to marry as an enlisted man, he was shipped back to the United States for discharge. He began to save money for a return to China, but after Pearl Harbor reenlisted in the Marine Corps. An old man of 26, Timmerman became an unlikely father figure for young Marines until his death in the tank named *Bonita*. Thompson:

> His brother and sisters wanted us to tell what we knew of him, because we knew more about him than they did. I asked the question "Did Timmerman's ring get home?" They didn't know anything about the ring.
>
> I said well, I figured someone got it and stuck it in their pocket. About four or five days after that I got a telephone call [from

Timmerman's brother]. He said. "Bob, you can quit worrying about the ring. I found it."

None of the family knew anything of it except his mother and dad, and they were both dead. They had all of his personal effects in a box, in storage. He said he went and got it, opened it up, and took everything out of it. Wrapped in a handkerchief in a corner of the bottom of the box was the ring.

I visited him a year or so later ... and I asked to see the ring. I picked it up in my hand. Held it. It has a very sentimental effect on you.

INTERVIEW SOURCES

The enlisted men and officers interviewed were a mixture of long-service professionals and hostilities-only Marines. They are also a modest group; one said of his Navy Cross "I'm a little bit uncomfortable even talking about it. I just did what I had to do. I'd have done it again." The men on the list below could contribute enough Navy Crosses, Silver Stars, Bronze Stars, Purple Hearts, and Naval Service Commendation Medals (the wound medal that pre-dated the Purple Heart for the Naval Services) to fill a sizable bucket. They didn't mention them, so I won't either.

C. B. ASH retired from the Marine Corps in 1963. After a brief period in the construction industry, he worked in radar construction and repair at the Long Beach Shipyard.

ED BALE stayed in the Marine Corps, served in Korea, and was a staff officer with the 1st Marine Division in Vietnam. He retired in 1968, then spent 10 years in the banking business.

BOB BOARDMAN became an ordained minister and non-denominational missionary, and worked for decades in Japan, Okinawa, and Korea. "It was a very traumatic experience for me to go to Japan. In fact, I was a reluctant volunteer. God had to draft me, because I didn't want to go. No Marine likes to be drafted, but God had to do it that way to me. I didn't hate the Japanese, I just didn't want to see them again. I didn't think they could accept me, and I didn't think I could accept them as former enemies. But God's ways are not our ways."

ROBERT BOTTS eventually ended up with a field commission. He declined a permanent reserve commission, and left the Corps after the war, "having used up about nine and a half of my nine lives." He farmed, worked for household appliance manufacturers, went into hospital maintenance, and eventually helped found a hospital engineering company. He offered me some advice: "Do everything you want to do before you retire, because after you retire you won't have the spare time."

CHARLES BURT "took about a year before I finally found out what I wanted to do, and became a sheet-metal worker." He retired in 1985 as general superintendent of a sheet-metal company specializing in large construction projects.

JIM CARROLL was discharged as a sergeant at the end of World War II, and in 1951 became an elementary school teacher. He joined the Marine Corps Reserve in 1953, became a Warrant Officer, and went back onto active duty in 1965. He served one tour in Vietnam, then returned to the 4th Tank Battalion, USMCR. He retired in 1987.

JIM CARTER "'bout starved to death" after the war. Joining the Marines at sixteen was scant preparation for a tight job market, so Carter did "about everything." In the 1950s he got into the lumber business, and founded a company that his sons now operate.

THOMAS CHESHIER'S later experiences included Typhoon Faye on Okinawa in 1957, where he forgot a tanker is safest. "We all went into the mess hall. It started peeling the tin off the mess hall, and most of us made it to the tanks. We should have been in them in the first place." He retired in 1961, and still owns and operates a transmission repair company.

DOUG CROTTS recovered from his wounds and went to college. He earned a Master's degree, and taught school for 32 years. "I had planned on it all my life. Before I went into the Marines, I couldn't afford to go to college, but that's what I would have done."

CLAUDE W. CULPEPPER was assigned to a medium tank crew for the invasion of Okinawa, but injured his ankle searching for enemy stragglers on Saipan. He was shipped Stateside for surgery, but neither that injury nor a later bout with polio kept him from three years in a steel mill followed by a 44-year career in law enforcement.

G. M. (MAX) ENGLISH retired as a lieutenant colonel after Korea. He joined Bob Neiman and Bob Reed (Neiman's Executive Officer in the 4th Tank) in the lumber business. He retired again, "went fishing in Louisiana," and stayed there. Max died in November 1998.

WILLIAM ORVILLE FINLEY returned to the Texas oil fields, farmed, and retired as a hospital maintenance worker. He and his wife had so many grandchildren and great-grandchildren that he "can't remember all their names." He spent an awful lot of time watching various grandsons either play or coach high school and college football. Bill died in March 2000.

CHARLES FREDERICK recovered from his wounds and returned to his prewar occupation as a mechanic.

ROWLAND HALL spent six years in the Marine Corps, and was a lieutenant colonel at the end of the war. He also returned to his prewar career, and retired after 43 years as an executive for a paper company. At age 83, he still flies his own airplane.

HAROLD HARRISON, with enough "points" to be shipped home, was seven days out of San Diego on an overloaded Liberty ship when the Japanese surrendered. The celebrations were over by the time the ship docked. He returned to school and became a refrigeration and air-conditioning mechanic. He reenlisted for Korea—in the 1st Engineer Battalion. "You think I'm going back in tanks? No way! That was an ammunition dump surrounded by armor plate!" He stayed with the engineers, retired in 1968 after a tour in Vietnam, then worked for the University of California until his second retirement.

BILL HENAHAN became a policeman in Detroit, and retired after 29 years. He served over 14 of those years in a precinct with one of the highest crime rates in the nation. The final 14 years were spent as a detective and special investigator.

ED HUTCHINSON left the Marines in late 1945, and returned to his father's small trucking company.

WILLIAM 'MAC' McMILLIAN retired to politics, serving several terms in the Louisiana State Legislature. He still serves as the gubernatorial appointee for his Parish Board of Elections Supervisors.

PHIL MORELL became a teacher. He was in the only Marine Reserve tank battalion when the unit was called up for Korea. He served at Inchon and the Chosin campaign as the 1st Tank Battalion Executive Officer. After Korea he was a teacher, counselor, and school principal.

BOB NEIMAN thought that "...for a young, single male who is at all interested in an outdoor life, there's nothing better than the Marine Corps. I loved it, and I think most Marines always do." But Bob decided he wanted a wife and family, so he and his best friend started a lumber business after the war.

CHARLES "CHILLY" NEWMAN attended the University of Houston and "hustled on the golf course." He helped build one of the major courses in the country, and still runs a major building-supply company.

HAROLD "HAL" ROGERS went to the 3rd Tank Battalion, then to 21st Marines as a radio repairman. He developed filariasis and was evacuated to the U. S., where a dormant case of malaria reappeared. He served at the Naval Depot at Schenectady, New York, where he met his wife. In 1950 he was recalled to active duty, and served as a Drill Instructor. After a lengthy career as a consulting engineer, Mr. Rogers died in late 1999.

ARTHUR ROWE was shipped stateside in 1944, first to a maintenance shop and then to the new radio school at the Philadelphia Navy Yard. After the war Rowe earned an associate degree in engineering "and that's when the good things started to happen." He worked at the Navy Electronics Laboratory, helping design the electronic Combat Information Centers. He retired after fifteen years at the laboratory.

ED SAHATJIAN was invalided back to the States after the Munda campaign in November 1943, still unpaid after his overseas duty. Ed served on Okinawa, in Korea and Vietnam, earned a commission, and retired as a captain in 1969.

JOHN SCARBOROUGH later commanded a rifle company, served in the Korean War, and retired from the Corps in 1958. He returned to his childhood home, where he sold real estate for another 14 years until his second retirement.

ROBERT SWACKHAMMER had seen peacetime duty and decided he "... didn't want any part of that." He joined the Missouri State Highway Patrol, and served for 29 years until compulsory retirement in 1975. He was troop commander for the Springfield District.

MELVIN SWANGO used his government benefits to train in the hotel business, his "lifelong love affair." He ended up managing ten hotel properties in a major metropolitan market.

G. G. SWEET retired as a captain in 1958. "At my retirement party they were asking me questions, and I would get up and answer them. He [a general] says 'What makes you think that after all these years as a Marine that you can get up and run a restaurant?' [I answered] 'Well, sir, 20 years ago I had 30 days mess duty'." Apparently mess duty was enough. Sweet became a successful businessman, owning—among other things—a string of restaurants.

ROBERT THOMPSON was shipped home after the battle for Tinian. "We were coming back for six months. I went to a Guard Company in Washington, D. C., on the Navy buildings. My name was already on the list to go to Camp Lejeune to head back when they dropped the bomb." He married a Marine, and "My kids have the honor of telling people that 'my mother and dad were both Marines'." Thompson worked for a major oil company until he retired in 1985.

EUGENE VIVEIROS became a tank gunnery instructor, first sergeant of a tank company, and sergeant major of an artillery battalion. He retired in 1959, became a firefighter, and retired again in 1975.

NOTES AND SOURCES

CHAPTER 1–INTRODUCTION

The history of the development of Marine Corps doctrine and equipment is drawn primarily from Allan Millett's *Semper Fidelis: The History of the United States Marine Corps*, and Frank O. Hough, Verle E. Ludwig, and Henry I. Shaw's *History of U. S. Marine Corps Operations in World War II, Volume I: Pearl Harbor to Guadalcanal*. Millett is particularly helpful in understanding the political struggles that led to the redefinition of the Marine Corps' role and operations in China, while Hough *et al* provide a detailed history of the development of equipment, particularly the landing boat development program. Rowland Hall's untitled letter (1994, Marine Corps Tanker's Association Newsletter) provides a concise summary of the organizational structure and function of the early tank companies. Richard Hunnicutt's *Stuart–A History of the American Light Tank*, and Peter Chamberlain and Chris Ellis's *Pictorial History of the Tanks of the World, 1915–1945* provide a developmental history of the American light tanks, and technical specifications for the early vehicles. The following notes refer to other sources listed in the Selected References.

1. Yahara, *Battle for Okinawa*, 12.
2. Tenth Army Prisoner Interrogation Report #28, reproduced in Yahara, *Battle for Okinawa*, 127.
3. Millett, *Semper Fidelis*, 361.
4. "History of Tanks in Marine Corps," compiled by Ken Estes on Marine Corps Tanker's Association website: www.mcta2000.com.
5. "History of Tanks in Marine Corps," compiled by Ken Estes on Marine Corps Tanker's Association website; Ken Estes, personal communication.
6. Ken Estes, personal e-mail communication, 10 June 2000.
7. Bob Neiman, telephone interview, 15 December 1998.
8. Hough, Verle, and Shaw, *History of U.S. Marine Corps*, 1:30.
9. Rowland Hall, telephone interview, 25 May 1998.
10. Neiman, interview.

11. Hall, interview.
12. Hough, Verle, and Shaw, *History of U.S. Marine Corps,* 1:39; Donovan, *Outpost in North Atlantic,* 1, 6.
13. Hough, Verle, and Shaw, *History of U.S. Marine Operations,* 1:84.

CHAPTER 2–GUADALCANAL AND THE SOUTHERN SOLOMONS

The history of the campaign is drawn from Frank O. Hough, Verle E. Ludwig, and Henry I. Shaw's *History of U. S. Marine Corps Operations in World War II, Volume I: Pearl Harbor to Guadalcanal.* Clifton Cates's "Leave Us Alone, We're Too Busy Killing Japs" provides a firsthand description of the destruction of the Ichiki Detachment in the battle of the Tenaru. The best resource on Japanese antitank weapons is Donald McLean's *Japanese Tanks, Tactics, and Anti-Tank Weapons.* The account of the former Marine tanks used by the army is drawn from John Miller's *Guadalcanal: The First Offensive.*

1. Isely and Crowl, *U.S. Marines and Amphibious War,* 116.
2. William McMillian, telephone interview, 25 May 1998.
3. Ibid.
4. Ibid.
5. Ibid.
6. "History and Lineage of 1st Tank Battalion" on Marine Corps Tanker's Association website: www.mcta2000.com.
7. Leckie, *Strong Men Armed,* 43.
8. Cates, "Leave Us Alone," in Smith, *United States Marine Corps,* 228.
9. Tregaskis, "The Grove: Mop Up," in Smith, *United States Marine Corps,* 235.
10. Vandegrift as quoted in Coggins, *The Campaign for Guadalcanal,* 60.
11. Cates, "Leave Us Alone," in Smith, *United States Marine Coprs,* 228.
12. Coggins, *Campaign for Guadalcanal,* 74; Miller, *Guadalcanal: First Offensive,* 112.
13. Numbers from Japanese sources provided by Akira Takizawa, personal e-mail communication, 25 August 1999.

CHAPTER 3–NEW GEORGIA

The most comprehensible account of this complex and often confusing campaign is D. C. Horton's *New Georgia–Pattern for Victory,* written by a participant in the campaign. Detailed accounts of the campaign are provided by Henry I. Shaw and Douglas T. Kane's

History of U. S. Marine Corps Operations in World War II, Volume II: Isolation of Rabaul, and Jeter A. Isely and Philip A. Crowl's *The U. S. Marines and Amphibious War: Its Theory and Its Practice in the Pacific.* Charles D. Melson's *Up the Slot: Marines in the Central Solomons* and John N. Rentz's *Bougainville and the Northern Solomons* provide useful accounts of tank operations.

1. Robert Botts, telephone interview, 19 November 1998.
2. Horton, *New Georgia,* 74.
3. Botts, interview.
4. Rentz, *Marines in Central Solomons,* 78.
5. Blake, "Death on Munda Trail," in Smith, *United States Marine Corps,* 423.
6. Ibid., 426.
7. Horton, *New Georgia,* 81.
8. Shaw and Kane, *History United States Marine Corps,* 103.
9. Horton, *New Georgia,* 88; Spector, *Eagle Against the Sun,* 236.
10. McLean, *Japanese Tanks,* 190–191.
11. Botts, interview.
12. Letter, Lt. Irving P. Carlson to Mrs. H. E. Botts, mother of Robert Botts, handwritten, dated 3 February 1944.
13. Ibid.
14. Ibid.
15. Ibid.
16. Hal Rogers, telephone interview, 23 November 1998.
17. Rentz, *Marines in Central Solomons,* 155.

CHAPTER 4–BOUGAINVILLE

The general outline of the Bougainville campaign is drawn from Henry I. Shaw and Douglas T. Kane's *History of U. S. Marine Corps Operations in World War II, Volume II: Isolation of Rabaul,* John Rentz's *Bougainville and the Northern Solomons,* and John C. Chapin's *Top of the Ladder: Marine Operations in the Central Solomons.*

1. Shaw and Kane, *History U.S. Marine,* 2:179-180.
2. Leckie, *Strong Men Armed,* 175.

CHAPTER 5–TARAWA

After Iwo Jima, Tarawa is likely the most written about battle of the Pacific war. The small size of the battle area, and the brief duration of the fighting make the battle one of the easiest to comprehend, and there are several excellent references. Henry I. Shaw, Bernard C. Nalty, and Edwin T. Turnbladh's *History of U. S. Marine Corps Operations in World War II, Volume III: Central Pacific Drive* is by far the most comprehensive, but Shaw's *Tarawa: A Legend Is Born* and Derrick Wright's *A Hell af a Way To Die–Tarawa Atoll, 20–23 November 1943* are excellent general accounts. Joseph Alexander's *Across The Reef: The Marine Assault of Tarawa* provides additional insight into the riddle of why the Japanese did not counterattack the beachhead on the first night.

1. Shaw, Nalty, and Turnbladh, *History of U.S. Marine Corps*, 3:31; Isely and Crowl, *U.S. Marines and Amphibious War*, 211; McKiernan, "Tarawa," in Bartlett, *Assault from the Sea*, 215.
2. Hunnicutt, *Sherman*, 143–152.
3. Ibid., 144; Bale, interview; Zaloga, *Tank Battles*, 4.
4. Boardman, *Unforgettable Men*, 16.
5. Doug Crotts, telephone interview, 20 July 1998.
6. Ed Bale, interviewCollege Station, TX, 26 June 1998.
7. Ibid.
8. Wheeler, *Special Valor*, 177.
9. Alexander, *Across the Reef*, 18.
10. McMillian, interview.
11. Ibid.
12. Bale, interview.
13. McCoy, letter in Sherrod, *Tarawa*, 189.
14. Bale, interview.
15. Bale, interview.
16. Alexander, *Across the Reef*, 18.
17. Bale, interview.
18. Shaw, Nalty, and Turnbladh, *History U.S. Marine Corps*, 3:83.
19. Alexander, *Across the Reef*, 17.
20. Shaw, *Tarawa*, 75.
21. Wright, *Hell of a Way to Die*, 80.
22. Bale, interview.
23. Wright, *Hell of a Way to Die*, 134.
24. Crotts, interview.
25. Shaw, *Tarawa*, 102.
26. McMillian, interview.
27. Ibid.
28. Shaw et al, p. 87
29. Alexander, 1993, p. 41

30. Shaw, Nalty, and Turnbladh, *History U.S. Marine Corps*, 3:90.
31. 2nd Tank Battalion Report, as quoted by Isely and Crowl, *U.S. Marines and Amphibious War*, 219.
32. McCoy, letter in *Tarawa* by Sherrod 188–189.

CHAPTER 6–CAPE GLOUCESTER

The general outline of the campaign is drawn from Henry I. Shaw Jr., and Douglas T. Kane's *History of U. S. Marine Corps Operations in World War II, Volume II: Isolation of Rabaul* and Bernard C. Nalty's *Cape Gloucester: The Green Inferno*. Frank O. Hough and John A. Crown's *The Campaign on New Britain* provides information on tank operations that is more detailed than is usual. Physical details for the new M5A1 and M4A1 tanks used in the campaign are available in R. P. Hunnicutt's *Stuart–A History of the American Light Tank*, and *Sherman–A History of the American Medium Tank*.

1. Nalty, *Cape Gloucester*, 6.
2. Wheeler, *Special Valor*, 218.
3. Nalty, *Cape Gloucester*, 11.
4. McLean, *Japanese Tanks*, 186, 188.
5. McMillan, "Struggle for Borgen Bay," in Smith, *United States Marine Corps*, 482.
6. Rowe, "I Am Not Qalified Tanker–The Who Is?," 6–9.
7. Shaw and Kane, *History of U.S. Marine Corps*, 2:394.
8. Holzimer, "In Close Country," 22.
9. Hough and Crown, *Campaign on New Britain*, 184.

CHAPTER 7–THE MARSHALLS

The course of the Marshalls campaign is drawn from Henry I. Shaw Bernard Nalty, and Edwin T. Turnbladh's *History of U. S. Marine Corps Operations in World War II, Volume III: Central Pacific Drive*, and Jeter A. Isely and Philip A. Crowl's *The U. S. Marines and Amphibious War: Its Theory and Its Practice in the Pacific*. Isely and Crowl provided clarification of the radio communication problems that led to the impromptu charge on Roi. The episode of Captain Denig's death is covered in detail in Robert D. Heinl and John A. Crown's *The Marshalls: Increasing the Tempo*, and Carl W. Proehl's *The Fourth Marine Division in World War II*.

1. Ed Hutchinson, telephone interview, 2 December 1998.
2. Neiman, interview.

3. Neiman, interview.
4. Ash, "First Thirty Minutes," in *Marine Corps Tankers Association Newsletter,* 6:4-93:16–17
5. Heinl, "Operation Flintlock," in Smith, *United States Marine Corps,* 570.
6. Ash, "First Thirty Minutes," in *Marine Corps Tankers Association Newsletter,* 6:4-93:16–17.
7. Neiman, interview.
8. Ash, "First Thirty Minutes," in *Marine Corps Tankers Assoc. Newsletter,* 6:4-93:16–17.
9. Shaw, Nalty, and Turnbladh, *History of U.S. Marine Corps,* 3:165.
10. Neiman, interview.
11. Chapin, *Breaking Outer Ring,* 9.
12. Shaw, Nalty, and Turnbladh, History of U.S. Marine Corps, 3:172.
13. Heinl and Crown, *The Marshalls,* 93.
14. Proehl, *Fourth Marine Division,* 30.
15. Leckie, *Strong Men Armed,* 285.
16. Proehl, *Fourth Marine Division,* 33.
17. Chapin, *Breaking Outer Ring,* 18–19; Heinl and Crown, *The Marshalls,* 132.
18. Isely and Crowl, *U.S. Marines and Amphibious War,* 297.

CHAPTER 8–SAIPAN

The course of the Saipan campaign is drawn primarily from Henry I. Shaw, Bernard Nalty, and Edwin T. Turnbladh's *History of U. S. Marine Corps Operations in World War II, Volume III: Central Pacific Drive* and Jeter A. Isely and Philip A. Crowl's *The U. S. Marines and Amphibious War: Its Theory and Its Practice in the Pacific.* The action in which GySgt. McCard won the Medal of Honor is described in Carl W. Proehl's *The Fourth Marine Division in World War II.* Richard Wheeler's *A Special Valor: The U. S. Marines and the Pacific War* provides a good description of the Japanese armored counterattack from the infantry's point of view.

1. Akira Takizawa, personal e-mail communication, 21 September 1999.
2. Isely and Crowl, *U.S. Marines and Amphibious War,* 327.
3. Bale, interview.
4. Hunnicutt, *Stuart–History of American Light Tank,* 372–379.
5. Leckie, *Strong Men Armed,* 320.
6. McMillian, interview.

7. Shaw, Nalty, and Turnbladh, *History of U.S. Marine Corps*, 3:275–276.
8. McLean, *Japanese Tanks,* 161–163; Chamberlain and Gander, *Anti-Aircraft Guns,* 34–35.
9. Ibid., 169–170; Ibid., 35; Akira Takizawa, personal communication.
10. C. B. Ash, telephone interview, 1 December 1998.
11. Medal of Honor citation in Proehl, *Fourth Marine Division*; Leckie, *Strong Men Armed*, 325–326.
12. Chapin, *Breaking Outer Ring,* 8.
13. Ibid.
14. Sherrod, "Green Beach Landings," in Smith, *United States Marine Corps,* 590.
15. Wheeler, *Special Valor,* 259.
16. Spector, *Eagle Against the Sun,* 306,
17. Chapin, *Breaking Outer Ring,* 14.
18. Shaw et al, *History of U.S. Marine Corps,* 3:329–330.
19. Ibid., 327.
20. Ibid, 327; Love, *27th Infantry Division,* 443.
21. Chapin, *Breaking Outer Ring,* 33–34.
22. Ibid., 34.

CHAPTER 9–TINIAN

The course of the Tinian campaign is drawn primarily from Henry I. Shaw, Bernard Nalty, and Edwin T. Turnbladh's *History of U. S. Marine Corps Operations in World War II, Volume III: Central Pacific Drive* and Richard Harwood's *Close Encounter: The Marine Landings on Tinian*. Details of the reorganization following the Saipan operation are provided in Jeter A. Isely and Philip A. Crowl's *The U. S. Marines and Amphibious War: Its Theory and Its Practice in the Pacific.*

1. Spector, *Eagle Against the Sun,* 318–319; Harwood, *Close Encounter,* 3.
2. Harwood, *Close Encounter,* 18.
3. Ibid., 5.
4. Shaw et al, *History U.S. Marine Corps,* 3:384.
5. Ibid., 381.
6. Harwood, *Close Encounter,* 17.
7. Johnston, *Follow Me!,* 247.
8. Harwood, *Close Encounter,* 24; Shaw et al, *History of U.S. Marine Corps,* 417.
9. Harwood, *Close Encounter,* 27.

CHAPTER 10–GUAM

The course of the Guam campaign in drawn from Henry I. Shaw, Bernard Nulty, and Edwin T. Turnbladh's *History of U. S. Marine Corps Operations in World War II, Volume III: Central Pacific Drive* and Cyril J. O'Brien's *Liberation: Marines In The Recapture Of Guam*. O'Brien also provides new background material on Tsuenaga's counterattack against the beachhead. Jeter A. Isely and Philip A. Crowl's *The U. S. Marines and Amphibious War: Its Theory and Its Practice in the Pacific* provides details of the unusual use of water obstacles by the Japanese. Bevan G. Cass's *History Of The Sixth Marine Division* provides considerable information on tank operations.

1. Isely and Crowl, *U.S. Marines and Amphibious War*, 386–387.
2. Morell, "Co 6 Tank," 5.
3. Phil Morell, telephone interview, 5 November 1998.
4. Letter of Col. Edward A. Craig, cited in Shaw et al, *History of U.S. Marine Corps*, 465.
5. O'Brien, *Liberation*, 17.
6. Ibid., 18.
7. Spiller, *The Longest Night*, 7.
8. Ibid., 7, 10.
9. Aiga, "Japanese Anti-tank Weapons," 112.
10. Morell, interview.
11. Chapman, "Guam Incident," 26.

CHAPTER 11–PELELIU

The background and course of the Palau campaign was provided by George W. Garand and Truman R. Strobridge's *History of U. S. Marine Corps Operations in World War II, Volume III: Central Pacific Drive* and Jeter A. Isely and Philip A. Crowl's *The U. S. Marines and Amphibious War: Its Theory and Its Practice in the Pacific*. Bill D. Ross's *A Special Piece of Hell* provided the background on the long-unspoken controversy concerning the awkward and inefficient command structure before and during the battle, and the effects of the brutal climate.

1. Ross, *Special Piece of Hell*, 88.
2. Ibid., 84, 89.
3. Spector, *Eagle Against the Sun*, 420–421.
4. Ross, *Special Piece of Hell*, 133.
5. Garand and Strobridge, *History of U.S. Marine Corps*, 4:88; Isely

and Crowl, U.S. Marines and Amphibious War, 398–399; Bill Henahan, telephone interview, 25 October 1998.

6. Garand and Strobridge, *History of U.S. Marine Corps*, 3:84–85.
7. Ibib., 155.
8. McLean, *Japanese Tanks*, 180–183.
9. Leckie, *Strong Men Armed*, 401.
10. Ross, *Special Piece of Hell*, 189.
11. Garand and Strobridge, *History of U.S. Marine Corps*, 4:122
12. Wheeler, *A Special Valor*, 317–318.
13. Watkins, Bruce R., *Brothers in Battle*, 19. (The appropriate passage appears on a privately maintained website: vm.uconn.edu/~don4762/brothers.htm.)
14. Garand and Strobridge, *History of U.S. Marine Corps*, 4:126.
15. Leckie, *Strong Men Armed*, 417.
16. Ross, *Special Piece of Hell*, 299.
17. Henahan, interview.
18. Ross, *Special Piece of Hell*, 303–304.
19. Ibid., 284.
20. Garand and Strobridge, *History of the U.S. Marine Corps*, 4:154.
21. Hallas, *The Devil's Anvil*, 114.
22. Garand and Strobridge, *History of the U.S. Marine Corps*, 4:155–156.

CHAPTER 12 –IWO JIMA

The background and course of the Iwo Jima campaign was provided by George W. Garand and Truman R. Strobridge's *History of U. S. Marine Corps Operations in World War II, Volume III: Western Pacific Operations* and Jeter A. Isely and Philip A. Crowl's *The U. S. Marines and Amphibious War: Its Theory and Its Practice in the Pacific.* Jeter and Isely also provide valuable information concerning the reorganization of the Marine divisions prior to the battle. Joseph Alexander's *Closing In: Marines in the Seizure of Iwo Jima* discusses the difficulties encountered in landing tanks and other heavy equipment. Howard M. Conner's *The Spearhead: The World War II History of the 5th Marine Division* is an excellent divisional history that deals with tank operations in some detail.

1. Spector, *Eagle Against the Sun*, 494; Leckie, *Strong Men Armed*, 426.
2. Conner, *The Spearhead*, 35.
3. U. S. War Department, pp. 47–48
4. Alexander, *Closing In*, 23.
5. Ibid., 28.

6. Isely and Crowl, *U.S. Marines and Amphibious War*, 433–434; Alexander, "Iwo Jima Amphibious Pinnacle, " 25.

7. Spector, *Eagle Against the Sun*, 496.

8. Conner, *The Spearhead*, 69.

9. Garand and Strobridge, *History of U.S. Marine Corps Operations*, 3:472.

10. Alexander, *Closing In*, 37.

11. Isely and Crowl, *U.S. Marines and Amphibious War*, 460.

12. Garand and Strobridge, *History of U.S. Marine Corps Operations*, 3:483; Isely and Crowl, *U.S. Marines and Amphibious War*, 458.

13. Robert Swackhammer, interview.

14. Ash, interview; Neiman, interview.

15. Neiman, interview.

16. Astor, *Operation Iceberg*, 480; Zaloga, *Tank Battles*, 65.

17. Isely and Crowl, *U.S. Marines and Amphibious War*, 462–463; Alexander, *Closing In*, 7; Alexander, "Iwo Jima Amphibious Pinnacle," 30.

18. Spector, *Eagle Against the Sun*, 500.

19. Charles Burt, telephone interview, 2 December 1998; Neiman, interview.

20. Garand and Strobridge, *History of U.S. Marine Corps Operations*, 3:509.

21. Newcomb, *Iwo Jima*, 99.

22. Ibid., 99; McLean, *Japanese Tanks*, 183–184.

23. Garand and Strobridge, *History of U.S. Marine Corps Operations*, 3:513.

24. Ash, interview.

25. Garand and Strobridge, *History of U.S. Marine Corps*, 4:515, 520.

26. Neiman, interview.

27. Proehl, *Fourth Marine Division*, 152.

28. Garand and Strobridge, *History of U.S. Marine Corps*, 4:548.

29. Wheeler, *A Special Valor*, 368.

30. Garand and Strobridge, *History of U.S. Marine Corps*, 4:531; Alexander, *Closing In*, 21.

31. Conner, *The Spearhead*, 71.

32. Ibid., 62.

33. Hengen, "Single-Handed Tank Act," in *Marine Corp Tankers Assoc. Newsletter*, 5.

34. Newman interview.

35. Radeleff, "Untold Story," in *Marine Corps Tanker's Newsletter*, 5.

36. Sweet, unpublished notebook, 4.

37. Radeleff, "Untold Story," *Marine Corps Tank's Newsletter*, 6.
38. Sweet, unpublished notebook, 6.
39. Garand and Strobridge, *History of U.S. Marine Corps*, 4:564.
40. Conner, *The Spearhead*, 80–81.
41. Ross, *Iwo Jima*, 163.
42. Swackhammer, interview.
43. Garand and Strobridge, *History of U.S Marine Corps*, 574.
44. Sweet, unpublished notebook, 8, 10.
45. Ross, *Iwo Jima*, 214–215.
46. Wheeler, *Special Valor*, 389–390; Sweet, unpublished notebook, 10.
47. Charles Newman, telephone interview, 15 May 1999.
48. Sweet, unpublished notebook, 12.
49. Hengen "Single-Handed Tank Act," in *Marine Corps Tankers Newsletter*, 5.
50. Ross, *Iwo Jima*, 240–241.
51. Sweet, unpublished notebook, 14.
52. Sweet, unpublished notebook, 16; Breard, "The Dude," in *Leatherneck*, October 1945.
53. Alexander, *Iwo Jima*, 33.
54. Sweet, unpublished notebook, 16.
55. Ibid., 18.
56. Ash, interview.
57. Sweet, inpublished notebook, 18, 22.
58. Garand and Strobridge, *History of U.S. Marine Corps*, 4:688.
59. Sweet, unpublished notebook, 20.
60. Breard, "The Dude," in *Leatherneck*, October 1945; Sweet, unpublished notebook, 22.
61. Arthur and Cohlmia, *Third Marine Division*, 251.
62. Isely and Crowl, *U.S Marines and Amphibious War*, 515–516.
63. Donahoe, "Flamethrower Tanks," in *Armor*, vol. CIII/1, 6.

CHAPTER 13–OKINAWA

The outline of Marine Corps operations on Okinawa is drawn from Benis M. Frank and Henry I. Shaw's *History of U. S. Marine Corps Operations in World War II, Volume V: Victory and Occupation* and Jeter A. Isely and Philip A. Crowl's *The U. S. Marines and Amphibious War: Its Theory and Its Practice in the Pacific*. Relevant Army operations are summarized from Roy E. Appleman, James M. Burns, Russell A. Gugeler, and John Stevens's *Okinawa: The Last Battle*. Bevan G. Cass's *History of the Sixth Marine Division* provides good coverage of tank operations by that division.

1. Hunnicutt, 1978, 328.
2. Alexander, *The Final Campaign,* 9.
3. Frank and Shaw, *History of U.S. Marine Corps,* 5:55; Isely and Crowl, *U.S. Marines and Amphibious War,* 540; Appleman et al, *Okinawa: The Last Battle,* 95; Alexander, *The Final Campaign,* 19; Yahara, *Battle for Okinawa,* 35.
4. Isely and Crowl, U.S. Marines and Amphibious War, 540–541.
5. Alexander, *The Final Campaign,* 34; Donahoe, "Flamethrower Tanks, in *Armor,* vol: CIII/1, 9.
6. Hunnicutt, 1978, 430; Henahan, interview.
7. Ibid.
8. Frank and Shaw, *History of U.S. Marine Corps,* 5:114.
9. Henahan, "Another 1st for the First," in *Marine Corps Tankers Newsletter,* 9:198, 4.
10. Ibid.
11. See photographs in Cass, *History Sixth Marine Division,* 55.
12. Appleman et al, *Last Battle,* 144–145.
13. Ibid., 144.
14. Ibid., 204.
15. Isely and Crowl, *U. S. Marines and Amphibious War,* 543–544.
16. Alexander, *The Final Campaign,* 31.
17. Cass, *History of Sixth Marine Division,* 109; Hallas, *Killing Ground on Okinawa,* 38.
18. Feifer, *Tennozoan,* 258–260.
19. Boardman, *Unforgettable Men,* 180.
20. Cass, *History of Sixth Marine Division,* 110.
21. Ibid., 123; Hallas, *Killing Ground on Okinawa,* 167.
22. Alexander, *The Final Campaign,* 46.
23. Hogg, *Encyclopedia of Infantry Weapons World War II,* 147.
24. Henahan, interview.
25. Cass, *History of Sixth Marine Division,* 133.
26. Frank and Shaw, *History U.S. Marine Corps Operations,* 5:316–318.
27. Cass, *History of Sixth Marine Division,* 157, 161.
28. Frank and Shaw, *History U.S. Marine Corps Operations,* 340; Astor, *Operation Iceberg,* 486–490.
29. McLean, *Japanese Tanks,* 208–209.
30. Boardman, *Unforgettable Men,* 186–196.
31. Feifer, *Tennozoan,* 504.
32. Neiman, interview.
33. Frank and Shaw, *History of U.S. Marine Corps Operations,* 368.

CHAPTER 14–ANTICLIMAX

Casualty estimates for the projected invasion of Japan have been revisited by a number of modern historians. Unfortunately the issue has become inextricably tied to the more emotional question of whether the use of the atomic bomb was justified. The author considers John Skates's *The Invasion Of Japan–Alternative to the Bomb* to be the most impartial treatment of this controversial subject.

1. Zaloga, *Tank Battles of Pacific War*, 72; Chamberlain and Ellis, *Pictorial History of Tanks*, 144; Akira Takizawa, personal e-mail communication, 21 September 1999.
2. Spector, *Eagle Against the Sun*, 544.
3. Warner and Warner, *Sacred Warriors*, 248; Spector, *Eagle Against the Sun*, 543; Skates, *Invasion of Japan*, 80–81, 256.
4. Warner and Warner, *Sacred Warriors*, 288.
5. Giangreco, "Casualty Projections U.S. Invasion of Japan," in *Journal of Military History*, 61:580–582.
6. For example, Harries and Harries, *Soldiers of the Sun*, 477.
7. Spector, *Eagle Against the Sun*, 557–558.
8. For example, Dower, *War Without Mercy*, 243.
9. Millett, *Semper Fidelis*, 449-451.

SELECTED REFERENCES

Aiga, Magoichi. "Japanese Anti-Tank Weapons (7): From the Nomonhan Incident to the End of World War II." *Tank Magazine*, vol. 13, no. 7 (1990): 108-113. (Text in Japanese)

Alexander, Joseph H. *Across the Reef: The Marine Assault of Tarawa.* Washington, DC: U.S. Marine Corps Historical Center (1993).

————. *Closing In: Marines in the Seizure of Iwo Jima.* Washington, DC: U. S. Marine Corps Historical Center (1994).

————. "Iwo Jima-Amphibious Pinnacle: U. S. Naval Institute Proceedings," vol. 121/2/1104 (1995): 28-35.

————., *The Final Campaign: Marines in the Victory on Okinawa.* Washington, DC: U.S. Marine Corps Historical Center (1996).

Appleman, Roy E., James M. Burns, Russell A. Gugeler, and John Stevens. *Okinawa: The Last Battle: United States Army in World War II, The War in the Pacific*: Washington, DC: Center for Military History, U. S. Army (1991).

Arthur, Robert A., and Kenneth Cohlmia. *The Third Marine Division.* Washington, DC: Infantry Journal Press, 1948.

Ash, C. B. "First Thirty Minutes in Combat." *Marine Corps Tanker's Association Newsletter*, vol. 6, no. 4-93 (1993): 16-17.

Astor, Gerald. *Operation Iceberg–The Invasion and Conquest of Okinawa in World War II–An Oral History.* New York: Dell paperback edition, 1996.

Blake, Robert. "Death on the Munda Trail." In *The United States Marine Corps in World War II*, edited by S. E. Smith, 416-427. New York: Random House, 1969.

Boardman, Bob. "The Gyrostabilizer." *Marine Corps Tanker's Association Newsletter*, vol. 9, no. 198 (1998): 16.

————. *Unforgettable Men In Unforgettable Times: Stories of Honor, Courage, Commitment and Faith From World War II.* Seattle, WA: privately published, Navigators,1998.

Breard, Harold. "The Dude." *Leatherneck*, October, 1945.

Carlson, Irving P. Letter to Mrs. Botts: handwritten, dated 3 February 1944.

Cass, Bevan G. *History of the Sixth Marine Division.* Washington, DC: Infantry Journal Press, 1948.

Cates, Clifton B. "Leave Us Alone, We're Too Busy Killing Japs." In Smith, S. E. (ed.), *The United States Marine Corps in World War II*, edited by S. E. Smith, 227-228. New York: Random House, 1969.

Chamberlain, Peter, and Chris Ellis. *Pictorial History of Tanks of the World, 1915-1945*. Harrisburg, PA: Galahad/Stackpole, 1972.

Chamberlain, Peter, and Terry Gander. *Anti-Aircraft Guns: World War 2 Fact Files* (series). New York: Arco Publishing, 1975.

Chapin, John C. *Breaking The Outer Ring: Marine Landings in the Marshall Islands*. Washington, DC: U. S. Marine Corps Historical Center, 1994 28.

————. *Breaching The Marianas: The Battle for Saipan*. Washington, DC: U. S. Marine Corps Historical Center, 1994.

————. *Top Of The Ladder: Marine Operation in the Central Solomons*. Washington, DC: U. S. Marine Corps Historical Center, 1997.

Chapman, John W., "Guam Incident Better Than Movies." *Marine Corps Tanker's Association Newsletter*, vol. 8, no. 195 (1995): 26. (Reprinted from CheVron, MCRD San Diego, 4 August 1945.)

Coggins, Jack. *The Campaign for Guadalcanal*. Garden City, NY: Doubleday, 1972.

Conner, Howard M. *The Spearhead: The World War II History of the 5th Marine Division*. Washington, DC: Infantry Journal Press, 1950.

Crost, Lyn. *Honor by Fire*. Novato, CA: Presidio, 1994.

Crowl, Philip, and Edmund G. Love. *The Seizure of the Gilberts and Marshalls*. Washington, DC: Center for Military History, U. S. Army, 1985.

Donahoe, Patrick J. "Flamethrower Tanks on Okinawa." *Armor*, vol. CIII/1 (1994): 6-10.

Donovan, James A. *Outpost in the North Atlantic: Marines in the Defense of Iceland*. Washington, DC: U. S. Marine Corps Historical Center, 1992.

Dower, John W. *War Without Mercy*. New York: Pantheon, 1986.

Feifer, George. *Tennozoan: The Battle Of Okinawa and the Atomic Bomb*. New York: Ticknor & Fields, 1992.

Frank, Benis M., and Henry I. Shaw Jr. *History of U. S. Marine Corps Operations in World War II, Vol. V: Victory and Occupation*. Washington, DC, Headquarters Marine Corps, Historical Branch, 1968.

Garand, George W., and Truman R Strobridge. *History of U. S. Marine Corps Operations in World War II, Vol. IV: Western Pacific Operations*: Washington, DC, Headquarters Marine Corps, Historical Branch, 1962.

Giangreco, D. M. "Casualty Projections For The U. S. Invasions of Japan, 1945-1946: Planning and Policy Implications." *Journal of Military History*, vol. 61 (1997): 521-582.

Gilbert, Ed. "Supplemental Tank Armor in the Central Pacific." *International Plastic Modeler's Society Quarterly*, vol. 22, no. 3 (1987): 35-39.

Graham, Michael B. *Mantle of Heroism: Tarawa and the Struggle For the Gilberts*. Novato, CA: Presidio, 1993.

Hall, Rowland. Untitled letter. *Marine Corps Tanker's Association Newsletter*, vol. 7, no. 494(1994): 5.

Hallas, James H. *The Devil's Anvil: The Assault on Peleliu*. Westport, CT: Praeger, 1994.

————. *Killing Ground On Okinawa: The Battle For Sugar Loaf Hill*. Westport, CT: Praeger, 1996.

Hammel, Eric. *The Munda Trail*. New York: Orion, 1989.

Harries, Meirion, and Susie Harries. *Soldiers of the Sun*. New York: Random House, 1991.

Harwood, Richard. *Close Encounter: The Marine Landings on Tinian*. Washington, DC: U. S. Marine Corps Historical Center, 1994.

Heinl, Robert D. "Operation Flintlock." In Smith, S. E. (ed.), *The United States Marine Corps in World War II*, edited by S. E. Smith, 563-575. New York: Random House, 1969.

Heinl, Robert D., and John A. Crown. *The Marshalls: Increasing The Tempo*. Washington, DC: Historical Section, Headquarters, U. S. Marine Corps, 1954.

Henahan, Bill. "Another First For The 1st!" *Marine Corps Tanker's Association Newsletter*, vol. 9, no. 198 (1998): 4.

Hengen, Bill. "Single-Handed Tank Act Brings Marine Navy Cross-Bronze Star." *Marine Corps Tanker's Association Newsletter*, vol. 8, no. 195 (1945): 5. (Reprinted from *CheVron*, MCRD San Diego, 4 August 1945.)

Hogg, Ian. *The Encyclopedia of Infantry Weapons of World War II*. Northbrook, IL: Bison Books, 1977.

Holzimmer, Kevin C. "In Close Country: World War II American Armor Tactics in the Jungles of the Southwest Pacific." *Armor*, vol. CVI, no. 4 (1997): 21-31.

Horton, D. C. *New Georgia–Pattern For Victory*. New York: Ballantine, 1971.

Hough, Frank O., and John A. Crown. *The Campaign on New Britain*. Washington, DC: Historical Section, Headquarters, U. S. Marine Corps, 1952.

Hough, Frank O., Verle E. Ludwig, and Henry I Shaw Jr. *History of U.S. Marine Corps Operations in World War II, Vol. I: Pearl Harbor to Guadalcanal*. Washington, DC: Headquarters Marine Corps, Historical Branch, 1958.

Hunnicutt, R. P. *Sherman–A History of the American Tank*. Novato, CA: Presidio, 1978.

Hunnicutt, R. P. *Stuart–A History of the American Light Tank*. Novato, CA: Presidio, 1992.

Isely, Jeter A. and Philip A. Crowl. *The U.S. Marines and Amphibious War: Its Theory and Its Practice in the Pacific*. Princeton, NJ: Princeton University Press, 1951.

Johnston, Richard W. *Follow Me! The History of the Second Marine Division in World War II*. Nashville, TN: Battery Press, 1948. (Reprint of original Infantry Journal Press edition.)

Keegan, John. *The Second World War*. New York: Penguin, 1989.

Leckie, Robert. *Strong Men Armed–The United States Marines Against Japan*. New York: Da Capo, 1997.

Love, Edmund G. *The 27th Infantry Division in World War II*. Nashville, TN: Battery Press, 1982. (Reprint of original Infantry Journal Press edition.)

McCoy, C. W. Letter in *Tarawa: The Story of a Battle* by Robert Sherrod. New York: Bantam paperback edition, 1983. (Letter dated 1953 does not appear in the original 1944 edition.)

McKiernan, Patrick L. "Tarawa: The Tide That Failed." In *Assault From The Sea–Essays on the History of Amphibious Warfare*, edited by Merrill L. Bartlett, 210-218. Annapolis, MD: Naval Institute Press, 1983

McLean, Donald B. *Japanese Tanks, Tactics, and Anti-Tank Weapons*. Wickenburg, AZ: Normount Technical Publications, 1973.

McMillan, George. *The Old Breed: A History of the First Marine Division in World War II*. Washington, DC: Zenger Publishing, 1949 reprint.

———. "The Struggle for Borgen Bay: First Phase." In *The United States Marine Corps in World War II*, edited by S. E. Smith, 477-484. New York: Random House, 1969.

Melson, Charles D. *Up the Slot: Marines in the Central Solomons*. Washington, DC: U. S. Marine Corps Historical Center, 1993.

———. *Condition Red: Marine Defense Battalions in World War II*. Washington, DC: U. S. Marine Corps Historical Center, 1993.

Miller, John. *Guadalcanal: The First Offensive*. Washington, DC: Historical Division, Dept. of the Army, 1978.

Millett, Allan R. *Semper Fidelis: The History of the United States Marine Corps*. New York: Free Press, 1980.

Morell, Phil. "President's Message." *Marine Corps Tanker's Association Newsletter*, vol. 7, no. 494 (1994): 2, 18.

———. "President's Message." *Marine Corps Tanker's Association Newsletter*, vol. 8, no. 195 (1995): 2-3, 8-9, 13, 25.

————. "A Co 6th Tank Has Surprise 'Mini Reunion'" (letter). *Marine Corps Tanker's Association Newsletter*, vol. 8, no. 297 (1997): 5.

Nalty, Bernard C. *Cape Gloucester: The Green Inferno*. Washington, DC: U.S. Marine Corps Historical Center, 1994.

Neiman, Bob. "I Shall Always Remember 'G M' English." *Marine Corps Tanker's Association Newsletter*, vol. 10, no. 199 (1999): 10-11.

Newcomb, Richard F. *Iwo Jima*. New York: Bantam paperback edition, 1982.

O'Brien, Cyril J. *Liberation: Marines in the Recapture of Guam*. Washington, DC: U. S. Marine Corps Historical Center, 1994.

O'Neill, Richard. *Suicide Squads*. New York: Ballantine, 1981.

Proehl, Carl W. (ed.). *The Fourth Marine Division in World War II*. Washington, DC: Infantry Journal Press, 1946.

Radeleff, Lyle R. "The Untold Story of LST 477." *Marine Corps Tanker's Association Newsletter*, vol. 9, no. 298 (1998): 5-6.

Rentz, John N. *Bougainville and the Northern Solomons*. Washington, DC: Historical Section, Headquarters, U. S. Marine Corps, 1948.

————. *Marines in the Central Solomons*. Washington, DC: Historical Section, Headquarters, U. S. Marine Corps, 1952.

Ross, Bill D. *Iwo Jima–Legacy of Valor*. New York: Vanguard, 1985.

————. *A Special Piece of Hell*. St. Martin's Press, 1993. (Originally published as *Peleliu: Tragic Triumph* by Random House, New York, 1991.)

Rowe, Arthur. "I Am Not A Qualified Tanker–Then Who Is?" (letter). *Marine Corps Tanker's Association Newsletter*, vol. 10, no. 199 (1999): 6-7.

Shaw, Henry I. *Tarawa: A Legend Is Born*. New York: Ballantine, 1968.

————. *First Offensive: The Marine Campaign for Guadalcanal*. Washington, DC: U. S. Marine Corps Historical Center, 1992.

Shaw, Henry I. Jr., and Kane, Douglas T. *History of U. S. Marine Corps Operations in World War II, Vol. II: Isolation of Rabaul*. Washington, DC: Headquarters Marine Corps, Historical Branch, 1963.

Shaw, Henry I., Bernard C. Nalty, and Edwin T. Turnbladh. *History of U. S. Marine Corps Operations in World War II, Vol. III: Central Pacific Drive*. Washington, DC: Headquarters Marine Corps, Historical Branch, 1966.

Sherrod, Robert. "Green Beach Landings." In *The United States Marine Corps in World War II*, edited by S. E. Smith, 584-592. New York: Random House, 1969.

Skates, John Ray. *The Invasion of Japan–Alternative To The Bomb*. Columbia, SC: Univ. South Carolina Press, 1994.

Spector, Ronald H. *Eagle Against The Sun*. New York: Vintage, 1985.

Spiller, Lou. "The Longest Night" (letter). *Marine Corps Tanker's Association Newsletter*, vol. 7, no. 494 (1994): 7, 10.

Stockman, James R. *The Battle for Tarawa*. Washington, DC: Historical Section, Headquarters, U. S. Marine Corps, 1947.

Sweet, G. G., Record of Events, 1st Sgt. Sweet, USMC, Iwo Jima. Unpublished notebook, 1945. (Photocopy provided by Charles Bell.)

Tregaskis, Richard. "The Grove: Mop Up." In *The United States Marine Corps in World War II*, edited by S. E. Smith, 229-237. New York: Random House, 1969.

U.S. War Department. *1944 Handbook on Japanese Military Forces*. Baton Rouge, LA: LSU Press reprint edition, 1991.

Warner, Denis, and Peggy Warner. *The Sacred Warriors: Japan's Suicide Legions*. New York: Avon (pb ed), 1982.

Watkins, Bruce R. *Brothers in Battle*. Manchester, CT: privately published memoir (no date given).

Wheeler, Richard. *A Special Valor–The U. S. Marines and the Pacific War*. New York: Harper and Row, 1983.

Wright, Derrick. *A Hell Of A Way To Die–Tarawa Atoll, 20–23 November 1943*. London: Windrow and Greene, 1996.

Yahara, Hiromichi, with commentary by Frank B. Gibney. *The Battle For Okinawa*. New York: John Wiley and Sons, 1995.

Zaloga, Steven J. *Tank Battles of the Pacific War, 1941–1945*. Hong Kong: Concord Publications, 1995.

INDEX

Index

Index